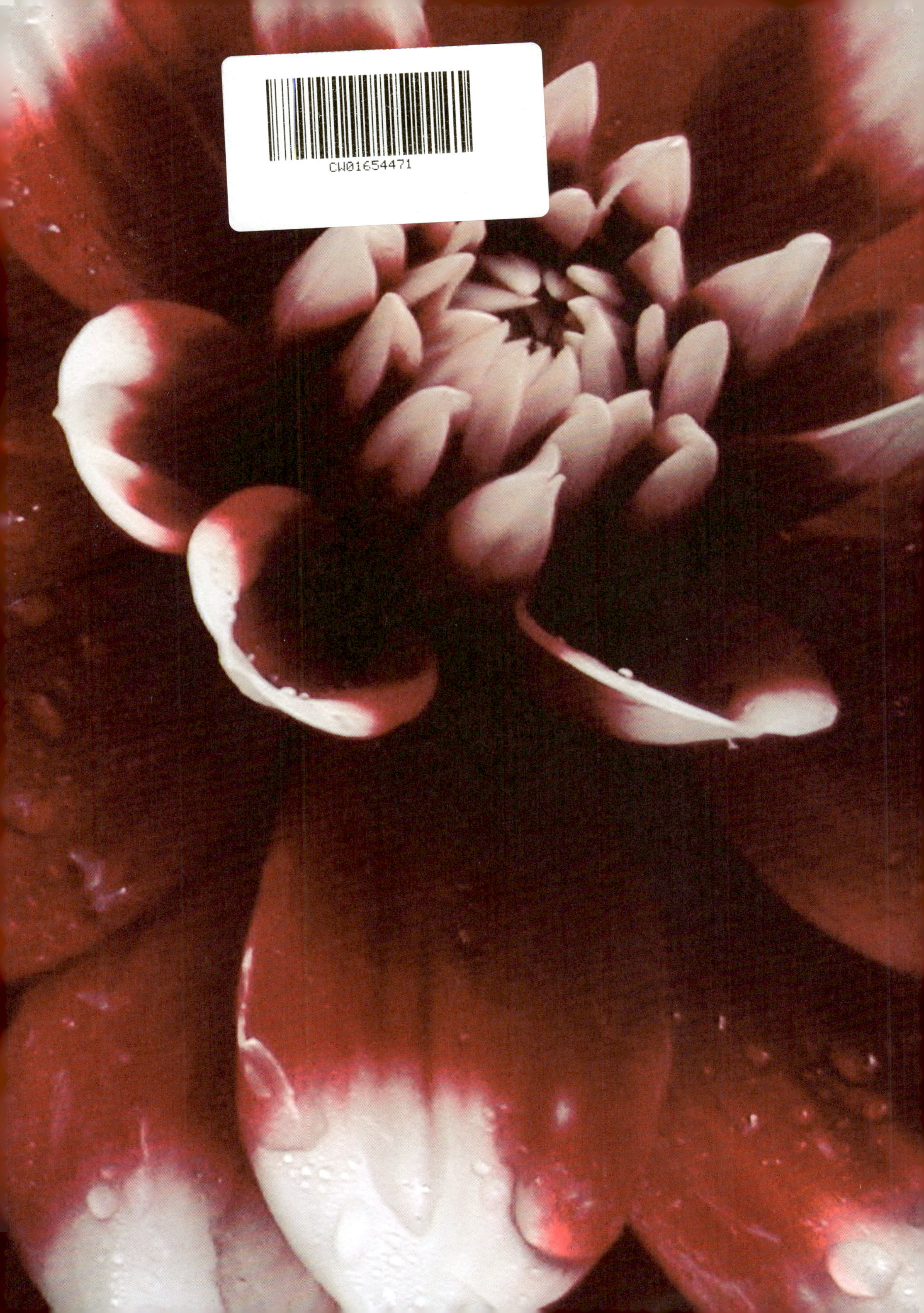

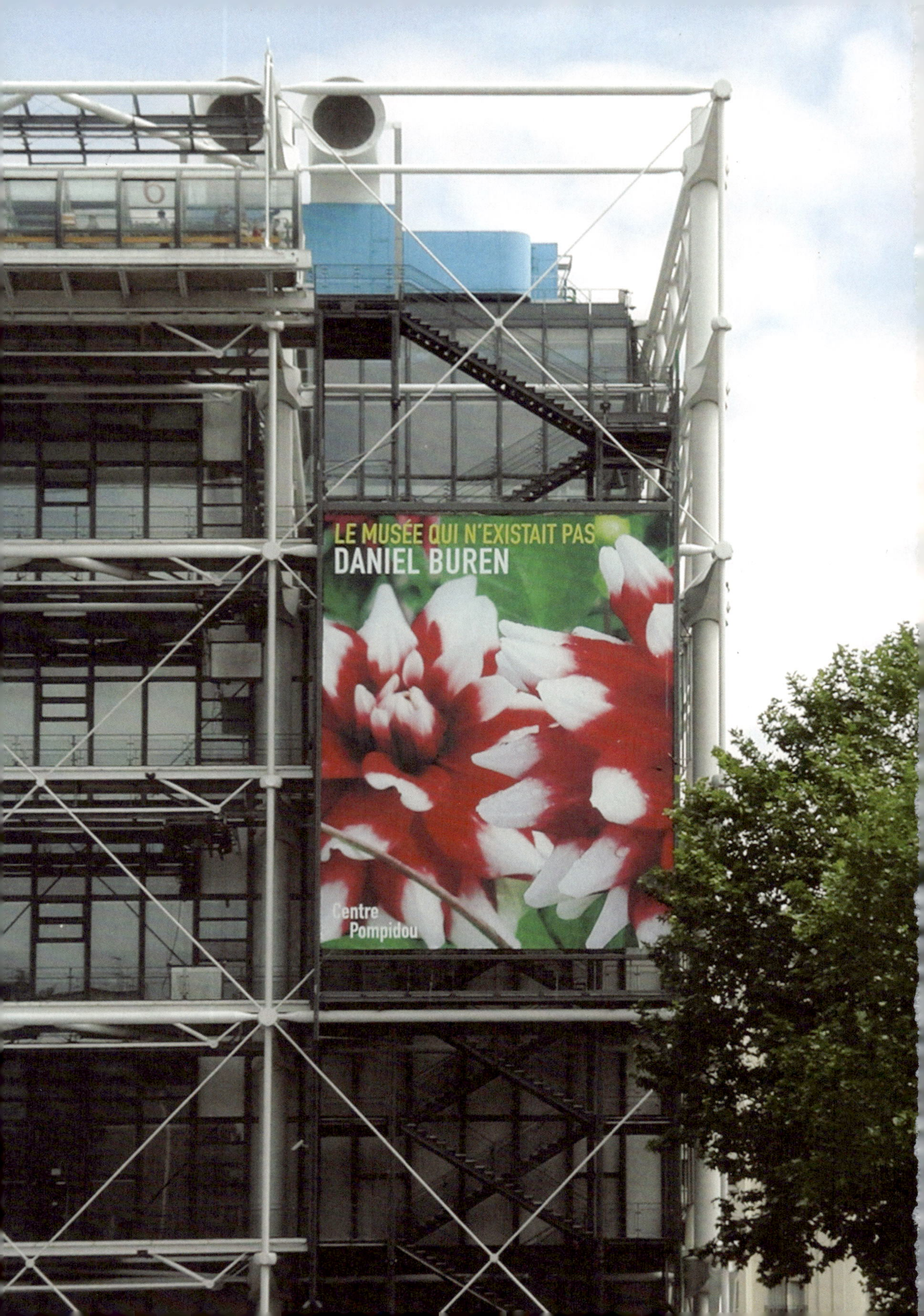
LE MUSÉE QUI N'EXISTAIT PAS
DANIEL BUREN
Centre
Pompidou

50

The Museum That Did Not Exist

The Museum That Did Not Exist

The Museum That Did Not Exist

Daniel Buren

PRESTEL
Munich · Berlin · London · New York

"Le Musée qui n'existait pas" (The Museum that did not exist) was shown at the Centre Pompidou from 26 June to 23 September 2002. In this book, Daniel Buren offers a photographic tour of this *in situ* work. All the photographs in this book are by Daniel Buren with the exception of the one reproduced on page 65.

Published by arrangement with Editions du Centre Pompidou /
Editions Xavier Barral, Paris
Original title: Le Musée qui n'existait pas

Foreword

In the spring of 2002, Jean-Jacques Aillagon, then President of the Centre Pompidou, and Alfred Pacquement, who had just taken over from Werner Spies as director of the Musée national d'art moderne, inaugurated the Daniel Buren exhibition "Le Musée qui n'existait pas" (The Museum That Did Not Exist).

Based on an idea mooted by Bernard Blistène, at that time Deputy Director of the Musée national d'art moderne, and since appointed inspector general of artistic creation at the commission of visual arts, the project was undertaken with the cooperation of Laurent Le Bon and Alison M. Gingeras, curators at the Musée national d'art moderne, the invaluable help of Patrick Bouchain, whose talent is currently being devoted to our mobile Centre Pompidou project, and the unwavering support of Guy Amsellem, visual arts representative.

The exhibition occupied many areas at the Centre Pompidou. This was what Daniel Buren wished. Gallery 2 on level 6 housed the large arrangement which extended to the terraces. There were many installations inside the building, which they revealed in all its complexity and diversity.

"Le Musée qui n'existait pas" was a very big success. For it, Daniel Buren came up with a series of highly inventive ephemeral propositions, which all dealt and dialogued with the outstanding building designed by Renzo Piano and Richard Rogers. Buren's remarkable project definitely contributed to a new generation of artists being offered these spaces hitherto reserved for others.

Daniel Buren conceived his appointment with the Centre Pompidou as a set of propositions which occupied the place in its entirety, and spilled over, as it were, into the impressive book titled *Mot à Mot* (Word for Word), created for the exhibition.

The catalogue for the exhibition itself remained to be produced, based on illustrative material largely made by the artist himself, and describing the exceptional diversity of the *in situ* ideas executed and then destroyed, as is his wont each time, at the end of the show.

This is why, in the wake of a conversation with Daniel Buren, I was keen to have this publication, for whose preparation it seemed quite natural to enlist the same team which planned the *maquette* of the earlier book.

I am pleased that this publication is thus ushering in a collection of books devoted to different shows held at the Centre Pompidou, whose layout and designs are essential milestones in contemporary museography, and make a crucial contribution to the history of the cultural institutions of our day and age. Other titles are in planning, one such being a book highlighting the diversity of the various ideas associated with the different ports of call of the exhibition "Dada", after its conception in Paris.

May all these works contribute to our knowledge of major moments in the Centre Pompidou's history and in our contemporary culture. And may this first title mark a new step in the hopefully ever more fertile relationship between artists and this incomparable venue.

Alain Seban
President of the Centre Pompidou

Daniel Buren at the Centre Pompidou

Bernard Blistène

Thought in Motion

Something to do with a history now past and buried resurfaces here. Images, "photos-souvenirs" which we know to be incomplete. They evoke, straight off, how and why "Le Musée qui n'existait pas" (The Museum That Did Not Exist) kindles thought in motion more than any other exhibition that I have had the privilege of working on. I have very vivid memories of the Daniel Buren show at the Centre Pompidou, after spending so much time walking round it, for the host of different perspectives it outlined led to itineraries that were forever being reinvented with each visit and as time passed. I have a vivid and, when all is said and done, special memory, for very few exhibitions offer so much freedom to their visitors. Few, too, have so determinedly refused to impose an itinerary. Few have been constructed with such a resolute idea about avoiding any scheduled, marked out route. Few have so determinedly sidestepped the initial story they were meant to tell. "Le Musée qui n'existait pas" was indeed a Daniel Buren retrospective, but it replaced its familiar form with a thoroughly novel space-time paradigm.

It is true that Buren wanted people to get lost in his show. No question of a beginning and an end, of any obligatory circuit or laid-out path, or even of any logic complying with an imposed pace. People would visit it as they pleased, going from one room to another, one space to another, just as they felt like, just as their whims and desires dictated: the journey rather than the destination.

The structure he elected to impose, as soon as negotiations – the word is apt – under way with the project's different partners encountered on the way, was not unfamiliar. Daniel Buren would immediately respond to the linearity of the year 2000 arrangements and their formatted spaces with a systematic gridding of the exhibition area properly so-called. He would contrast the system punctuating and imposing its scansions with a master scheme that he would slap and overlay on the structure, discourse versus discourse, narration versus narration: here, this time around, commenced the "sanction of the museum"[1].

At the outset, then, there was the invitation extended to Daniel Buren to think about the idea of a retrospective… A question posed to the artist who, for more than forty years, had been working *in situ*, and refusing to regard the temporary exhibition space, as opposed to the museum space, as a memorial place. Buren, incidentally – and this is just one point among others that sets him apart from his contemporaries – is not the memorial sort; he has doubts about all forms of commemoration. He probably prefers the notion of celebration to that of commemoration and all that attaches thereto: past against present, the proposal made to him probably did not consist, for him, for one split second, in going back to his existing work, but in going forward, with the idea of advancing by "zigzagging[2]", yes, but obviously well removed from any confinement involving the collection of works from the past. Had he, for a moment, imagined any such thing, the *in situ* notion together with the method peculiar to a very large part of his work would have stopped him.

We are aware that the art of the exhibition, for Daniel Buren, does not have to do with the past, but with the activation of the present. Neither past nor anywhere else but, like his contemporaries, a "here and now" to

1 We are acquainted with the story, often told by Daniel Buren, about a mistaken reading of a handwritten text penned in New York in 1970, which he sent to the Museum of Modern Art in Oxford in 1973, erroneously published under the title "Sanction of the Museum" and in fact titled "Function of the Museum". The full significance of this error would be confirmed over the years, to such a degree did the artist's work assert itself as a critical look at the way institutions operate. See Daniel Buren, *Les Écrits*, vol. I (1965-1976), "Fonction du musée", pp. 169-173, and vol. III (1984-1990), pp. 373-389, Bordeaux, capcMusée d'art contemporain, 1991.

2 See Jean-Claude Lebensztejn, *Zigzag*, Paris, Flammarion, 1981. This collection of thoughts on Dubuffet, Stella, Matisse, Klee, kitsch, the zigzag and Bataille, the frame, and whiteness represents a noteworthy example of critical analysis, off the beaten track. By zigzagging, Lebensztejn formulates a wandering line of thought in which one can establish a parallel with many projects contemporary with Daniel Buren. "Reading, wrote Michael Androula in *Critique d'art*, n° 19, spring 2002, at times linear, at others elliptical, playing with the cut, the margin and/or margins, borrows from the Borgesian image of 'forking paths', and different directions."

whose introduction and formulation Daniel Buren incidentally largely contributed. An essentially innovative present when a large number of the artists of his generation was embarking on their œuvre in order to recall or, as Racine said about literature, to talk of a "distant land[3]". A "here and now" whose challenge, as we well know, consists in remaining anchored in the present reality, so as to act upon it. So, right away, Buren posited – the apt word, once again – one of the essential principles of his method in answer to the proposal made to him. an exhibition, to wit. After all, he was the last (of the French artists, anyway) of his generation to be invited to show the whole of his work at the Centre Pompidou. An exhibition, but in the immediate sense of the word: "a project", as people say of things aspiring to put forward hypotheses (self-projection), to construct (an architect's project), of a situation contingent upon a place, a surface, a building or a site, its limitations, its ambiguities, its beauty, its complexity, its vagaries, its means… in a nutshell, everything that makes an exhibition happen or not happen. So the fight was just beginning…

The "fight"? A warlike metaphor which Buren would not contradict. Art has a set-to with reality. It cannot avoid it. It can do nothing other than seize it. It cannot conclude just in terms of space, nor even in just the patience of time, but rather by immediately envisaging the way it functions in a set of discursive networks, where the centre Pompidou, by its very nature and by the way it works, appears like favourable terrain.

So something of that past exhibition is coming back: a history, needless to say, nearly eight years ago, and the vivid memory of discussions, faxes and exchanges at numerous meetings about what the project might be and the need to immediately take "the measure" of the building.

3 In *Sur Racine*, Paris, Seuil, 1960, Roland Barthes analyses the signifying structure of tragedy through a reading of places (chamber, antechamber, exterior). He deciphers Racine's theatre like a game of chess, with its rules and its own space. See, among others, the pages on the theme of the hidden to be found in images of dark places (hell, labyrinths, forests). This world is related to that of the earth: Aricia and her brothers are the descendants of the goddess Earth; Theseus is a chthonic hero (of the Earth): Barthes analyses the metaphor of his descent into hell and the labyrinth See, *inter alia*, chapter 1, "L'Homme racinien", 1. La structure, pp. 9-14.

I recall Daniel Buren taking a few photographs of the space which we eventually offered him, after much in-house discussion. I recall the hesitation over giving him the building's level 6, something which I, for my part, was adamant about. I can still see him, clutching a tape measure, assessing the real size of the place. I can remember his scepticism about the estimates of the area being offered and the intelligence with which he turned the lack of precision in the plan provided for him to his own advantage. I can still remember the mischievous way he caught us out. The institution's "sanction", again, in relation to the problem with taking the measure, literally and figuratively, of the place, and producing, year in year out, exhibitions whose real surface area turned out, in the end of the day, to be somewhat random. And Buren recalling that the *in situ* notion could not be satisfied with improbable calculations as long as it was grappling with the truth of the reality all about it. In Daniel Buren's praxis there is the art of the surveyor, and the art of the assertion whereby the effective transformation of a space can only result from a proper appreciation of its measure and what it contains. Therefore, everything was set up for the exhibition to turn reality against itself. So we paced up and down gallery 2 on level 6 and agreed to say that the measurements announced did not in any way tally with reality. Deceit was in the air. Buren would quickly give us the "corrected surface area", the same that you give to a real estate agent or a proprietor to let you know that he has fooled you and that you must now negotiate, or else the contract will be broken... But wherever the contract might be broken, Buren immediately found an alternative. He had been promised more space. It would have to be found, come what may. Buren suggested that the exhibition be opened out and now developed *extra muros*, outside the setting hitherto meant to contain it. In so doing, he would point out the lost room space and the ineffectiveness of the division of the building's level 6 into three galleries, as it had been set up for its re-opening. This time around, Buren would invert the initial proposition, and turn the space of the exhibition into the actual exhibition of the space. He responded to the 960 square metres [10,000 square feet] offered him, way below the 1,200 [13,000] initially promised, corresponding in effect to the area of the present-day south gallery on the Centre Pompidou's ground floor, with a proposal that would factor in the long corridor designed to provide two different access points to the three linked shows on level 6. Negotiations got under way and, with them, his litany of questions which would make this exhibition one of those most rooted in the building's history. Buren had instantly grasped that exhibiting at the Centre would presuppose the introduction of a dialogue, not to say an ongoing confrontation with Piano and Rogers's building. A confrontation, but also an experiment in the sense that the Centre Pompidou, for him, was the distinctive feature of a "desirous machine", a system with its contradictions, its paradoxes and its utopias: there is an analysis to be made of Buren's work using the yardstick of the Deleuzian model[4]...

So I recall memorable discussions with Jean-Jacques Aillagon, then President of the Centre Georges Pompidou, about the project's nature, about the challenge it represented, and about the idea of a structure which, *de facto*, and to be persuasive, had to be projected beyond the space meant to contain it and occupy the whole building. I still remember the paper that Buren probably kept, the plan made by Jean-Jacques Aillagon's hand sketching out the possibility that, once it lacked the promised area, the exhibition could be extended beyond the agreed boundaries, and propose many different interventions in different places.

Then came the idea of a grid. Unless it was already there... A rigorous grid like a parlour game, running counter to the linearity introduced by the 2000 arrangements, and suggesting a placement

4 See Gilles Deleuze and Félix Guattari, *L'Anti-Œdipe*, Paris, Minuit, 1973, chap. 3 ("Sauvages, barbares, civilisés"), § 10 (" La représentation capitaliste"), p. 306. In, *Lire,* May 2008, Alain Rubens comments on the book and writes: "Desire must be open to the four winds. Everyone becomes a desirous machine and enjoyment will occur here, there and everywhere. This is a desire/factory for producing multiple arrangements. Desire is arrangement." Buren often emphasized the impact that the writings of Deleuze and Guattari had on his own thinking.

between the structure's layout and main beams, a gridding of the surface in such a way that this would develop a set of spaces, rooms, and sites of equal dimensions.

There is much to be said (and written) about this grid idea, and about the reasons which led Buren to be keen, very quickly, to assert thereby the overall form of his project. Let us note, first and foremost, that this is a recurrent principle of his œuvre. The principle of elementary geometry that consists in dividing the space into squares of identical area is at once simple and effective, wherein lies the history of many types of representations, starting with the use of tiles and perspective in painting. This principle is also the one that Daniel Buren applies to himself in countless projects that he has carried out, or imagined. It prompts him to take the measure of the space involved, like an archaeologist dividing his dig into squares, when he starts his excavations. There is something here involving an archaeology of the place, even an "archaeology of knowledge", and we might also say that *Les Deux Plateaux* is one of the outdoor examples emblematic of Buren's œuvre and method[5].

But there is something else, too. In his painstaking observation of the gradual arrangement of the Centre Pompidou's spaces, Buren was able to emphasize how the notion of the initially open and flexible set was henceforth rigidified, in the course of time and the pressure of a model against which the Centre Pompidou had been devised by its originator. The grid highlighted how the organization of the spaces had, as re-arrangement followed re-arrangement, blocked the principle of open circulation, and the fluidity of sets freely offered to the designers and artists invited to work there. The open space notion had gradually given way to a linear principle: the idea of a street crossing the building from north to south, leading to the construction of a huge partition oriented towards the window, a partition on which, from one show to the next, it is only possible to write the title of the work, and, at best, the various chronological and biographical details of the different artists being exhibited. Not without irony, Buren emphasized that the longest of the Centre Pompidou's picture rails was in fact an impossible surface, a wall that served solely to make the exhibition sanctuary-like behind a wall (or perhaps an enclosure) away from all natural light, and away from the city which the building nevertheless calls upon in its very principle, through and through.

So the grid made it possible to both demonstrate and sidestep this. It presupposed a simple principle which was in contrast with the existing structure, denied its validity, and, in an even more subtle way, helped people to understand in the name of what refusal and for what reasons this picture rail had been installed. It thus clearly highlighted the primacy of a model which Buren's art has been constantly questioning since the mid-1960s: the supremacy of the pictorial form over all others, not to say its predominance. In an insidious way, Buren here pointed a finger at the primacy of the picture over any other form of artistic expression, and the subordination of exhibition areas to their conventions. And he

5 On this subject, see the different analyses of the public commission made by the Ministry of Culture from Daniel Buren, *Les Deux Plateaux*, sculpture *in situ* 1985-1986, Cour d'honneur du Palais-Royal, Paris. We should here emphasize the collaboration established between Daniel Buren and Patrick Bouchain who would meet through Bernard Tschumi. Buren called on Bouchain who was helped by the theatre builder, Vito Schavelzon, to execute the work *La Rencontre des sites* as part of the Grande Halle de La Villette, for the Nouvelle Biennale de Paris in 1985, then, obviously enough, for the implementation of the Palais-Royal project. Bouchain would subsequently become the accomplice in many of his works and, with the help of Paule Thévenin, would form the work's back-up committee. Patrick Bouchain's role in the execution of the Centre Pompidou show was also quintessential. As soon as François Belfort, the Centre Pompidou's director of exhibition production, had suggested that the technical realization of the project should be farmed out, Buren wanted Bouchain to be in on it, assisted by Nicole Concordet, first to think it right through, and then to actually produce the arrangement with the technical help of Patrick Ferragne, for its making and assembly. It is clear that Buren raises crucial questions about the relation between his own work and architecture and, in a more general way, about that between the visual artist and the architect in the contemporary period. On the relation to the public place, please also refer to the analyses of Hal Foster, *The Return of the Real. The Avant-Garde at the end of the century*, Cambridge (Massachusetts)/London, The MIT Press, 4th ed., 2001. In this important book, Foster shows, *inter alia* how the distance and perspective done away with in the flatness of the surface are not just signs of the loss of what Clement Greenberg called "the only surrender of painting to its medium", but an evolution of the art scene where the subject is seeking its place, where the order of things is broken. Daniel Buren would broach the Centre Pompidou like a monument conceived as an element symbolizing the public dimension of the city and its organization, and as what Foster calls "a discursive network of different praxes".

also pointed his finger all the more subtly since his own œuvre, absolutely contemporary as it was in its conceptual maturity and formulation in relation to the Centre Pompidou project, would lead him to give up on the principle of traditional hanging, and transform the picture into a "visual tool", capable of revealing the structural and symbolic functioning of the spaces in which he would be invited to exhibit.

In the moment of examining the elaboration of his project, there is – and it is perhaps important to underline this here – an absolute contemporaneousness between the invention of the Centre Pompidou and the invention of Daniel Buren's œuvre, objectives which must be analysed in their exact historical similarity. The renunciation of the picture, as such, for Daniel Buren, in favour of the formulation of a critical praxis based on the "arrangement" notion, the principle of open, modulable space for Renzo Piano, Richard Rogers and Gianfranco Franchini.

The grid thus pointed to the paradoxes of the present time – are they paradoxes? – which had gradually led to a preference for the fixedness of partitions obstructing light in the name of the conventions governing the pictorial model. This fact, for Buren, was merely more significant insomuch as it peremptorily and paradoxically affirmed the supremacy of one genre over another, whereas the contemporary creation of the building of the Centre Pompidou would affirm more than ever the intermingling of disciplines, and could hope to find therein the most appropriate place for its new experiments.

Buren "entered" the Centre Pompidou in 2000 and from then on was bound to point the finger at that closed development of the permanent and temporary exhibition areas, and want his project to be based on the place's anatomy, and its operational potential, with the wish not to submit to its new logic, but to find its founding principles. So the grid was not simply going to be the affirmation of a specific temporary exhibition system, but also the construction of an implicit principle which, in being superposed over the existing structure, would shatter its straitjacket.

There was something here akin to a meeting of two discourses and the demonstration of two contradictory systems of logic: the one tending to shut the space, and enclose it; the other, to open it up, to the point of going beyond its boundaries. We know how much the "boundary" notion is essential in Daniel Buren's œuvre, and to what degree it is a notion that is part and parcel of his theoretical principles. It runs right through his writings and his ideas. Buren's art is continually "an experiment with boundaries", not in the sense presupposed by poetry, but in the sense whereby the boundary notion refers firstly to the aesthetic and political challenges of modernity, the issue of the frame, and its edges, and so on. Going beyond boundaries is going beyond restrictions. It assigns to the artist the duty to reveal that going-beyond. It extends the aesthetic idea to the whole of reality, which it breaks up in order to bring forth the way it works. As Jean-Marc Poinsot has written: "We must be done with the idea whereby the site, the installation framework, even the context might contain the work. It is, quite to the contrary, the work which contains the features and fragments of the site in which it is installed. ... The primary link between the work and reality is thus that of its own integrity[6]".

Buren's whole œuvre presents itself as going beyond the boundaries wherein he recognizes a limitation of both content and style, a refusal of the expanse, a framing, and hence a restriction. Daniel Buren has never seen his relation to the institution other than by envisaging it, in its very reality, as a boundary *per se*. With Buren, art is openness in the field of possibilities. After the restriction and the "semantic asepsis" towards which he would steer his œuvre in 1967, this latter has been forever opening out and broadening. This is why, incidentally, I have said how markedly his project, in its initial definition, appeared to me like an indexation of the

6 Jean-Marc Poinsot, in his book titled *Quand l'œuvre a lieu. L'Art exposé et ses récits autorisés* (Geneva, Les Presses du Réel, coll. "Mamco", 2008), has rightly underlined how the attention paid to the context as a battle ground where there is a clash between the critical analyses of artists and the institutional materialization of power is due to a critique of European origin more accustomed to political analysis.

baroque thinking whose distinctive feature is that it opens out *ad infinitum*. Since 1968, Buren's project has been constructed in accordance with this assertion. In a way, it is a Leibnizian project in the sense in which, as Gilles Deleuze points out, everything, in his work, "folds, unfolds and re-folds". As such, Buren's entire œuvre results from a "monad[7]". We shall see how the diagram of the exhibition that he proposed for the Centre Pompidou turned out to be its perfect affirmation.

As a two way movement between the frame and its rejection, constraint and its denial, the diagram worked out thus represented the guiding principle of his project. Nothing if not shrewd, Buren let it be known that once accepted in its principle, the grid eluded him and found its execution beyond its own intent. It would thus negotiate the wall, develop in the corridor, pass the large window and multiply in the void, in a state of equilibrium... above the museum's terrace. Buren's project found its accomplishment in the folds and renewed folds and the unfurling of the form in space, until its encounter with a significant void. Buren ushered in a baroque structure which he unfolded, like Josef Albers's origami at the Bauhaus, to spread and draw multiple figures.

In all this there was a spatial and philosophical movement, a form of merry deductive determinism, a singular path, incisive and lighthearted, which would then jostle more than a few, jostle, too, the institution's conventions and the way it operates, and the rules governing the building's use, provide some of its departments with a thousand and one reasons for refusal and gradually for negotiations with the artist. I have never seen such a project come into being with so many problems, and in the end enjoy every manner of complicity. I have never seen an exhibition win over so many sceptics and opponents. Buren, it is true, has know-how.

7 The "monad" notion is definitely a notion stemming from metaphysics extended to the artistic arena, not to say to the specificity of the work of art, originally signifying "unity". But the monad signifies just as much a minimal unity as a maximal unity. So it is possible to see in the arrangement of "Le Musée qui n'existait pas" the materialization of this double meaning.

The grid thus proposed a diagram of seventy-one identically-sized compartments which would regularly and repetitively structure all the space on level 6, henceforth given over to the show. Each one of these compartments would define a room of some thirty square metres [325 square feet]. The whole would form the largest of the "situated cabins" which Buren had made to date. I have incidentally attempted to highlight the function of the "cabins" in Buren's œuvre. It goes without saying that they took a thoroughly specific turn in the Centre Pompidou's architecture. More than anywhere else in the artist's œuvre, they were the precarious and temporary construction opposite the "evolving spatial diagram" initially devised by the building's architects. Perhaps they are not that removed, in their initial intent, from Mario Merz's igloo, with which they were contemporary: an overall and standard form, a provisional architecture, a fragile construction whose old-fashioned architectural paradigm was not far from the wooden shed which Le Corbusier built for himself to contrast with the dreams of the Plan Voisin, the desire for a concrete utopia...

Buren's system was thus not so much constructed against the Centre Pompidou's architecture in itself as against what it had become. It revealed the initial underlying structure, and its possibilities. It was placed in the space with the firm intention of denying the way it functioned at the time. It played against it in order to show its museum future and the endless possibilities of the space when it is returned to its initial flexibility.

To take things further still in what we might call "a veritable deconstruction of space", Buren decided to work on the oblique. By leaving the corners of each of the boxes open, in such a way that they became zones of passage and circulation, Buren suggested infinite vanishing lines. Faithful to the ongoing analysis of the history of forms that fuelled his idea, he brought back into the picture, both literally and figuratively, the scheme initiated for the plan of the picture by Theo Van Doesburg, by creating "a spatially open work" and by applying the principle of the

1920 *Manifesto of Constructivism* advocating the production not of a painting or a sculpture, but a "construction in space". He redeployed the principle of the first "kinetic constructions", where the form determines the rhythm and movement of space-time. He used, in his own way, light materials so as to design a project that grappled directly with the architecture. He reactivated the theoretical principles of the IZO workshop which he knew well, principles that had led Katarzyna Kobro to produce her many writings on "sculpture and volume[8]". In proposing a total and organic organization of space, determined by all the open volumes, Buren resolutely incorporated his project in the tradition of reflections coming out of the historical avant-gardes, the contrary of a moment of plastic artistic creation preferring, at that precise instant, pathos and narrativeness over all other forms. Daniel Buren's project thus linked up with constructivist history and had every intention of assuming it. Construction versus architecture, Buren put his work in direct relationship with the history of plastic utopias of modernity, for which he cannily proposed, for his Centre Pompidou show, close to the museum housing the twentieth century collections, a critical summary of the relation between contemporary creation and its historical models.

8 The art of Katarzyna Kobro (1898-1951), in search of a radical objectivism, tries to construct itself, not to say deduce itself, from experimentation and analysis. At the root of her research, Kobro props up her idea on the abstract concept of "infinite space". Space thus conceived is homogeneous and has no specific link, no reference point (as the centre might be, in a system of coordinates). Based on this, Kobro tends, through her works, to construct the organization of space so that the works co-exists with the environment or incorporates this latter. From this notions issues, in effect, the elimination of the notion of centre. Since the 1920s, through the notion of "spatial composition", Kobro had a significant link with the Praesens group of architects, such that we can read, from the pen of certain critics, includinhg Mieczysław Treter: "Madame Kobro makes sculptures which do not merit this name" (magazine *Europa,* n° 2, 1929). Several theoretical writings by Kobro, some of which were written with Strzemiński, would underscore her intentions: "Sculpture is a part of the space in which it is. Sculpture enters the space and the space enters the sculpture." It is as well to "take the form in the rhythm of calculating time and space" (in *Formy* ["Les Formes"], 1936, n° 4). In *Głos Plastyków* (["The voice of visual artists"], 1937, n° 1-7), she wrote again: "Sculpture is a part of space. This is why its link with space is the condition of its organism. … The energy of the forms which follow in space creates the rhythm of time and space." In the many books she devotes to Kobro and Strzemi ski, the Polish art historian Małgorzata Kitowska-Łysiak, of the Instytut Historii Sztuki, specifies: "Over and above Suprematism, unism seeks to 'compose space'".

Beyond the "zero of form", as Malevich formulated the initiatory principles of Suprematism, beyond that "degree zero" of the painting of his own works in the years 1966/67, Buren here evolved towards "the objectless world" which Malevich was hoping and praying for: a division of space, support for endless propositions but this time round more ephemeral, with the application of the idea that "form fades in the unlimitedness of vision" and that, to reactivate Aleksandr Rodchenko's intention, "the domain of reality is that of practical construction[9]". By accentuating the dynamic state breaking with frontality and encouraging openness by slant and angle, Buren introduced a twofold movement between the interior of successive spaces and the movement of the visitor's body capable of constructing in that deliberately "disorienting" space his own narrative. Still the monad and the Leibnizian perception of the soul which, itself "is a monad with neither door nor window, and draws from a dark background all its clear perceptions". Still the monad which can only be confused by analogy with the interior of a Baroque chapel where the light arrives through apertures that cannot be seen by the onlooker inside. Here, says the philosopher, "the soul is full of dark folds[10]". Here, Buren's project is also a metaphor of shadow and light in the different rooms offering a sequence of chromatic and plastic variations, an area of particularly dynamic investigation for an œuvre open to all possibilities. Colour, as we shall see, and his free will, will obviously play a decisive part in it.

Text to be continued page 47

9 See Andrzej Turowski, "Théories de la sculpture en Europe de l'est, 1910-1920", in *Revue de l'art,* n° 76, 1987, pp. 85-87.

10 It is also worth referring to the work by Gilles Deleuze, *Le Pli, Leibniz et le Baroque*, Minuit, Paris, 1988, which shows how the baroque takes the fold ad infinitum, with the aim of once again grasping a world slipping away.

Buren came and put a large white frame, bordered with the "visual tool" recognisable by one and all, over all the signs and notices prepared by the Swiss graphic designer Ruedi Baur for the refitting of the Centre Pompidou's forum in 2000: Buren appropriated the Centre Pompidou and steered the spectator. Image took precedence over words: the show has already begun.

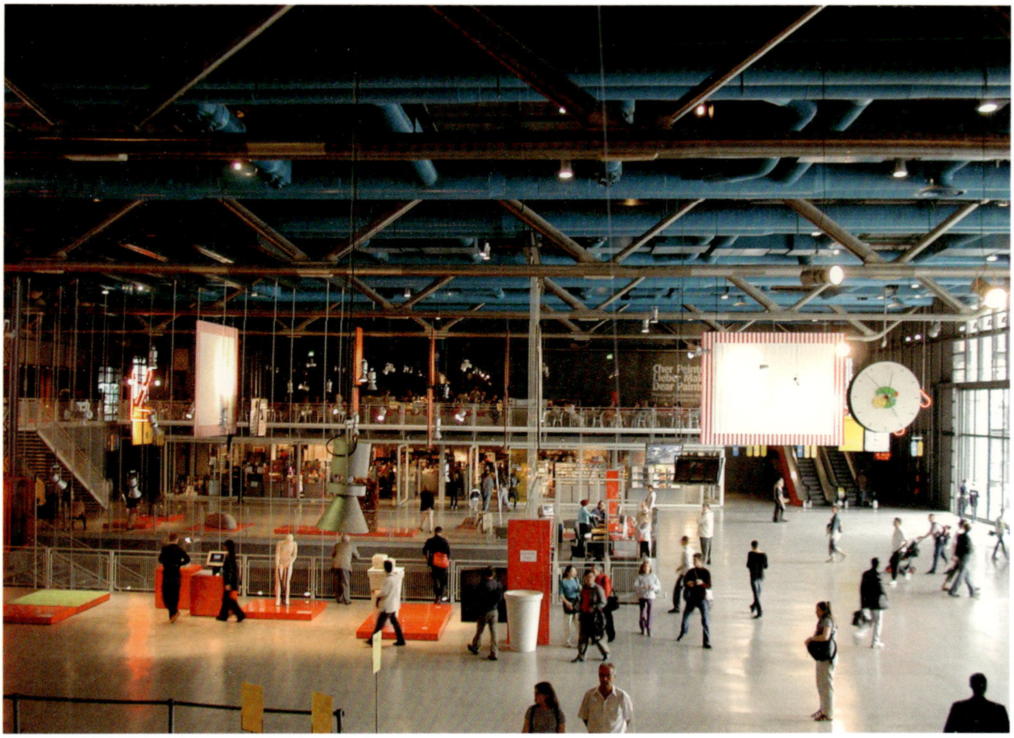

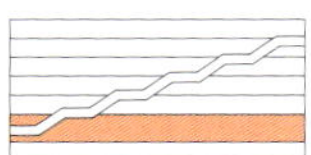

Forum

Photo-souvenir: "Making a Sign", works *in situ* (front)
Canvas, silkscreen, cables, steel tubes

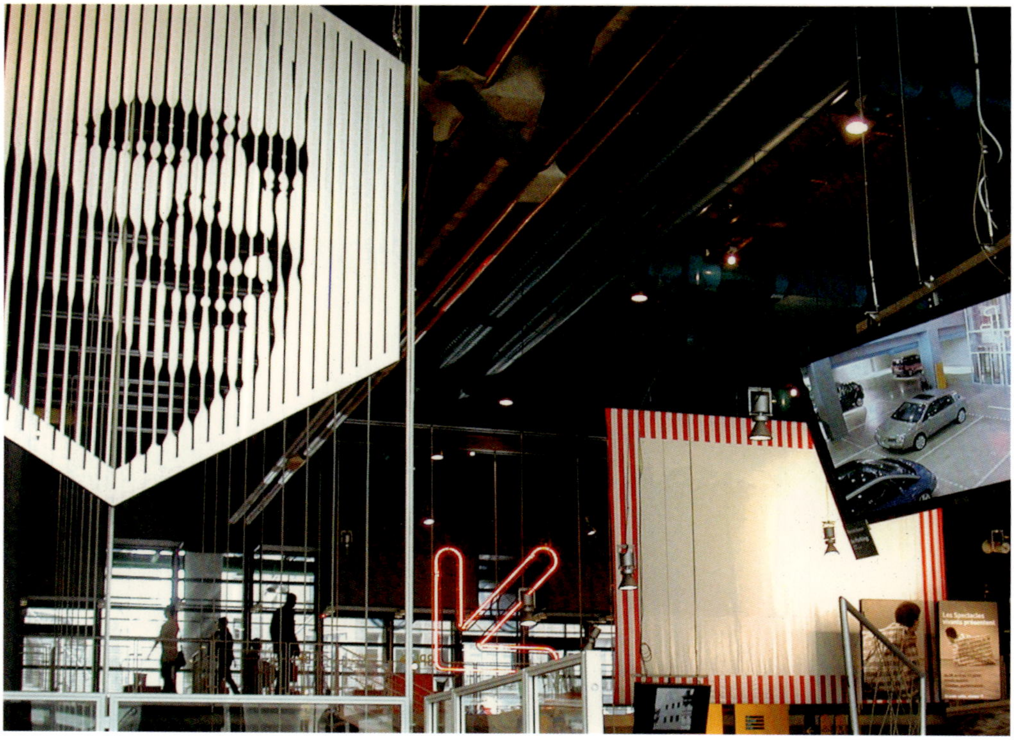

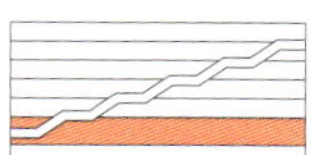

Forum

Photo-souvenir: *"Making a Sign"*, works *in situ* (front)
Canvas, silkscreen, cables, steel tubes

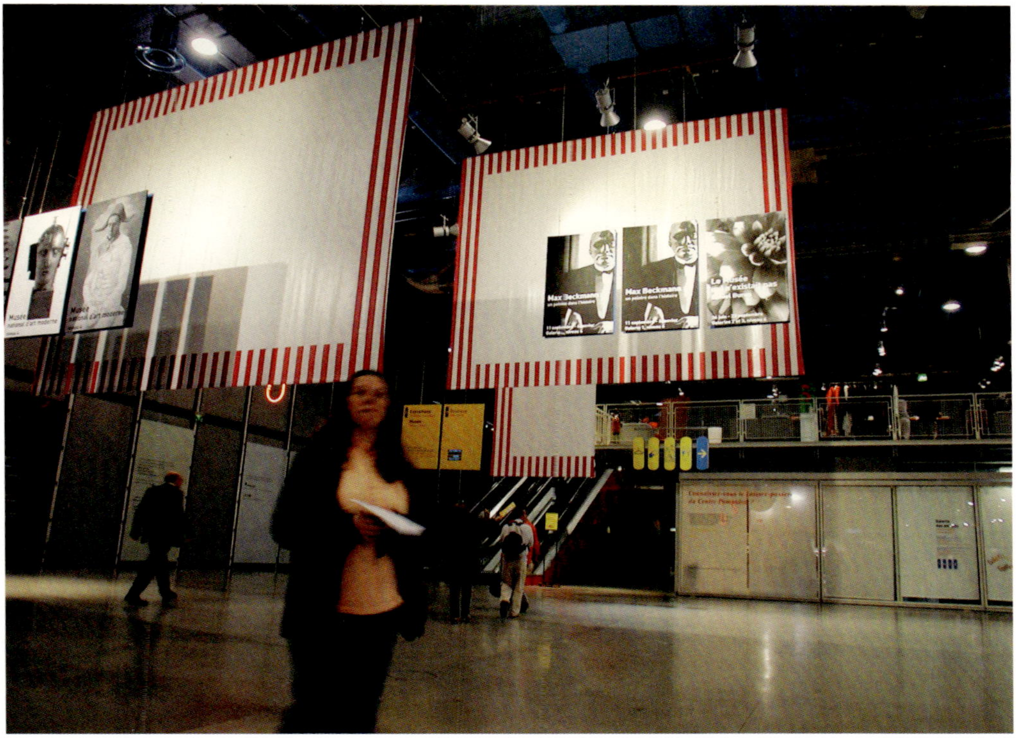

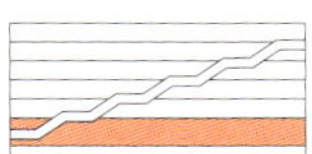

Forum

Above and on following pages:
Photos-souvenirs: "Making a Sign", works *in situ* (front and back)
Canvas, silkscreen, cables, steel tubes

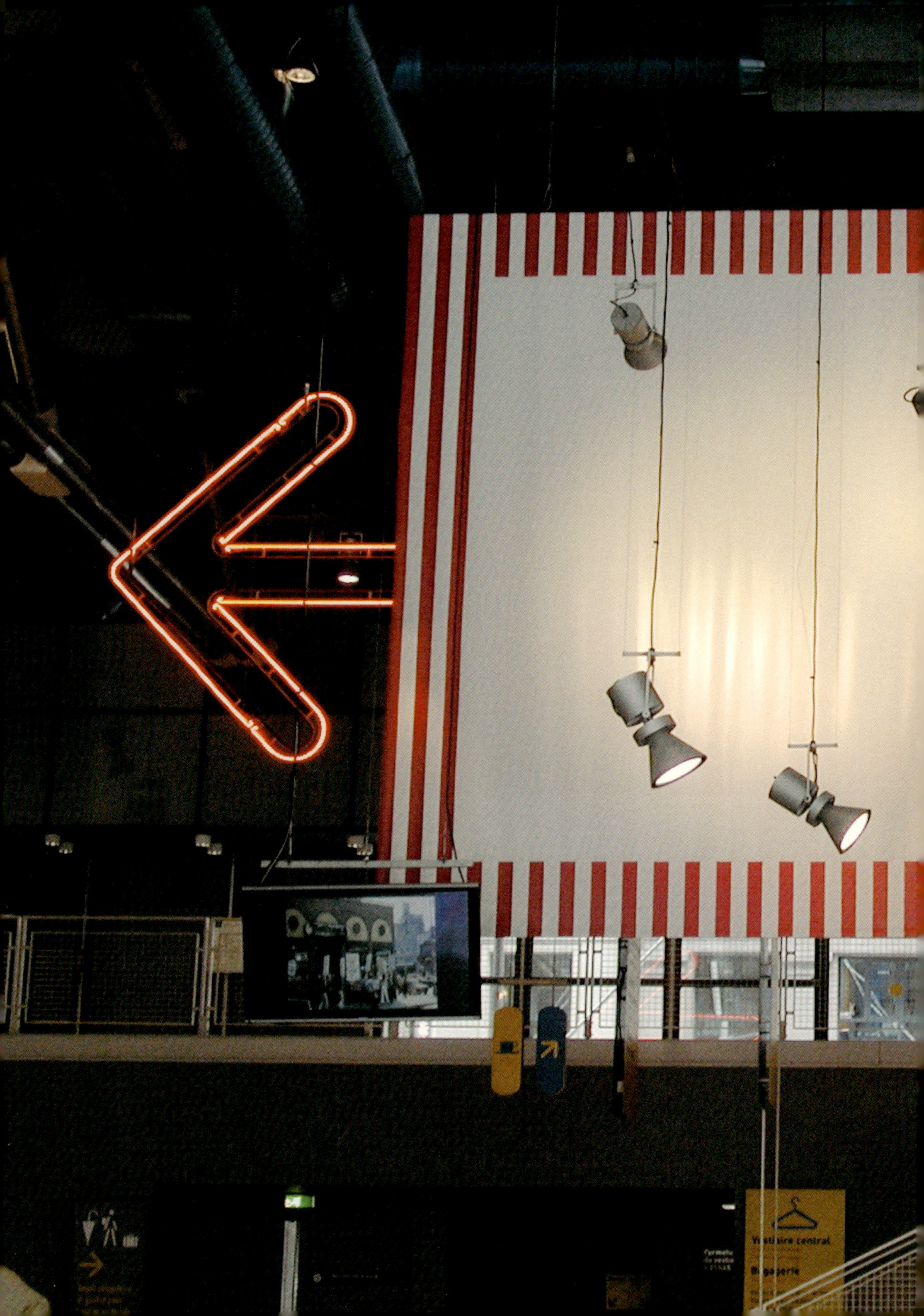

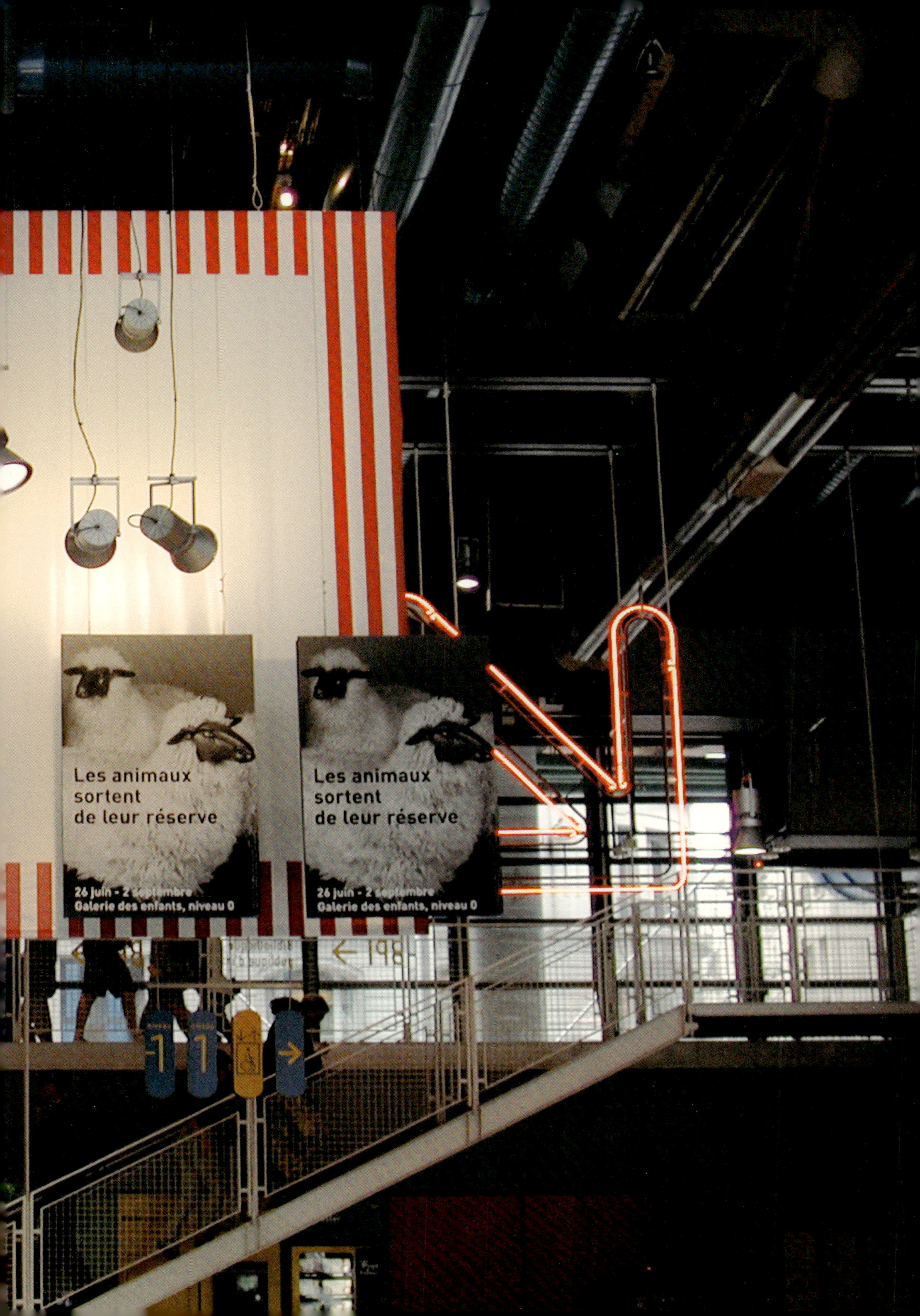
Les animaux
sortent
de leur réserve
26 juin - 2 septembre
Galerie des enfants, niveau 0
Les animaux
sortent
de leur réserve
26 juin - 2 septembre
Galerie des enfants, niveau 0

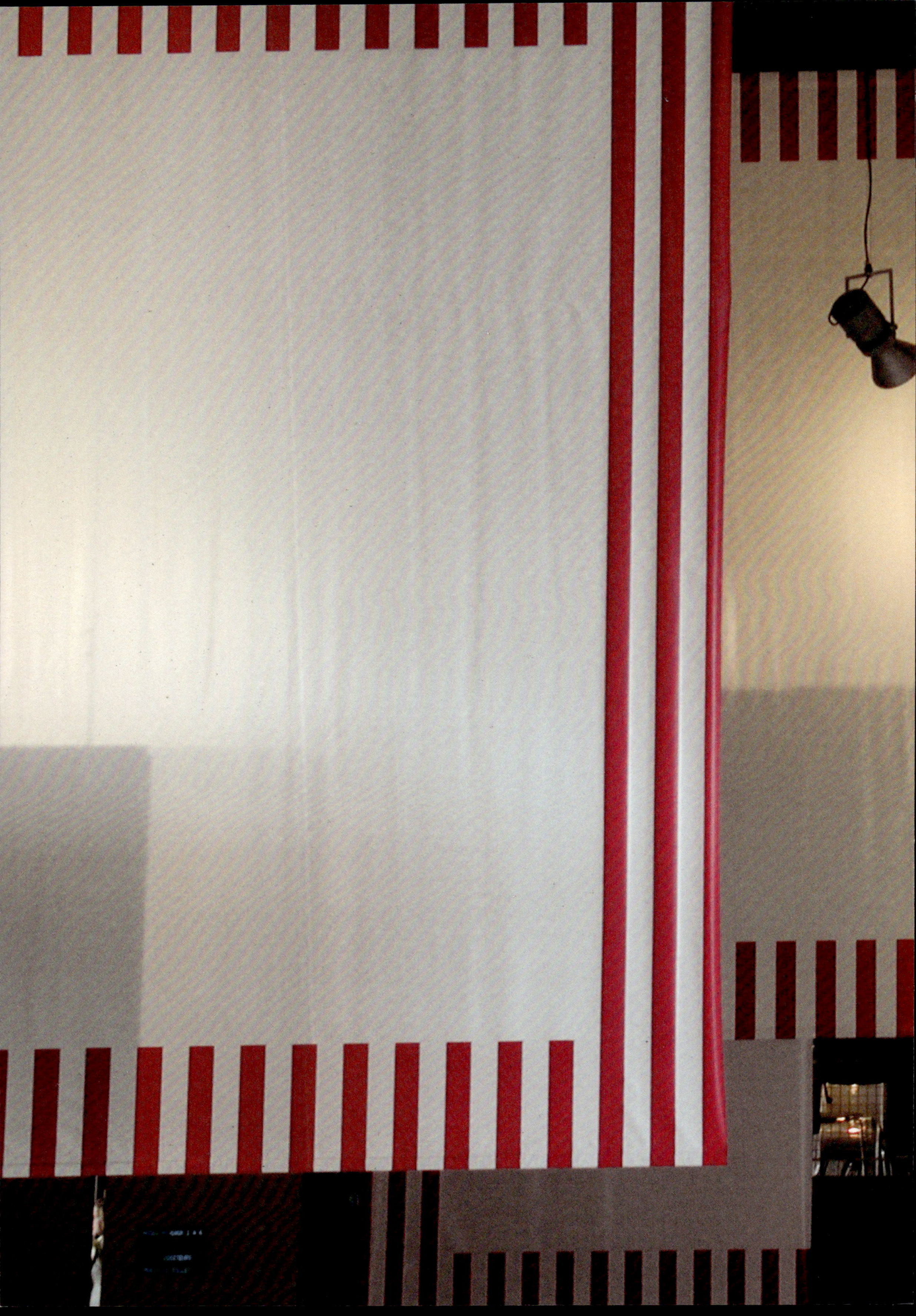

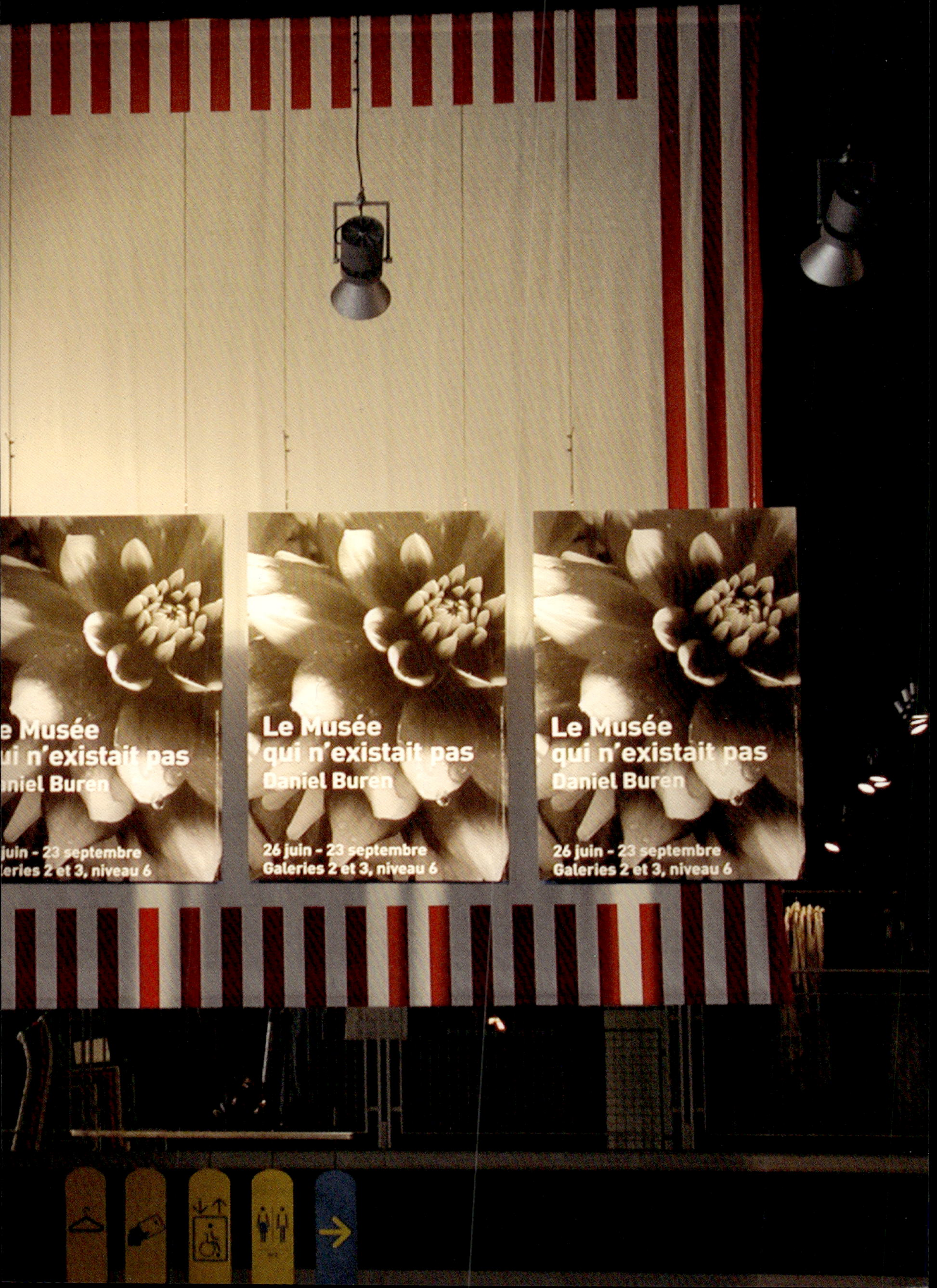
Le Musée
qui n'existait pas
Daniel Buren
26 juin - 23 septembre
Galeries 2 et 3, niveau 6

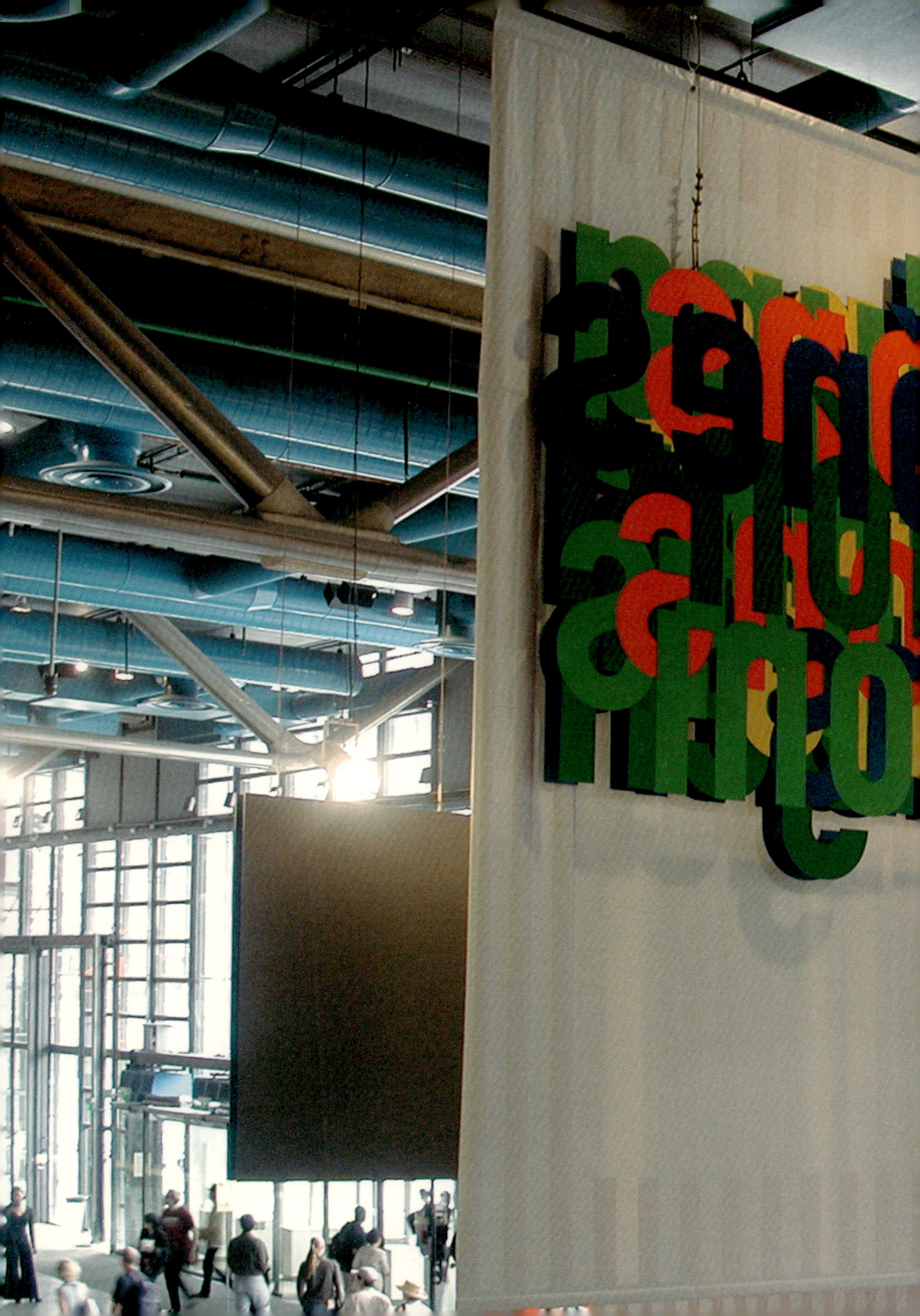

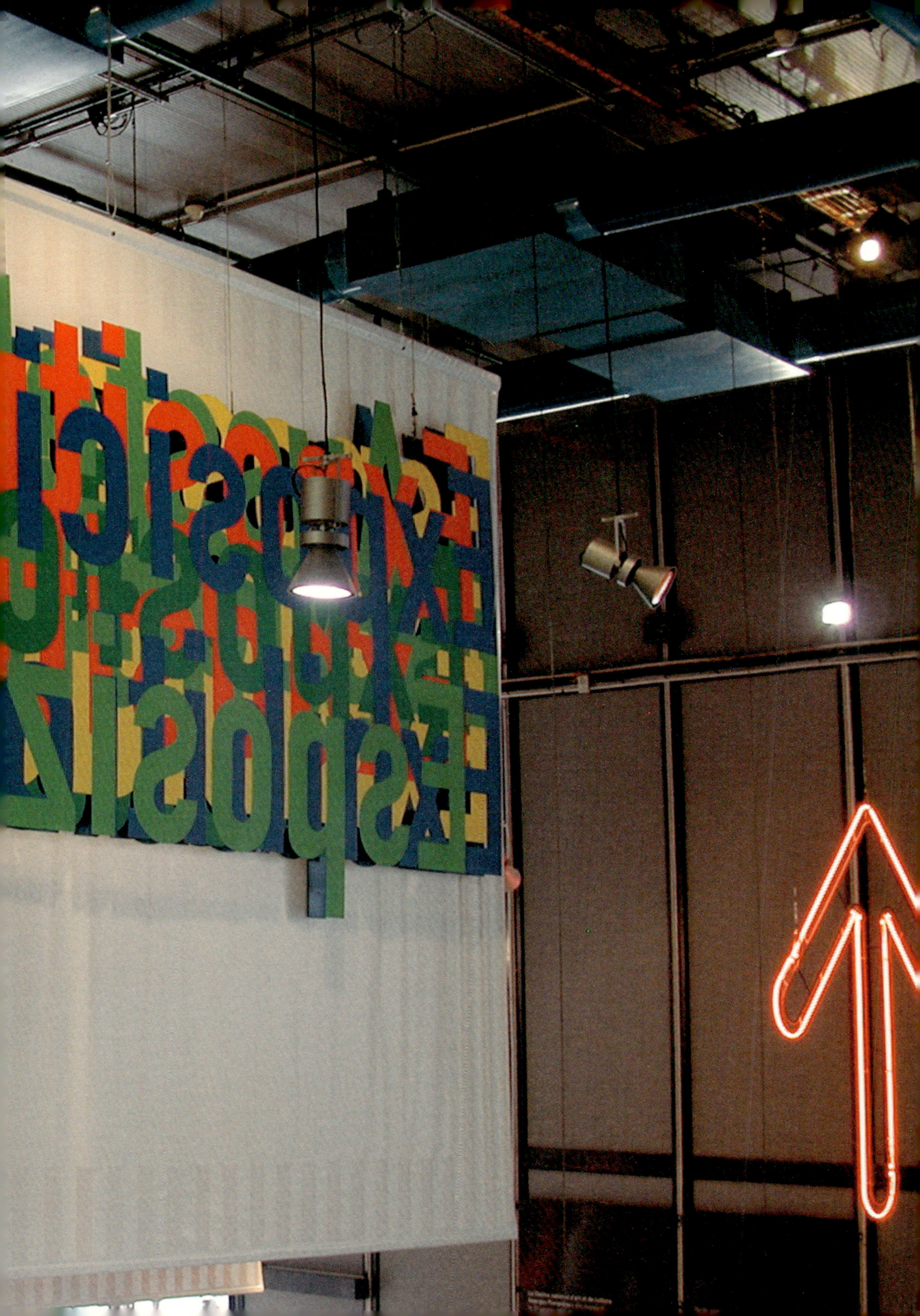

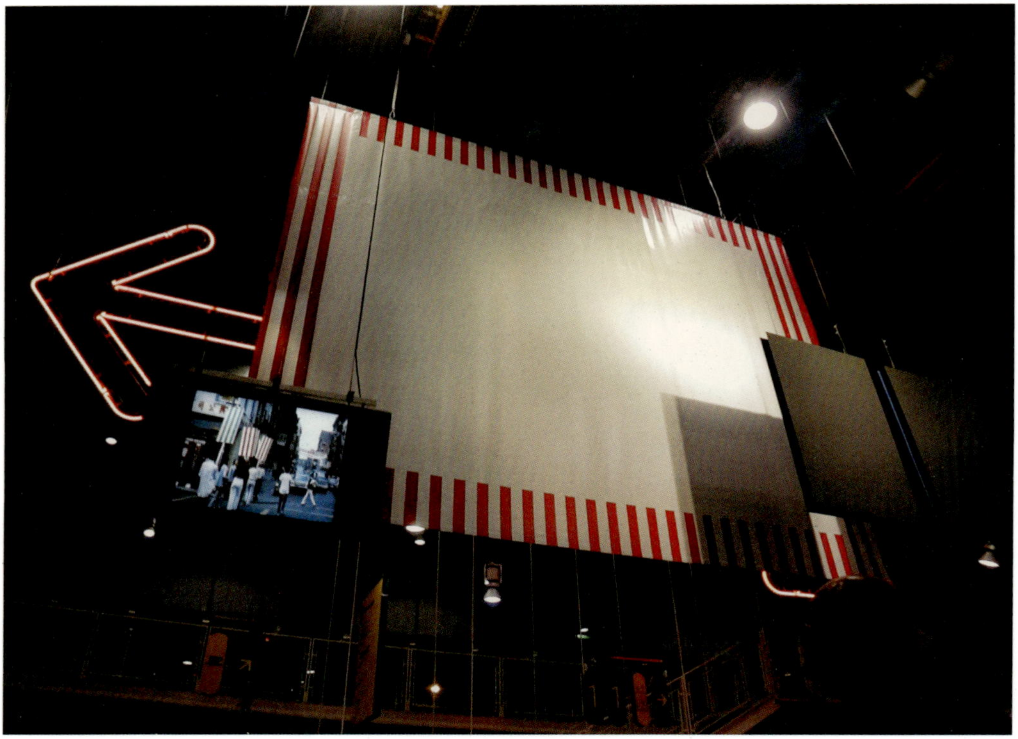

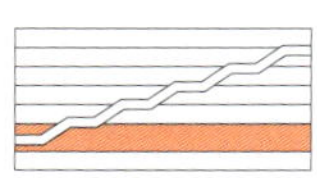

Forum

Photo-souvenir: *"Making a Sign"*, works *in situ* (front)
Canvas, silkscreen, cables, steel tubes
Screens scattered in the hall of the Centre Pompidou rebroadcast views of the exhibition and some non-exhibited Daniel Buren works.

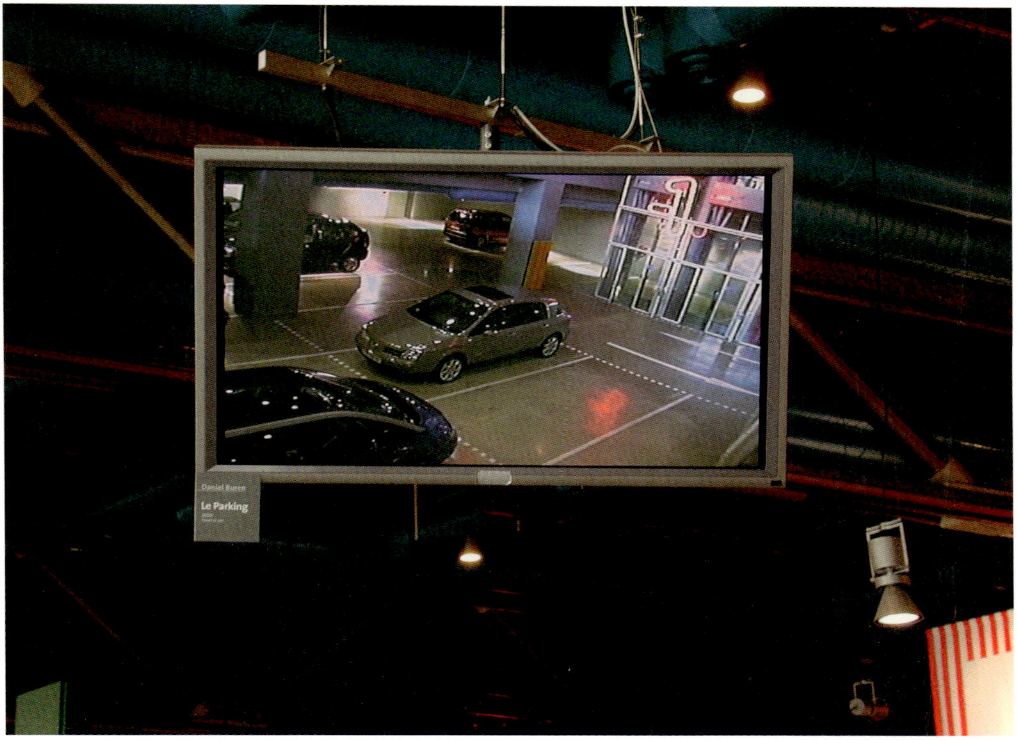

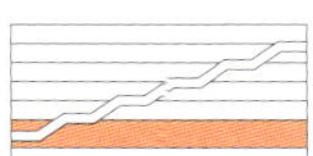

Forum

Photo-souvenir: *"Making a Sign"*, works *in situ* (front)
Canvas, silkscreen, cables, steel tubes
Screens scattered in the hall of the Centre Pompidou rebroadcast views
of the exhibition and some non-exhibited Daniel Buren works.

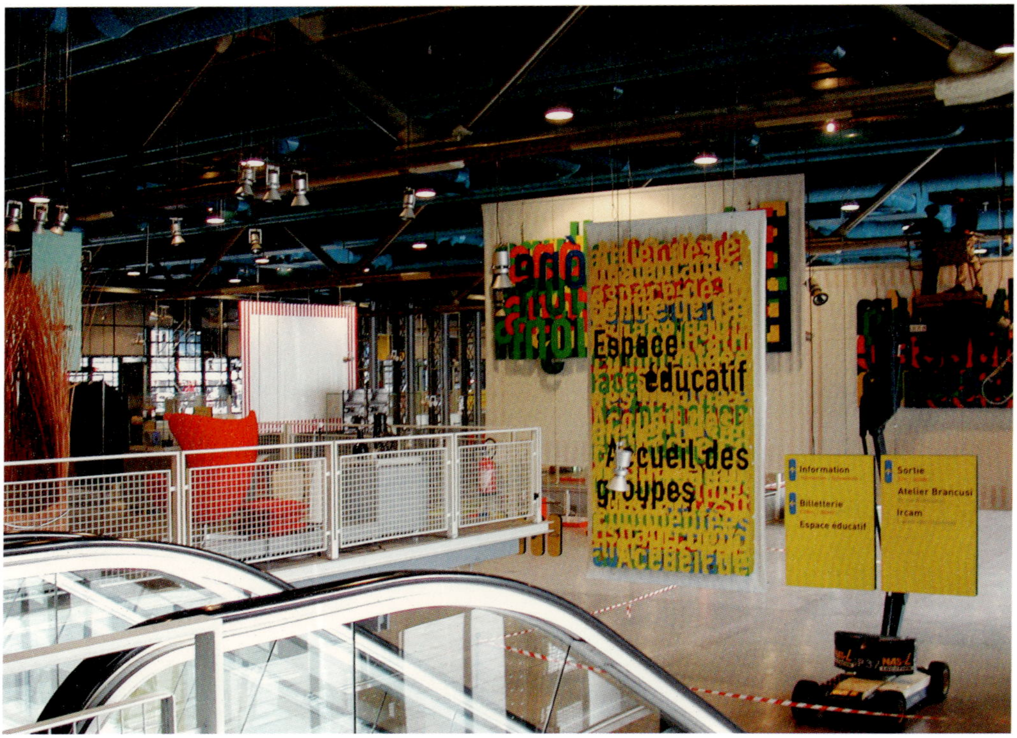

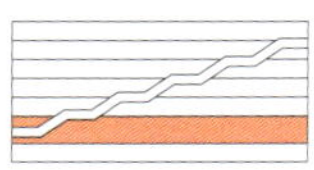

Forum

Photo-souvenir: "Making a Sign", works *in situ* (both sides)
Canvas, silkscreen, cables, steel tubes

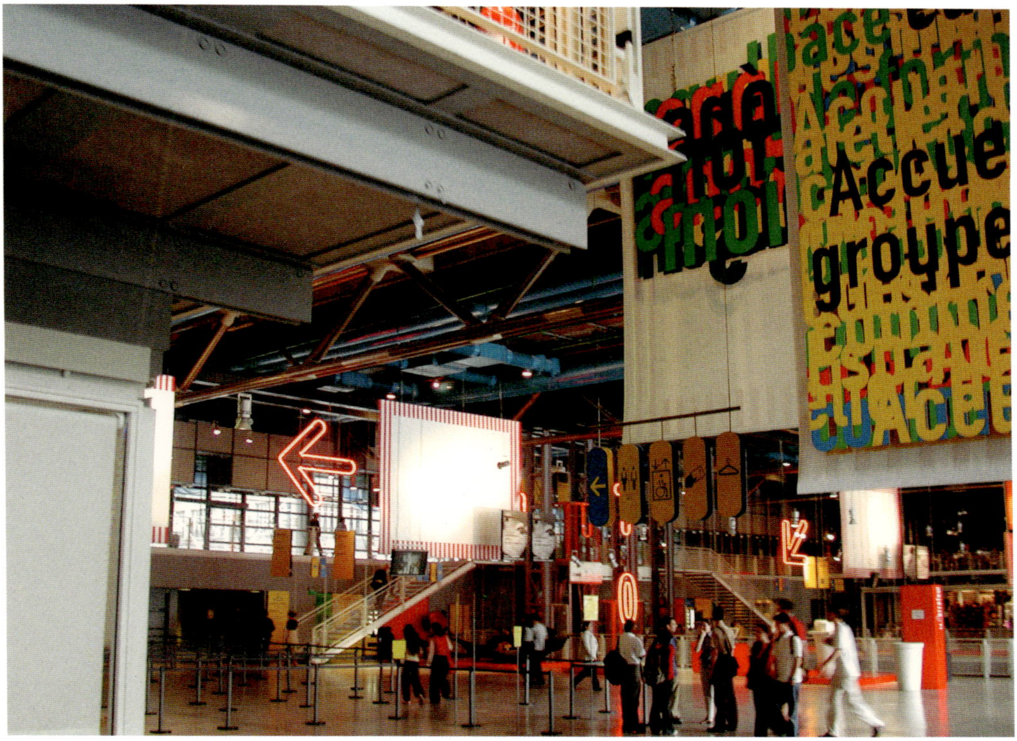

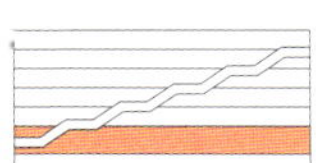

Forum

Photo-souvenir: *"Making a Sign"*, works *in situ* (both sides)
Canvas silkscreen, cables, steel tubes

Buren temporarily transformed the forum -1 of the Centre Pompidou into a car park. Or how to reveal a place initially given over to exhibitions which had become, from one building refit to the next, a space that had lost all cultural identity — an identity that it has since regained... When it comes to Buren, American thinking talks about "an institutional criticism".

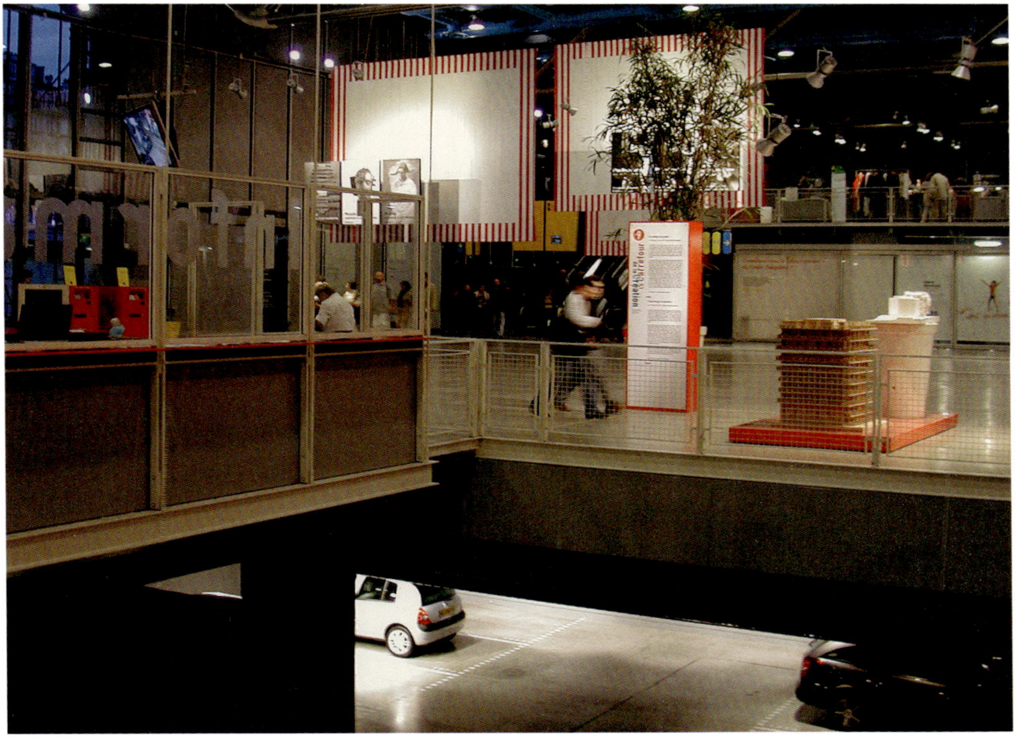

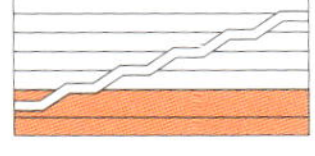

Forum and Level -1

Photo-souvenir: "Making a Sign" (front), *"Car park"*, works *in situ*
Canvas, silkscreen, cables, steel tubes
White acrylic stripes, cars

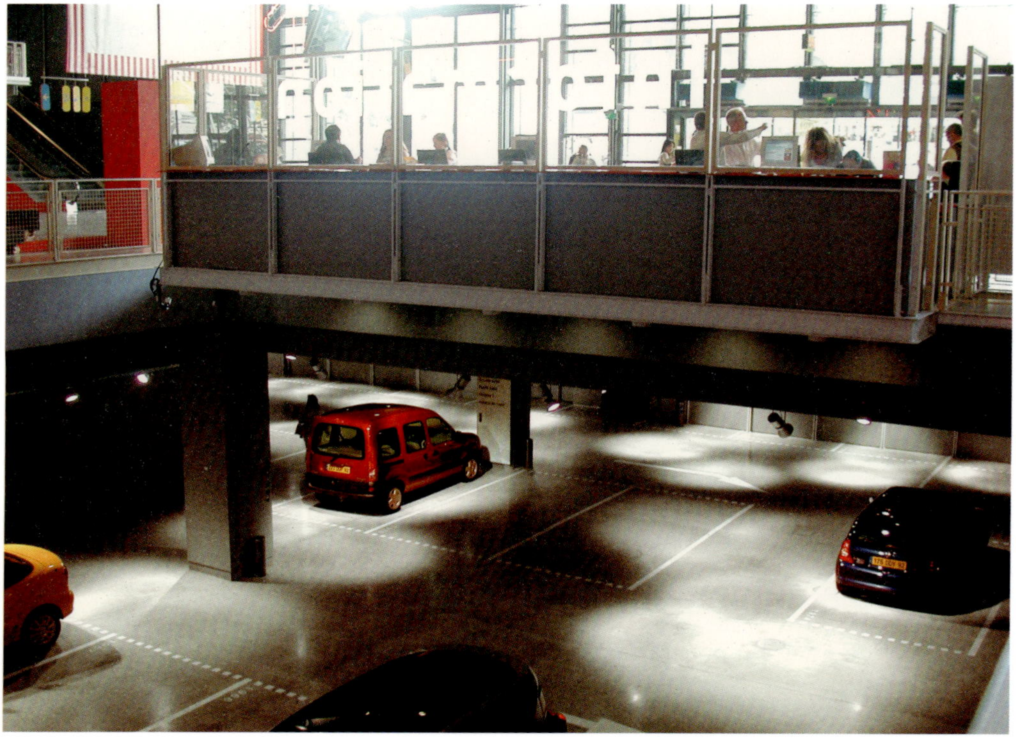

Forum and Level -1

Photo-souvenir: "Making a Sign" (front), *"Car park"*, works *in situ*
Canvas, silkscreen, cables, steel tubes
White acrylic stripes, cars

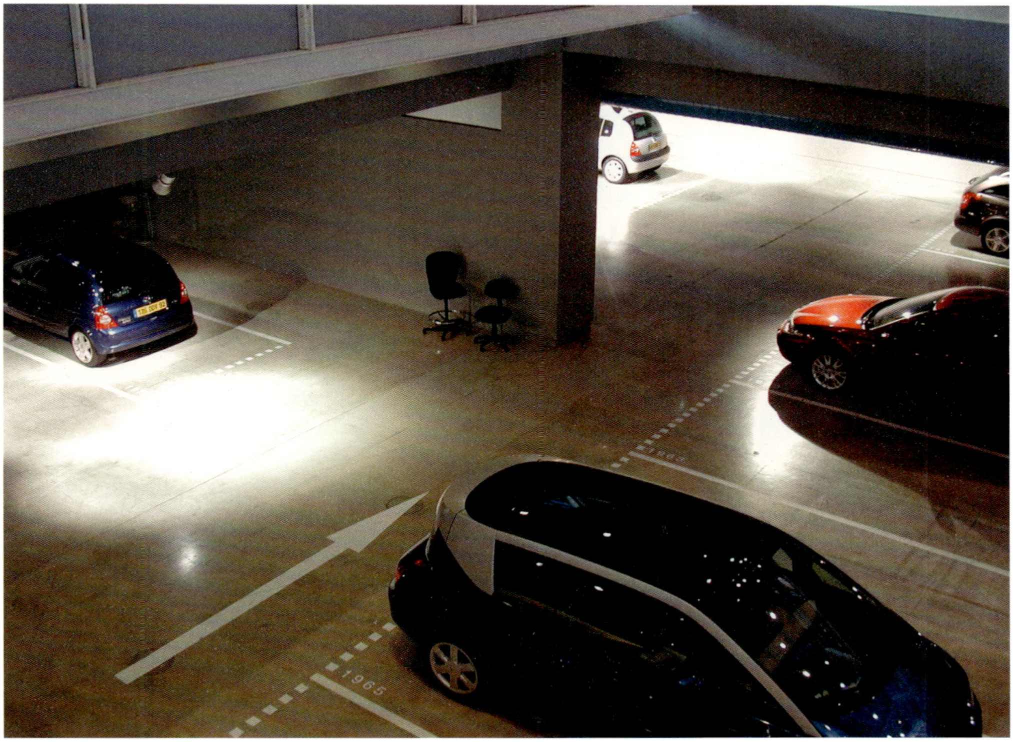

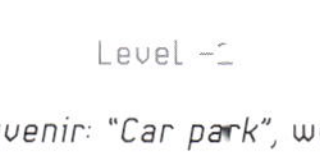

Level -1

Photo-souvenir: "Car park", work in situ
White acrylic stripes, cars

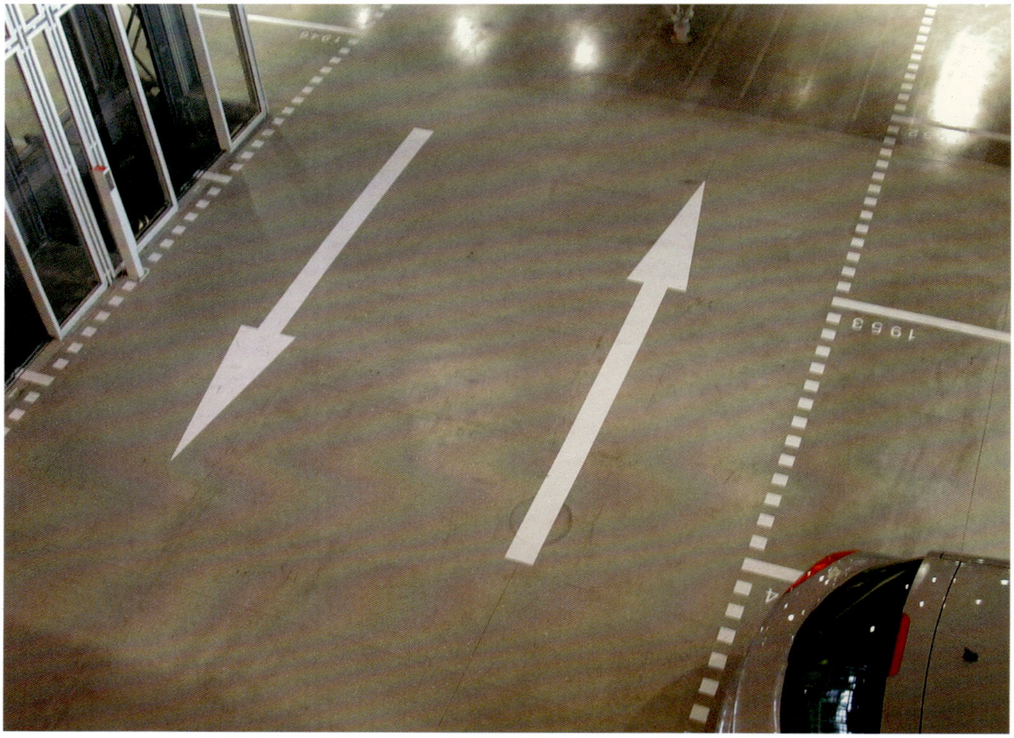

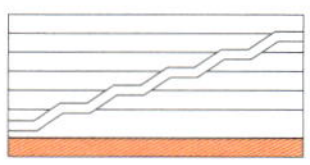

Level -1

Photo-souvenir: "Car park", work in situ
White acrylic stripes, cars

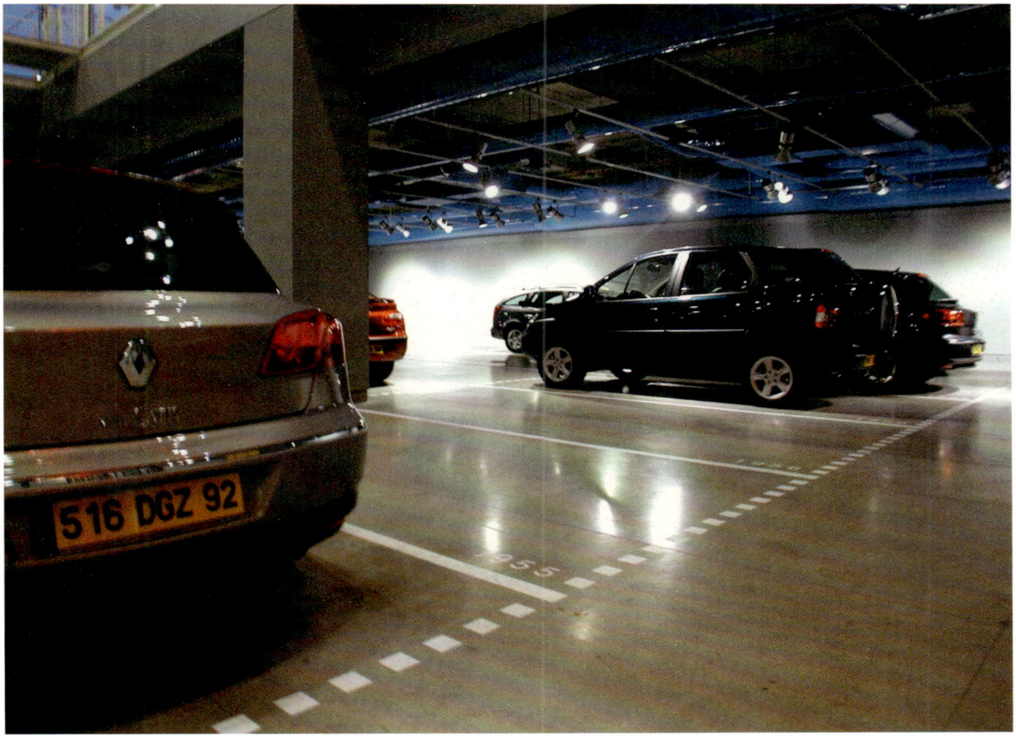

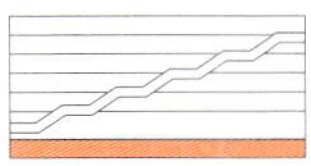

Level -1

Photo-souvenir: "Car park", work in situ
White acrylic stripes, cars

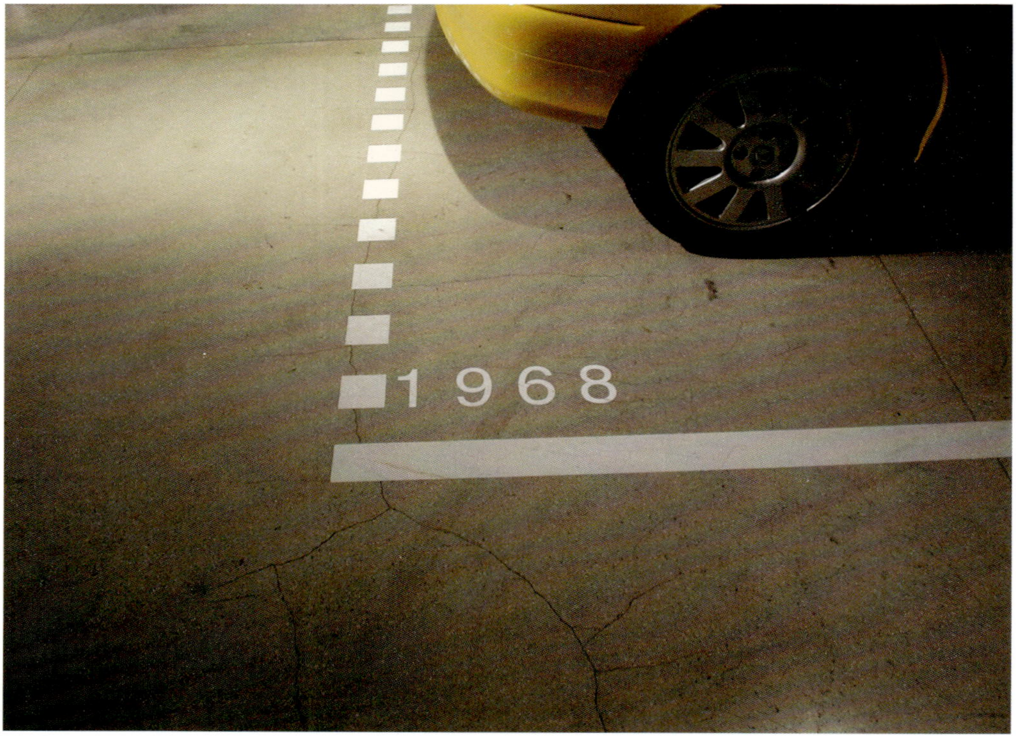

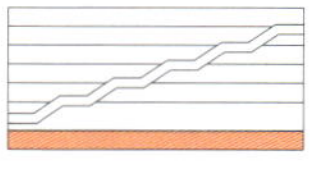

Level -1

Photo-souvenir: "Car park", work in situ
White acrylic stripes, cars

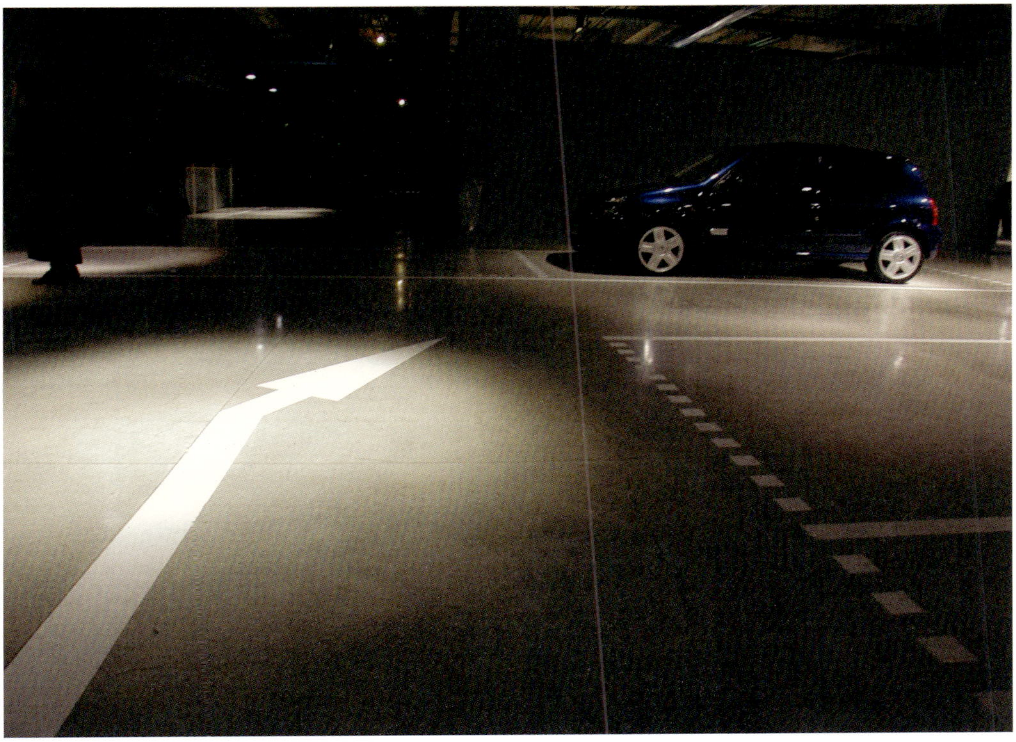

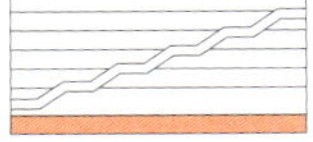

Level -1

Photo-souvenir: "Car park", work in situ
White acrylic stripes, cars

The Labyrinth

At this stage in the project's development, the diagram initiated by Buren, with its basic structure and the geometry thus engendered, led him towards a rational division of space. While he proposed a structure *per se* and its gradual diminution outside the building, Buren would nevertheless push still further the initiatory principle for turning the initial grid into a chequerboard, or even a set, in such a way that a full compartment would alternate with an empty one. Here probably lies an essential factor of the arrangement which we should dwell on.

Once the initial arrangement was okayed, Buren obtained a principle whose main merit was that it offered a large number of possibilities for systematically elaborating therein a set of propositions in which most of us saw a demonstration of the different aspects and variations of his work. But while it was expected that each one of the boxes obtained be the site of a possible intervention, Buren would swiftly decide to leave every other one empty. After months of negotiations to get more space, Buren left half the spaces won empty. Each one of these free zones then became a space of repose, "a grey zone" which Buren in fact wanted to paint grey, a sort of intermediary "non-place" but also an arithmetical operation bordering on total irony: Buren had secured almost double the space initially offered him. Henceforth he would leave half of it empty, simply by not occupying it. He was free to do as he wished. "The site's turn, your turn", he wrote back in 1985[11].

This is definitely one of the most intriguing aspects of the artist's method, a method in which I readily recognise a display of the principle of creative freedom to which Buren is forever referring. Faced with the restrictions that he had to manage to get round, Buren became master of the space by winning one part of it and ceding back another.

11 Daniel Buren, *La Rencontre des sites*, in Jean-Marc Poinsot, *Quand l'œuvre a lieu. L'Art exposé et ses récits autorisés,* Geneva, Les Presses du Réel, coll. "Mamco", 2008, p. 301.

He invented a grid which he made at once a chequerboard and a chessboard, once again suggesting his attachment to the practical and symbolic systems of spatial mathematisation constructed throughout the history of painting and architecture. He also emphasized the fact that the invention of the game into which he wanted to draw us presupposed, above all, the invention of a specific space so that "the work can take place[12]".

Painting and architecture, of course, but also the praxis of art submitting the viewer to a rule which the artist – each and every artist – has to be past master of, a rule on the scale of the body moving about in it, a rule presupposing that once in the labyrinth, one grasps the principle, one visualizes the openings, one ventures and proceeds therein along the winding layout in a succession of forks, dead ends and false leads. A labyrinth, therefore, in which we know how much Buren and his contemporaries saw a motif and a representation of man's relation to creation, but a labyrinth which, needless to add, here responded neither to the figure of the Minotaur nor to that of Mannerism, but rather to that of the contemporary rhizome, where each path can cross another, without any centre or delimited space. The rhizome is blurred and thus undefined. It is subject to all manner of conjecture, which we know to be suppositions based on appearances. The permanent exhibition would make this demonstrable.

A labyrinth, lastly, as an archetype of knowledge and profane space, all at once: an adjustment in the given space and the desire to go astray in the heart of the work to raise the issue, right away, of the spectator's place in his/her relation to the work, and, by contrast, create an imposed route, the need for an artistic experience at the heart of a living space. "The labyrinth", said Walter Benjamin, "is the homeland of hesitation."

12 *Ibid.*

Roaming Thoughts

From this labyrinth prompting roaming thoughts, set up in the exhibition's initial space like a principle essentially differing from that of the re-arrangement of the museum's permanent collection areas, Buren would quickly make a model applicable to all the Centre Pompidou's areas and spaces which he was determined to use. After all, the invitation extended to him confronted him implicitly with the building and involved him in conceiving his proposition beyond just the exhibition areas. Right away, Buren had also made it clear that he wished to intervene in different places. He identified strategic spaces, in such a way as to be able to present his project to be read in several emplacements. Buren was unable to envisage his project on any scale other than that of the Centre itself, and in so doing he would point to the place's overall functioning, the contrasts between common spaces and exhibition spaces, the relation between the museum and the temporary spaces and, *de facto*, the "specific" place of this in the building. While some thought that he would construct a critique of the museum in the Centre, Buren would, quite to the contrary, highlight the museum's subordination to the Centre, in a nutshell, "The Museum that did not exist". While others detected a desire for hegemony of the artist over the place, Buren highlighted the real place of artwork in the building and the subordination of the exhibition to specific places. By gradually working his way in to different places, ranging from the building's basements to its terraces, horizontally and vertically alike, Buren introduced an overall system and arrangement whose primary function was to retake possession of the places and, in so doing, get back to the initial project of the Centre Pompidou made up of spaces not earmarked for any allocated function. Here there was not so much an idea of conquest as of reconquest of the premises, which had gradually been snatched from art to become zones subject to different kinds of rites other than those of creative activity. Places versus non-places. Exhibition places for art and works. "One can try", said Jean-Marc Poinsot, "to shed light, one by one, on the issue of space and the issue of otherness based on two contrasted and complementary spatial realities ...: that of the place, a place which I have called anthropological place because the identity, relations and history of those in it are incorporated in the space; that of the non-place, meaning by that the areas of circulation, distribution and communication, where neither identity, nor relations, nor history can be grasped, and which seem to me specific to contemporary history[13]."

Buren thus worked on the divisions between social space and art space, highlighting how these latter were organized within the Centre Pompidou itself. He worked on the boundaries between place and non-place. The Centre Pompidou became the archetype of a space where art's function gradually found itself facing that of merchandise. In his criticism of the institution where, more than ever, to borrow Jean-Luc Godard's words, "culture and art are clash like the rule and the exception", Buren's subtle and insidious approach aimed at highlighting the spectacle-in-the-making of the cultural institution and the museum's subordination to the space of which it is a department, appears to be one of the essential challenges of his proposal. This time around, Buren turned his project into the means of an investigation of the social space of art, and brought to the fore the dovetailing between the exhibition of the space and the space of the exhibition. It was not simply a matter of underlining any old compartmentalization between the museum and the Centre Pompidou, but of giving readability to the ongoing linkage between the way the institution functions in its entirety and the way the museum works as part of an overall system. Let me once again borrow Jean-Marc Poinsot's words, writing about the "exorcized monument": "If the organisation of institutions, the economy, and the professional arena defines the social space of art and

13 *Ibid.*

the ways it finds its way into the whole of the human space, it does not seem possible to me to think of the "sites" where art encounters the social outside of the art institution. Otherwise put, the history of the non-places of art is in a way the other side of the history of the institution[14]."

It is here that Daniel Buren's exhibition enjoyed its full reverberation even beyond the space allocated to him. It is here that, invited to consider a proposal from the Musée national d'Art moderne by the Centre Pompidou's President, Daniel Buren pointed the finger at the singularity of the way the institution functioned, and decided to respond to the proposal by working at once in the gallery offered to him and in the building's shared spaces. He immediately underscored the fact that the exhibition venues were, furthermore, not so much those of the museum as those of the Centre in its entirety. He highlighted, in an insidious and decisive way, the museum's place within the Centre Pompidou, and the unusualness of the relations enacted therein.

As was his wont, Buren then used the areas made available to him like so many possible but different investigations. He dealt with the organization of gallery 2 on level 6 by extending it beyond itself, to the point of prolonging it into the bookshop adjoining the space, and to the Restaurant Georges beside the exhibition venues, as well as to the terraces giving onto the city. But Buren also extended his appropriation of the building's entrance foyer and its signs and notices, level -1 and its common areas, the tracks of the escalators leading to the different levels, and he conspicuously reinstalled in the museum the most invisible of his pieces, *The Forms: paintings*, a work made up of several rebounds, "visible" just by way of the notices informing viewers of their presences beneath the pictures in the museum collection, freely chosen by the curator in charge of the hanging. The Centre Pompidou was henceforth "taken to task".

14 *Ibid.*

It is surprising, and Buren was probably the most surprised, that the requests he then made were all accepted. Perhaps there was a desire to give the artist the possibility of implementing his different propositions? Perhaps there was also the feeling that, whatever the daring and the controversial dimension, they could only give the Centre Pompidou back its essentially experimental dimension, which was what befitted it? Perhaps there was, herein, an awareness that, in the logic peculiar to the artist's work, the building could only be "grasped" in its entirety? Perhaps there was the idea that the invitation extended to Buren was not so much the affair of just the museum as of the Centre itself, and in so doing, it was important to get the artist to signify as much?... In any event, an essential aspect of the project was asserted, an aspect where the artist and the Centre would come to an agreement over a set of propositions, in which both would be in evidence... It is odd to observe here how the formulation of the project was gradually made up of exchanges between the president's office and the artist, and how an unusual contract was drawn up between the two parties. Buren wanted at once to mark out the forum with panels shaped like large frames with white and pink stripes, encompassing an entirely white space, which would cover the existing signs and notices. He would suggest replacing information in words with sign information. For the signs telling the public where the different spaces were, he would propose that they be masked and, when all's said and done, dispensed with. While he was told that there was the risk of disorienting the public – something which probably did not displease the artist – Buren retorted that he was proposing to try it out, and that he would accept that everything should be dismantled if visitors got lost. Here lay an endless raft of questions that the artist, for the nonce master of the premises, prepared to bring to the fore. Buren, as we know, is unrivalled when it comes to pinpointing the ideological and practical contradictions of each and every institution.

There was neither complaint nor confusion. As if by some natural reflex, the public went on walking around and getting its bearings in the building without having to ask the way. If the truth be told, people did not notice much, except that they had to walk around and move about as they wished. With signs and notices more or less in abeyance, apart from a few small notices for temporary shows, the Centre was there for everyone to discover at will, like that "discursive network of different praxes" which Hal Foster talks about and which people strode and visited with the idea of constructing their own itinerary and their own set of tracks. With its written signs done away with, the Pompidou Centre found itself given over to the power of the sign rather than to that of the written word and the artistic proposition, to the building's total space rather than to an assigned place. When visitors entered the building, they could thus see that level -1 had become a car park. In it Buren had put cars that Renault had agreed to lend for the occasion, for the vehicles could not be any old make, and they also had to be "prepared" for reasons of security, in order to be shown. This was probably one of the most impulsive proposals Buren suggested, a reflection on the future of this place, also reconfigured during the reconstruction works between 1998 and 2000, and the opinion, shared by many today, that the way it was now reduced meant that it had lost its initial potential. It is hard to gauge how the strength of the proposal was all the more radical since it went unnoticed by most visitors. Buren had used the white stripes applied directly to the grey surface of the ground to mark out the space into so many potential parking places, for vehicles which visitors could incidentally notice were all of the same make: a "Jacques Tati-like" development of a space which the artist turned into a garage.

And then, once past the forum and the level -1 areas, Buren also wanted to install a piece in the track of the escalators[15]. Televisions were set up and broadcast one of the artist's old sonic video works

15 Daniel Buren, *The Colours : sculptures*, 1984-2002, outside escalators, Centre Pompidou, second project for "The Museum that did not exist".

where you glimpsed his hands handling and tearing sheets of paper with different coloured stripes, superposing them and adjusting them, in such a way that they keep the 8.7 centimetre [3.4 inches] gap representing the standard motif on which the artist's visual work is based... In an implicit way, the piece had a specific connotation. It ushered in the motif and the sign peculiar to the whole of Buren's œuvre. It also suggested, in its very form, that the praxis of art is not far removed from conjuring. It reminded people, as well, that at the beginning of the Centre Pompidou this place of passage had been occupied by certain artists including Robert Wilson who had installed therein, at Pontus Hulten's request, continuous loop short video pieces produced by the Centre Pompidou[16]. Last of all, it highlighted the particularly strategic function of this space. Buren subjected the Centre Pompidou to his sign/image informing the building. This would recur in the museum's permanent collections, where, for the occasion, two of the artist's most emblematic pieces would be installed: *The Forms: paintings* and *The Colours: sculptures*, both introduced like two *in situ* proposals deeply incorporated within the history of the collections of the Musée national d'art moderne, since these latter had found their way into the Centre Pompidou.

The choice of presenting these two pieces didn't come about by chance. In many ways it would symbolise the complete idea behind the show, clearly expressing, on the one hand, Daniel Buren's relation to the museum as well as to the Centre Pompidou, and, on the other, that of the museum to the Centre.

As we know, the two pieces were acquired by the museum during its installation and opening at the Centre Pompidou in 1977. Although they may be shown separately, they clearly form a whole because they play both with plane and volume, with the museum's interior space and the outside area of the level 6 passageway, where telescopes were

16 For the presentation of new acquisitions, Pontus Hulten, then director of the Musée national d'Art moderne, had installed Robert Wilson's video works in the track of the Centre Pompidou escalator. This is one of the rare uses of this space to have been made to date.

to be installed to make them visible. Whereas *The Forms: paintings* address the "onlooker" and can be installed, just as the curator chooses, behind paintings in the permanent collections, *The Colours: sculptures*, for their part, can only be seen from the Centre Pompidou through telescopes set up for the occasion. As we can once more see, the protocol was precise and involved the institution in an endless number of transactions with those in charge of different establishments, public and private alike, on whose roofs a striped flag was hoisted for the period of the presentation. *The Colours: sculptures* was actually so difficult to install and the permits so complicated to obtain, so deeply do they question the relation between power and its own representation, that the piece has been put in place only once in its entirety, since the Centre Pompidou opened. The opportunity was too alluring for Buren not to decide to go for it...

As a result the two pieces here became a major challenge in the general arrangement that Buren was setting up. In addition to evoking Buren's presence in the permanent collections of the Musée national d'art moderne since its installation at the Centre Pompidou, and thus the ongoing but paradoxical relation between artist and museum, they clearly symbolized the battleground upon which the artist's critical analyses clashed with those of every manner of institution. Here it is worth remembering the analysis made about those pieces by Benjamin H.D. Buchloh, then a great champion of Daniel Buren, whom he only want to comment upon and understand through the prism of political critique[17]. We are acquainted with the quarrels which since then pitted the historian of German extraction installed in the United States against the artist, and Buchloh's difficulty in grasping the development of Buren's œuvre in its particularly spectacular and conspicuously decorative dimension. It was nevertheless this dimension, conceived as a

17 Benjamin H.D. Buchloh was one of the first to explain Buren's work. His different essays about the artist, including the one published in Daniel Buren, *The Colours : Sculptures. The Forms : Paintings*, Paris, Centre Georges Pompidou / Halifax, Presses du Nova Scotia College of Art & Design, 1981, attest to an understanding of the development of his work, while certain others stirred up controversy between

necessary artifice, re-incorporated in its relation to the subject and its own place in its relation to the work, which, from the 1980s to today, would make Buren's work so quintessentially topical.

The Colours: sculptures and *The Forms: paintings* thus did indeed form the two centres of an activation of the space at the Centre Pompidou, even inside the building, and outside it. It may not be timely, at this juncture, to remind readers that what we had here was a critical approach to the relation of dependence of the work on the institution's space, and in so doing, of the relation of the readymade to the museum, but it is nevertheless important to underline that those two pieces, which became part and parcel of the general arrangement of Buren's project for his solo show at the Centre Pompidou, acted as essential referents. In addition to their participation in the organization and general distribution of the signs within the various spaces and areas, by playing at once with the place where art is meant to be validated as such (the museum) and intended to face reality (the public place), they were part of that desire for contamination and dissemination which Buren had made one of the "poetic and political" stakes of his project. Here I am intentionally borrowing this notion from Marcel Broodthaers who shares with Buren both the critical analysis of contexts and of the decorative and ambiguous function of art in the social space. *The Colours: sculptures* and *The Forms: paintings* were in a way the two pieces of one and the same game which would lead at once to returning to the museum and escaping from it, a centripetal and centrifugal movement, a movement in any event, not to say a dynamic definitely *in situ* but also, as Buren himself observed in the split second of analyzing the way his work functions, *in vivo*[18].

the critic and the artist. See also Daniel Buren, "Sur les avant-gardes" [interview with Benjamin Buchloh], in cat. A *Autour de "Ponctuations"*, Lyon, Le Nouveau Musée, 1980, unpaginated, French, English. Excerpt taken from "Autour de *Ponctuations/I* – Sur les avant-gardes", in cat. *A Points de vue*, Paris, ARC, Musée d'Art moderne de la Ville de Paris, 6 May-12 June 1983, unpaginated.

An Art of Time

Conceived as a possible succession of encounters with the Centre Pompidou's different spaces, "The Museum that did not exist" traced endless vanishing lines and gave greater importance to subjectivity than any obligatory itinerary. Further still, the general proposition on the scale of the place accommodating it restored the notion of subjectivity to its essential function by contrasting it with organized visits of all sorts. The exhibition was not conceived as a collective and pluralist visit, but as a deeply special experience, an attempt to reject the museum organization aiming at a staked-out route. It came across as a meditation on the future making of the institution. The museum that did exist, its linearity, its chronology, and all its markers and signs, responded to the time of an exhibition, the possibility of a "museum that never was".

What springs to mind here is that the exhibition, in its full and complete etymological sense, had to do with a consummate art of the spectacle. As a perfect pyrotechnician, Buren had immediately conceived the dramatic factor in a novel mode, because he had wanted it to develop in such a way that it encouraged visitors to stroll about, and even included sets of paths. In the strolling factor, Buren clearly saw the immediate possibility of sidestepping the orthodoxy of an imposed itinerary and the vague desire to walk about on a basis of fantasy, with no precise goal. By offering the public a possible series of rebounds throughout the building, Buren would radically transform the exhibition's protocol and, in so doing, that of the initial project proposed to him. To overly determined and smooth spaces he would respond in the manner of Gilles Deleuze and Félix Guattari's *Mille Plateaux*, by making the most of a "striped space"[19], literally and figuratively as far

18 Daniel Buren, *La Rencontre des sites*, in Jean-Marc Poinsot, *Quand l'œuvre a lieu, L'Art exposé et ses récits autorisés*, collection Mamco-Les Presses du Réel, Geneva, 2008, p. 108.

19 Gilles Deleuze et Félix Guattari, *Mille Plateaux*, Minuit, Paris, 1980. In this second volume of *Capitalisme et schizophrénie,* we find on p. 244, in the chapter titled "Trois nouvelles ou "Qu'est-ce qui s'est passé ?" :

as he was concerned. He would strive to highlight individual consciousness in the face of the State apparatus incarnated by the institution inviting him. He would show a preference for the being over the State, and what is becoming to what is. In the first instance, he would organize his project like "the antechamber" of a star-studded, fragmented narrative, a constellation. No beginning and no end, but a succession of possible meetings, signs and signals capable of keeping the mind alert. He would conceive each set like so many moments of intensity suggesting possible tracery work, designing multiple combinations and dovetailings. From the tarpaulin announcing the show outside the Centre Pompidou, on which he wanted to reproduce one of his own "photos-souvenirs" of dahlias, so that the potential onlooker might be at once intrigued by the unexpected image and tempted to enter to "be introduced into its history" (the intention was Mallarméan)[20], to level -1 transformed not without a cruel dash of irony into a parking lot for want, henceforth, of being able to be anything else, the proposition had to do with a succession of alerts which gradually led to the very heart of the project. But when people found themselves in the exhibition space, its prismatic structure suggested a whole host of colours and signs which, like shards in the light, evoked, in many places, the structure of a kaleidoscope; a kaleidoscope, like an interplay of mirrors reflecting *ad infinitum* and in colours the light outside; a kaleidoscope

"My territories are priceless, and not because they are imaginary, but because I am in the process of drawing them… I am no more than just a line." *Le Musée qui n'existait pas,* in its very title, suggests combinations between contradictory forces and arrangements of ideas, capable of transforming the institution's social space.

20 In his enthralling essay devoted to Daniel Buren, published by Flammarion in 2001, Guy Lelong's intent is to grasp and understand the artist's œuvre using Mallarmé as a yardstick. "Buren", writes Lelong, "has introduced into the visual arts a conceptual upheaval equivalent to the one introduced by Mallarmé to poetry. While the one refuses to comply with the previously determined sense of language, the other reverses the relation between the works and their exhibition venues with his notion of *in situ* work. Henceforth, the work of art is conceived on the basis of his exhibition venue and it fully incorporates its characteristics."

which, like the space that Buren had organized as seventy-one identically-sized compartments, suggests a finite number of elements in a finite and closed space, and authorises an indefinite (and not infinite) number of combinations.

As a tangible and symbolic illustration of the way it is possible to create something new by re-arranging what exists, the kaleidoscope is akin to a figure reconciling the opposite terms of permanence and change. It also makes it possible to grasp and illustrate at one and the same time an idea underpinning the fact that it is not the elements which make the whole but the form taken on by their combination: the whole of the kaleidoscope cannot be reduced to the sum of its parts. The kaleidoscope is a world of snippets and bits which is organized by the movements of the person handling it. It is a special *topos*, subject to spinning and the order of vision.

Unlike the principle of contemplation, Buren thus proposed, by way of strolling in the Centre Pompidou's actual itinerary, the idea of thought in motion. In so doing, walking here took on its full metaphorical dimension. The walk from one place to another in the show, without any preconceived route, within the arrangement as well as outside it, at the whim of discovery, symbolized, by contrasting with the linearity of the route of a history of art conceived in its chronological and evolutionary dimension, the philosophical and existential movement of anyone accepting to be freely summoned by the goings-on of life and mind.

Conceiving one's own path as a succession of walks and pauses. Conceiving the time of the walk as that of exploration, of new thoughts, of listening and encounter. Conceiving the walk as the time of freedom and, with it, in the instant of setting out to discover space, without any preconceived path, grasping that art history has probably been written, in the same way as philosophy, to the detriment of the Epicureans. "Le Musée qui n'existait pas" also had to do with the art of time.

An Art of the Spectacle

For anyone who visited "Le Musée qui n'existait pas", the experience was immediately akin to those offered by certain scenic devices such as Baroque theatre developed in the classical age. Baroque theatre and the principle of increasing the number of spaces, a reality carved up which unsettles and disrupts our perception in order to establish the conditions of roaming thinking and letting us go into the nets of chance.

The principle of circulation, like the spectator's errant situation in Daniel Buren's arrangement led to going astray in the space more than to finding the way. At a bend in a room, there was nothing to guide the visitor to any defined place; nothing, if not an attraction for a motif, a colour, or just a desire to plunge still further into the "house of wonders". Never had the Centre Pompidou offered this kind of possibility. Never had it been as close to those entertainment arenas which the Baroque age and its theatre had turned into metaphors of knowledge. Never had we been so committed "to taking incompletion seriously".

Much to the displeasure of a critique persuaded that Buren's œuvre would only find its full justification in its ideological criticism of power by turning its back on all aesthetic temptation, Buren responded for all to see by lending the whole of his project an unmatched spatial and temporal beauty. To the readily simplistic principle of the early works, to the lack of means, to their obliteration to the point of disappearing from the only field of view, Buren here responded by enlarging his project in ways unexpected. From being a visual contradiction, Buren's œuvre became an art with special and unusual variations. From being an intentionally secret and furtive form, the exhibition became a splendid piece of stage machinery, and an imperative pleasure for the eye.

By pushing back the décor so that the public no longer knew if it was on the stage or in the wings, the complete arrangement was carried along by a determinedly driving idea: that which opens does not draw to a close, but is referred back to time.

"Le Musée qui n'existait pas" would be that openness, with no fixed point, that sequence of singular variations prompting us to construct our own capacity to get lost. Because machinery usually remains the hidden aspect of technical implementation, it was exhibited here as never before. While the stage remained the place where just the artist evolved, the construction in its entirety urged the public to get lost but also to change states, to shift from the status of spectator to that of actor, to reverse roles to the point of becoming set designers of the space and inventing an improvised narrative along the itinerary, Buren's theatre at once set the world in motion and the illusions governing it. Buren here thought of the world as theatre, and the entire œuvre was its "endless duplication" or "*mise en abyme*".

We know the criticisms, not to say the violence of the views of the same ones who had recognized in the artist's early works an ascetic quality and a discipline bordering on obliteration. We know how much today's stage machinery throws them, such is its break with the spectator's position in relation to space, and does away with perfect symmetry and the casting of roles on which the looking-at/looked-at relation of modern criticism was based.

"Le Musée qui n'existait pas" obviously caught them out. Going into the Hall of Mirrors and the House of Wonders, even hiding, disappearing the better to re-appear, forgetting the courtyard side and the garden side, the stage and the wings, raising the eyes and lowering the head... Moving and letting oneself go at the risk of abandoning the behaviour imposed by the museum... Playing, inventing postures, positions, and attitude with each room operating like an individual set for each one of us... Inventing your own choreography, sets of gestures, seeking the echo, enhancing the voice, listening to the sounds captured elsewhere[21] and ending up slap bang in the middle of colour and its

21 This was one of Pierre Bourdieu's intentions, an intention actually never realized, that of capturing the words of the public outside and inside the exhibition, as it was to compile a questionnaire on which the sociologist would then have worked. Daniel Buren and Pierre Bourdieu had met at the Institut des hautes

reflections, thinking about your own position at the heart of the narrative... In a nutshell, reinventing a history of space where each motif works like a backdrop to the bodies moving about there, and making the exhibition what neither the museum nor the common spaces authorize. Perhaps the art of *flânerie* and lazing about which Walter Benjamin talks about, an art where the only consummation is that of the past, where there is nothing to take away except for memory, where, like other forms of artistic expression far too overlooked to understand Buren's art, it is definitely not a matter of a subject opposite the painting, but of the painting opposite its subject: so a curling up where the projection becomes a gyrovague, escaped, and draws vanishing lines, Deleuze again, and the Centre Pompidou given back its "Mille Plateaux".

Bernard Blistène

études en arts plastiques in 1993. Their relationship grew thanks to the complicity of the sociologist Patrick Champagne, husband of Annick Boisnard, one of Daniel Buren's long time associates. The collaboration between Daniel Buren and Pierre Bourdieu, during the preparation of the show at the Centre Pompidou, a collaboration which would develop around what the artist Tino Sehgal for his part, with regard to his own work, calls "scenographed situations", changed during the various interviews between artist and sociologist, and right up to the last meetings between the two men, when Pierre Bourdieu was in hospital. It came to an end, needless to say, with his death, on 23 January 2002. Anxious not to misinterpret Bourdieu's intentions, Buren then decided that, rather than being poorly executed in the very space of the exhibition, his propositions would be the object of an insert in *Mot à Mot,* Paris, Éditions du Centre Pompidou/Xavier Barral/La Martinière, 2002, a work dedicated to him. On pages 84-91 you will find the sociologist's working notes then published with the kind authorization of his family, plus a short text titled "Comprendre", which lends its title to a chapter in the book in which Pierre Bourdieu vehemently explains why it is up to the sociologist to unravel the complex threads of the struggle against contemporary art. Among the numerous projects left unfinished, Pierre Bourdieu was at work on the preparation of a book on Manet, in whom he saw a major figure of the symbolic revolution that founded the autonomy of the modern art arena.

The hands are Daniel Buren's. They could not be anyone else's, like Matisse's "cutting straight into colour". Matisse cuts out, Buren tears. Nuance is essential here. The piece was first made in 1984 at Middelburg. It was made again in 2002, while preparing for the Centre Pompidou show. It echoes many of the artist's propositions, including a 1982 piece, *Couleurs superposées*, several times "interpreted", always under his supervision.

The meticulousness of the coloured stripes on paper printed for Buren, and their geometry, is countered by the principle of folding and the unforeseen nature of tearing, a principle which Sol LeWitt would also apply. Buren adjusts the sheets of paper, juxtaposes them, and superposes them: he "composes" under the camera's eye. Like Baudelaire observing about colour that it is "the forced harmony of two shades", Buren makes sure that the colours are randomly married. Nothing here is subject to any complementary principle. Everything complies with the artist's choice. Needless to add, Buren has said a great deal about colour and how it can be handled. In August 1985, he wrote about the piece: "... Using video with its specific quality to produce a work is what most interests me. Here, in Middelburg, I've used video to improvise a work on colour. Passages of colour. A wordless story, words having been replaced by a handmade interplay of colours, superpositions, disappearance and striping of striped material, all used for manipulation ...."

But over and above the piece itself and the idea that the work invents itself by destroying itself, there is the wish for everything to be accomplished through the prism of the camera, based on the logic of a static and overhead shot which, in a way, forms a frame within which Buren executes his project. It is the artist at work, the aspect of the manufacture of the work, not to say the magic, which are here the subjects offered to the eye. This is the endless set of variations that Buren records, installs and projects in the track of the Centre Pompidou's escalators, a way of preparing the viewer who will discover on the building's level 6 the labyrinth of "Le Musée qui n'existait pas".

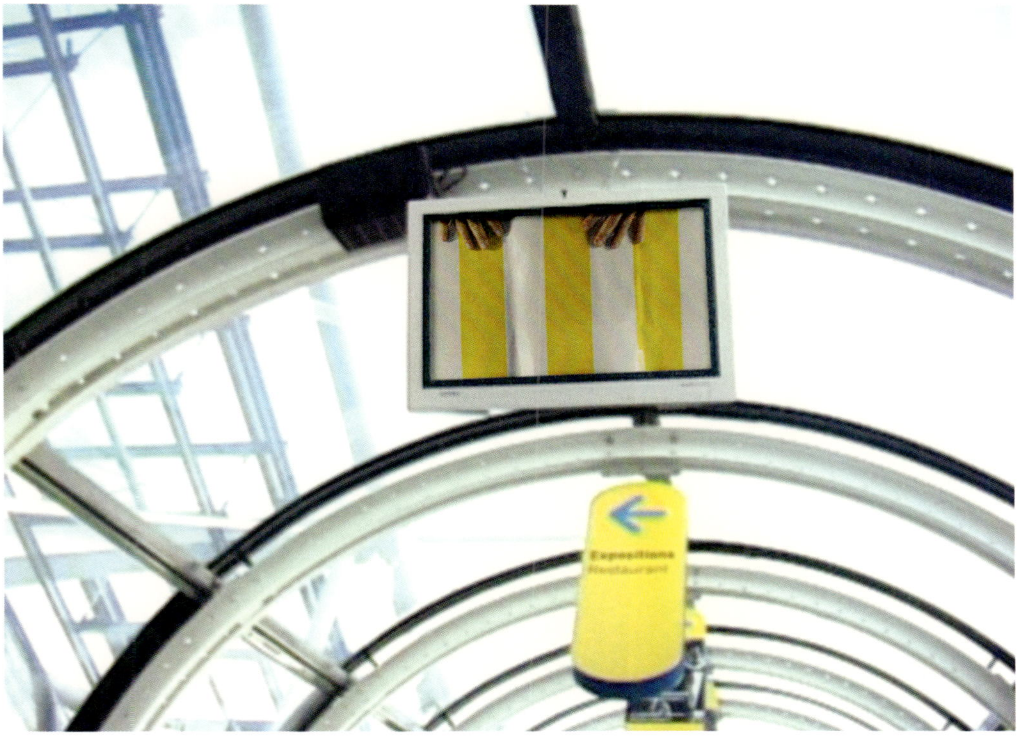

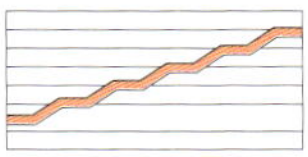

Escalators

Above and on following pages :
Photos-souvenirs taken from the video *Colours*, 1984-2002,
Shown on each level of the Centre Pompidou's outside escalators

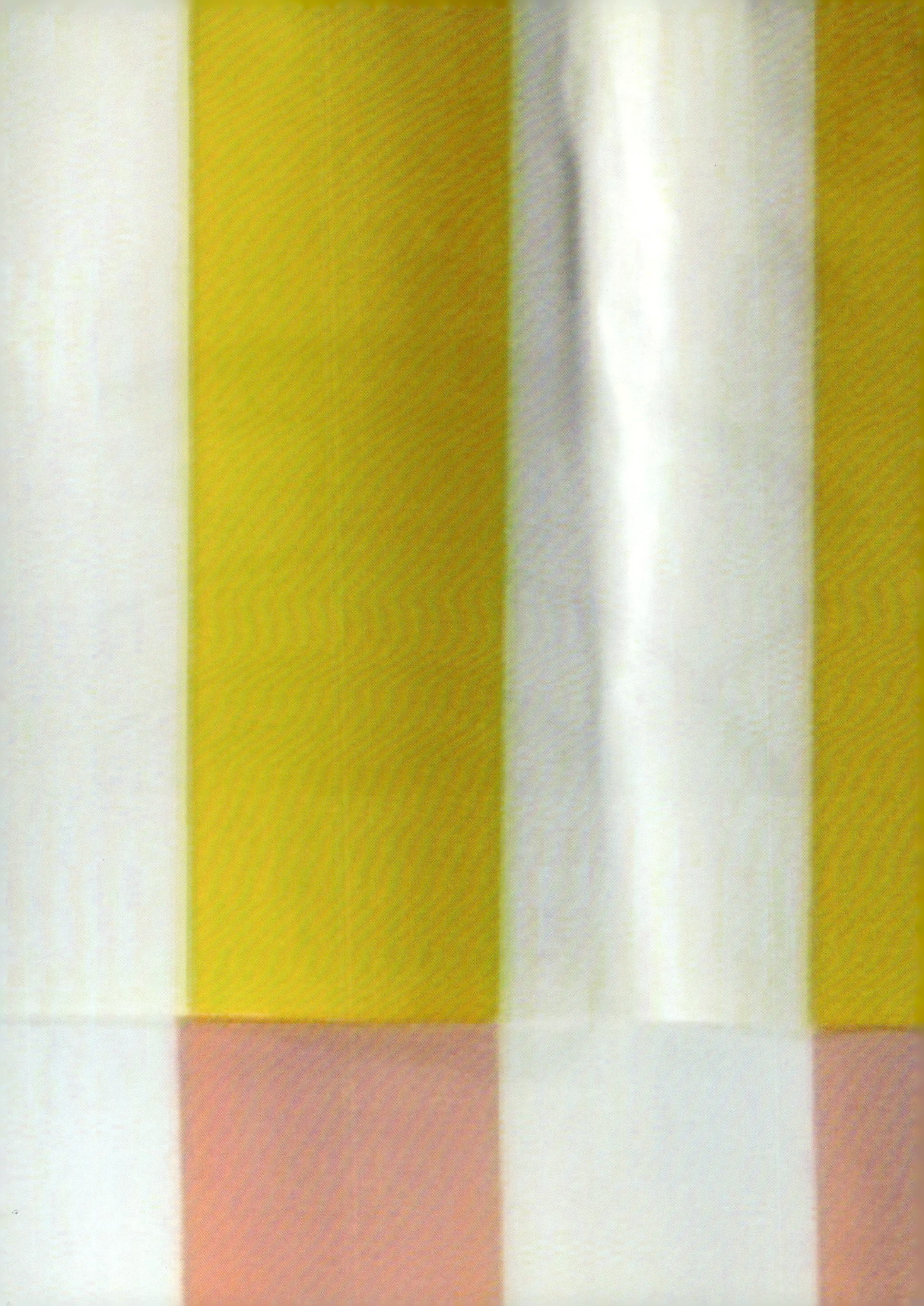

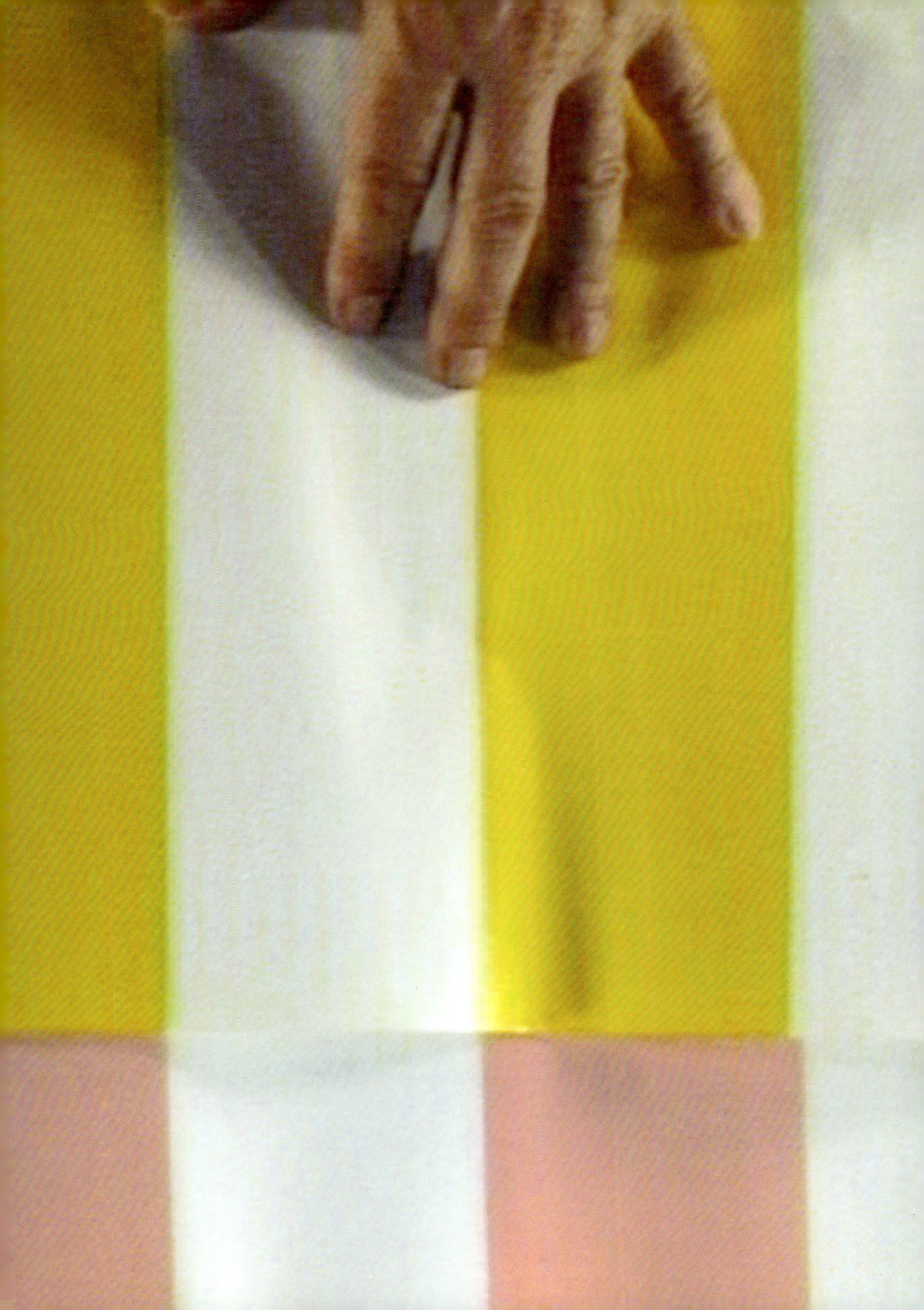

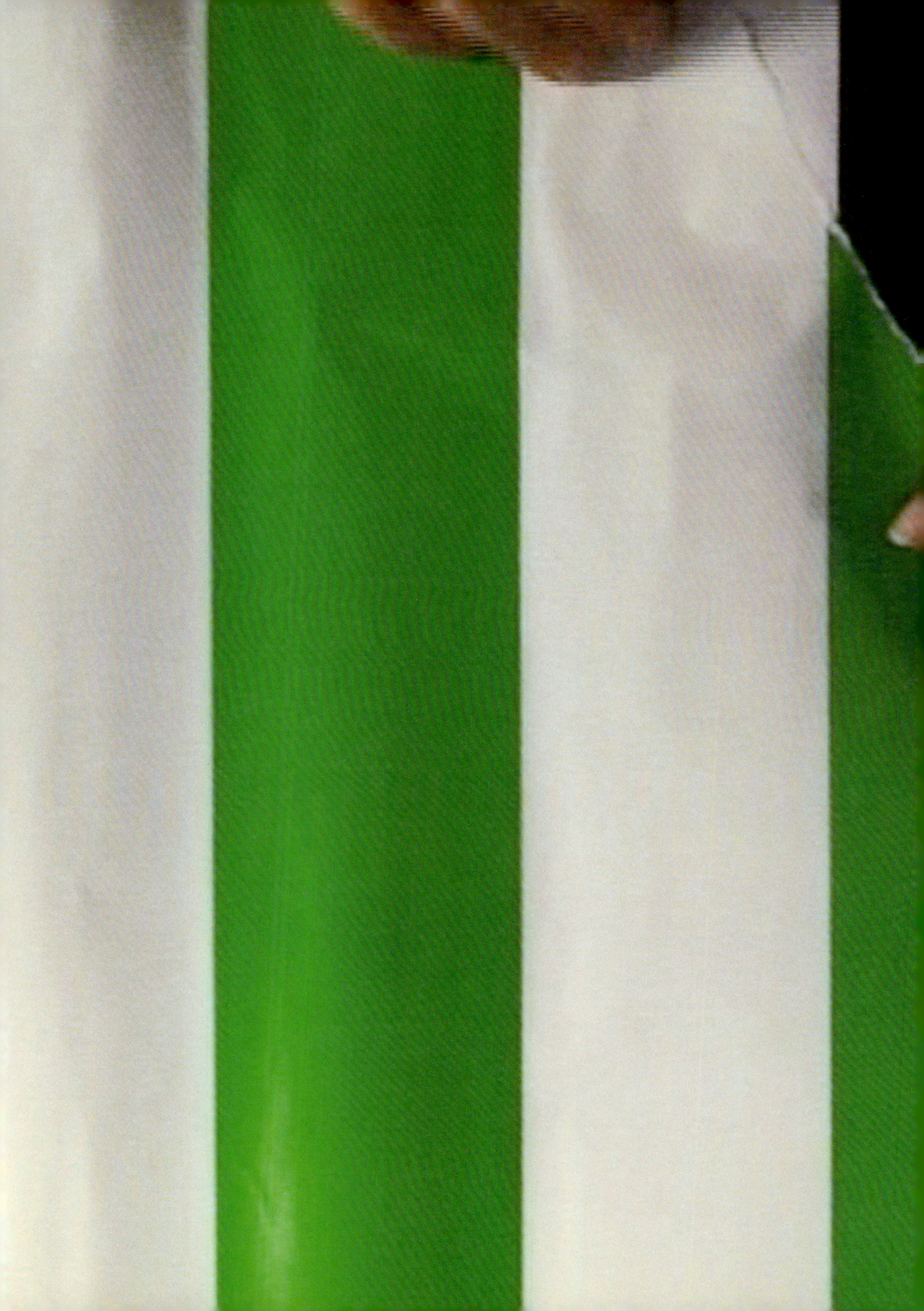

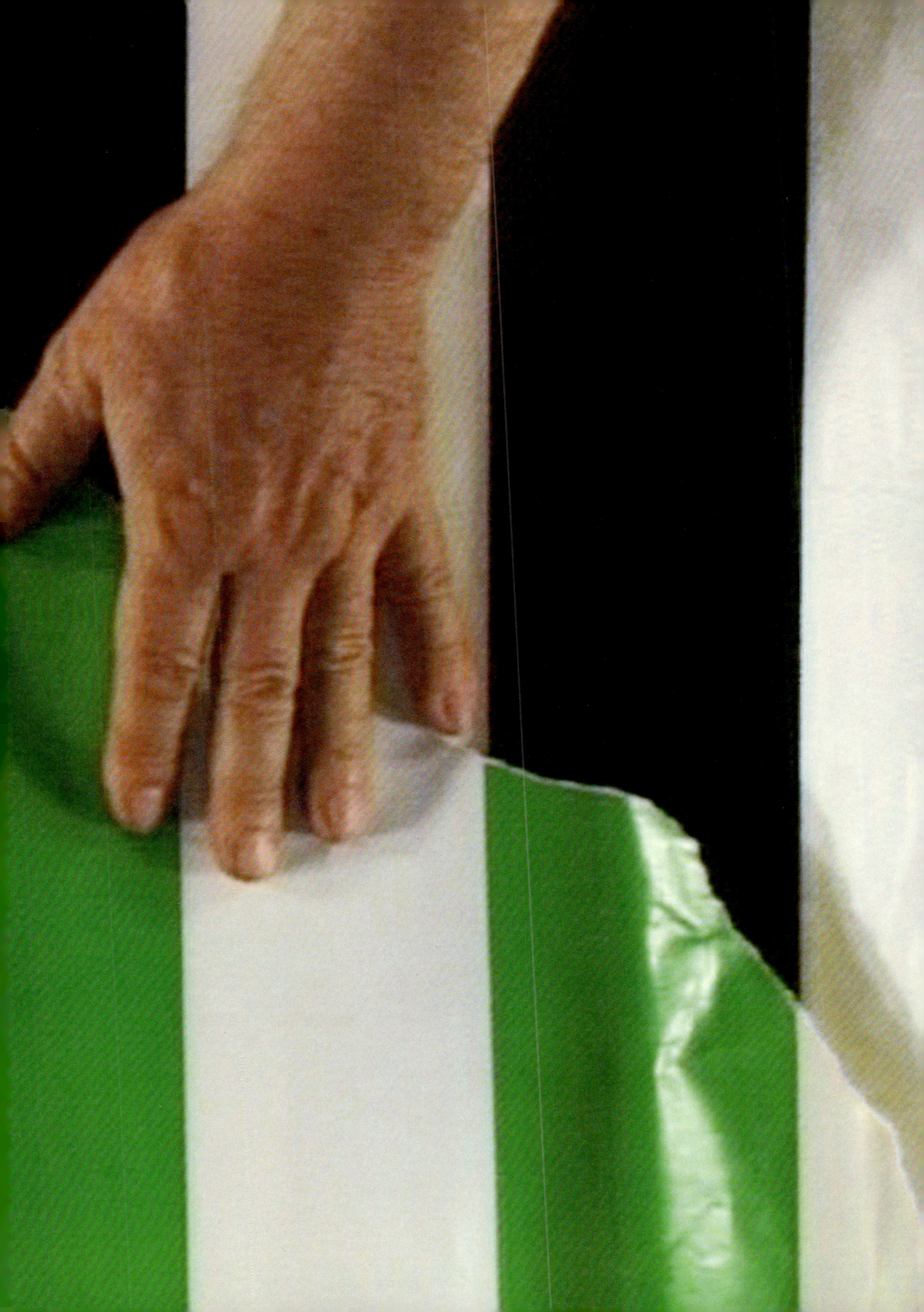

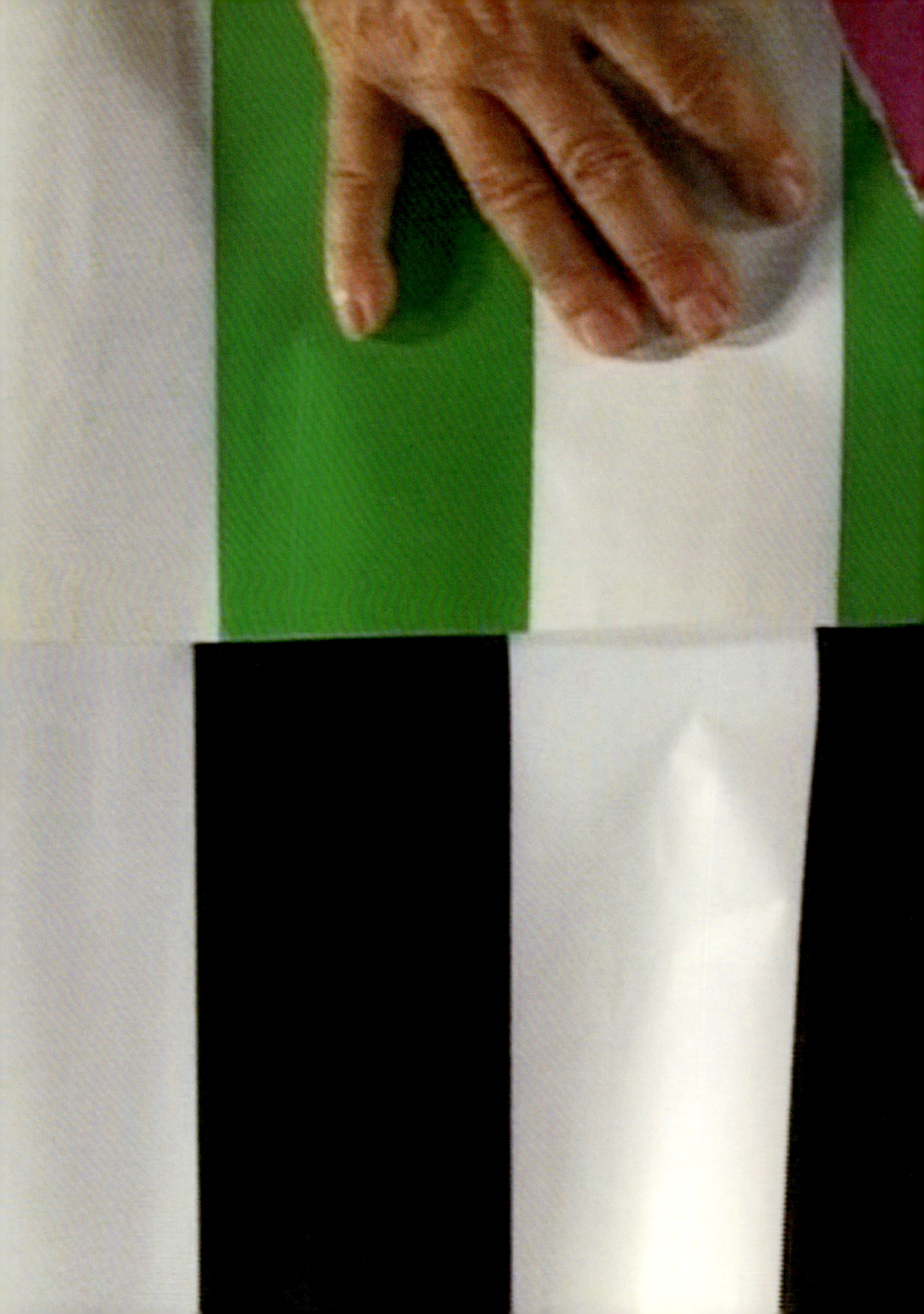

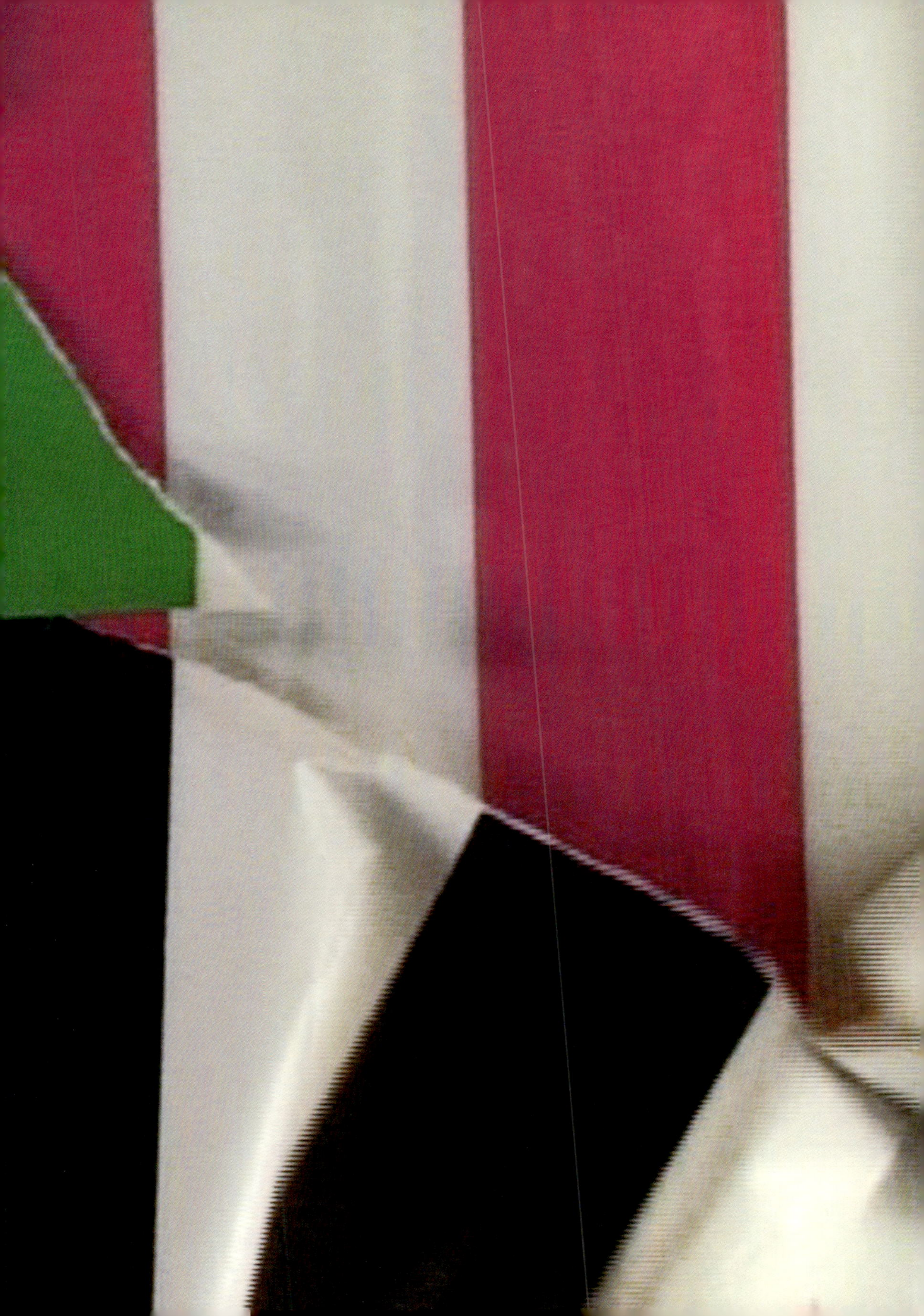

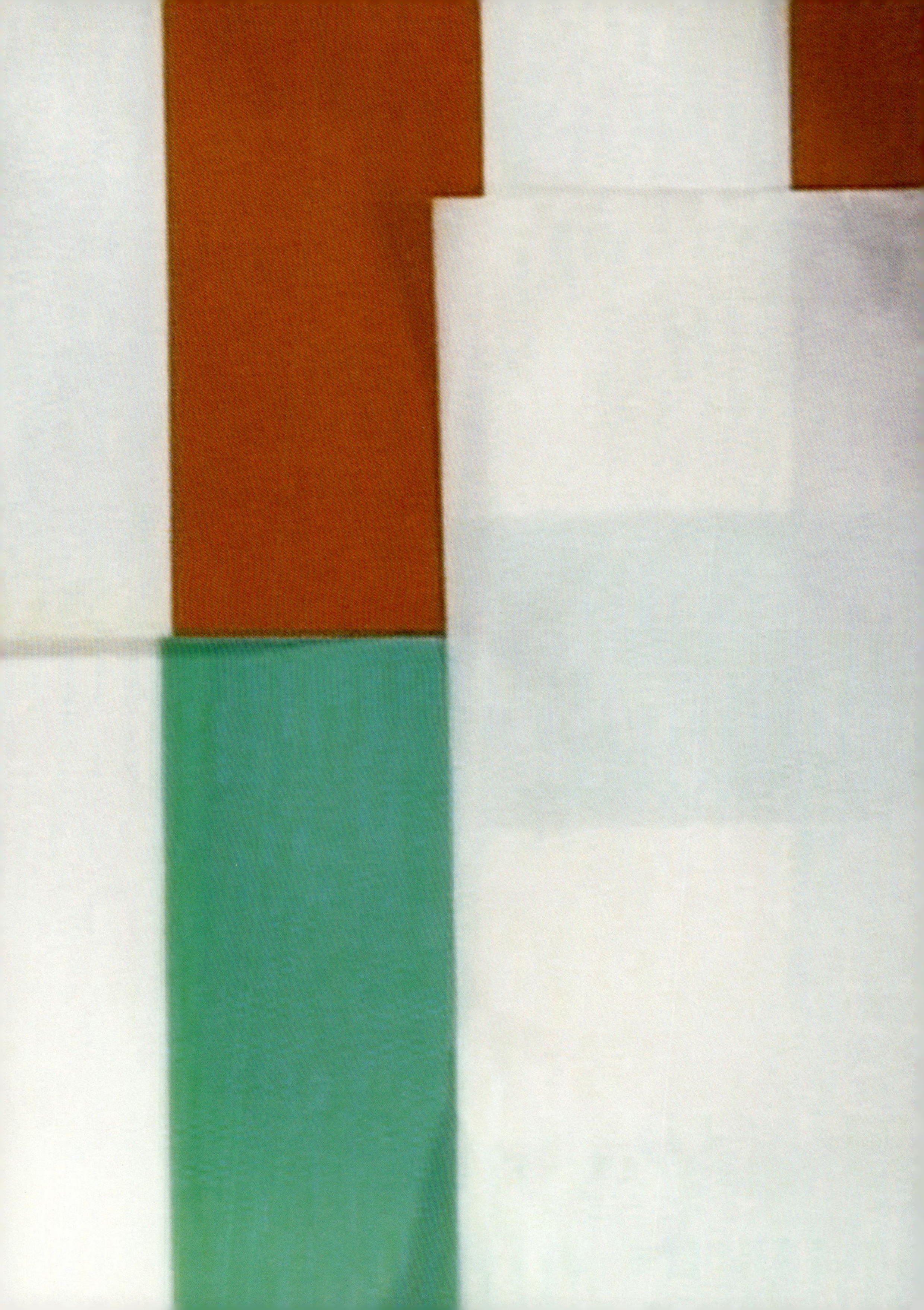

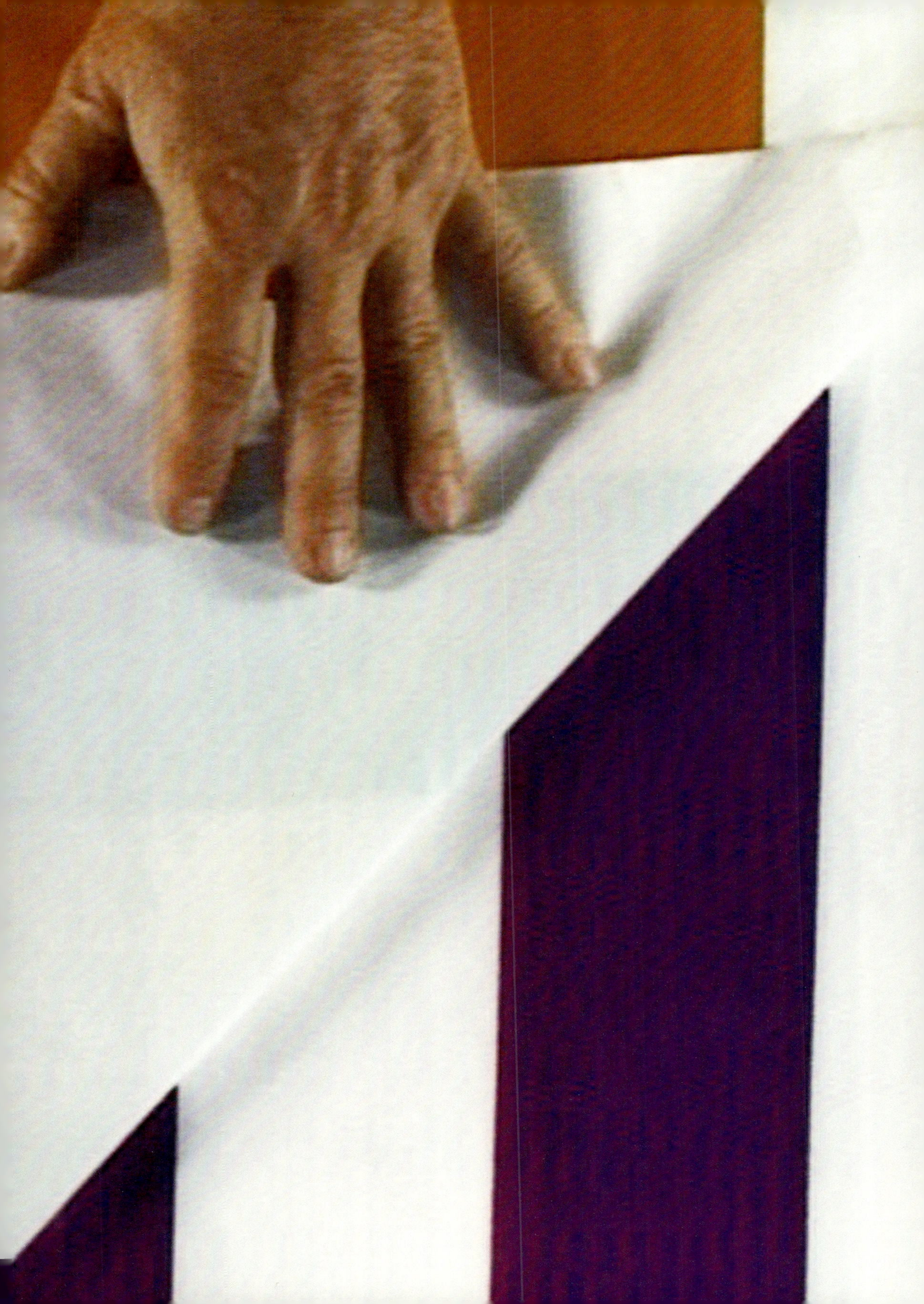

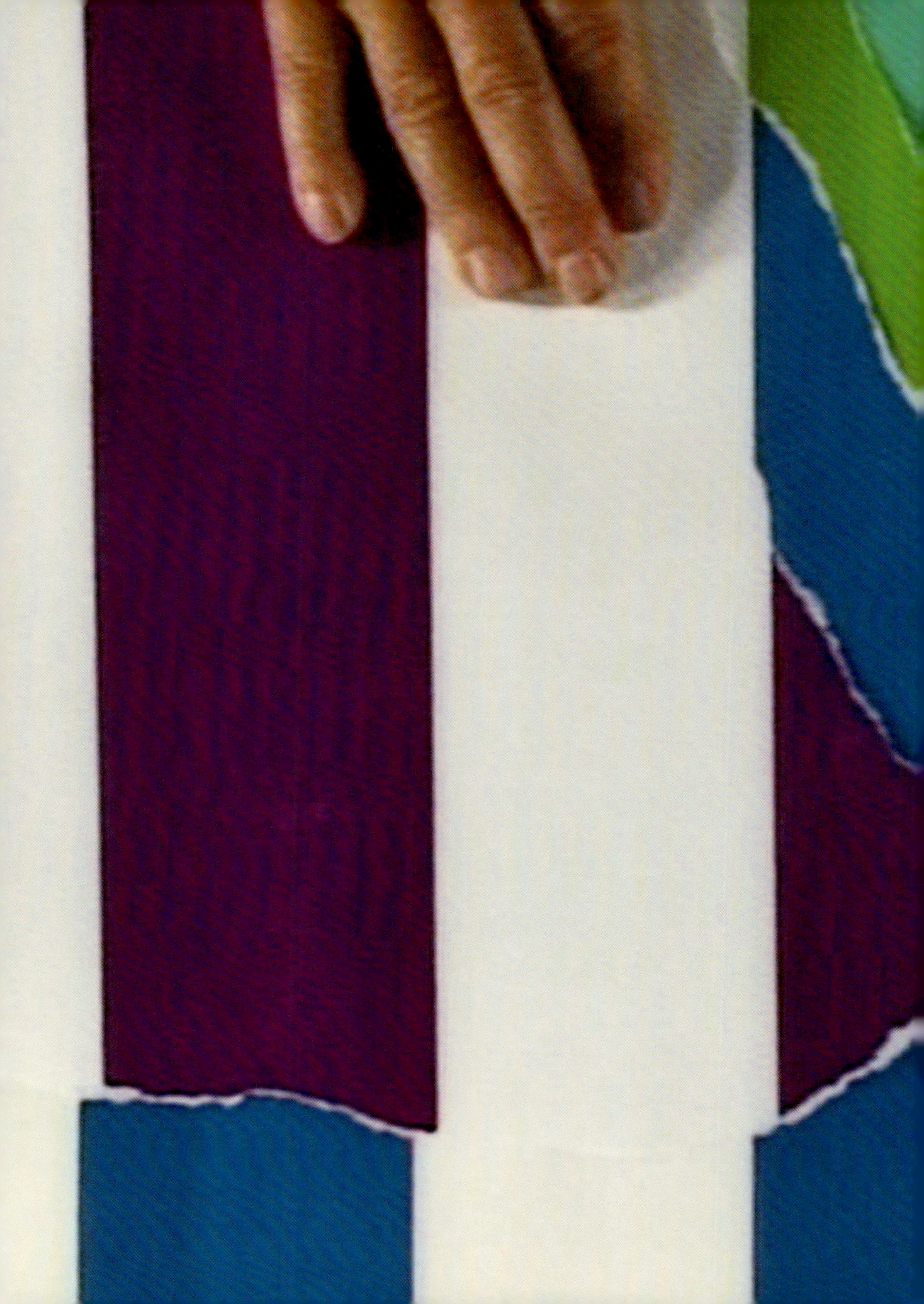

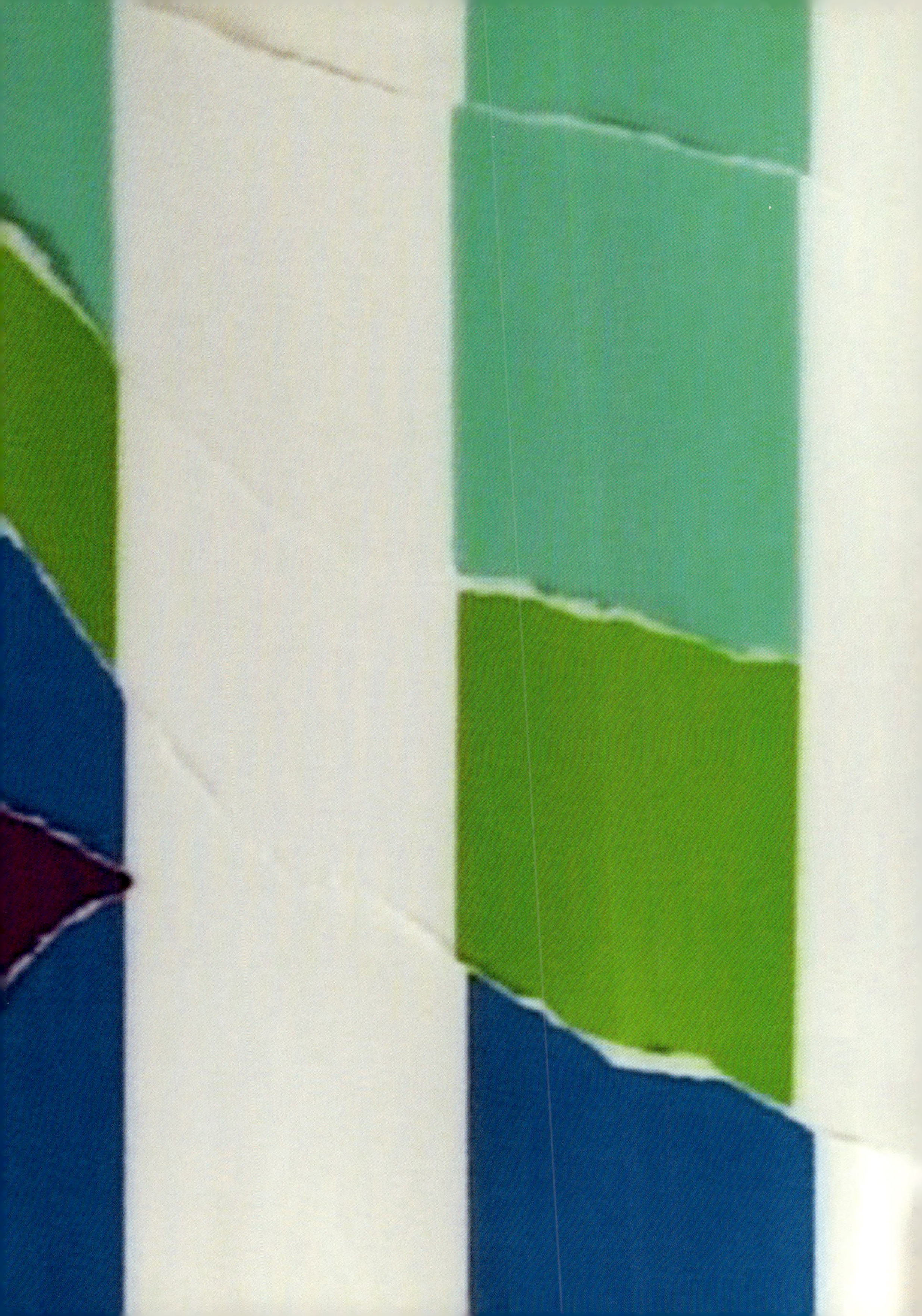

Made up of pieces of black and white striped fabric, and installed in accordance with a precise protocol beneath at least five works in the permanent collections of the Musée national d'art modern – here, among others, Picabia's *L'œil cacodylate* – *The Forms: paintings* are probably one of the most emblematic propositions involving Buren's relation to the museum institution. Conspicuously re-installed for the exhibition, the piece takes on a specific tone because it is thus part of the permanent collections of the Musée national d'art moderne, as if echoing the many arrangements which Buren simultaneously scatters in different places in the building.
The work has an unusual history. Acquired by the museum the year of its installation at the Centre Pompidou, its intent was to act on the actual collections by questioning what Buren calls "the place of visibility of an artwork". Fixed on a rail behind certain works selected at random by a curator in the course of the itinerary, and renewable depending on hangings, it carries within it the invisible trace of its presence. An identical notice to the one accompanying the painting, tells us "there is a work underneath". If there is nothing to see other than the description of the work, what there is to be understood is what no work can show: what names it, what denies it as a visible object, and confirms, as Buren points out. That "the place where a work of art is seen is its frame."
There is probably something else, associated, in this precise case, with the circumstances of the re-installation. *The Forms: paintings* are indeed in place for the Buren show on level 6 of the building, but they are probably among the pieces most invisible to the eye that the artist has ever invented. In the essay that the philosopher Jean-François Lyotard devoted to Buren in 1981, he wrote: "With *The Forms: paintings*, it is the other side, the unseen aspect of the visual object that is questioned". They are a secret and active presence, a sign among the signs which will be echoed at the same time by the installation of *The Colours: sculptures*, visible from the building's passageways. Buren chose to have two works re-installed, slipping away from the place accommodating them. The art of the exhibition like the exhibition of the art have an evident strategy with Buren.

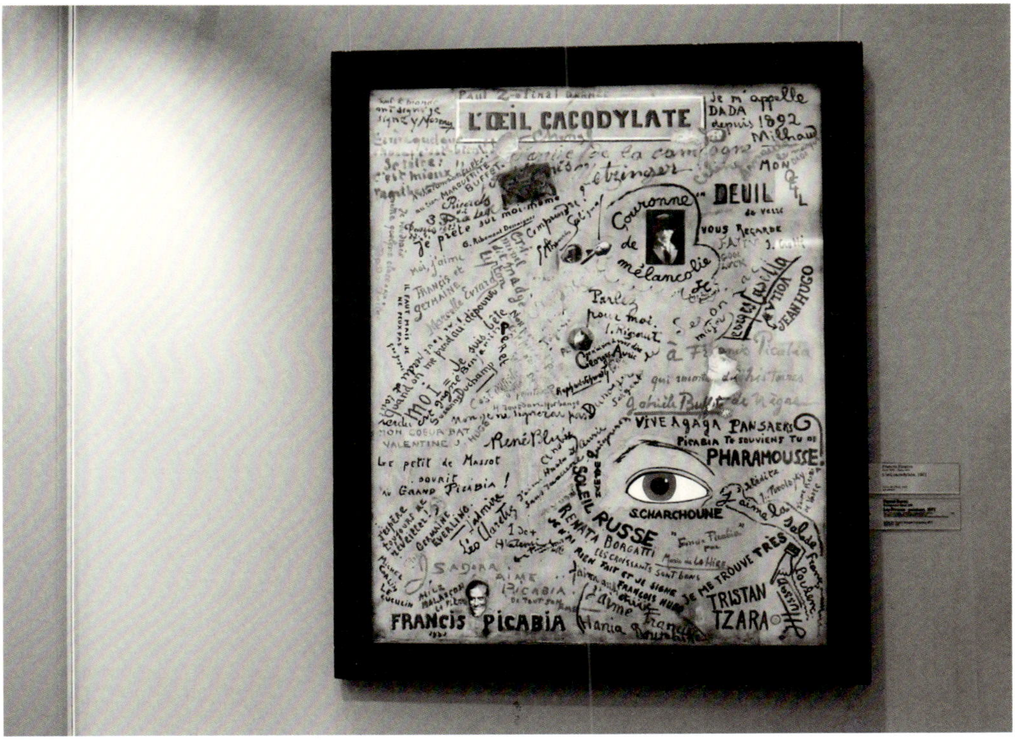

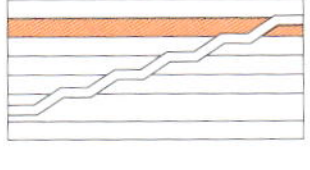

Level 5

Photo-souvenir: *"The Forms : paintings"*, work *in situ*, 1977-2002
Permanent collection of the Musée national d'art moderne, Centre Pompidou

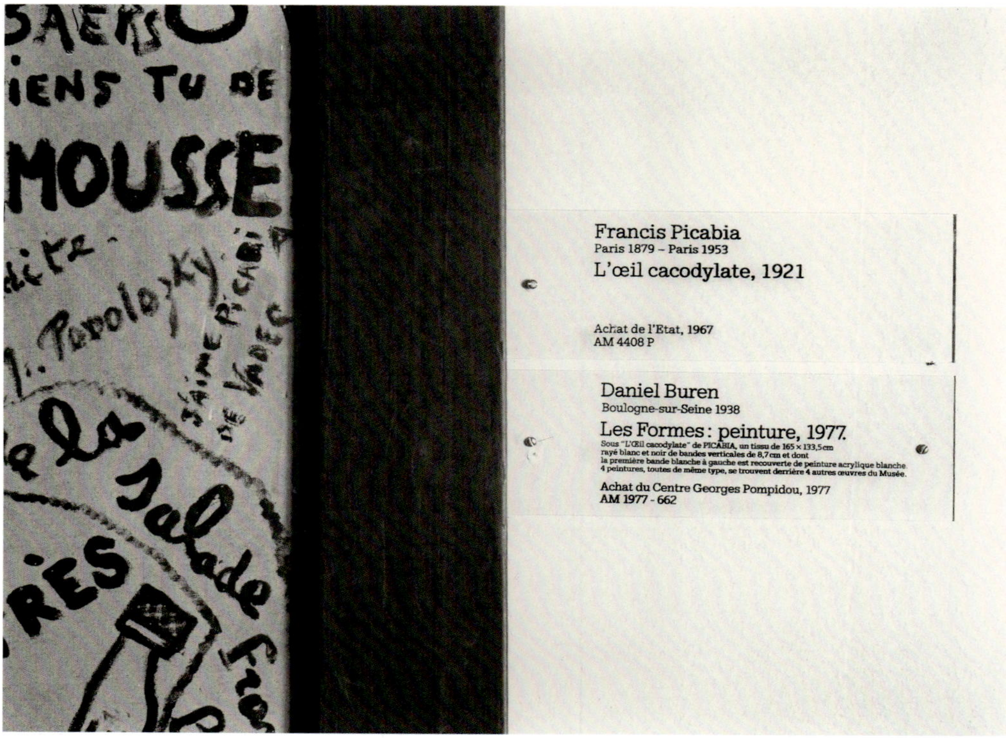

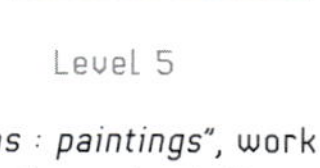

Level 5

Photo-souvenir: "The Forms : paintings", work *in situ*, 1977-2002
Permanent collection of the Musée national d'art moderne, Centre Pompidou

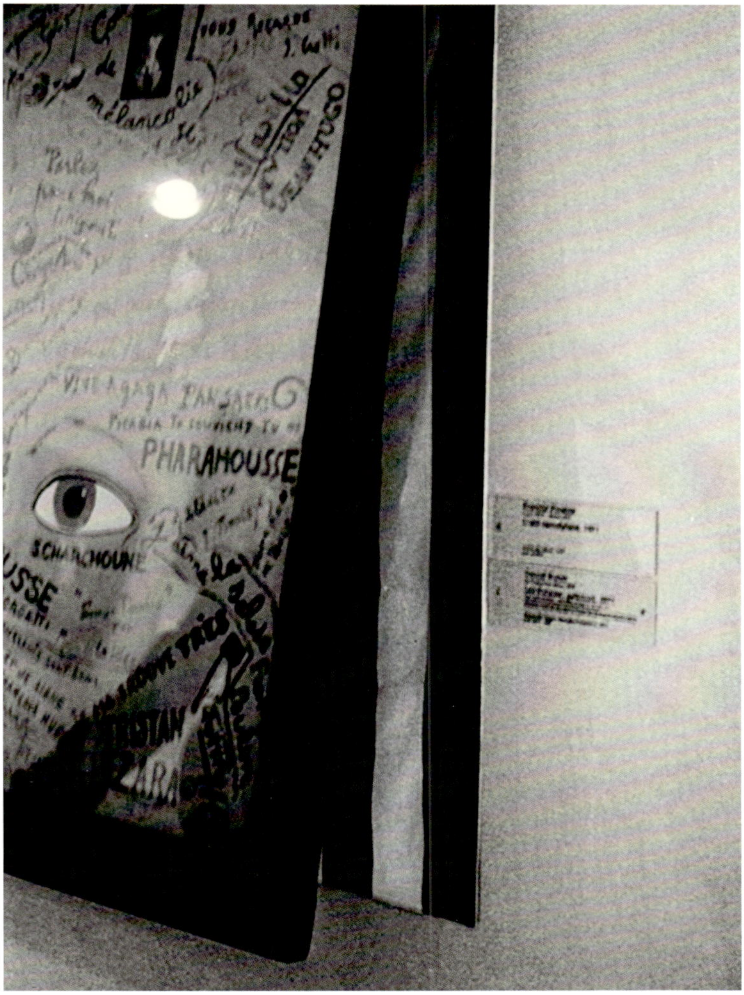

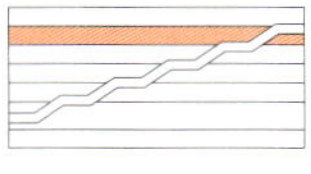

Level 5

Photo-souvenir: "*The Forms : paintings*", work *in situ*, 1977-2002
Permanent collection of the Musée national d'art moderne, Centre Pompidou

LEVEL 6

Arrangement of the room

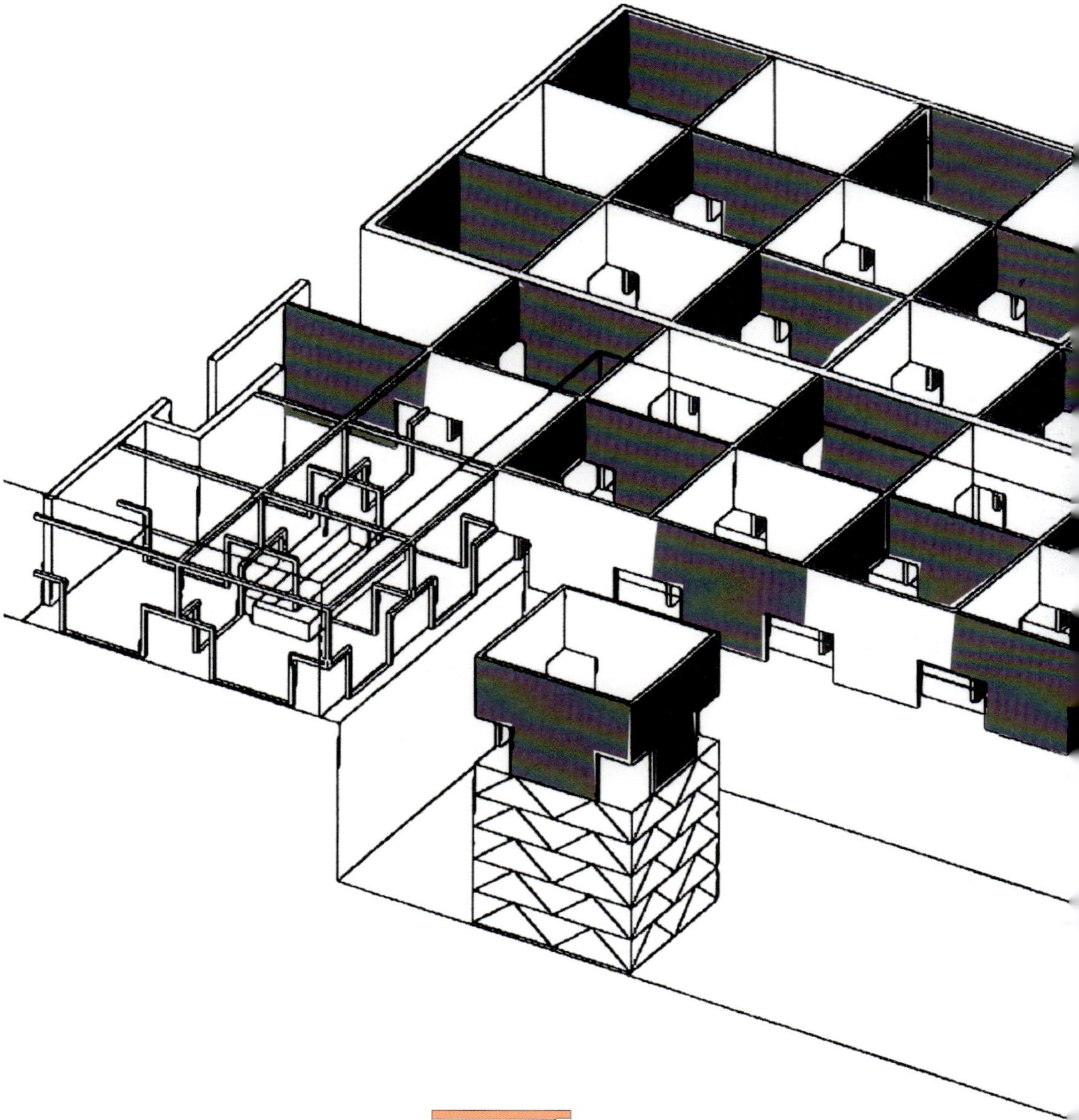

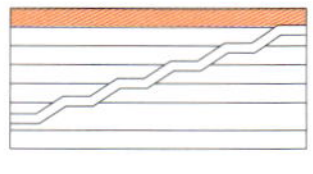

Level 6

The exhibition has been conceived as a chequerboard. Every other room consists just of four walls covered with deep grey paint and lit by a single central light, making these rooms relatively dark in relation to the others. These rooms do not contain any exhibition objects.

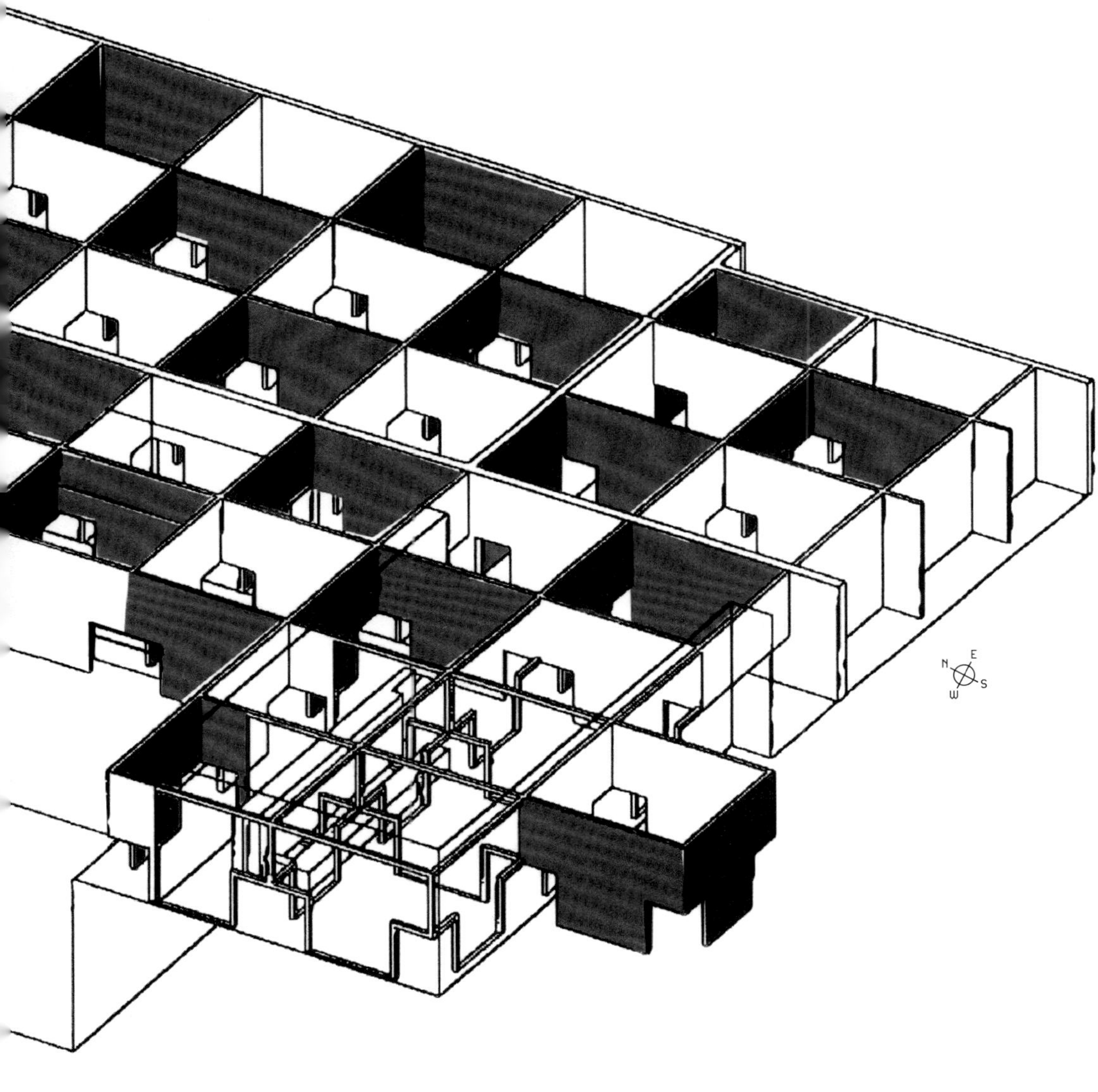
N
E
S
W

LEVEL 6

Index of the rooms

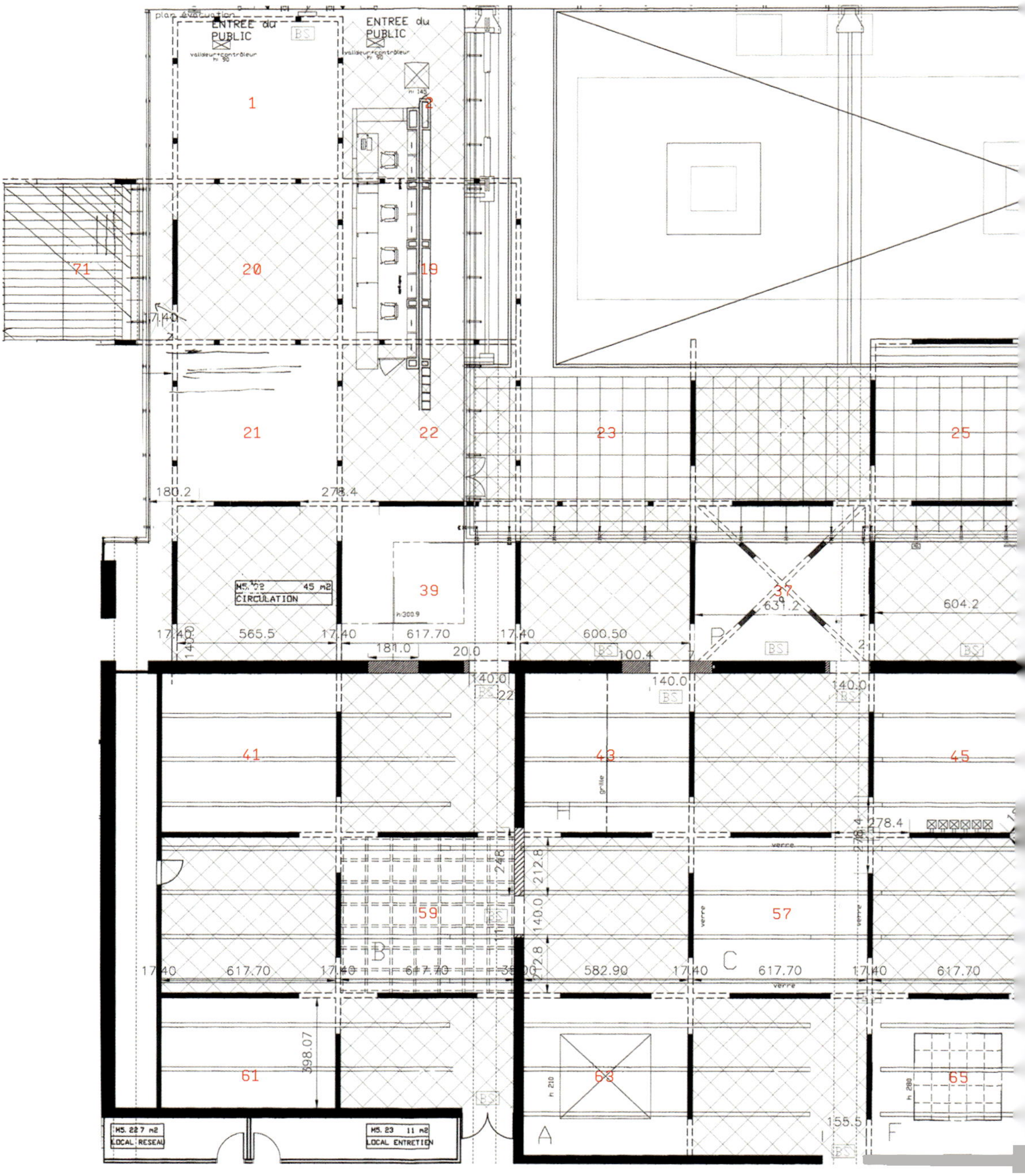

1-2-9-10-11-12-19-20-21-22-29-30- The framework of the rooms | 7- The floating island | 23- Truncated space | 25- Colour projection | 27- The transparent red roof | 31- The three lanterns | 33- The exploded cabin with 4,432 holes: lace | 35- The sliding wall | 37- 45° space | 39- Transparent walls | 41- Projection of 50 motifs | 43- The grid | 45- At a single glance | 47- Oblique walls | 49- Fragmented colour | 51- Around the return of a

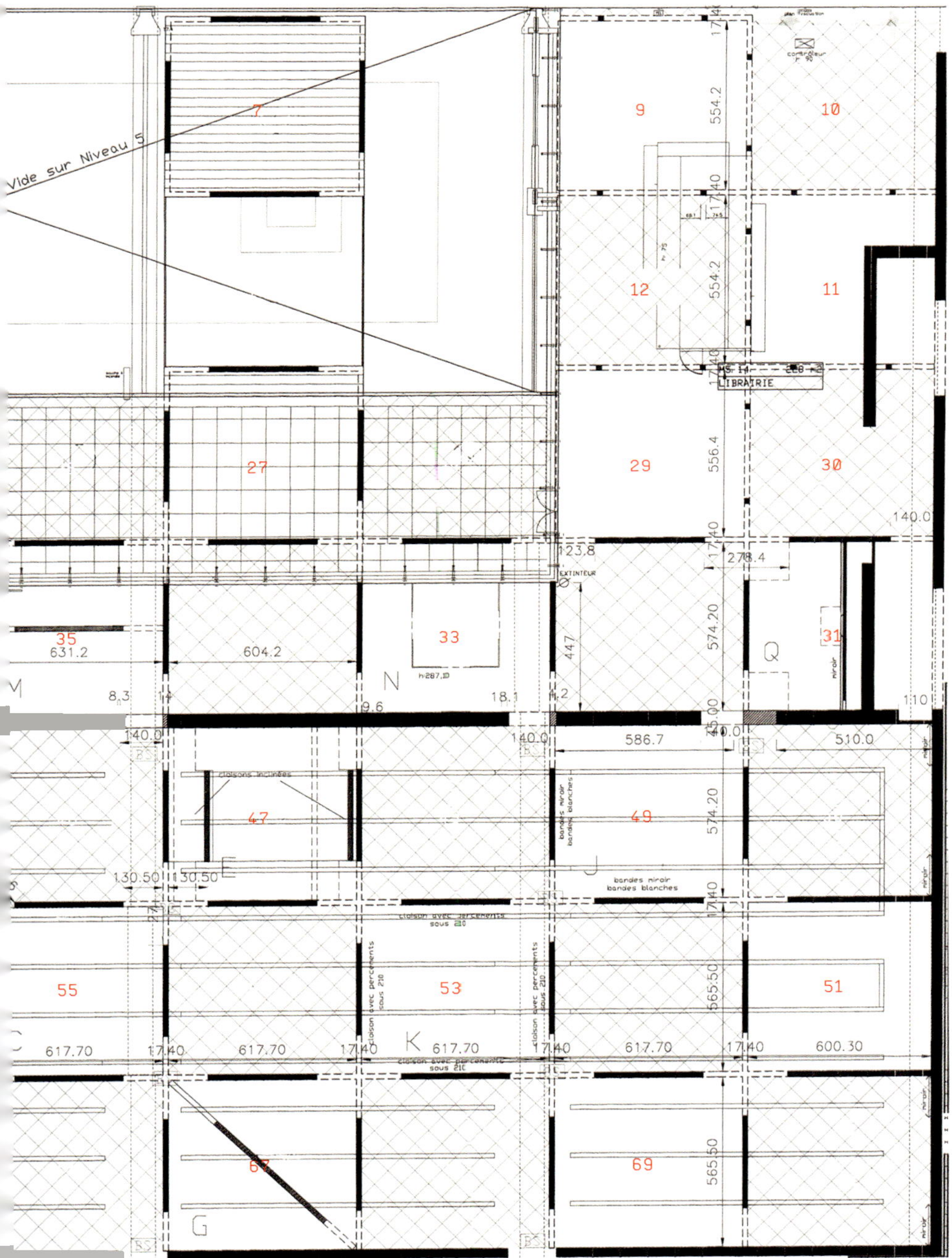

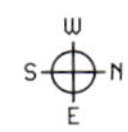

detour | 53- The imploded cabin: Distant murmur from the city | 55- The endless ceiling floor | 57- Under glass | 59- The suspended ceiling | 61- Video room | 63- The colour box | 65- The cabin with three ceilings | 67- Three colours make four: the oblique diagonal 69- Projection of light | 71- The dining room | 24-26-28-32-34-36-38-40-42-44-46-48-50-52-54-56-58-60-62-64-66-68-70- Grey rooms

A prismatic space, a kaleidoscope: you circulate in the exhibition properly so-called as in a labyrinth. The space is diffracted. Colour, shadow and light set the tone. The Centre Pompidou is turned into an optical machine. The building's windows tally with the Altuglas walls which here structure the venue. Buren emphasises the interaction he intends to set up between closed space and open space. "Le Musée qui n'existait pas" is a fluid *in situ* arrangement and the assertion that any exhibition venue catalyses a set of economic, political and sociological parameters which have an influence on the work whose autonomy is just a decoy, not to say an optical illusion.

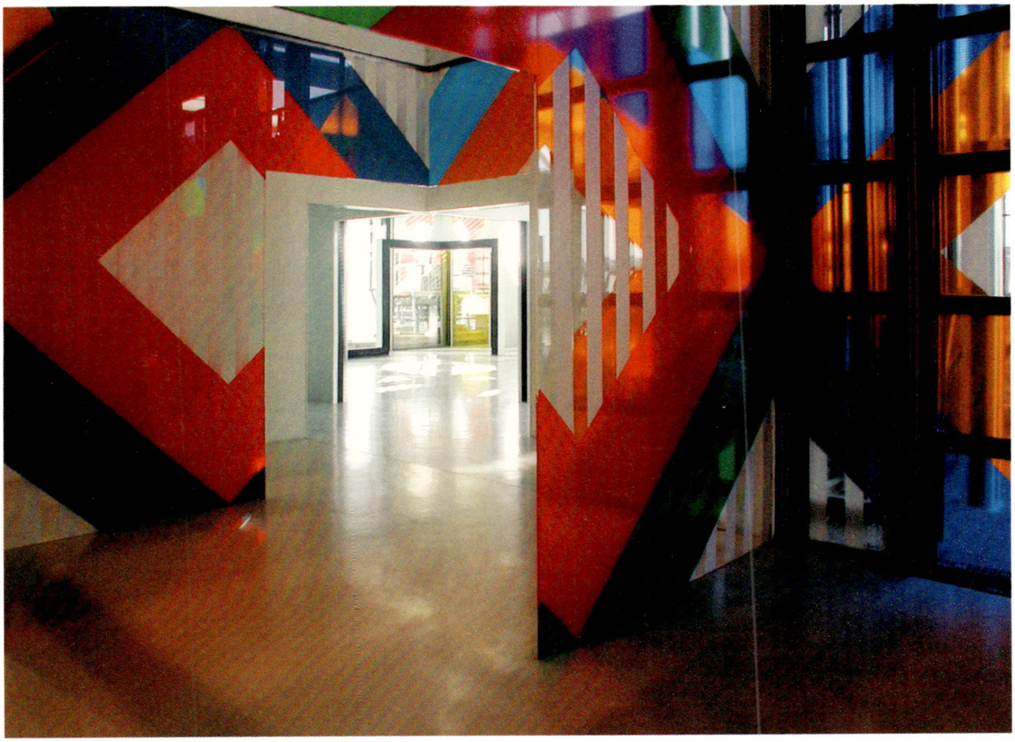

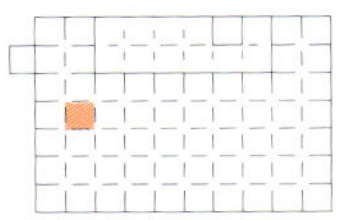

Room 39

Photo-souvenir: "Transparent walls", work *in situ*
Altuglas, coloured filters, glue
In the distance, room 21, *The framework of the rooms*, and room 71, *The dining room*

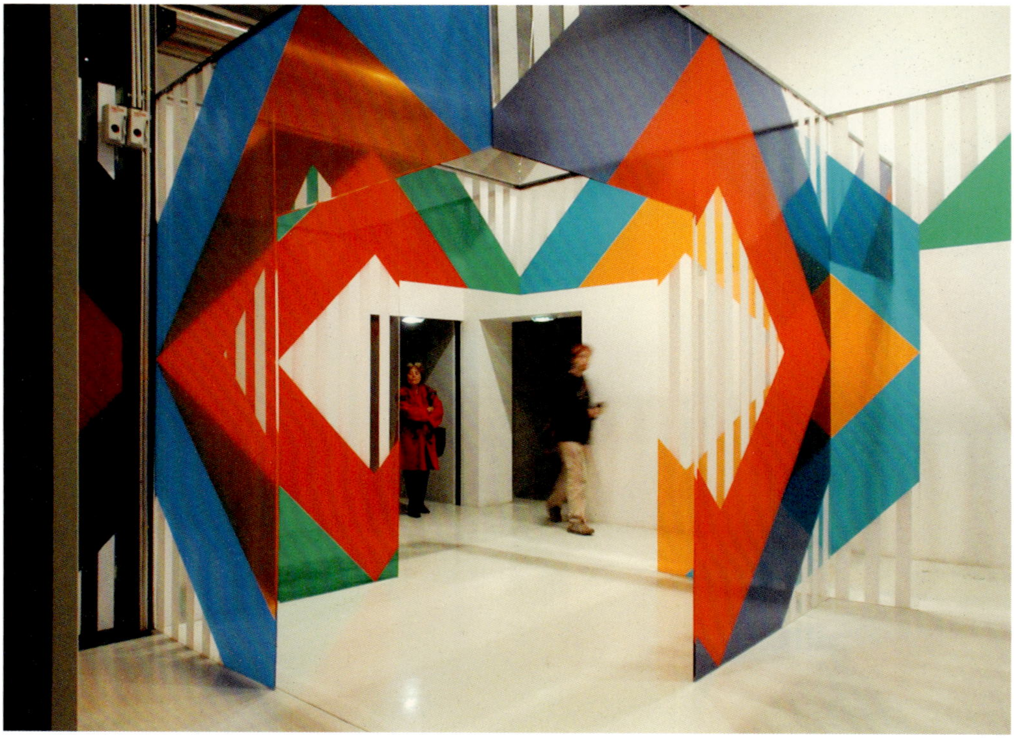

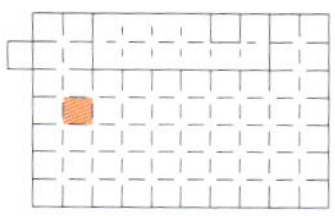

Room 39

Photo-souvenir: "Transparent walls", work in situ
Altuglas, coloured filters, glue
View from room 21, *The framework of the rooms*

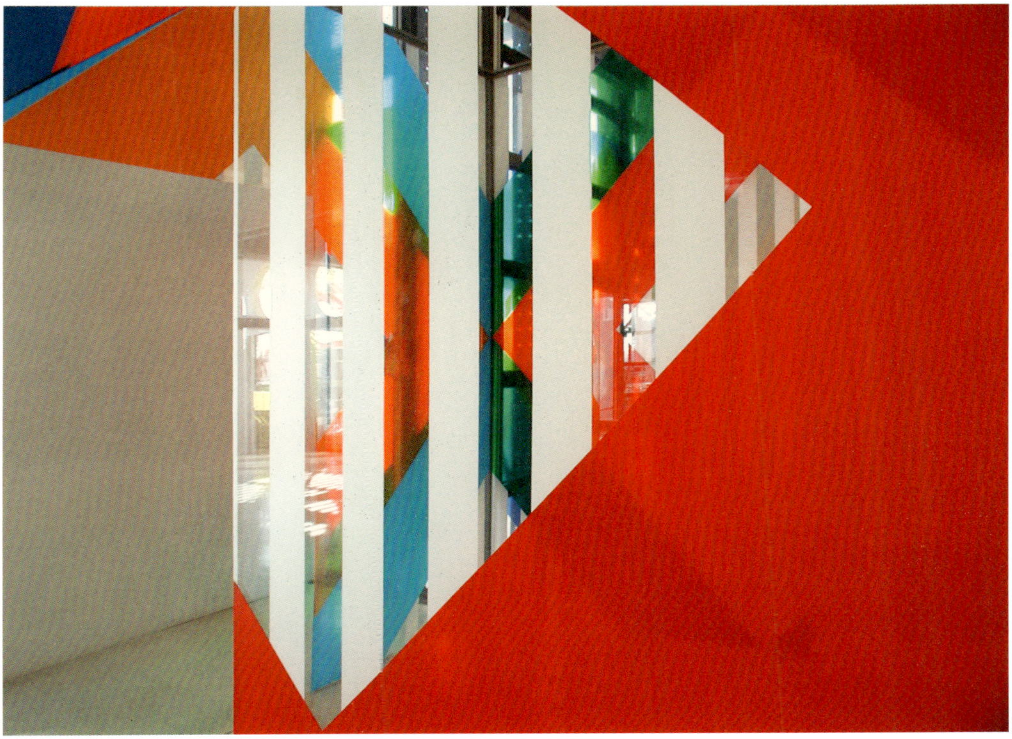

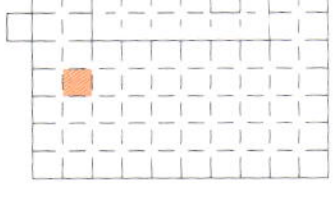

Room 39

Photo-souvenir: "Transparent walls", work *in situ*
Altuglas, coloured filters, glue

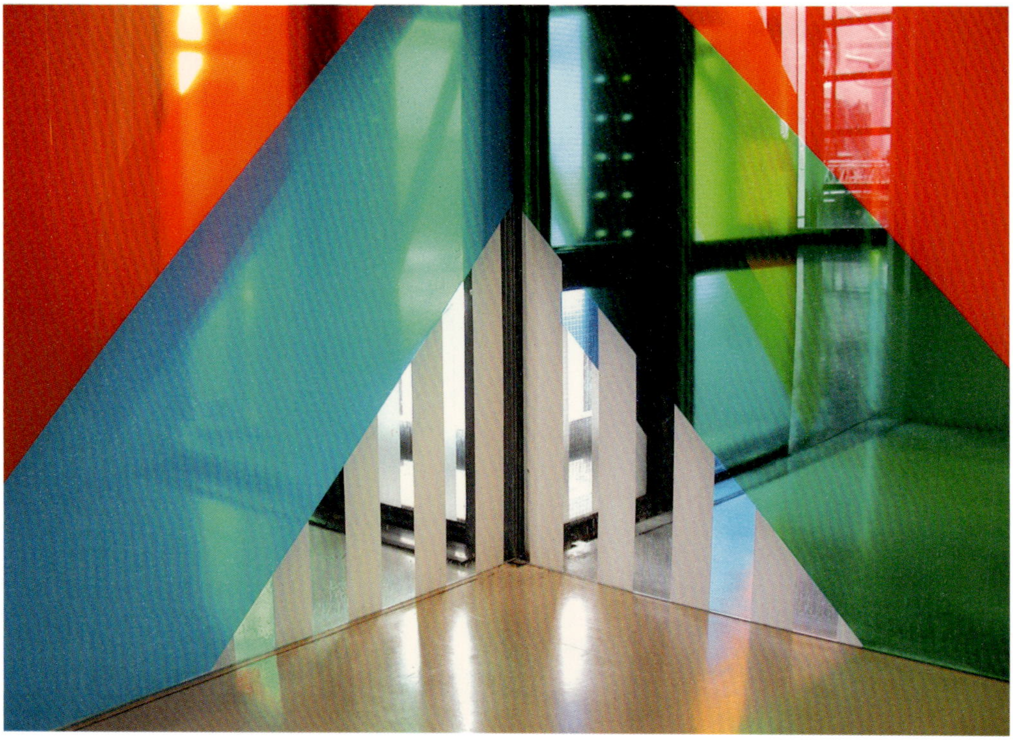

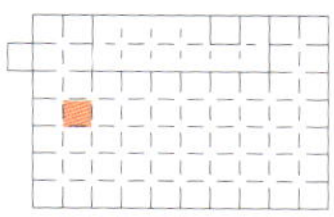

Room 39

Photo-souvenir: "Transparent walls", work in situ
Altuglas, coloured filters, glue

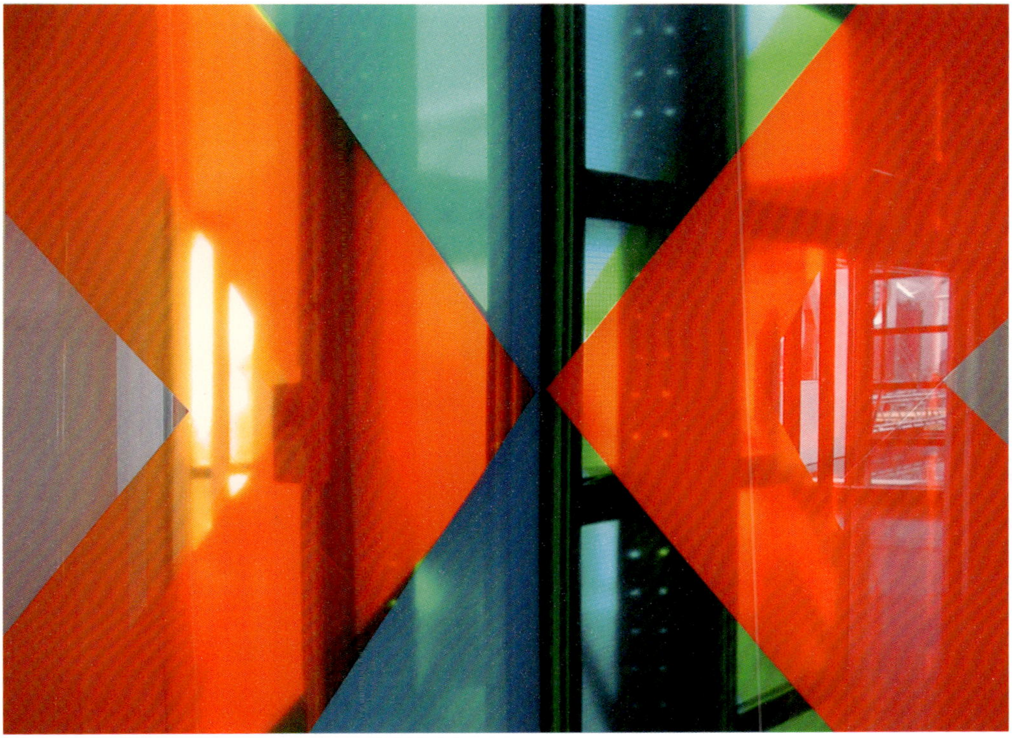

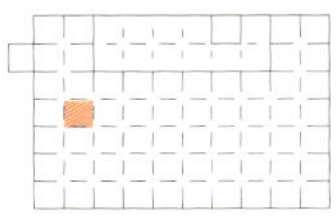

Room 39

Photo-souvenir: "Transparent walls", work *in situ*
Altuglas, coloured filters, glue

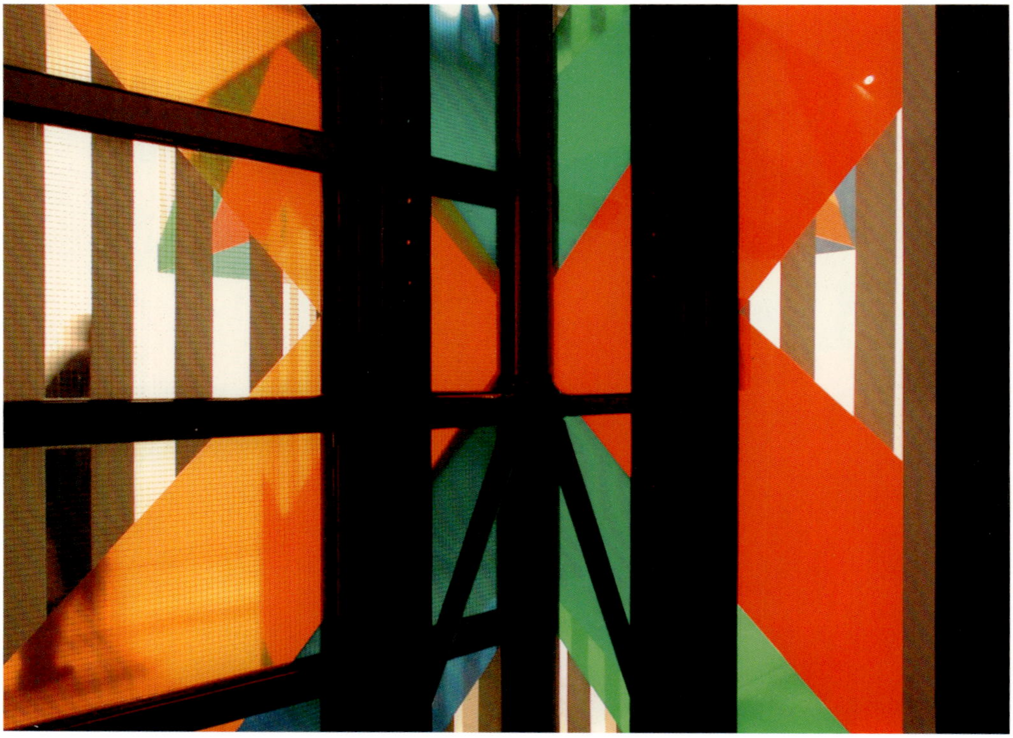

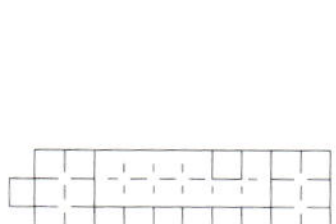

Room 39

Photo-souvenir: "Transparent walls" work in situ
Altuglas, coloured filters, glue

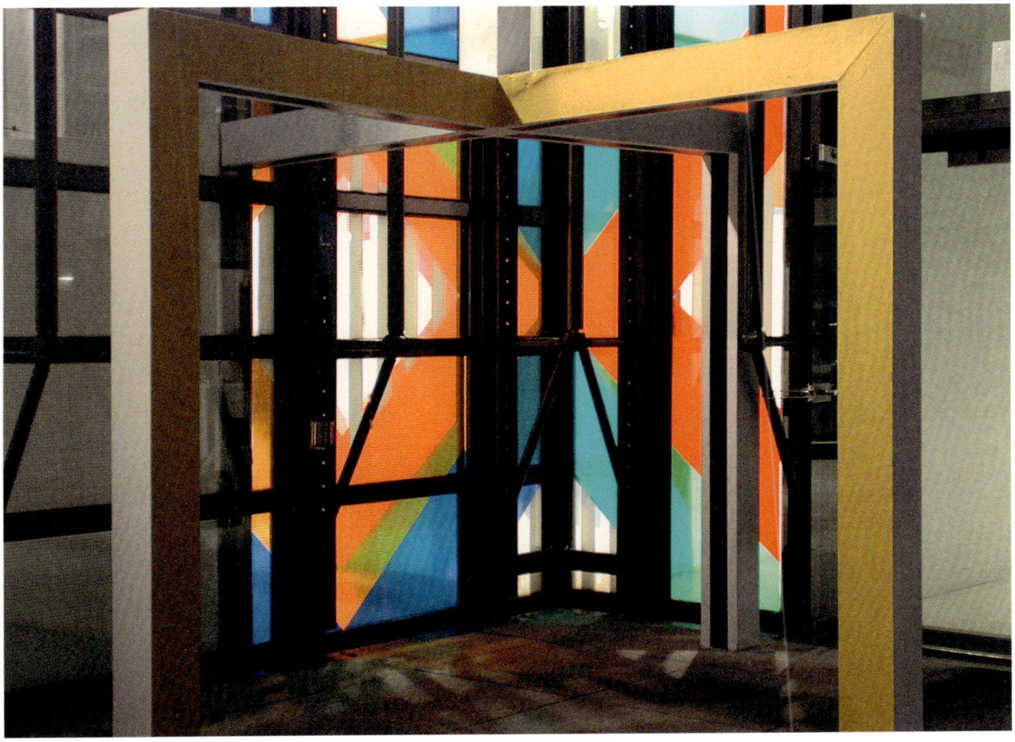

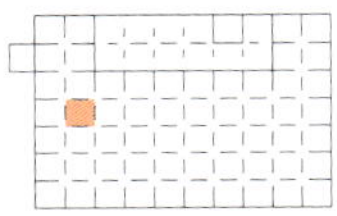

Room 39

Photo-souvenir: *"Transparent walls"*, work *in situ*
Altuglas, coloured filters , glue
View from room 22, *The framework of the rooms*

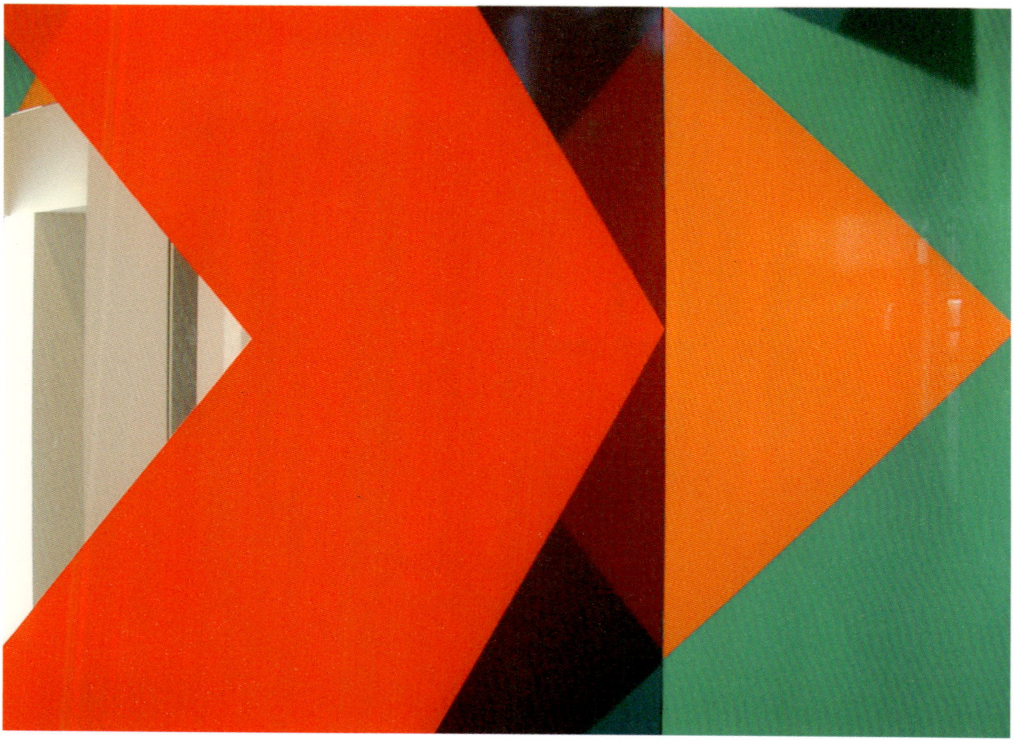

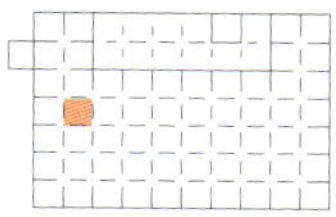

Room 39

Photo-souvenir: "Transparent walls", work in situ
Altuglas, coloured filters, glue

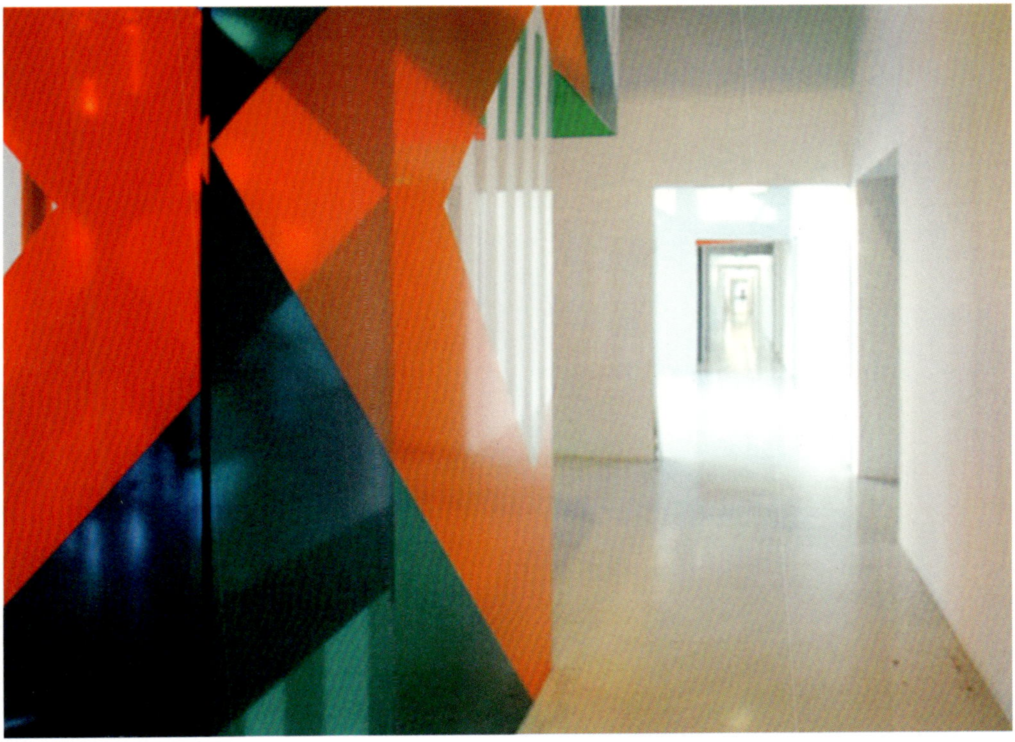

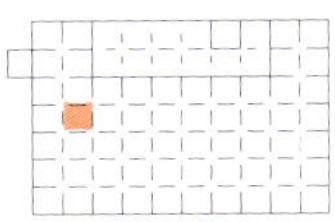

Room 39

Photo-souvenir "Transparent walls", work *in situ*
Altuglas, coloured filters, glue
Adjcining, rooms 38 to 31
In the distance, a mir-or in which all the doors are reflected

At different moments in his career, Buren unrolls his work on the ground. In addition to the historic bonds linking him with Carl Andre, and with the very few artists who, in the late 1960s, ushered in a relation between viewer and work in a hitherto unseen space-time dimension, it should be emphasized that Buren's system is thus developed through many different propositions aimed at suggesting, by the use of mirrors, an ad infinitum duplication of space. Buren is a topographer and a surveyor. He sees the very hub of the exhibition like a theatrical mirror and what Jurgis Baltrusaïtis calls "*a cabinet-salon*" of mirrors: "Le Musée qui n'existait pas" is nothing less than a catoptric machine.

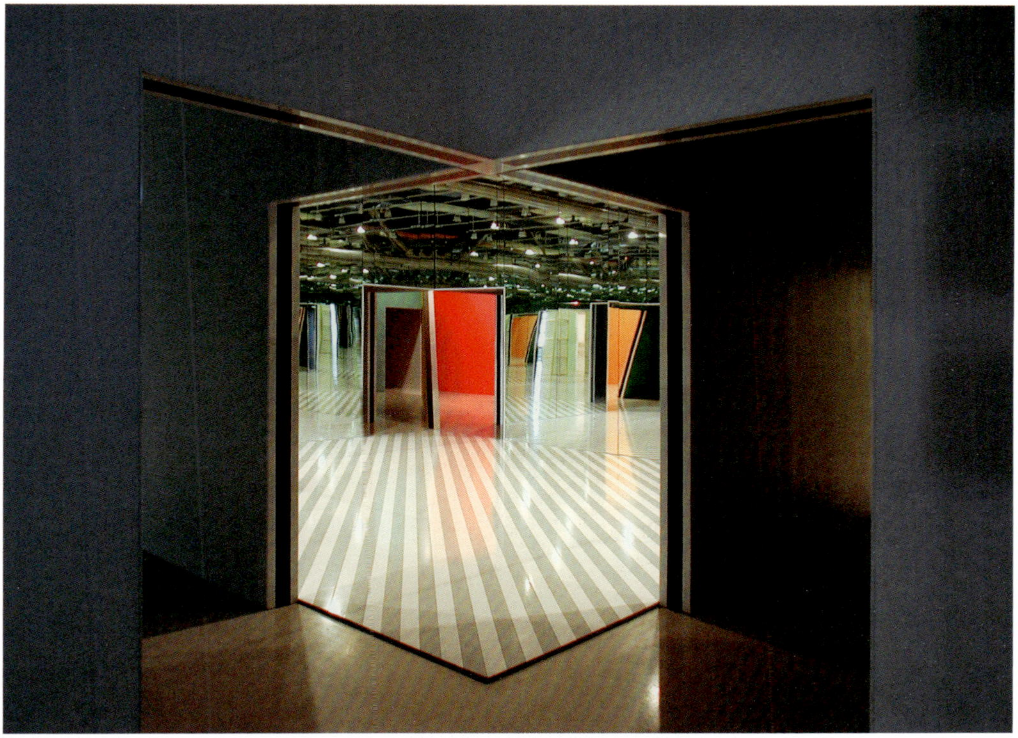

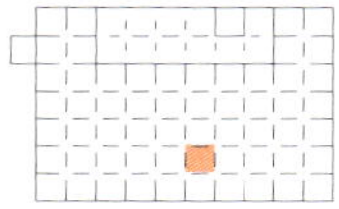

Room 55

Photo-souvenir: "The endless ceiling floor", work *in situ*
Painted wood, self-adhesive vinyl, mirrors, sheetrock, paint
View from room 45, *At a single glance*

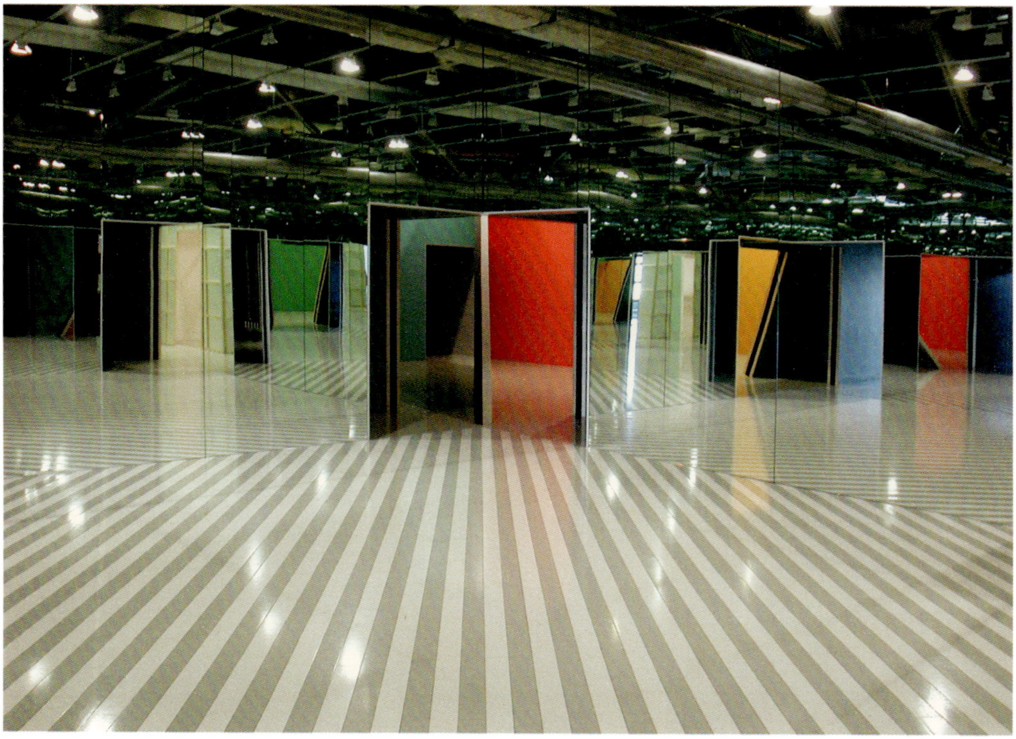

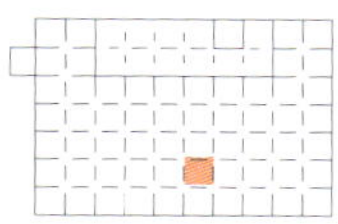

Room 55

Photo-souvenir: "The endless ceiling floor", work in situ
Painted wood, self-adhesive vinyl, mirrors, sheetrock, paint
Opposite, room 67, *Three colours make four: the oblique diagonal*

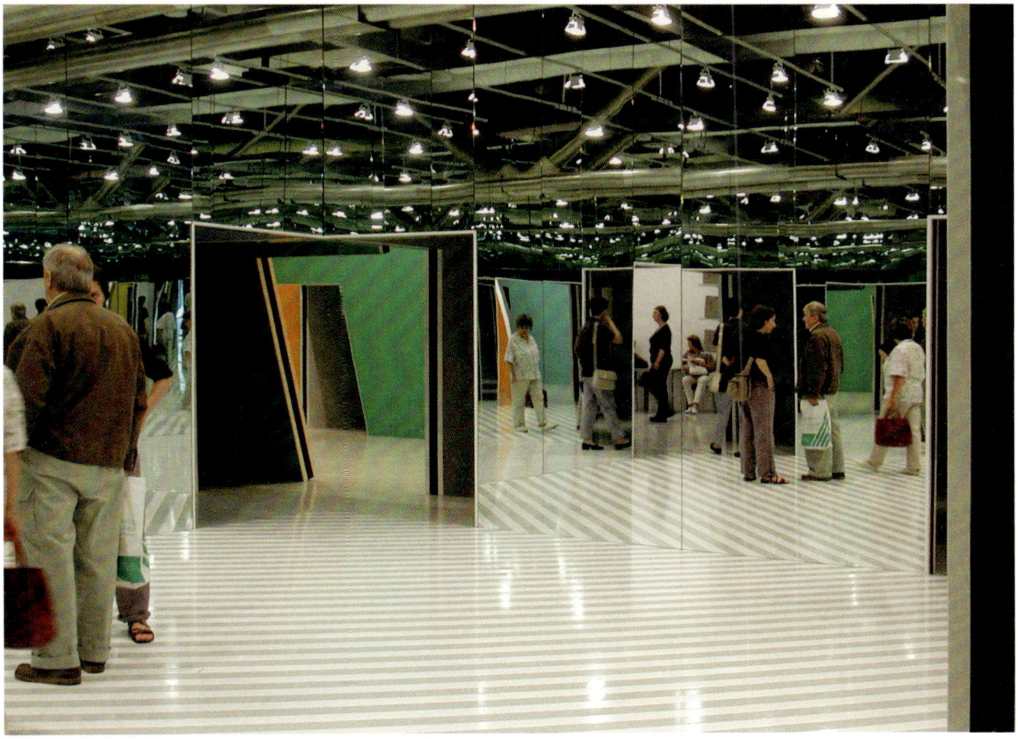

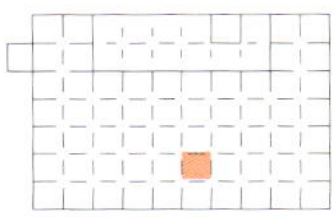

Room 55

Photo-souvenir: "The endless ceiling floor", work *in situ*
Painted wood, self-adhesive vinyl, mirrors, sheetrock, paint
Opposite, room 47, *Oblique walls*

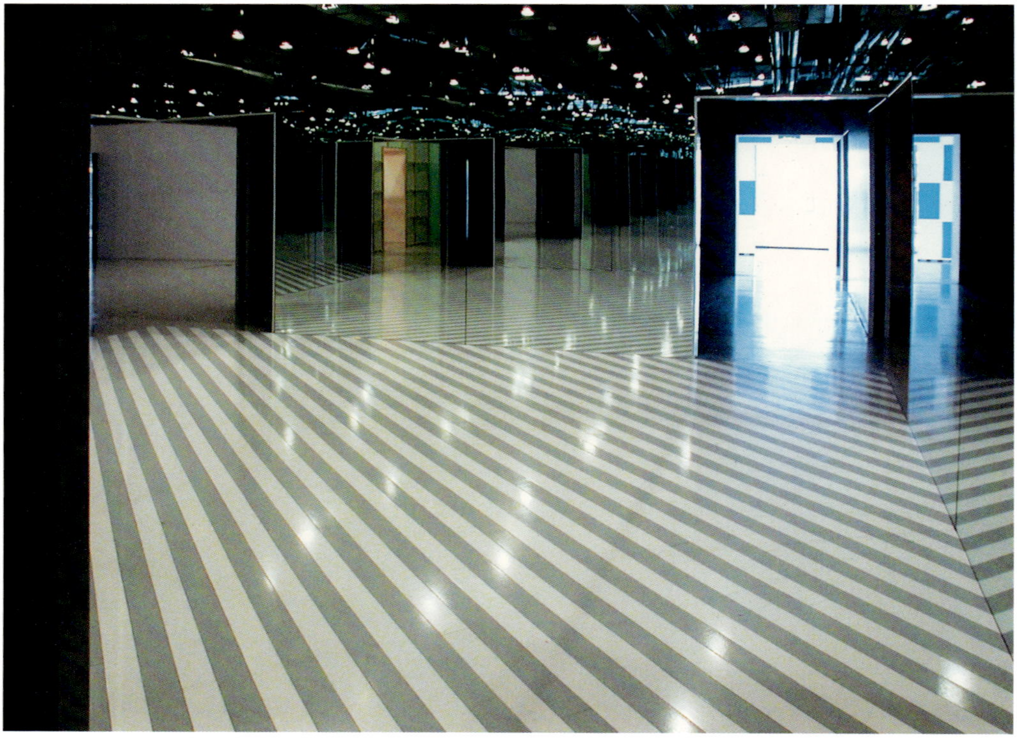

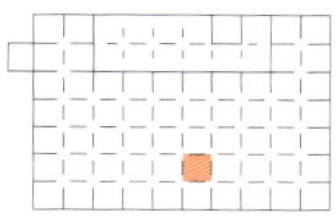

Room 55

Photo-souvenir: "The endless ceiling floor", work in situ
Painted wood, self-adhesive vinyl, mirrors, sheetrock, paint
Right adjoining, room 46 and room 35, *The sliding wall*
Left, room 45, *At a single glance*

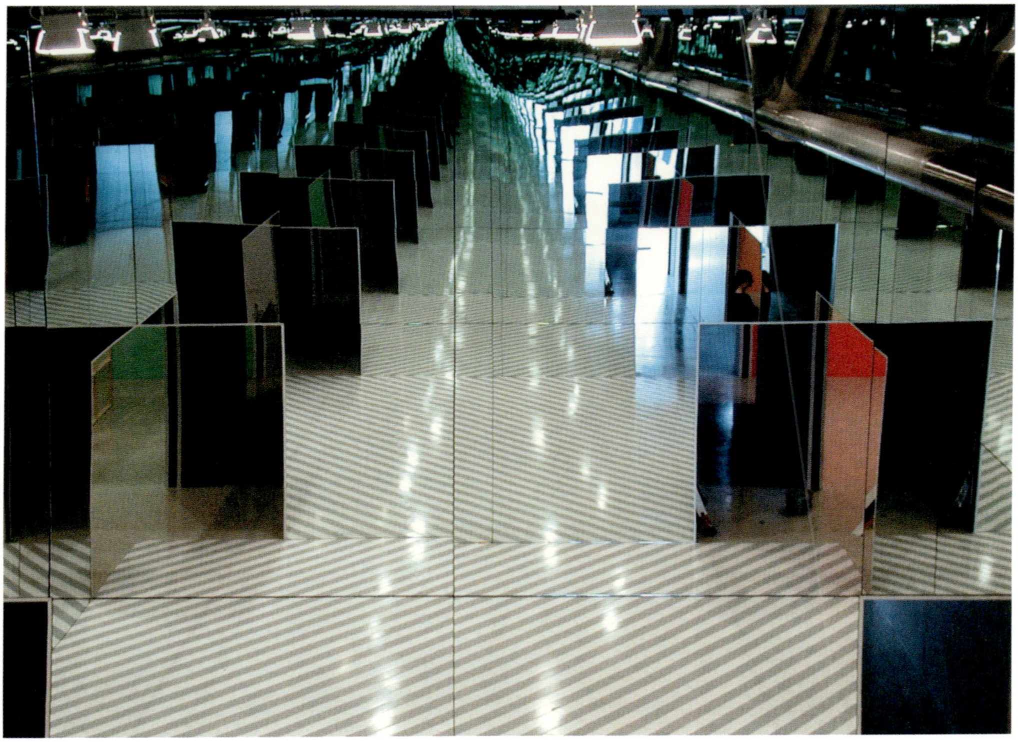

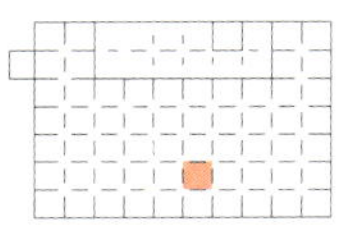

Room 55

Photo-souvenir: "The endless ceiling floor", work *in situ*
Painted wood, self-adhesive vinyl, mirrors, sheetrock, paint
Left, room 65, *The cabin with three ceilings*, and right,
room 67, *Three colours make four: the oblique diagonal*

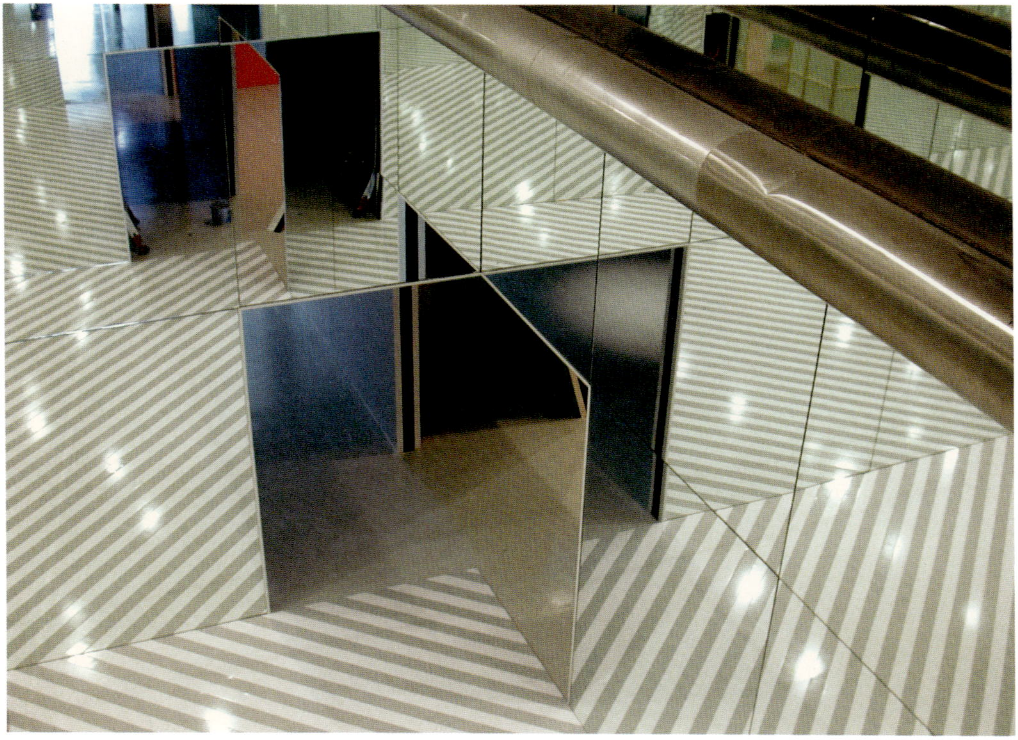

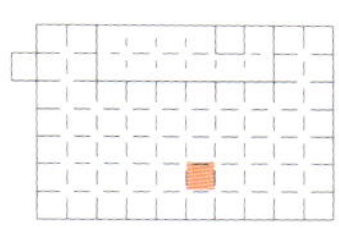

Room 55

Photo-souvenir: "The endless ceiling floor", work in situ
Painted wood, self-adhesive vinyl, mirrors, sheetrock, paint

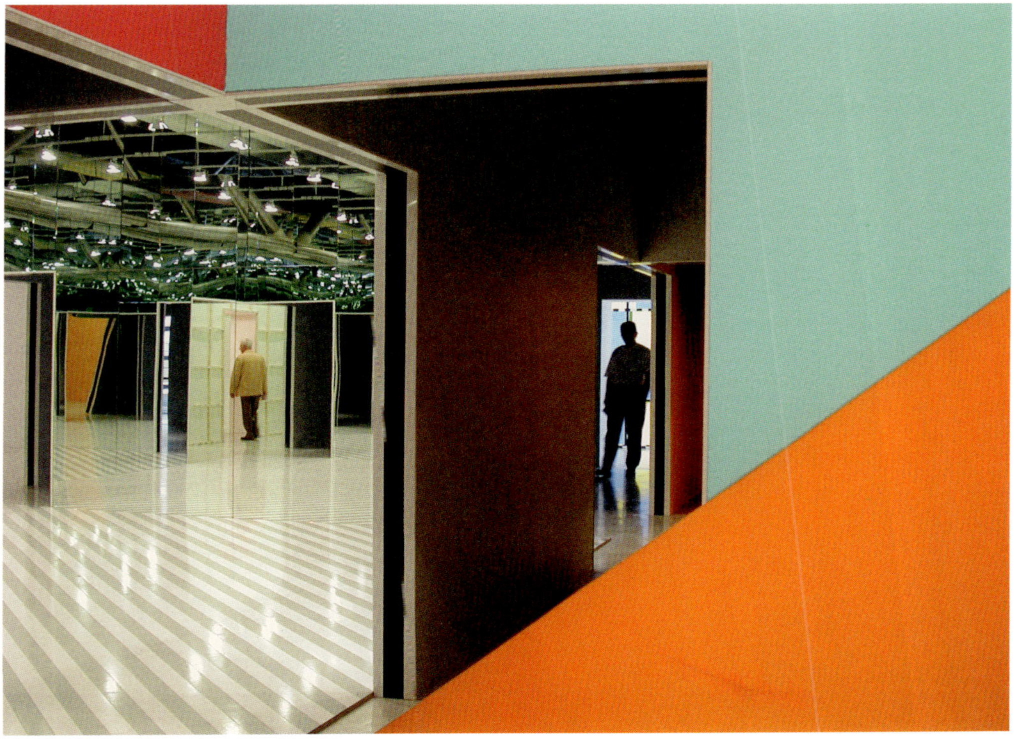

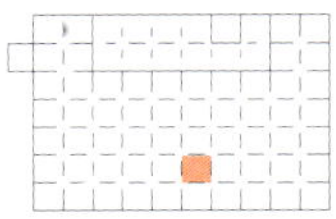

Room 55

Photo-souvenir: "The endless ceiling floor", work *in situ*
Painted wood, self-adhesive vinyl, mirrors, sheetrock, paint
View from room 67, *Three colours make four: the oblique diagonal*
Right, room 54

The only groins the passages bear the sign of the "visual tool" whereby Buren's work marks and takes possession of the space. The painted wall, as well as the oblique and the diagonal trace out a consummate art of geometry in space and unsuspected perspectives, shattering the authority of the white cube into a set of deliberately dissonant chromatic variations. In Buren's work, colour breaks with complementaries. It is pure presence. Back in 1965, the art critic Sarane Alexandrian subtly noted that: "Buren takes his colours without choosing them."

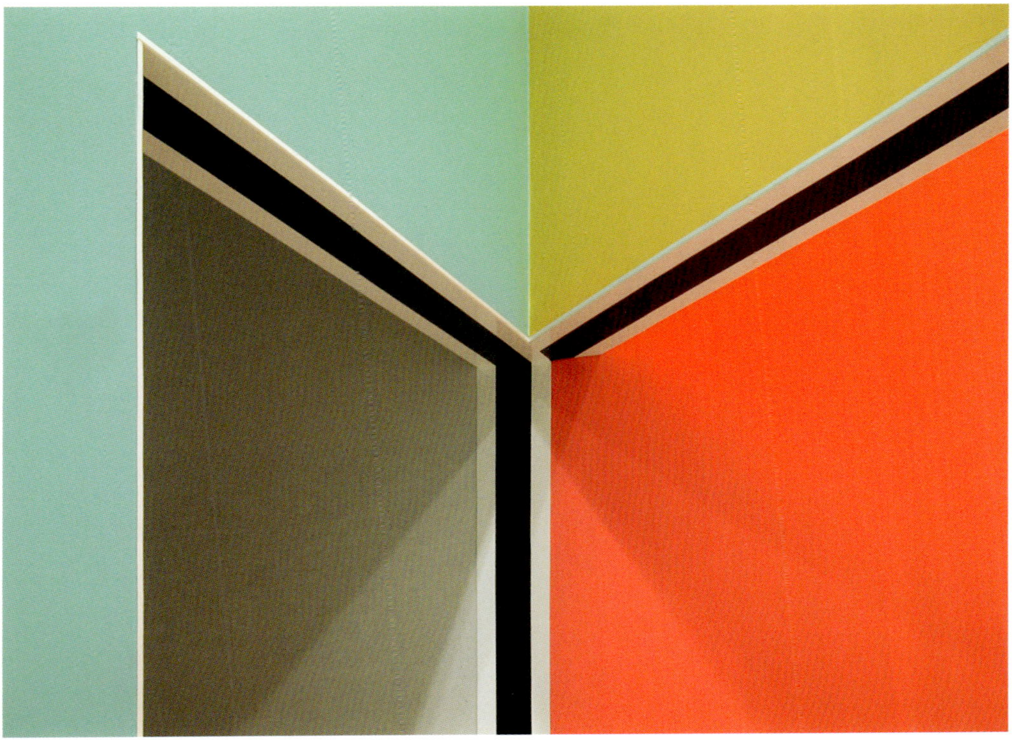

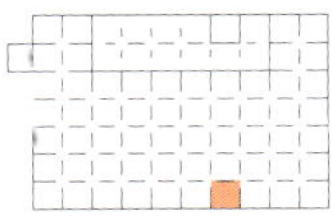

Room 67

Photo-souvenir: "Three colours make four: the oblique diagonal", work *in situ*
Sheetrock, 4 colours, self-adhesive vinyl

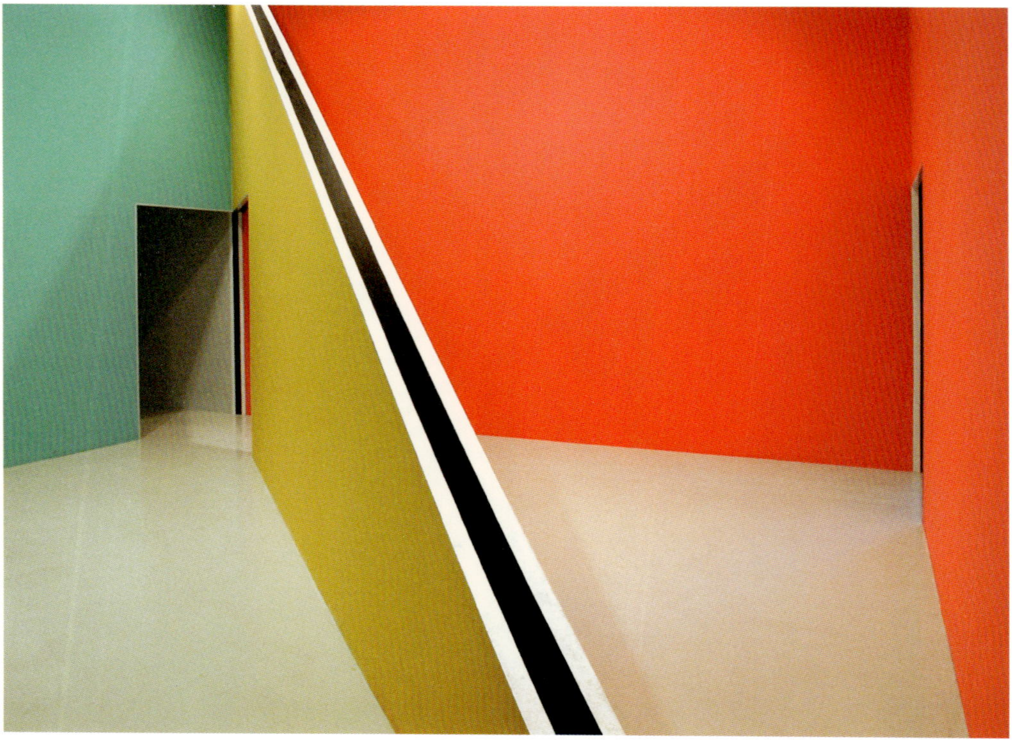

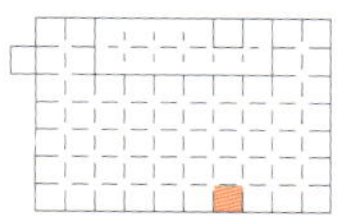

Room 67

Photo-souvenir: "Three colours make four: the oblique diagonal", work in situ
Sheetrock, 4 colours, self-adhesive vinyl

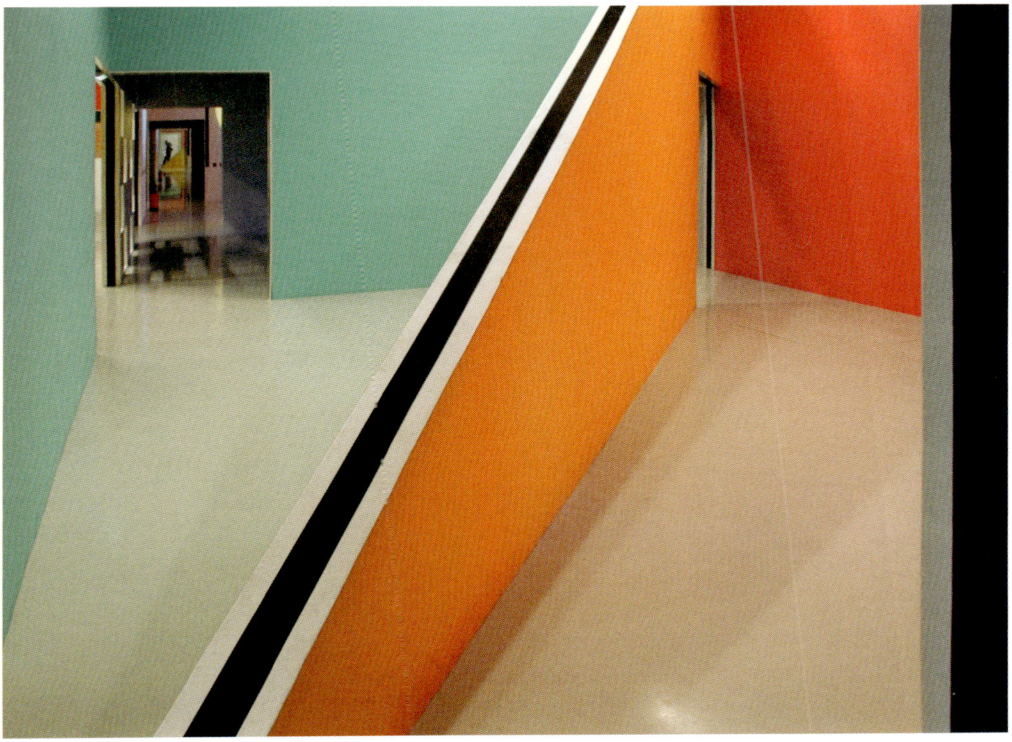

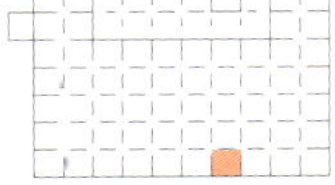

Room 67

Photo-souvenir: "Three colours make four: the oblique diagonal", work *in situ*
Sheetrock, 4 colours, self-adhesive vinyl
Left, adjoining, rooms 68 to 70
In the distance, a mirror n which all the doors are reflected

The toppling of space and the wall of colour underscores the particularly artificial dimension of the construction. It destabilises and alters the serial logic of the different cells, all identical in size. From one room to the next, each proposition is specific to the place and radically different from all the others. Each one is a fragment of a whole which the eye glimpses through the diagonal openings made by the artist. Buren's art has to do with deconstruction. It breaks the linearity of the geometric structure of space into an infinite host of variations and "whims", in which the eye circulates and is lost. What is involved is clearly taking possession of the place.

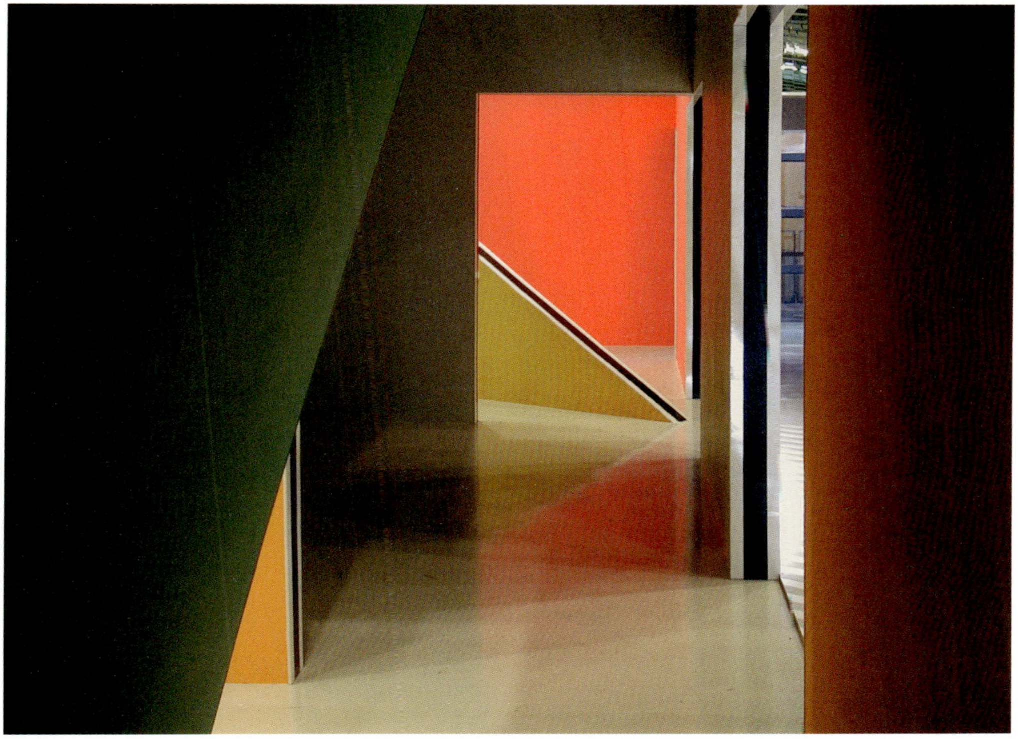

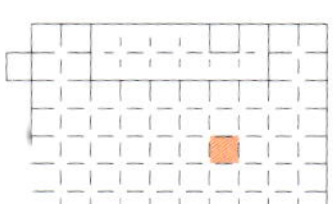

Room 47

Photo-souvenir: *"Oblique walls"*, work *in situ*
Sheetrock, metal structure, 2 colours, self-adhesive vinyl
Opposite, room 54 and room 67. *Three colours make four: the oblique diagonal*

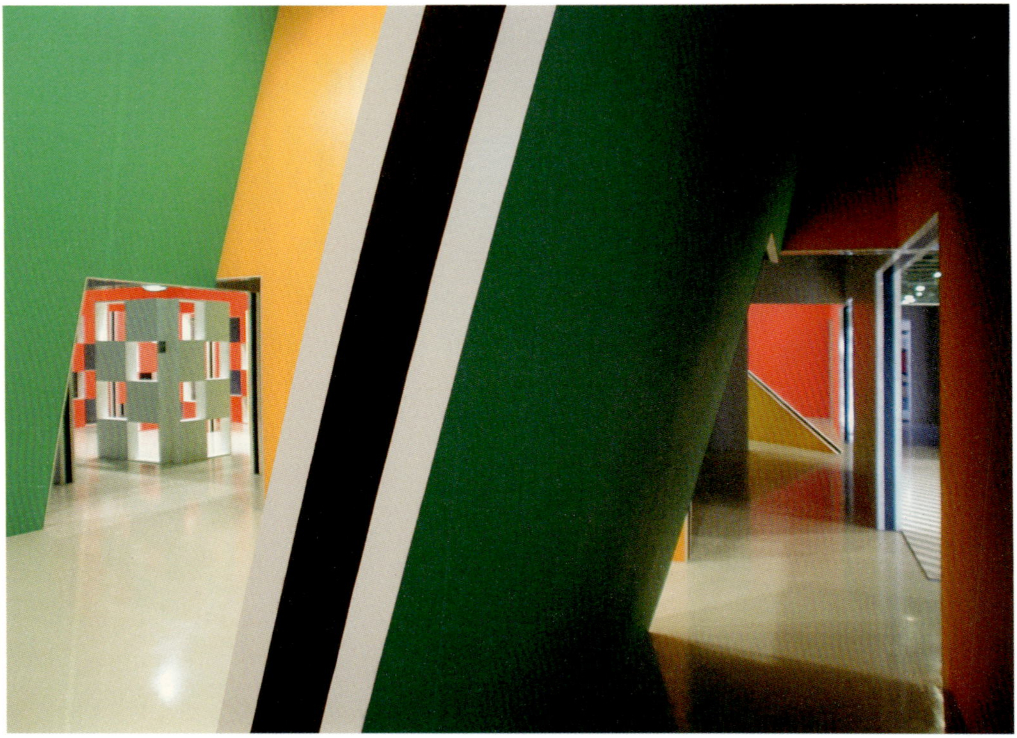

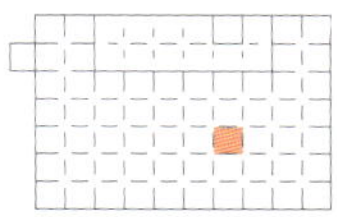

Room 47

Photo-souvenir: "Oblique walls", work *in situ*
Sheetrock, metal structure, 2 colours, self-adhesive vinyl
Left, room 53, *The imploded cabin: Distant murmur from the city*
In the distance, room 54 and room 67, *Three colours make four: the oblique diagonal*

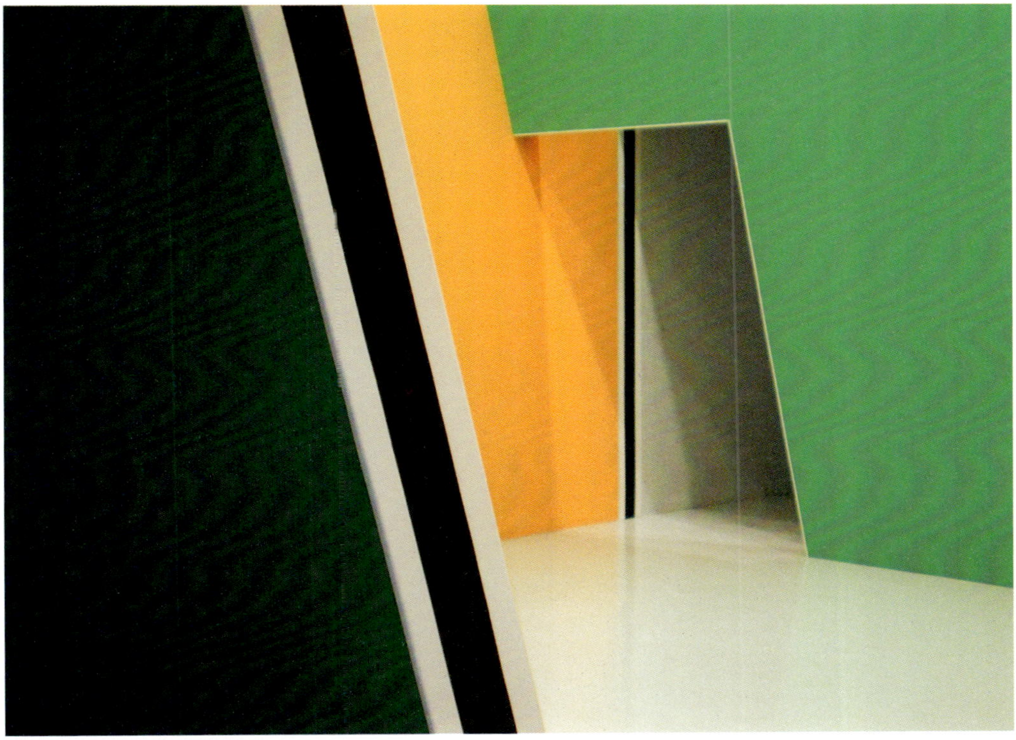

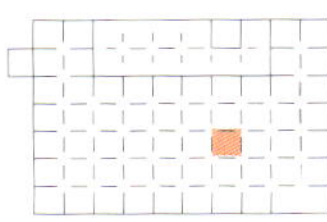

Room 47

Photo-souvenir: "Oblique walls", work in situ
Sheetrock metal structure, 2 colours, self-adhesive vinyl

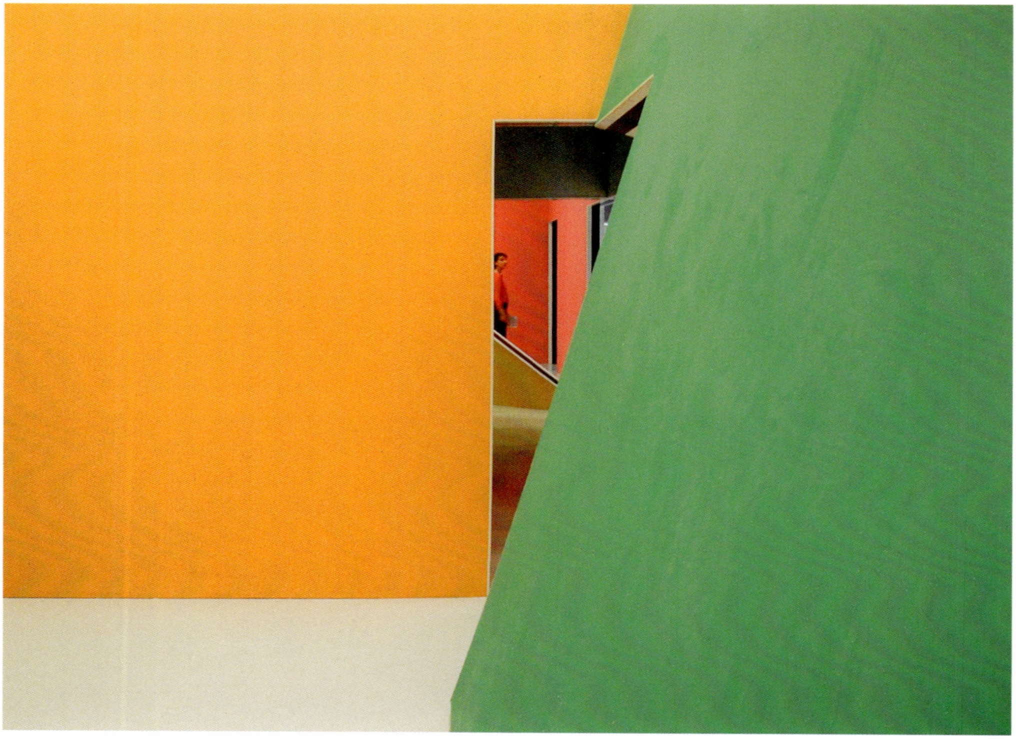

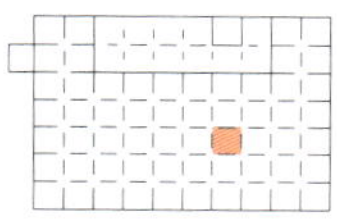

Room 47

Photo-souvenir: "Oblique walls", work *in situ*
Sheetrock, metal structure, 2 colours, self-adhesive vinyl
Opposite, room 54 and room 67, *Three colours make four: the oblique diagonal*

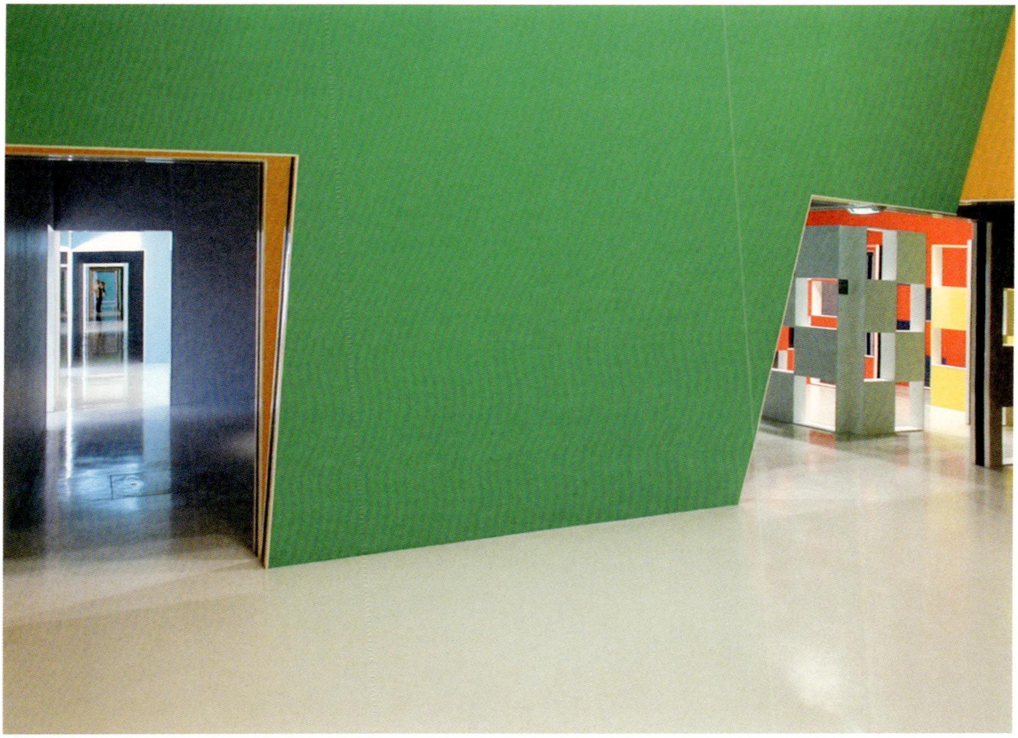

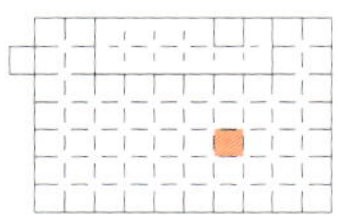

Room 47

Photo-souvenir: "Oblique walls", work *in situ*
Sheetrock, metal structure, 2 colours, self-adhesive vinyl
Left, adjoining, rooms 48 to 50
In the distance, a mirror in which all the doors are reflected
Right, room 53, *The imploded cabin : Distant murmur from the city*

In 1975, the "cabin" notion was part of the criticism of place which the artist has forever been formulating. "By definition", Buren points out, "any cabin takes its place of presentation as part and parcel of its visual result. Any cabin is thus associated with the place accommodating it, which it simultaneously reveals".

The art historians Alexander Alberro and Nora M. Alter have shown the crucial role played by the "exploded cabins" in the relation between viewer and work and their principle involving deconstructing the artefact of architecture. As Buren himself puts it: "...cabins thus form a very simple architecture situated within an existing architecture where they are exploded, the wrapper and what is wrapped are thus totally liaised. They are sites within sites, places within places". The logic of the cube which Buren immediately smithereens, the manhandling of the place and of the perception of this place under the eyes of viewers walking around it, seem to guide the logic of the "cabin".

Here, though, the principle is reversed: the cabin is not so much "exploded" as "imploded". The logic is not so much that of the shattering of the form and the smithereening of its component parts within the walled environment enclosing them, as the principle of the outside walls cut up and reducing the central nucleus to a completely fragmented volume. The movement is no longer made from the inside towards the environment of the walls framing the piece, as from the external walls towards a centre reduced to a principle of juxtaposed forms in a quincunx arrangement. Whereas the principle involving the shattering of the "exploded cabins" tears and fragments the component parts of the architecture and suspends them in the environment of the walls framing them, the "imploded cabins" proceed towards a fragmentation of the place. The corners are open and the perspective is oblique. At the point where the four spaces meet, visitors take the route they wish. The work's subtitle: *Distant murmur from the city*, underscores the fact that at the centre of the piece are gathered the sounds which Buren wanted to capture live from the piazza, on the Centre Pompidou's forecourt. While the "exploded cabins" developed in a centrifugal way, the "imploded cabin" is here asserted as a centripetal idea, bringing forms and sounds alike to the heart of the space.

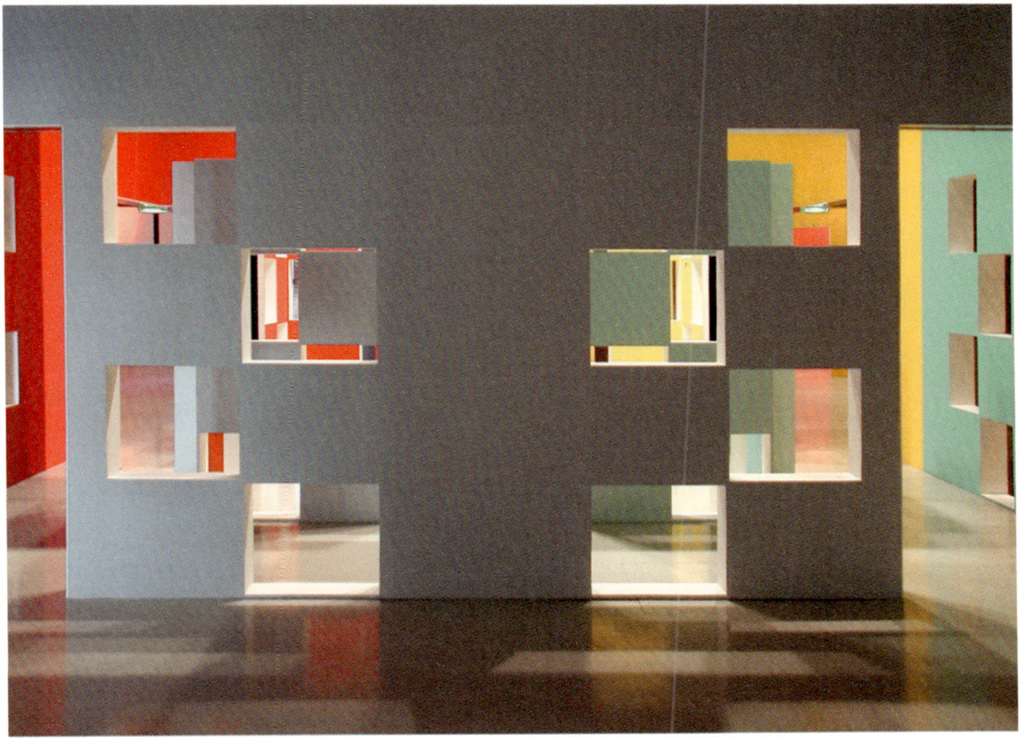

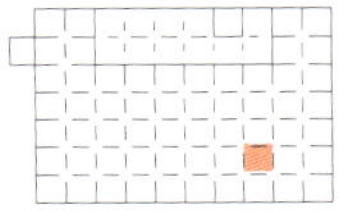

Room 53

Photo-souvenir: "The imploded cabin : Distant murmur from the city", work in situ
Sheetrock, metal structure, 3 colours, self-adhesive vinyl, loudspeakers
View from room 68

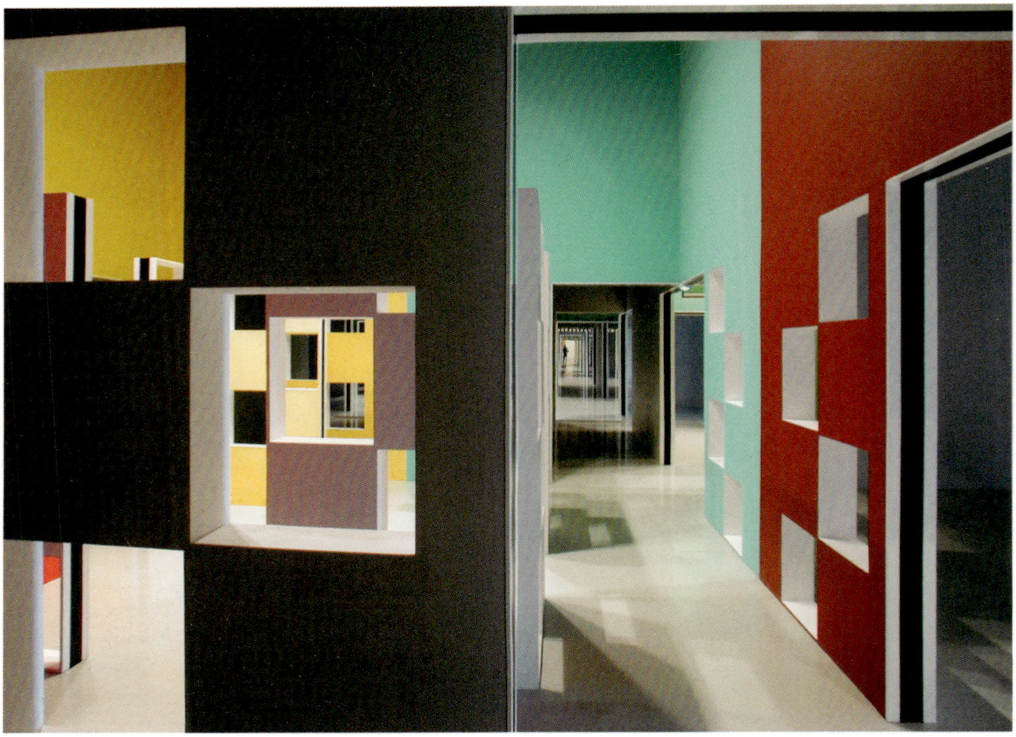

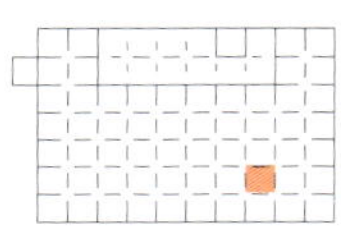

Room 53

Photo-souvenir: "The imploded cabin : Distant murmur from the city", work *in situ*
Sheetrock, metal structure, 3 colours, self-adhesive vinyl, loudspeakers
View from room 54; adjoining, room 52 and room 51, *Around the return of a detour*
In the distance, a mirror in which all the doors are reflected

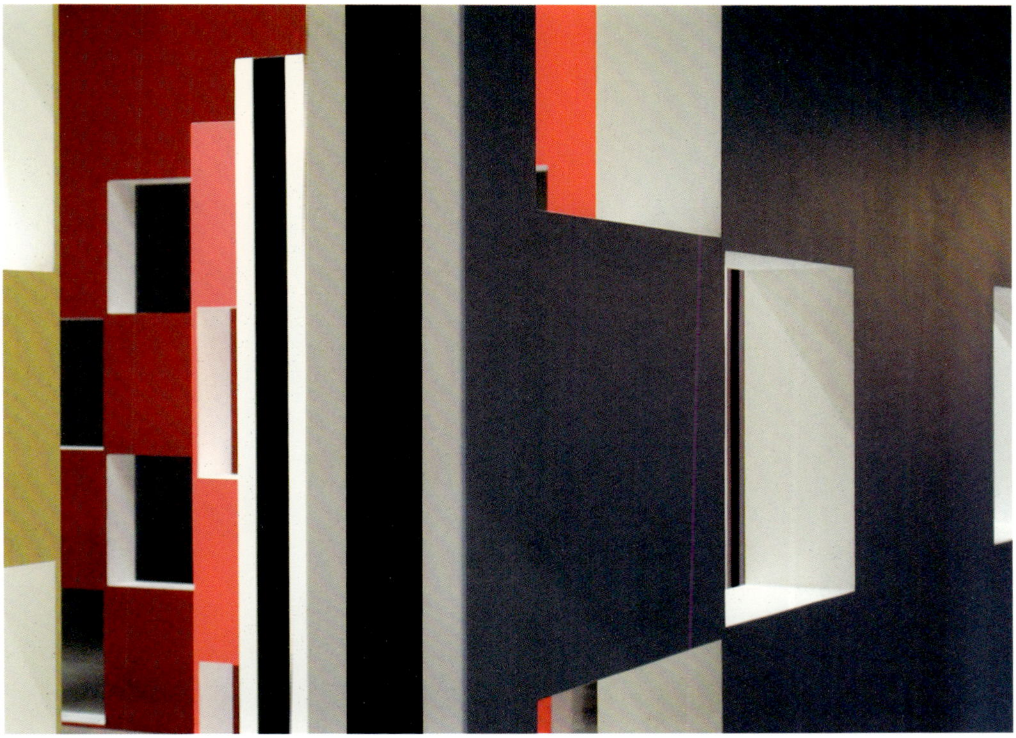

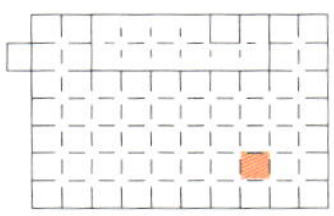

Room 53

Photo-souvenir: "The imploded cabin : Distant murmur from the city", work in situ
Sheetrock, metal structure, 3 colours, self-adhesive vinyl, loudspeakers
View from room 52

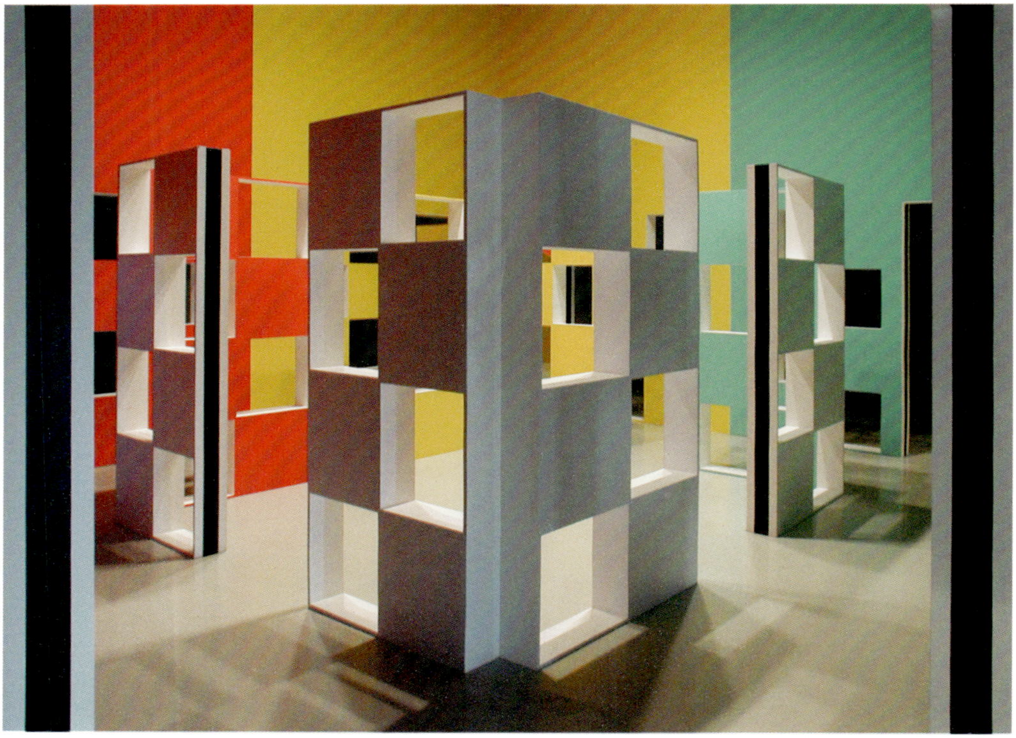

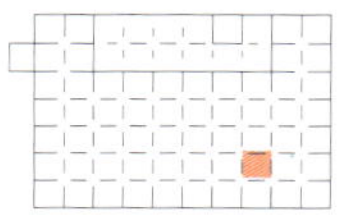

Room 53

Photo-souvenir: "The imploded Cabin : Distant murmur from the city", work in situ
Sheetrock, metal structure, 3 colours, self-adhesive vinyl, loudspeakers

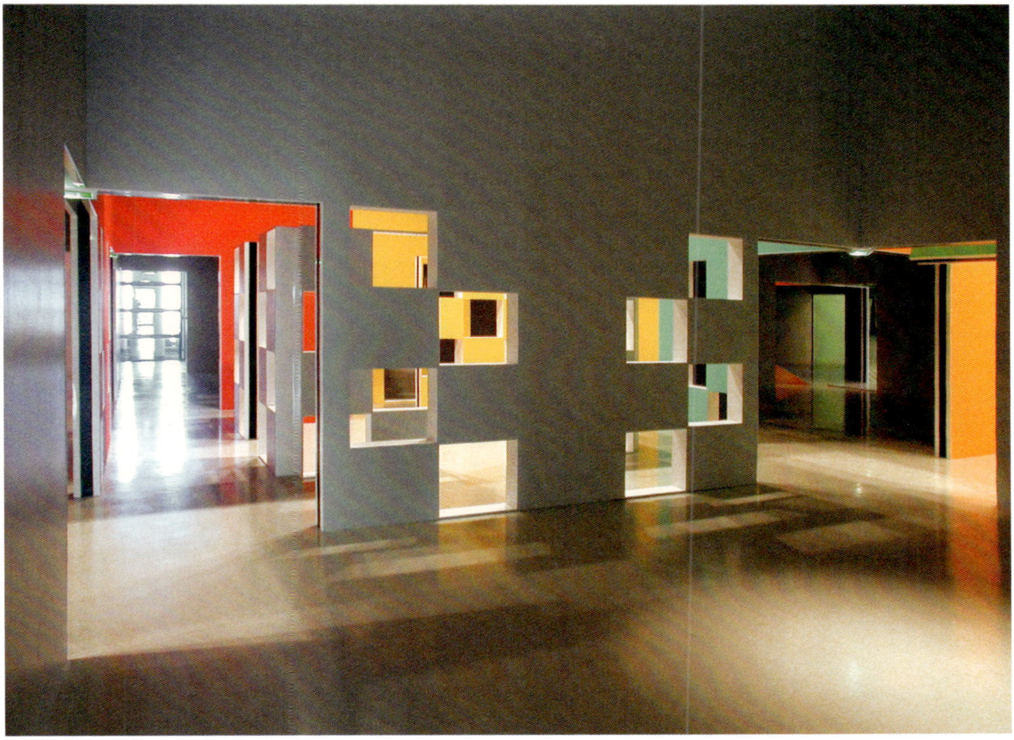

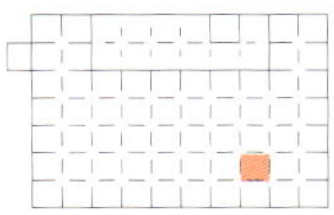

Room 53

Photo-souvenir: "The imploded cabin: Distant murmur from the city", work *in situ*
Sheetrock, metal structure, 3 colours, self-adhesive vinyl, loudspeakers

The "photo-souvenir" clearly highlights the extreme diversity of the ideas that Buren introduces. But if these variations are peculiar to each cell in the arrangement, they are just as often peculiar to the interior of the same space.
So it is, for example, with *Fragmented Colour*, whose principle is based on the contrast between the monochrome wall and the glass surface covered with strips of self-adhesive vinyl in which colour is reflected. Here, Buren sets up a cinematic principle which we find in many of his proposals. The chromatic unity is broken in the visual tool which thus fragments the vision. Time is put forward as one of the essential subjects of the artist's work. "Buren's approach", writes Thierry Laurent, "is a real educational method of seeing and looking at things".
With *Fragmented Colour*, viewers find themselves between two parts of one and the same room which they cannot completely grasp except by being reflected therein themselves – the active and moving part of a fixed, static arrangement. The use of the mirror thus refers as much to the idea of a broken unity as to anything else. This is what Buren had to say about it in 1985: "...it integrates within it "another" reality, alien to its form. The mirror emphasizes by its use that any old work is never other than a fragment of a whole. The mirror used introduces into the very corpus of the work in question thousands of elements which are not only alien to it but which are also never the same." Essential point: Buren's work cannot envisage grasping reality in its entirety.

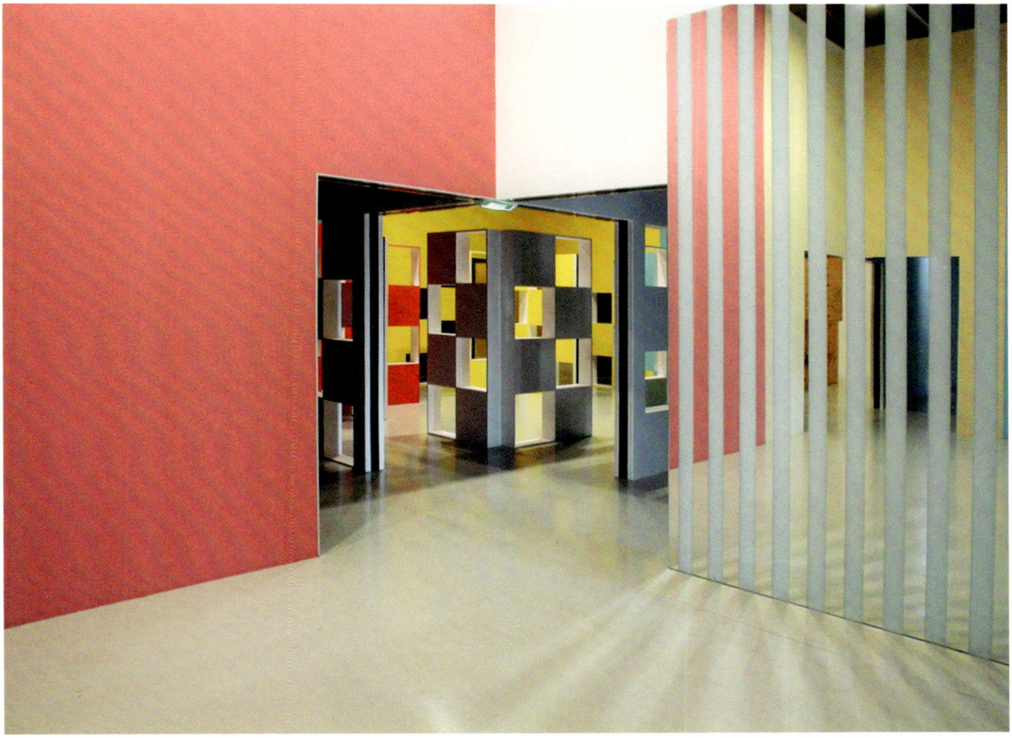

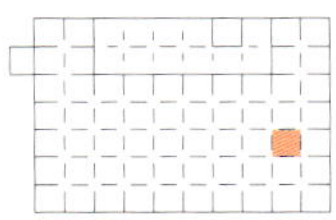

Room 49

Photo-souvenir: "Fragmented colour", work *in situ*
Mirrors, self-adhesive vinyl, glue, colours, metal structure
Opposite, room 53, *The imploded cabin : Distant murmur from the city*

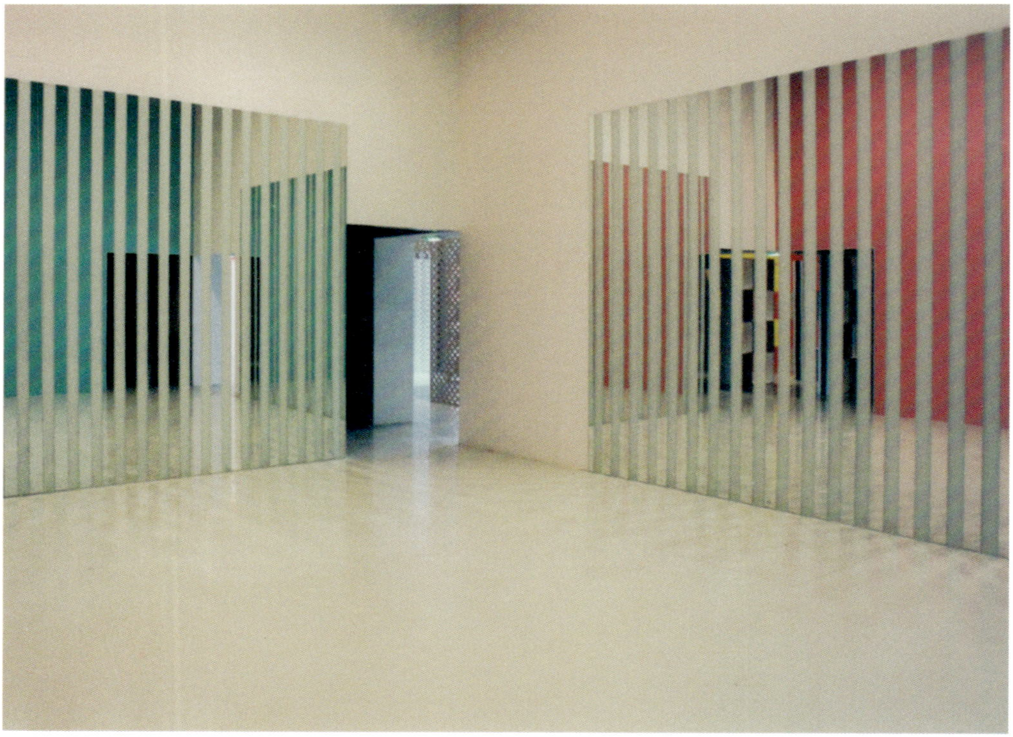

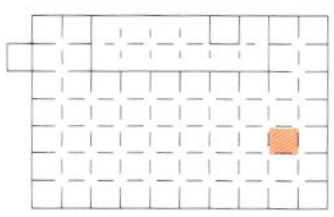

Room 49

Photo-souvenir: *"Fragmented colour"*, work *in situ*
Mirrors, self-adhesive vinyl, glue, colours, metal structure
Left, adjoining, rooms 48 to 41
Opposite, room 33, *The exploded cabin with 4,432 holes: lace*

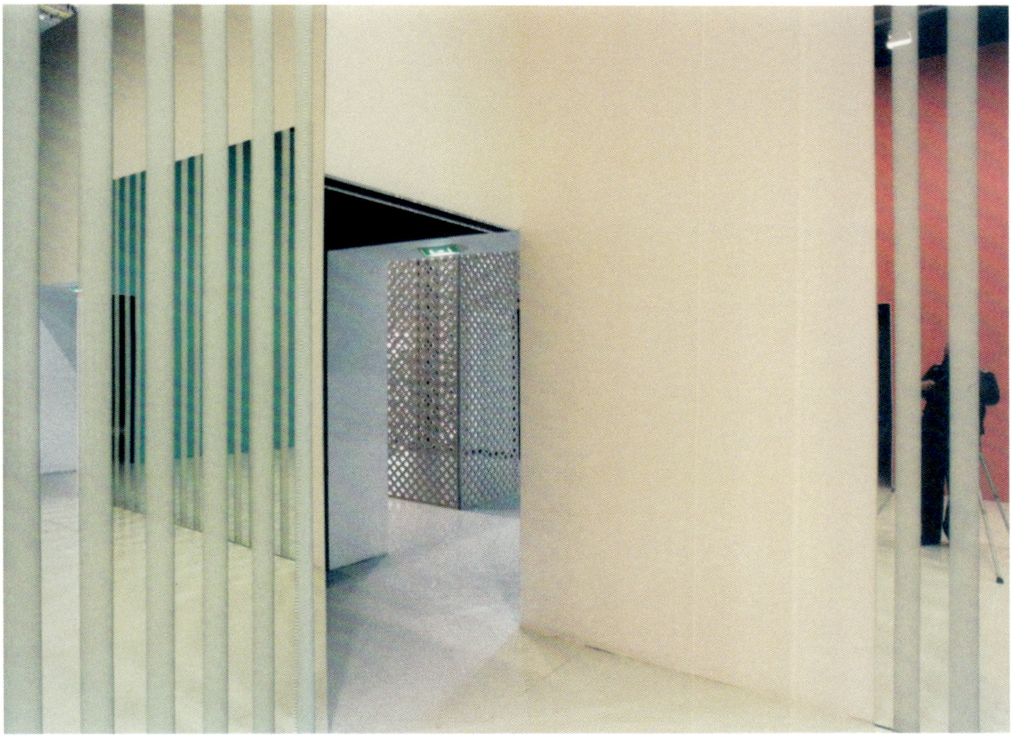

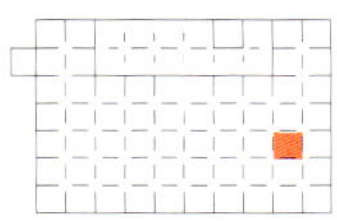

Room 49

Photo-souvenir: "Fragmented colour", work in situ
Mirrors, self-adhesive vinyl, glue, colours, metal structure
Oppcsite, room 33, *The exploded cabin with 4,432 holes: lace*

"Le Musée qui n'existait pas" was intended as a celebration of colour, an implicit response to too many works which, at the beginning of this twenty-first century, only found any legitimacy in illustrating the world's misfortunes. In the very earliest stages of his work, Buren wanted to take note of as much. Wherever it might be, the exhibition would be subject to a protocol in which colour and light would play a crucial part.
So it is with *Light Projection*, for which Buren uses colour gelatin which he projects directly onto the walls of the room at their maximum dimension. Light exposed, echoing many of the artist's propositions, and those of some of his contemporaries; light as subject of the work, but also the framed lighting of the "visual tool": a way of appearing to be "scouting around" and accentuating the especially spectacular, not to say scenographic and theatrical, dimension of "Le Musée qui n'existait pas".

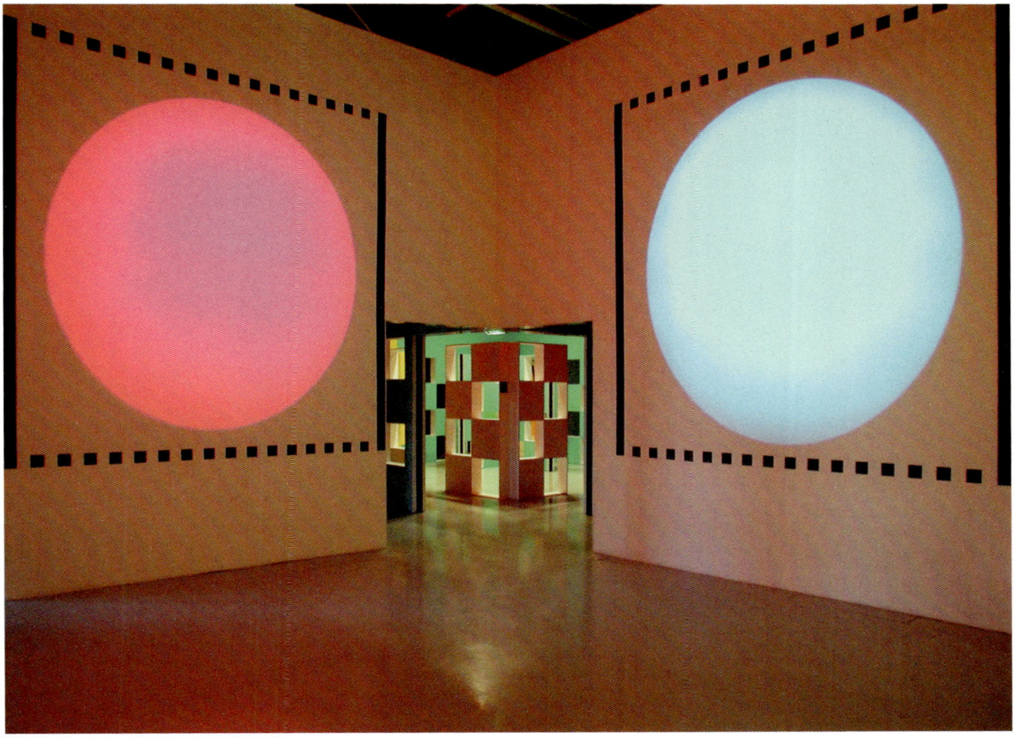

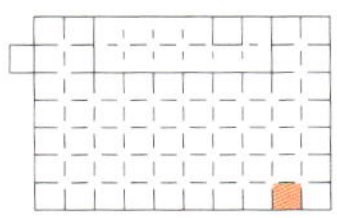

Room 69

Photo-souvenir: "Projection of light", work *in situ*
Sheetrock, self-adhesive vinyl, theatre projectors, metal structure
Opposite, room 53, *The imploded cabin : Distant murmur from the city*

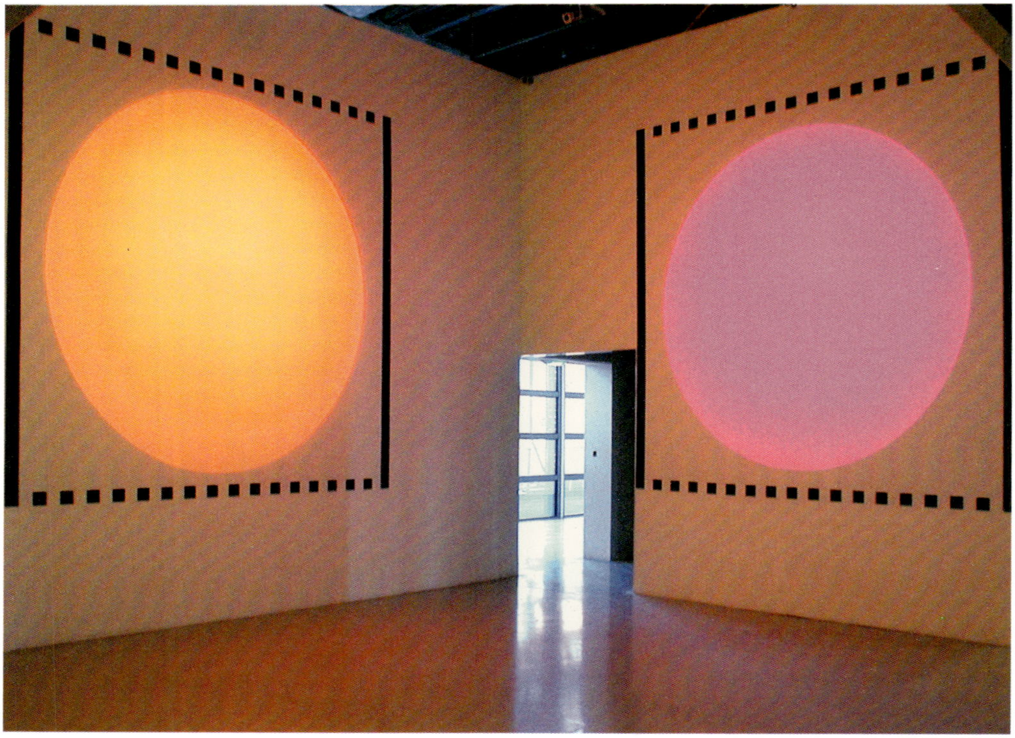

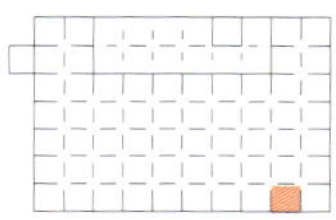

Room 69

Photo-souvenir: "Projection of Light", work *in situ*
Sheetrock, self-adhesive vinyl, theatre projectors, metal structure
In the distance, view of the windows at the back of the Centre Pompidou, east side

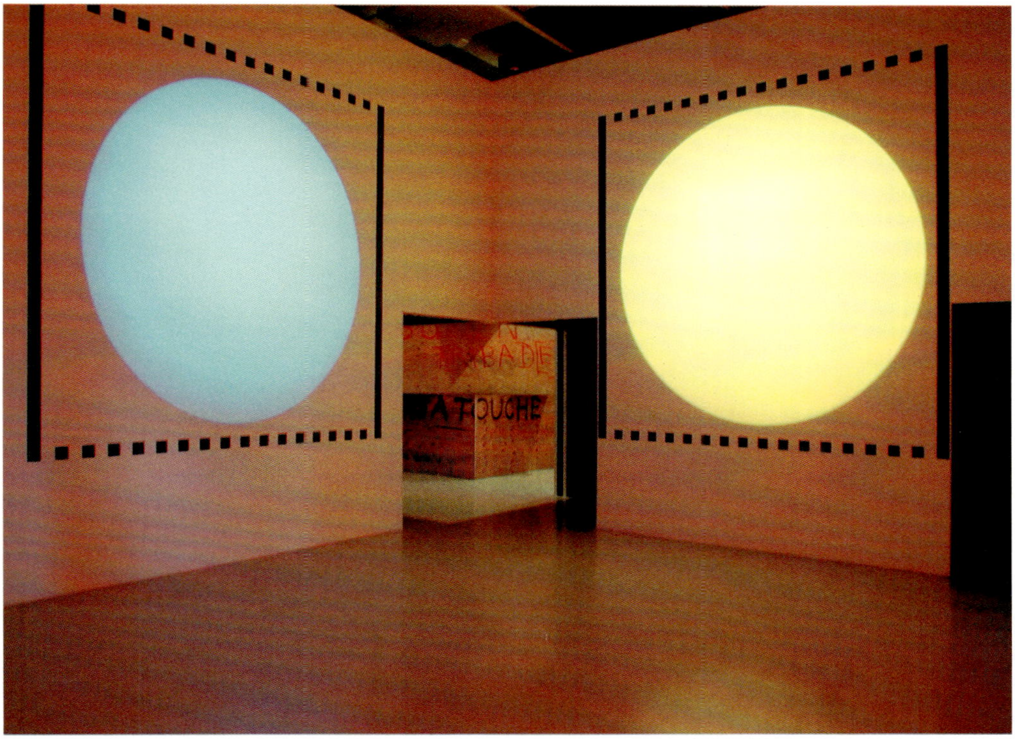

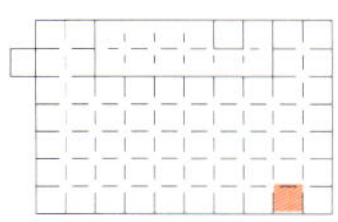

Room 69

Photo-souvenir: "Projection of Light", work *in situ*
Sheetrock, self-adhesive vinyl, theatre projectors, metal structure
Opposite, room 51, *Around the return of a detour*

In the opening of the passage made at each corner, we glimpse, piled one on top of the other, like a house of cards, some of the fences and palings from the Palais-Royal site which Buren retrieved when construction was over, and reversed order to turn them against the very ones that had been spread out poured out here and had covered them with all kinds of graffiti. Robert Cantarella, Margot Meyer, Sophie Streefkerk, and Julie Pellegrin, whose voices can be heard, were asked to read and record the different phrases and snippets of meaning which were methodically taken down.
In 1988, at the Le Magasin art centre in Grenoble, the site paling from the Palais-Royal courtyard gave rise to one of the most fascinating situation reversals ever produced by Daniel Buren. The whole thing was re-installed and indexed by the artist, in such a way that the graffiti covering it became food for thought about the relation between work and public place.
The elements on view in the Centre Pompidou in a way rekindled a discussion which, as we know, was one of the emblematic controversies involving contemporary art in the 1980s. *Around the Return of a Detour* is a tremendous final insult delivered to all those who tried to prevent the execution of the most radical public commission of the period, a reversal of the situation to the artist's advantage.

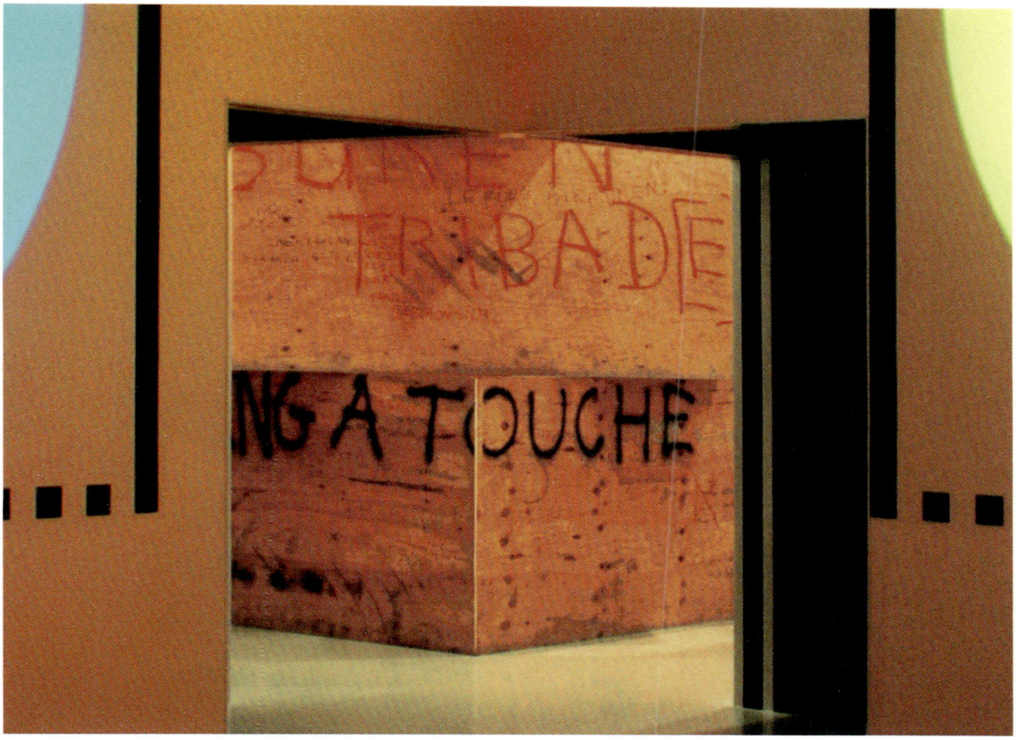

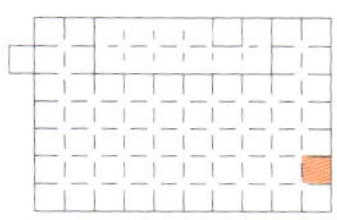

Room 51

Above and on following pages:
Photo-souvenir: "Around the return of a detour", work *in situ*, 1988-2002
12 fences taken from the 62 surrounding the Palais-Royal construction site between 1985 and 1986
Wood, paint, loudspeakers, recorded tape
View from room 69, *Projection of light*

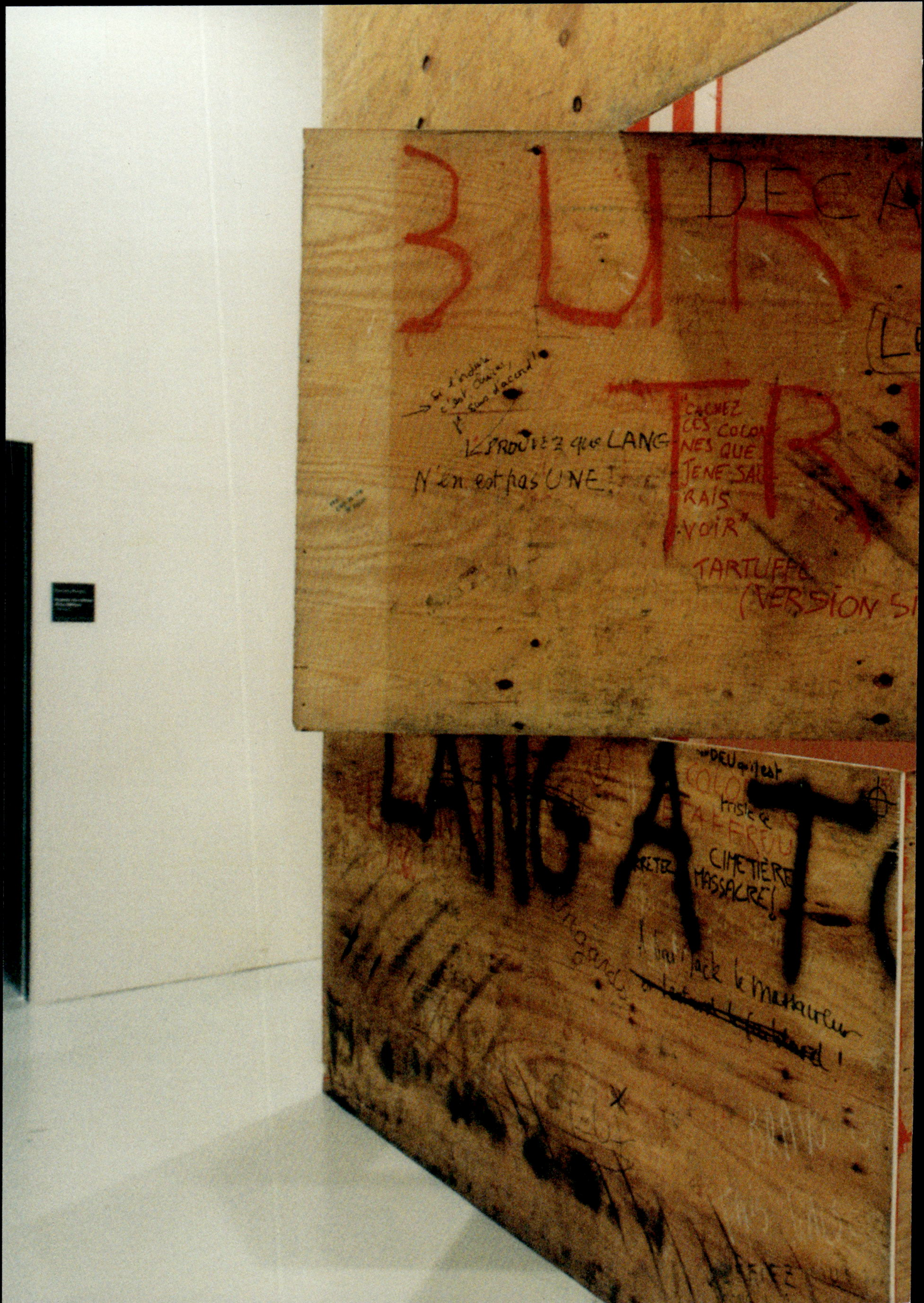
DECA
PROUVEZ que LANG
N'en est pas UNE!
"CACHEZ CES COLONNES QUE JE NE SAURAIS VOIR"
TARTUFFE
(VERSION S
LANG A T
CIMETIÈRE
MASSACRE!

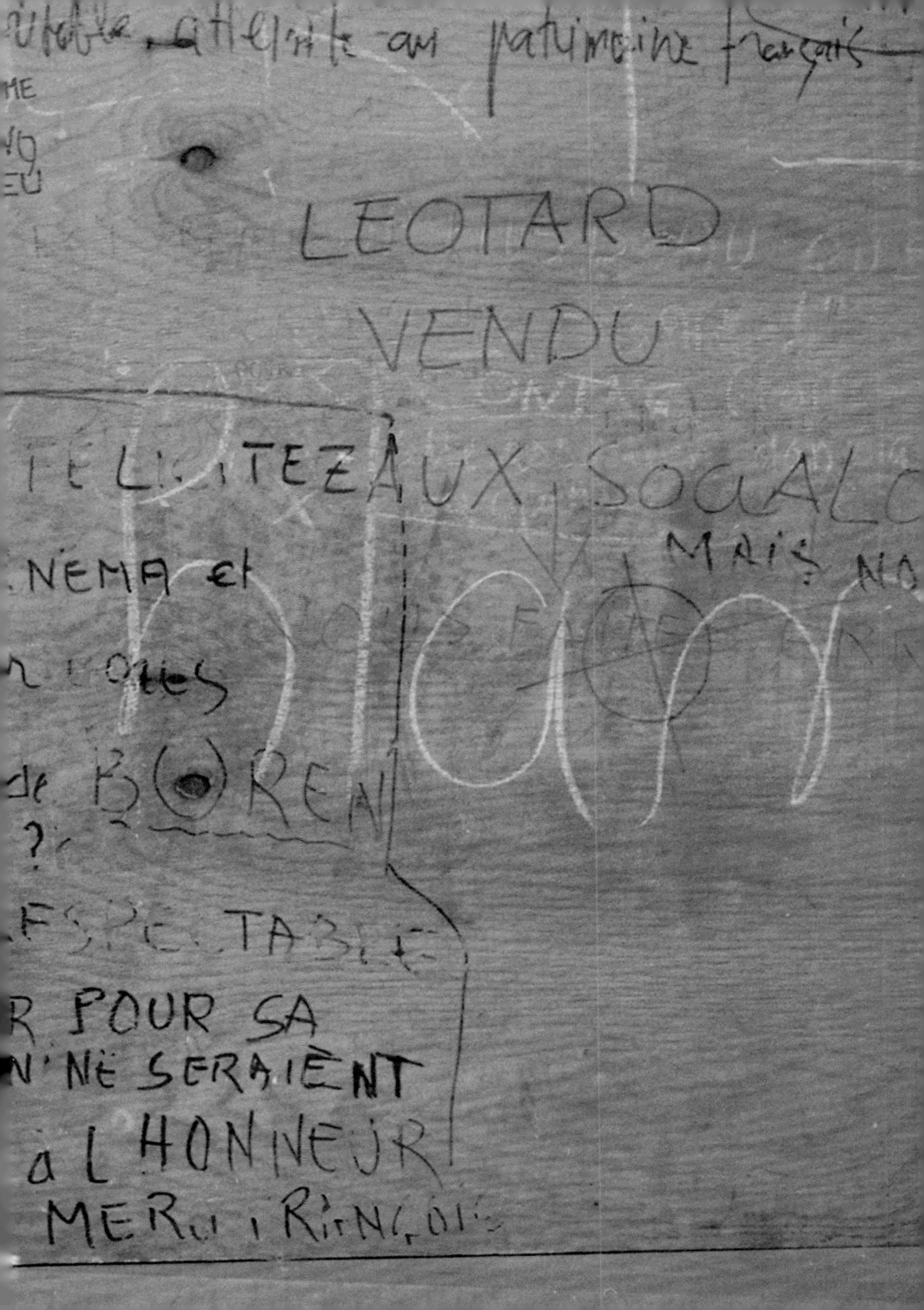
atteinte au patrimoine français
LEOTARD
VENDU
AUX SOCIALO
MAIS NO
NEMA et
de BOREN
R POUR SA
N'NE SERAIÈNT
à L HONNEUR

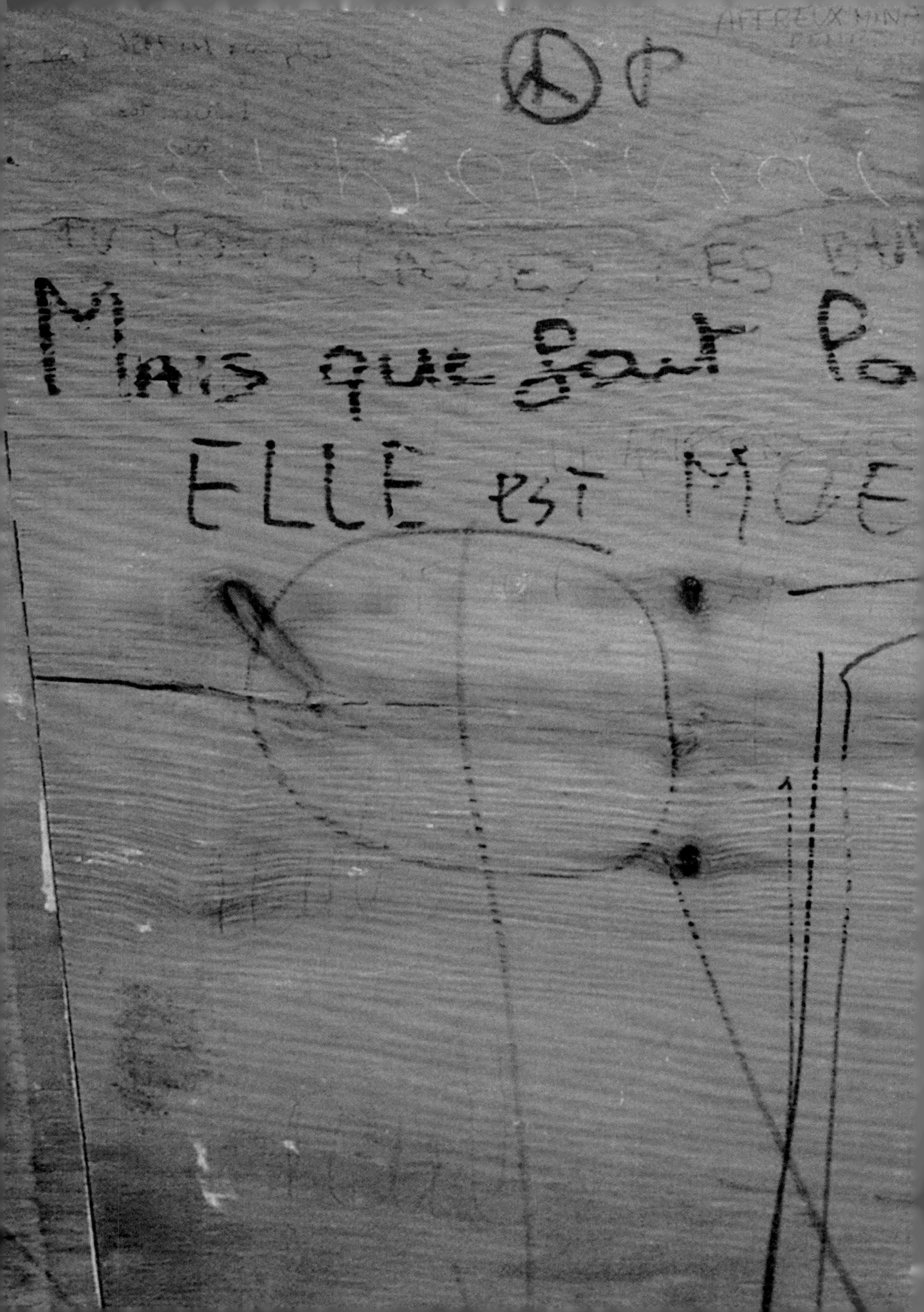
Mais que faut Po
ELLE est MOE

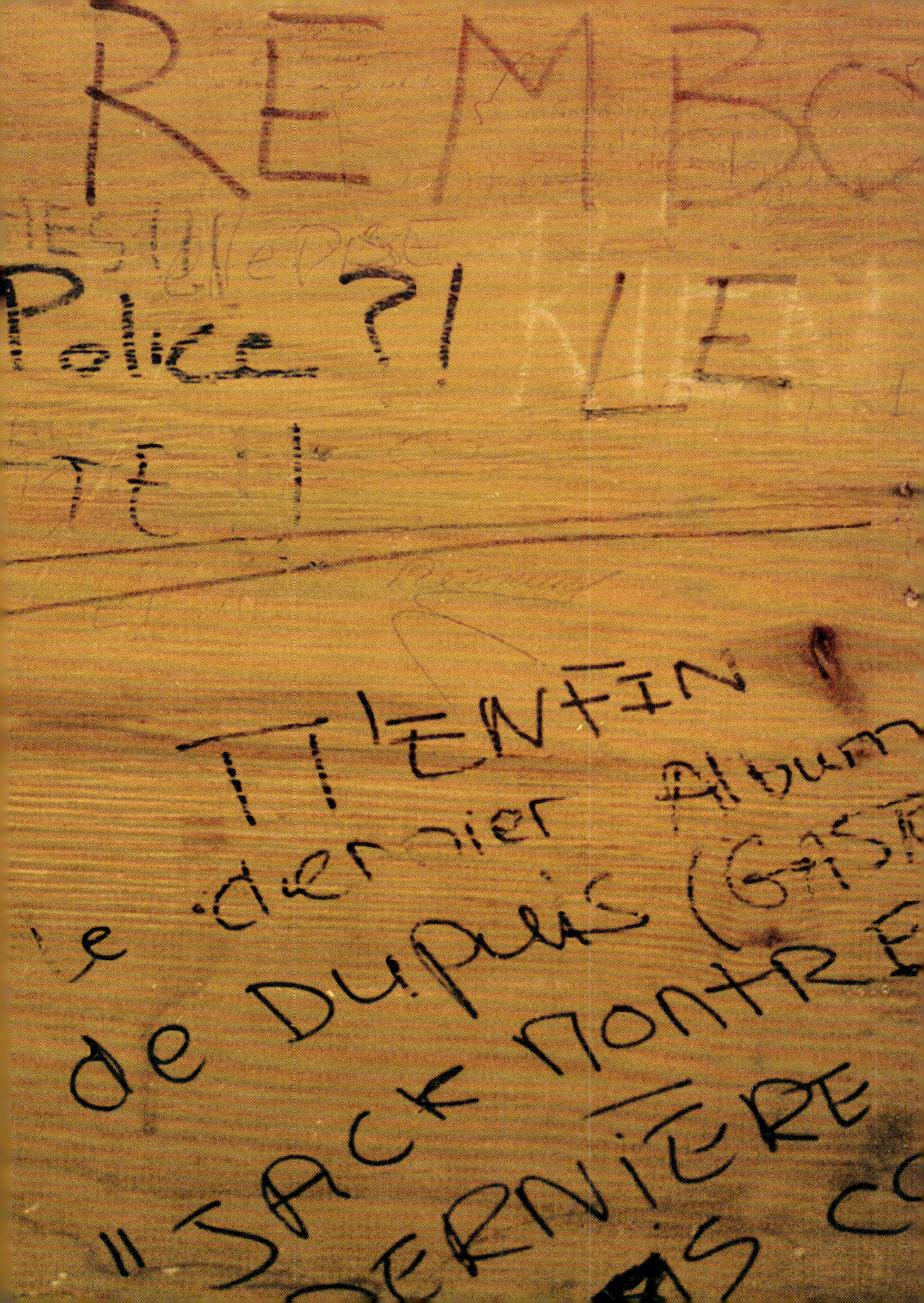
REMB
Police ?!
LE
ENFIN
dernier album
le
de Dupuis (GAS
de
MONTRE
"JACK
DERNIÈRE

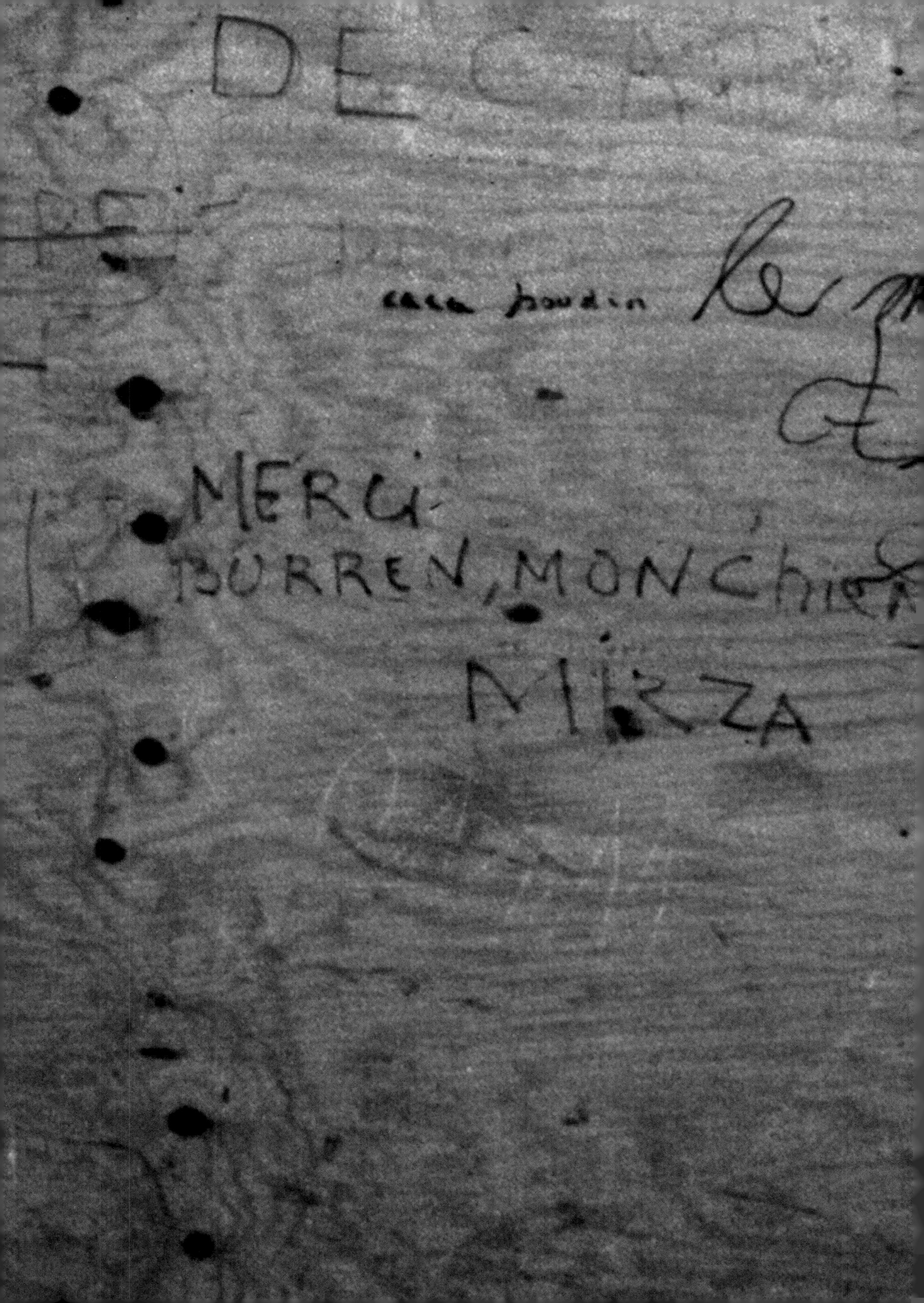
DE
caca boudin
MERCI
BURREN, MON
MIRZA

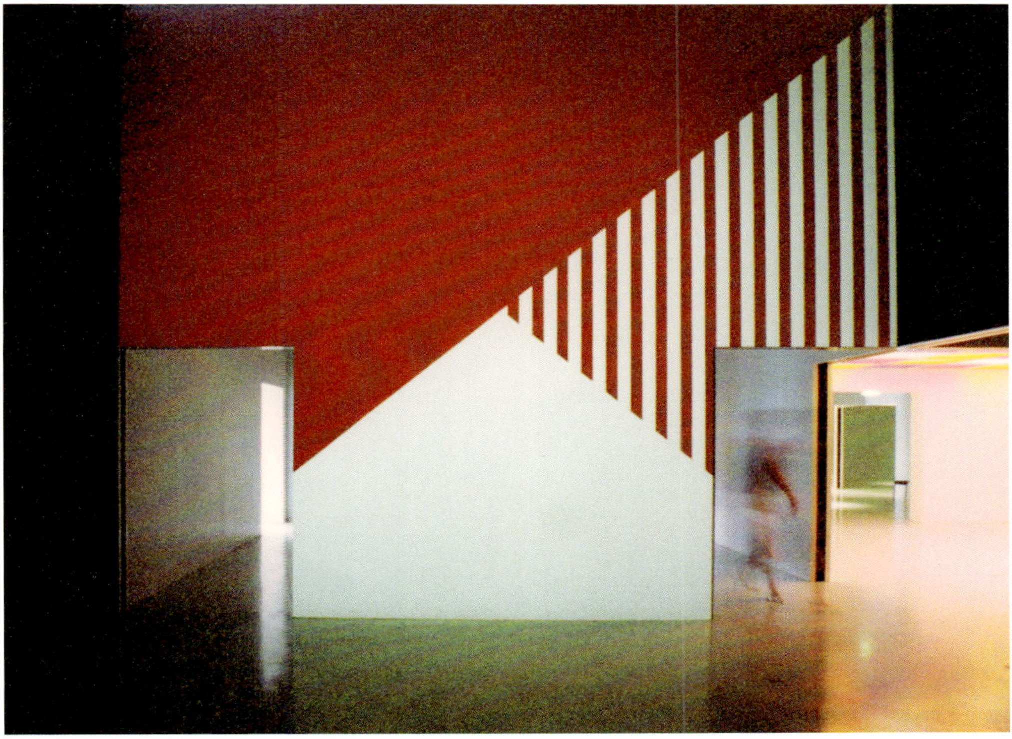

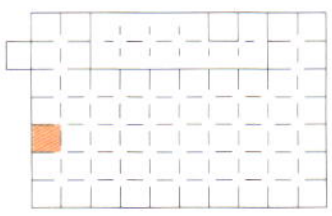

Room 41

Photo-souvenir: "Projection of 50 motifs", work *in situ*
Projector, 50 views, sheetrock, metal structure, paint
Right, view of room 59, *The suspended ceiling*
Left, room 42

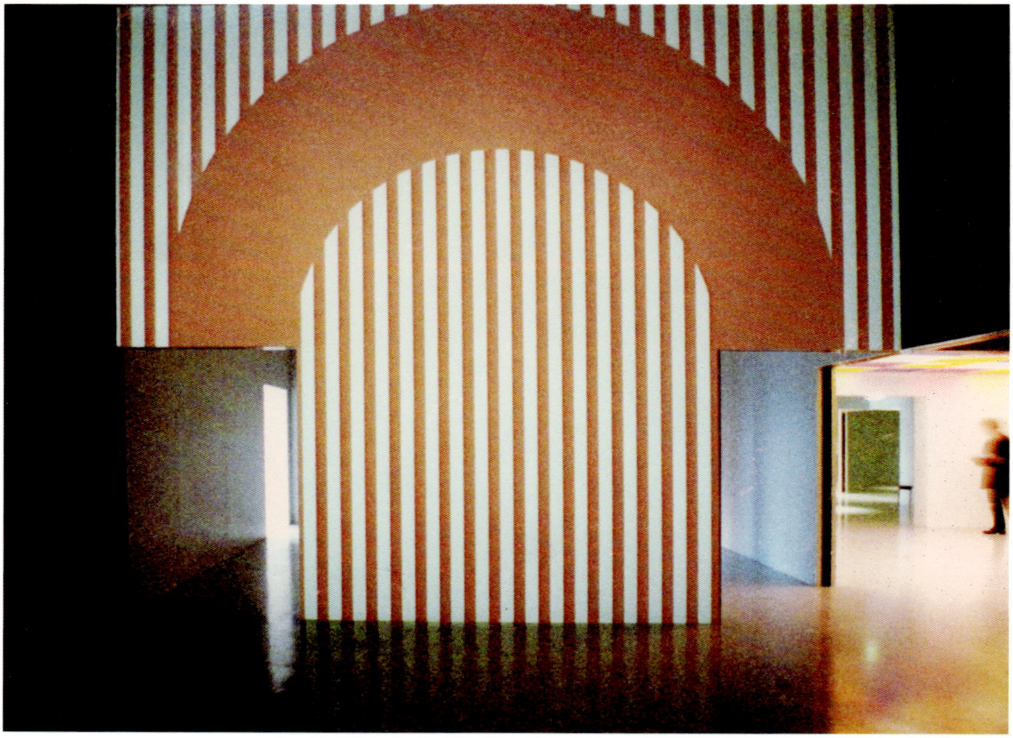

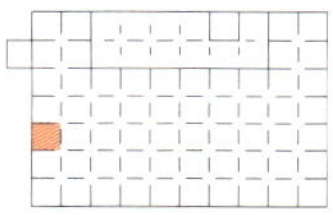

Room 41

Photo-souvenir: "Projection of 50 motifs", work *in situ*
Projector, 50 views, sheetrock, metal structure, paint
Right, view of room 59, *The suspended ceiling*
Left, room 42

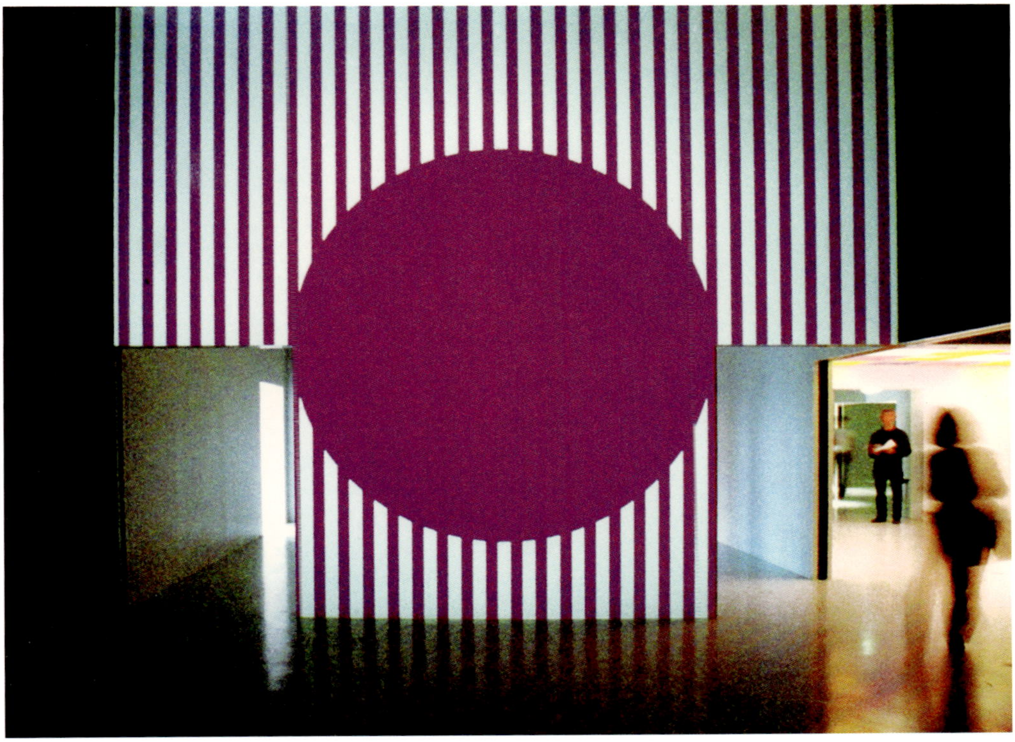

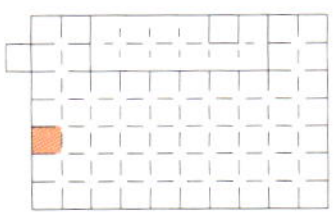

Room 41

Photo-souvenir: "Projection of 50 motifs", work *in situ*
Projector, 50 views, sheetrock, metal structure, paint
Right, view of room 59, *The suspended ceiling*
Left, room 42

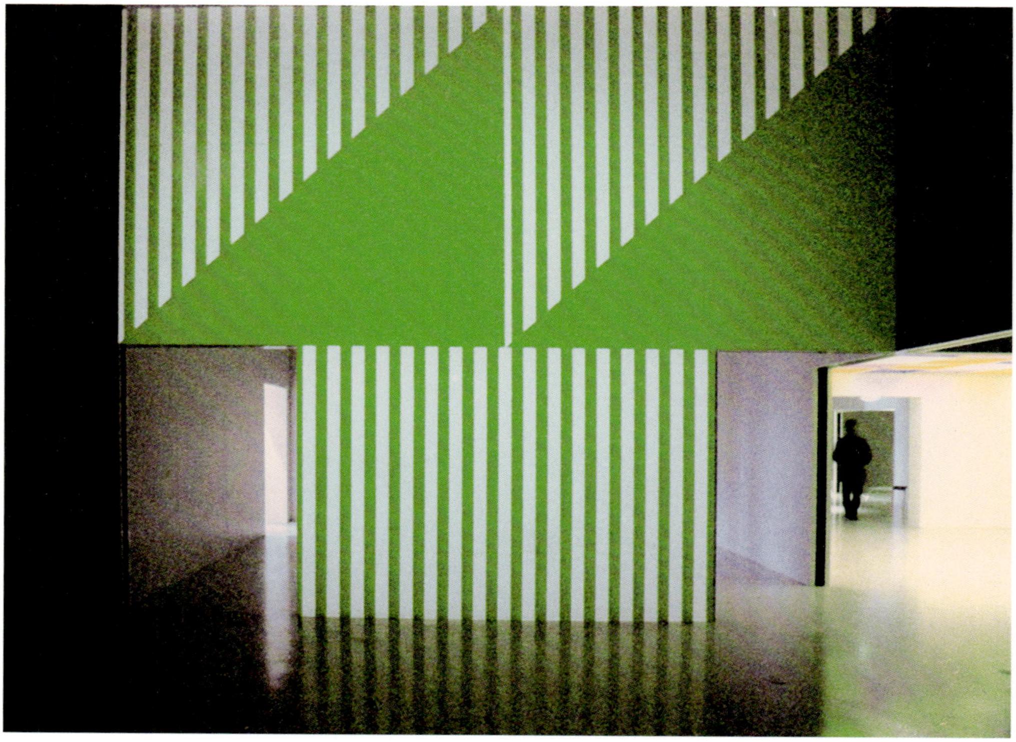

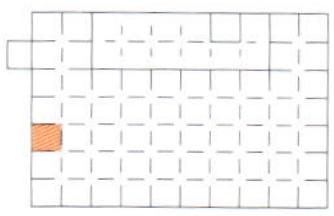

Room 41

Photo-souvenir: "Projection of 50 motifs", work *in situ*
Projector, 50 views, sheetrock, metal structure, paint
Right, view of room 59, *The suspended ceiling*
Left, room 42

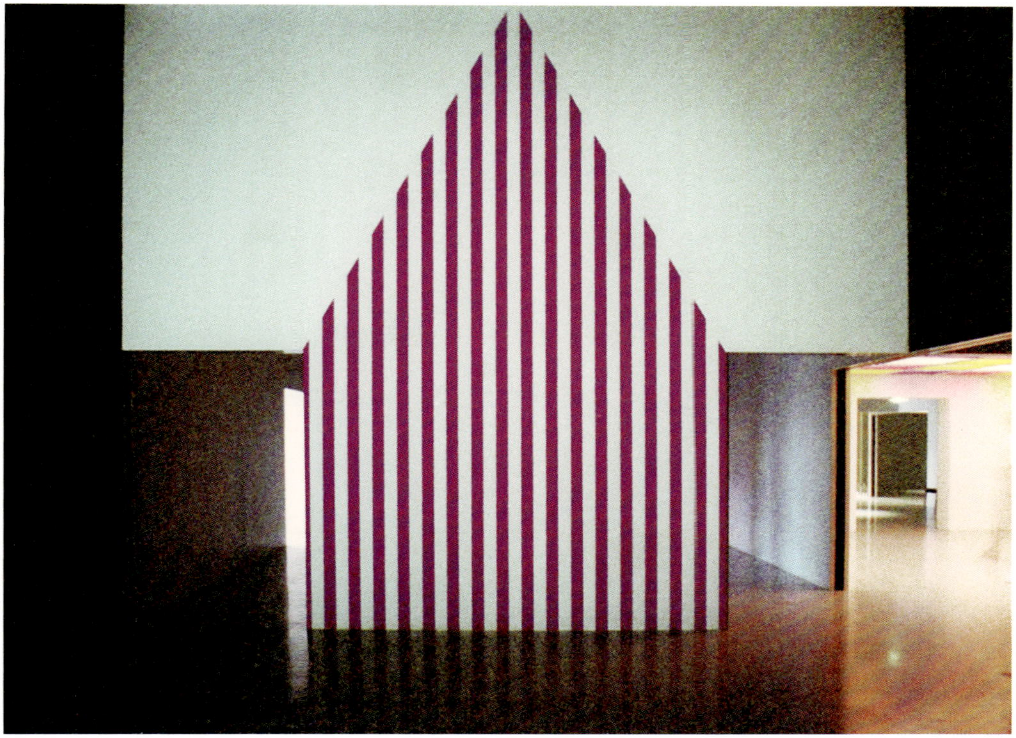

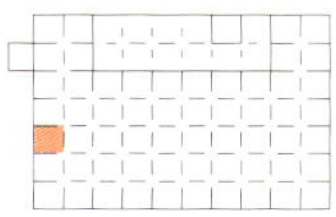

Room 41

Photo-souvenir: "Projection of 50 motifs", work *in situ*
Projector, 50 views, sheetrock, metal structure, paint
Right, view of room 59, *The suspended ceiling*
Left, room 42

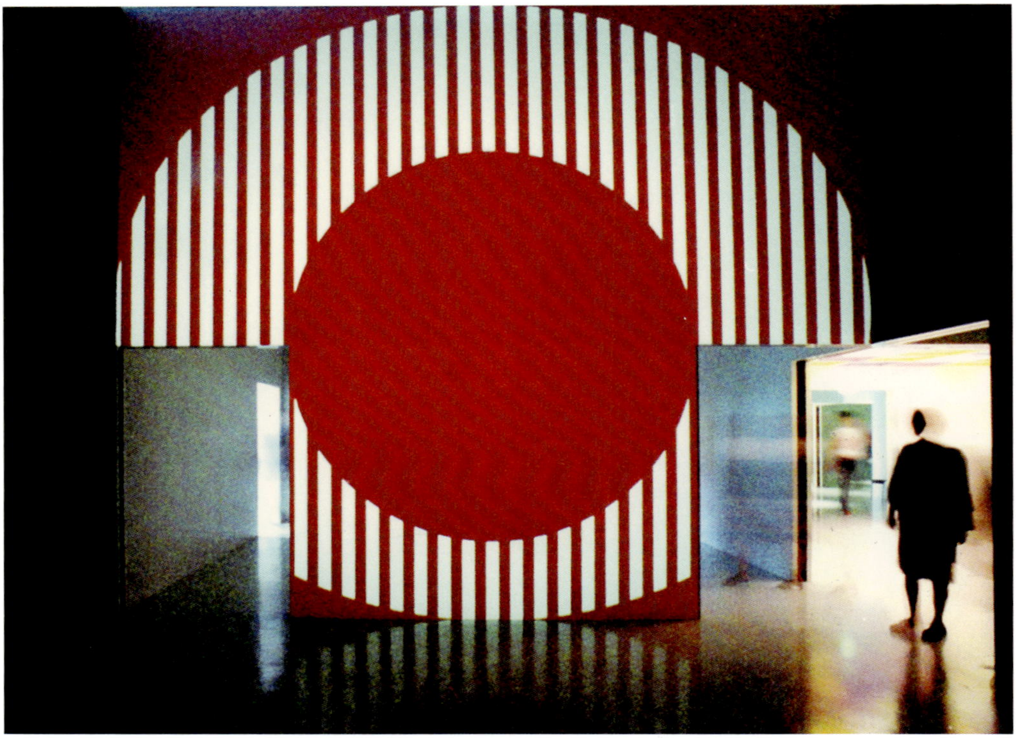

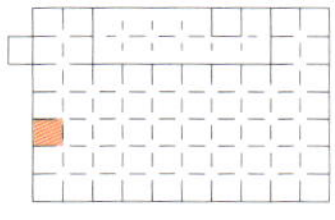

Room 41

Photo-souvenir: "Projection of 50 motifs", work *in situ*
Projector, 50 views, sheetrock, metal structure, paint
Right, view of room 59, *The suspended ceiling*
Left, room 42

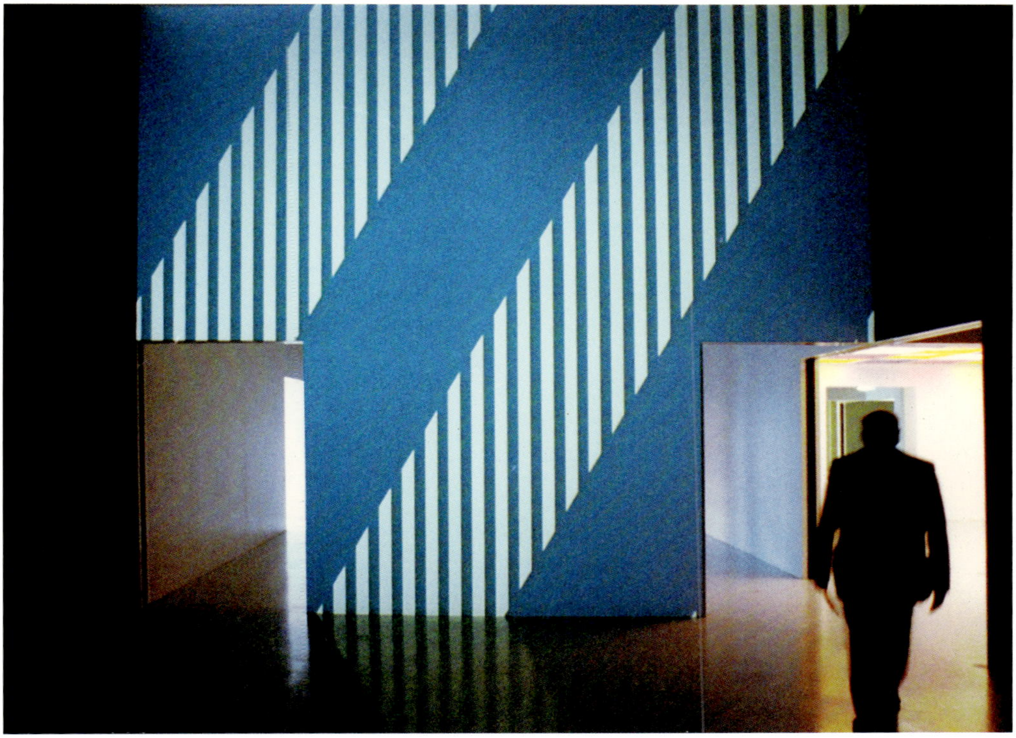

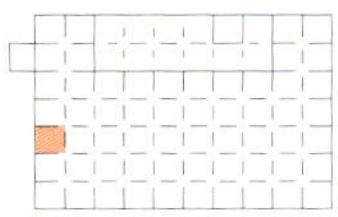

Room 41

Photo-souvenir: "Projection of 50 motifs", work *in situ*
Projector, 50 views, sheetrock, metal structure, paint
Right, view of room 59, *The suspended ceiling*
Left, room 42

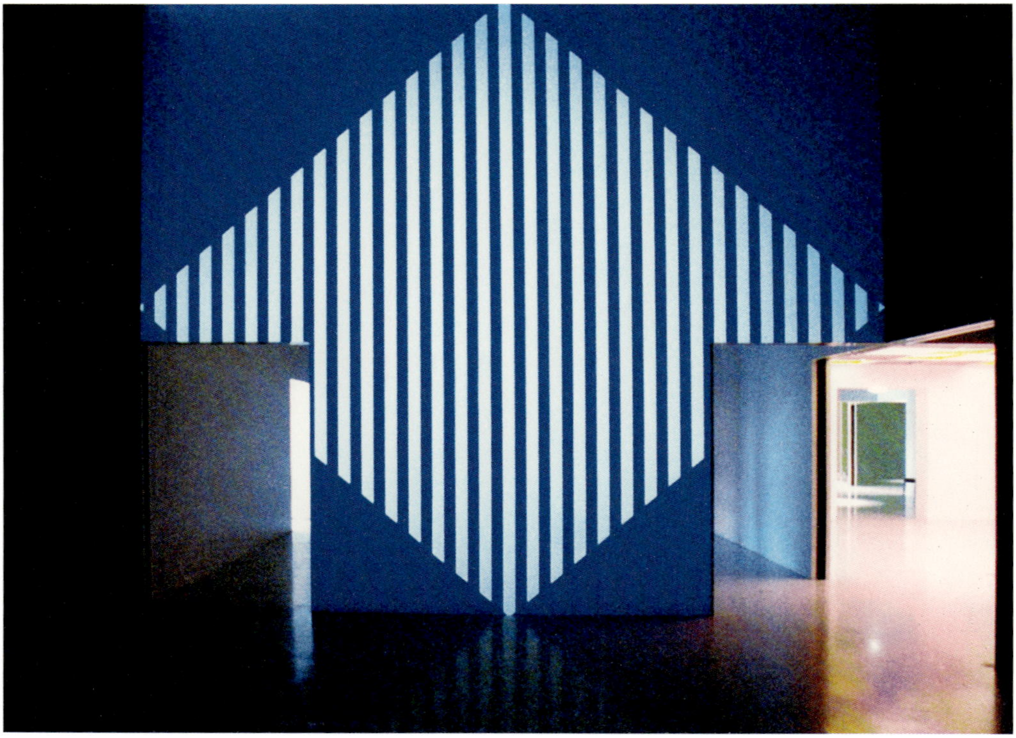

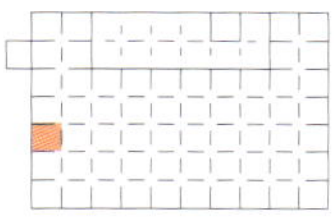

Room 41

Photo-souvenir: "Projection of 50 motifs", work *in situ*
Projector, 50 views, sheetrock, metal structure, paint
Right, view of room 59, *The suspended ceiling*
Left, room 42

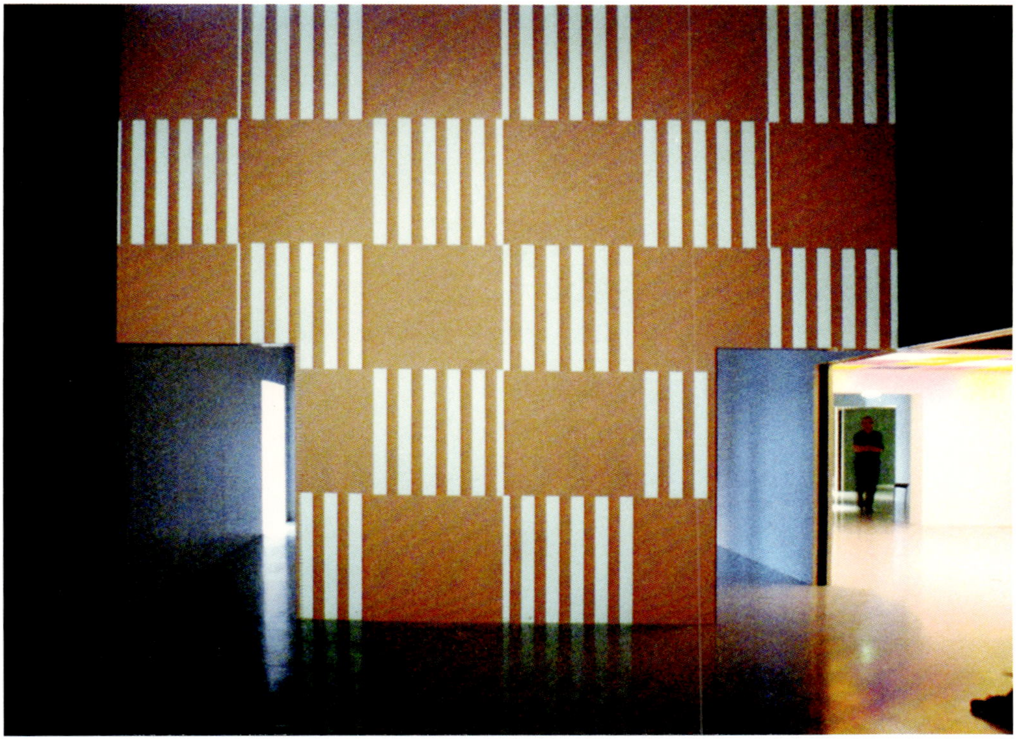

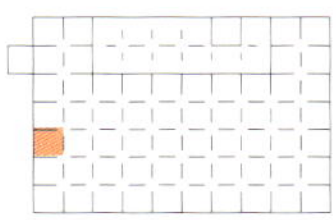

Room 41

Photo-souvenir: "Projection of 50 motifs", work *in situ*
Projector, 50 views, sheetrock, metal structure, paint
Right, view of room 59, *The suspended ceiling*
Left, room 42

Daniel Buren prosaically explains the reasons which led to the organization of the space: "The exhibition was conceived like a chequer-board. Every other room is made solely of four walls covered with deep grey paint and lit by a single central light, making these rooms relatively dark when compared with all the others. These rooms do not contain any exhibition objects."
The description would be simple and the result edifying if they did not highlight the actual history of "Le Musée qui n'existait pas" and the many dealings which culminated in the final grid of the building's level 6. Buren actually wanted the area initially offered him to be respected. Again and again he proposed (and found) solutions to capture areas which would enable him to develop his project with a greater scope. The indexing of the circulation corridor, dividing the two exhibition galleries, then the extension of the proposal to the terraces, gave him almost twice the area which had in the end been granted him.
In the moment of distributing the different ideas in each one of the cells, he proposed leaving every other one empty — a way of arranging a moment for the eye to have exposure time (and to pause), but also to remind people that he intended to be master of the premises.
The choice of grey is obviously not haphazard. Grey is the non-colour of non-colours, with which Manet covered the background of many of his pictures, and Richter, Buren's contemporary, made into an initial objective principle. Grey is not a colour but a value of luminous brightness, the perception of which for the human eye lies somewhere between white and black. It goes without saying that Buren measured its effect.

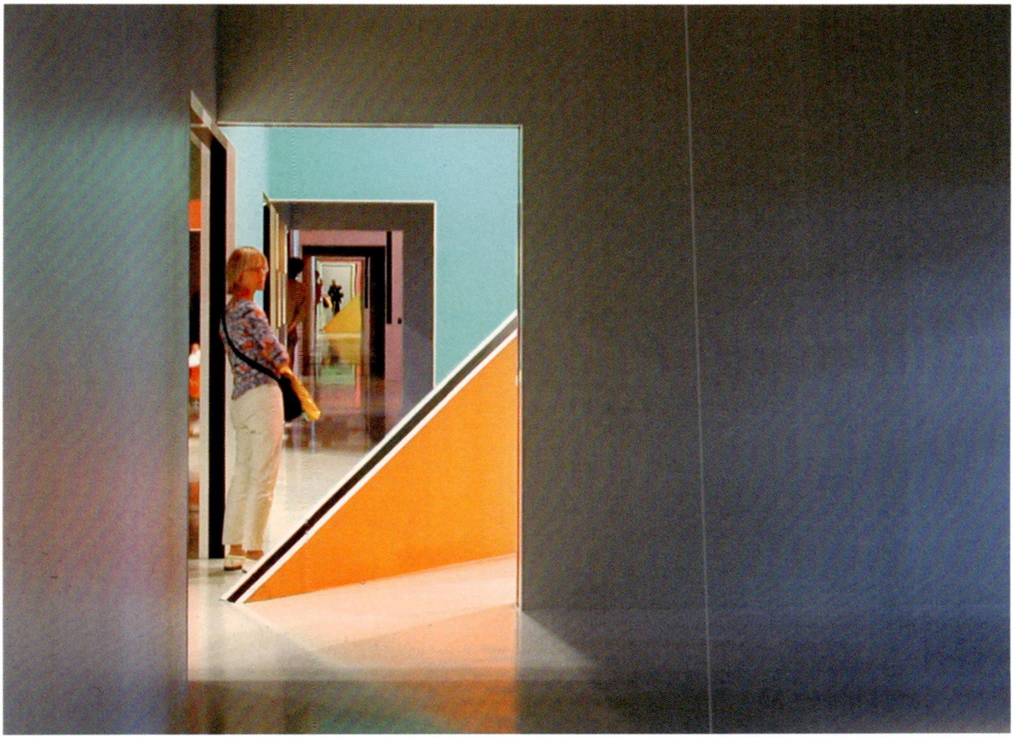

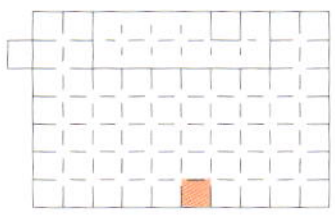

Room 66

Photo-souvenir: "Grey Room", work *in situ*
Sheetrock, paint, artificial light
Adjoining, rooms 67 to 70
In the distance, a mirror in which all the doors are reflected

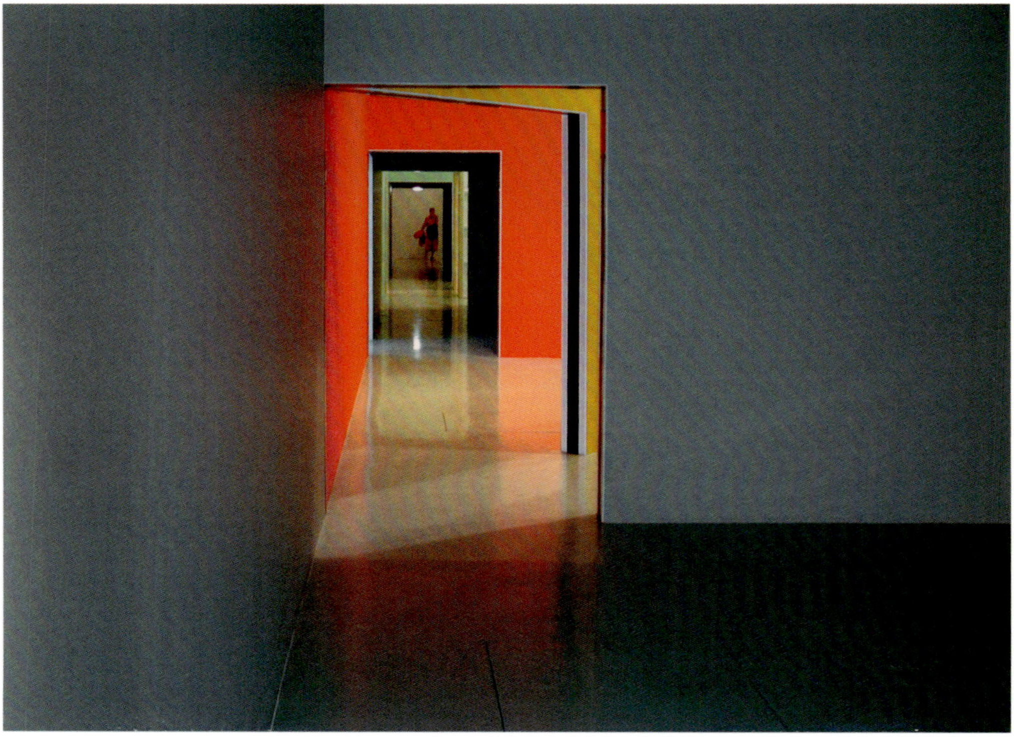

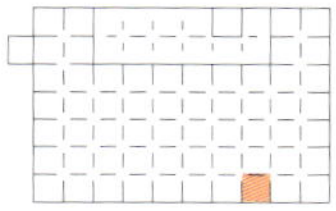

Room 68

Photo-souvenir: "*Grey room*", work *in situ*
Sheetrock, paint, artificial light
Adjoining, rooms 67 to 63
In the distance, a mirror in which all the doors are reflected

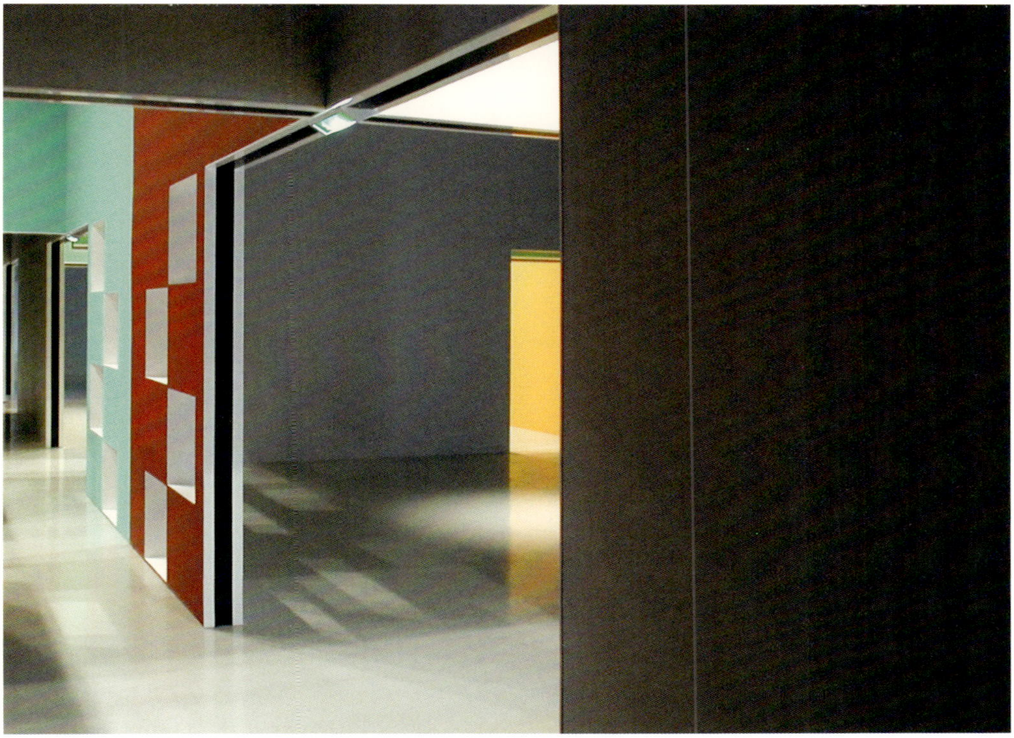

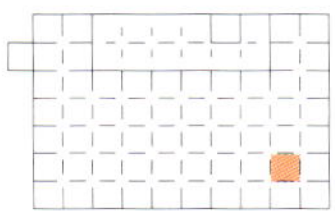

Room 52

Photo-souvenir: "Grey room", work *in situ*
Sheetrock, paint, artificial light
Right, room 48 and room 47, *Oblique walls*
Left, room 53, *The imploded cabin : Distant murmur from the city*

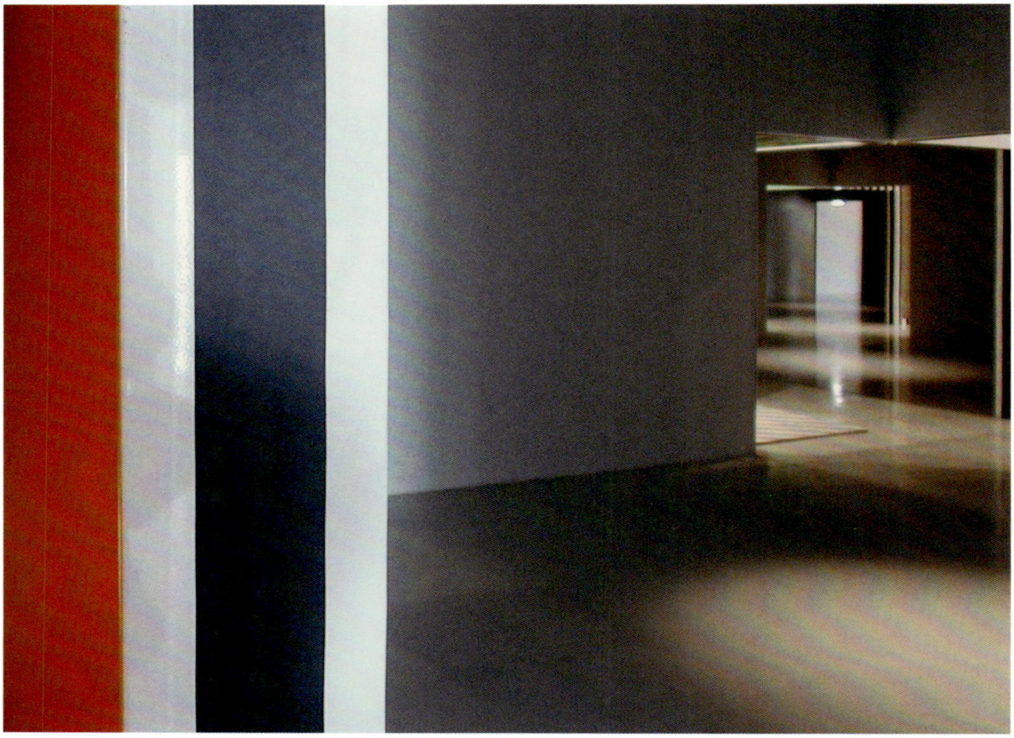

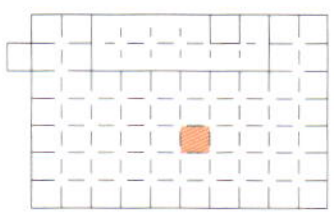

Room 46

Photo-souvenir: "Grey room", work in situ
Sheetrock, paint, artificial light
Right, adjoining, room 55, *The endless ceiling floor*, room 56 and room 64

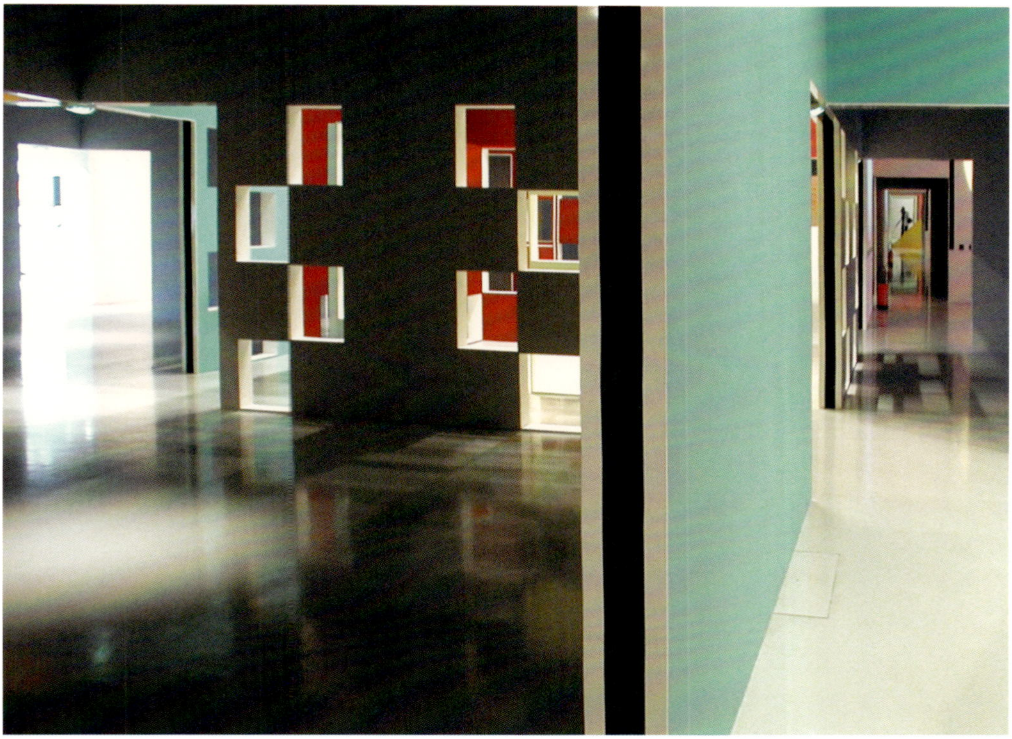

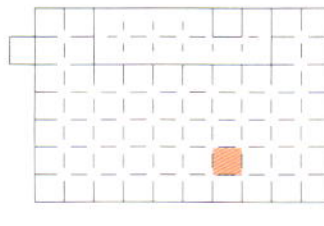

Room 54

Photo-souvenir: "Grey room", work *in situ*
Shetrock, paint, artificial light
View from room 47, *Oblique walls*
Right, adjoining, rooms 68 to 70
In the distance, a mirror in which all the doors are reflected
Left, adjoining, room 53, *The imploded cabin : Distant murmur from the city*, and room 48

During the various meetings dealing with the project's preparation, it appeared that the Centre Pompidou would obviously be unable to bring together the considerable number of guards and security personnel necessary for each one of the rooms in the arrangement imagined by the artist. So Daniel Buren seized upon this situation to develop, in one of the areas, a piece that was at once critical and effective: critical because it referred the Centre Pompidou to the obvious impossibility of providing the surveillance necessary in the areas he wanted to plan; effective, because the proposal solved the problem by concentrating the control of the entire arrangement in a system of closed-circuit surveillance and cameras installed above each room, under the watchful eye of one and the same attendant.
Daniel Buren had come up with a similar system for the labyrinth in the exhibition "C'est ainsi et autrement", held at the Bern Kunsthalle in 1983. It should be emphasized here that he was anticipating an art trend in the years to come in which the issue of panoptic devices such as closed-circuit surveillance would become essential subjects of the critique of the repressive mechanisms of our contemporary world. The arrangement incorporated within the exhibition venues thus became a piece in its own right which the artist would in fact title: *At a Single Glance.*

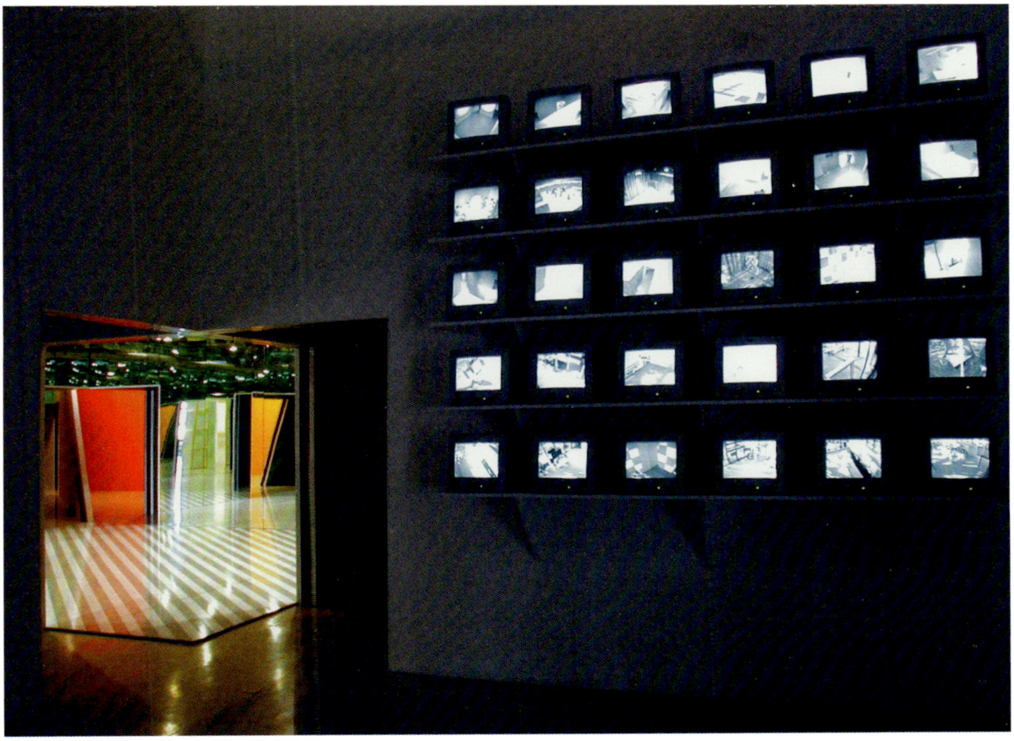

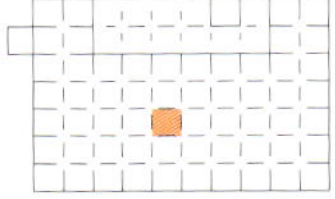

Room 45

Above and on following pages:
Photo-souvenir: "At a single glance", work *in situ*
Sheetrock, paint, metal structure, 30 monitors watching 30 different rooms
Left, room 55, *The endless ceiling floor*, and room 56

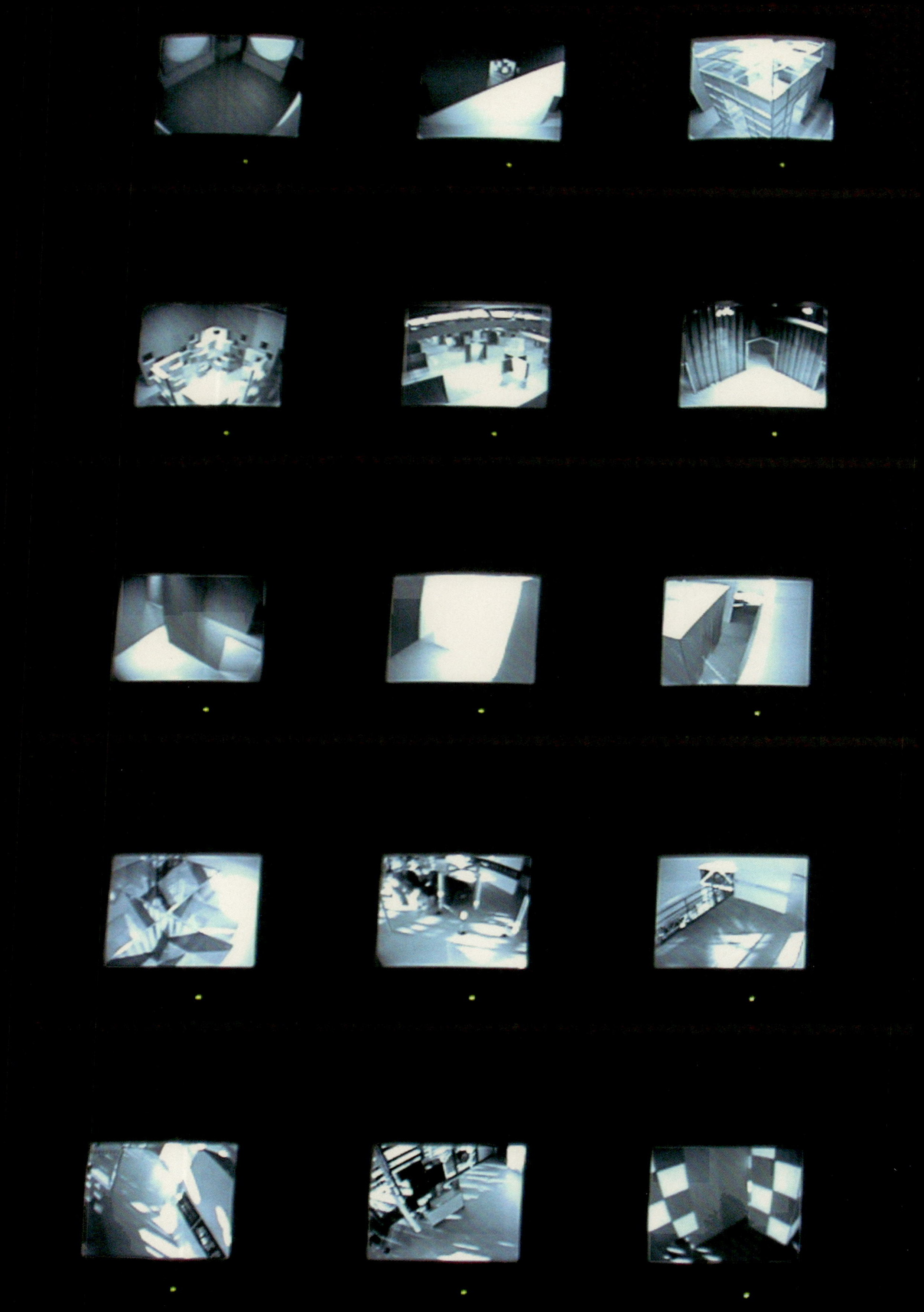

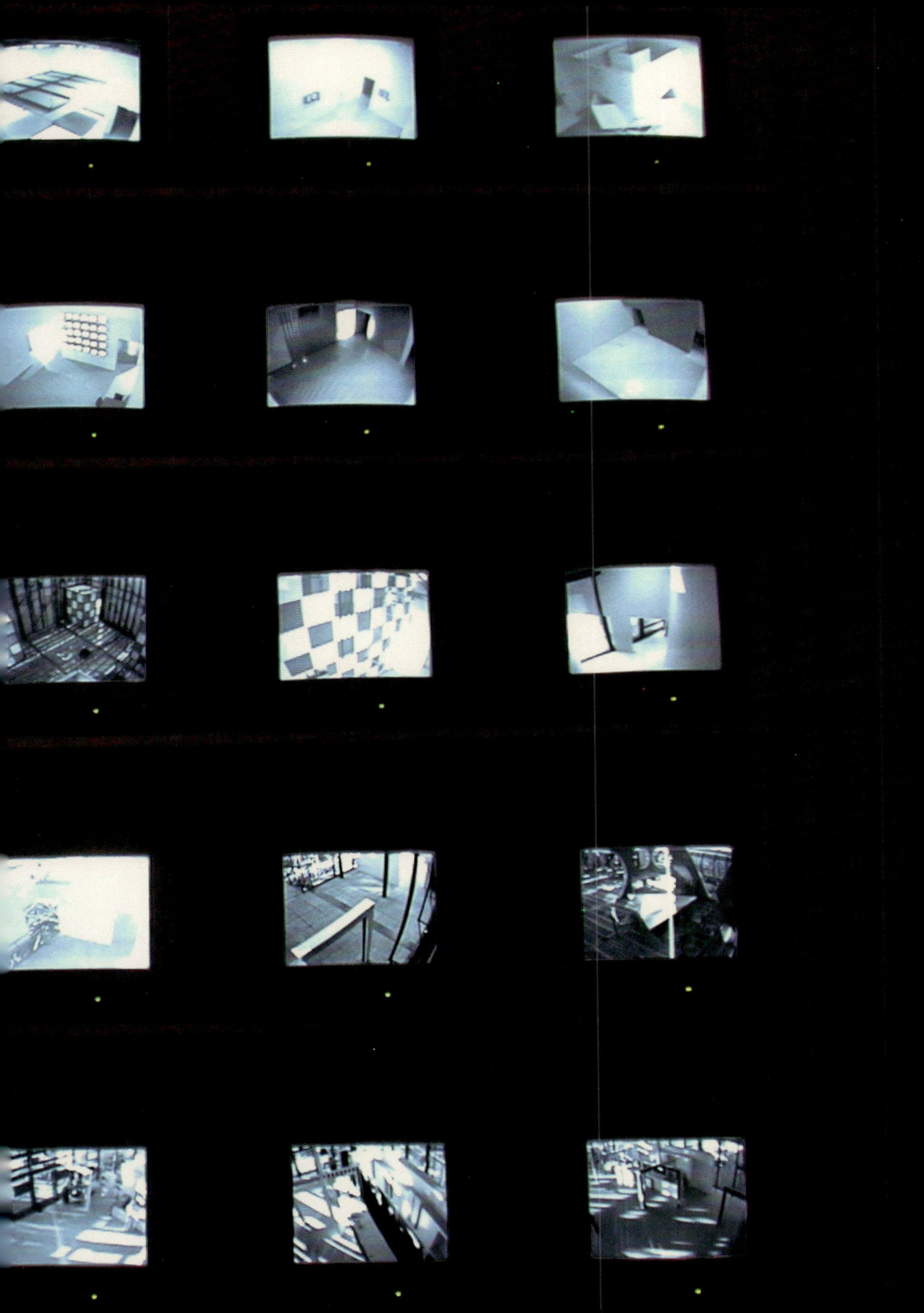

The other side of the picture reveals metal structures and the back of panels of sheetrock forming the whole set-like structure of the show. Covered with panes of glass, it becomes a proposition set off by the adhesive black and white stripes which hold it. Buren is keen to expose the hidden side of the arrangement – its flipside. He reveals the principle behind the building of the construction. He deconstructs the space of the representation by getting the spectator into the wings. This time around, deconstructing, for Buren, is not so much destroying as "trying to show another type of construction". The arrangement displays its conditions of formulation and assembly. It is also an opportunity to fight against the sole viewpoint of the work of art so as to prompt visitors to grasp "Le Musée qui n'existait pas" in all its complexity. The visit becomes exploration and stroll seeking spaces and forms where the exhibition's structure becomes the work's subject. "Le Musée qui n'existait pas" is a "general system" in which the place of the spectator is being forever re-thought.

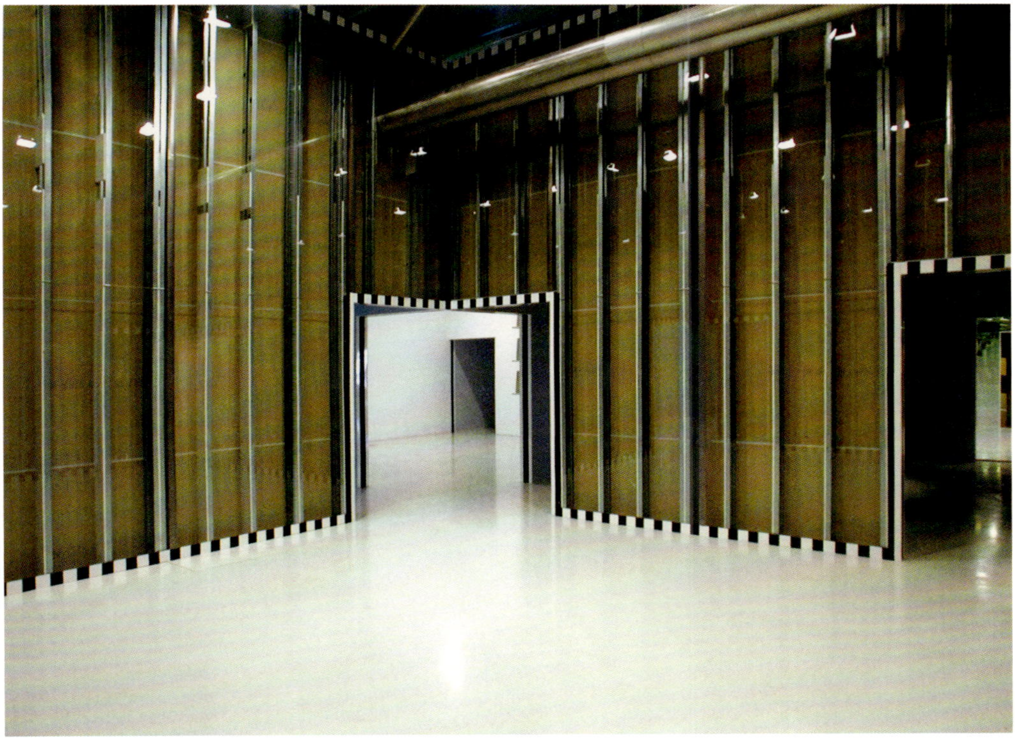

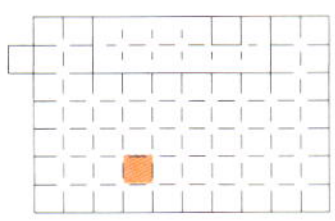

Room 57

Photo-souvenir: *"Under glass"*, work *in situ*
Metal structures, sheetrock, self-adhesive vinyl, glass
Opposite, room 45, *At a single glance*

Whereas all the arrangements and systems devised for "Le Musée qui n'existait pas" are unchanging, this "museum" is conceived as an alterable space which spectators can modify as they see fit. A sliding door thus makes it possible to superpose two same-sized yellow and blue panels and to obtain, through the interplay of complementarities and translucent surfaces, a green-coloured panel. Buren plays with the endless possibilities of the system that he himself worked out. The game dimension is without any doubt one of the most essential of his intention. Another point worth emphasizing that many of the artist's propositions reveal: we can see that all the pieces presented depend on the place but never belong to it. They can be seen but let themselves be seen, and assert, as a principle, that they will also reveal everything that is alien to them.

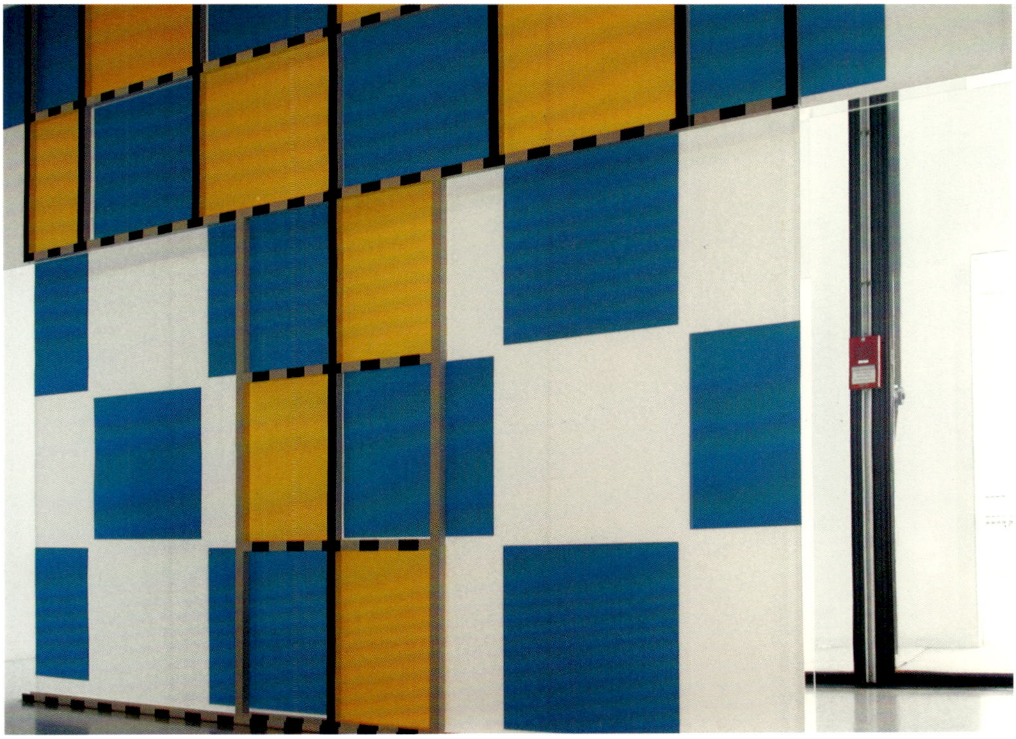

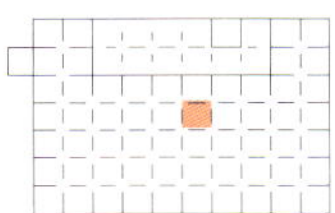

Room 35

Photo-souvenir: "The sliding wall", work *in situ*
Metal structure, sliding modular structure, translucent and coloured Plexiglas
Right, through the glass, view towards the Piazza and the west of Paris

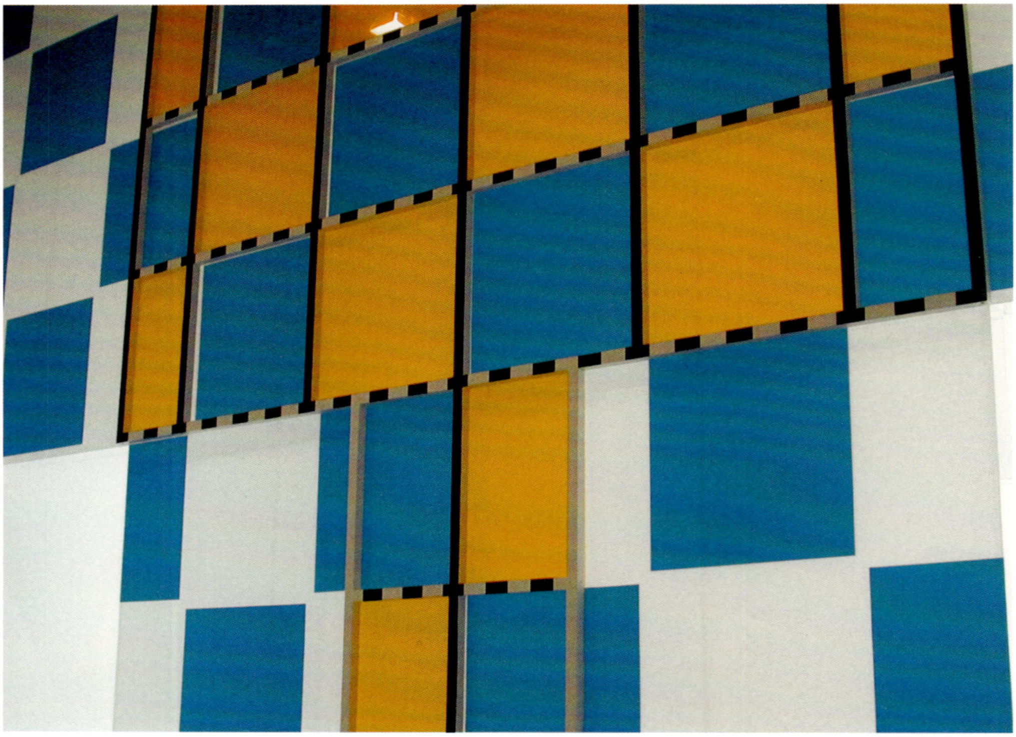

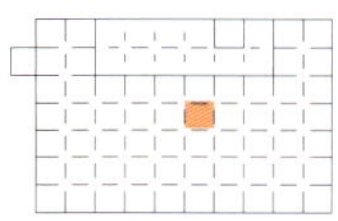

Room 35

Photo-souvenir: "The sliding wall", work *in situ*
Metal structure sliding modular structure, translucent and coloured Plexiglas

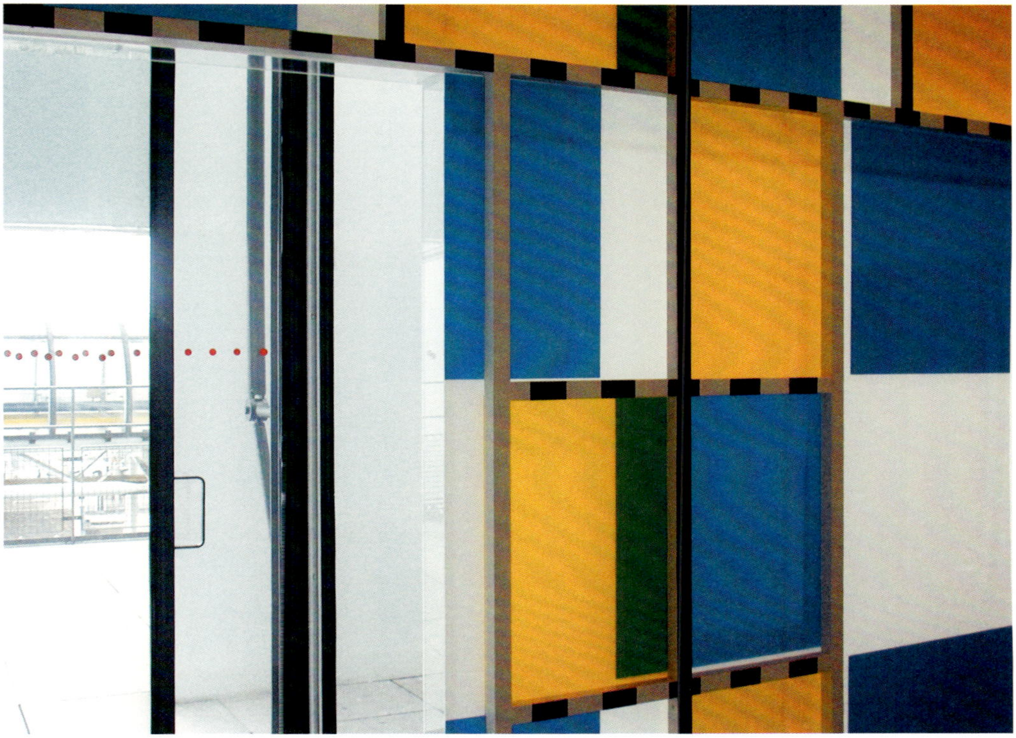

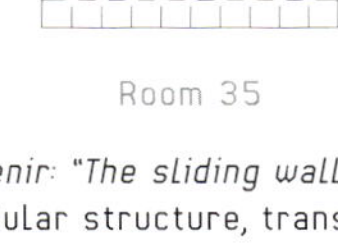

Room 35

Photo-souvenir: "The sliding wall", work in situ
Metal structure, sliding modular structure, translucent and coloured Plexiglas

The "photo-souvenir" highlights the complexity of the proposition once this latter indexes, in its very principle, the slightest nook and cranny of the spaces, and broadens its perimeter beyond the usual exhibition space. Buren tries both to optimise the place's possibilities and point to its limits. Here the space is pivoted at 45o and breaks the linearity of the overall grid of the exhibition's general arrangement. It is an angular and sharp-edged interpolation in the circuit, a broken angle which traces a set of vanishing lines and infinite openings.

A manifesto-like text, written for the presentation of his work produced at the Städtisches Museum in Mönchengladbach in 1975, highlights the principle of disclosure upon which the artist's approach is constructed: "The work of art should open the eyes and not blind them, make them master of their angles of view and not subject them to one and the same angle. Free the eye and not subject it. The work of art, all full of itself as it is, has gradually reached the latent paradox of blinding in order to be seen .... The work of art deprives the eye (thought) of its capacities, both by dazzling it and paralysing it, like a stiff neck."

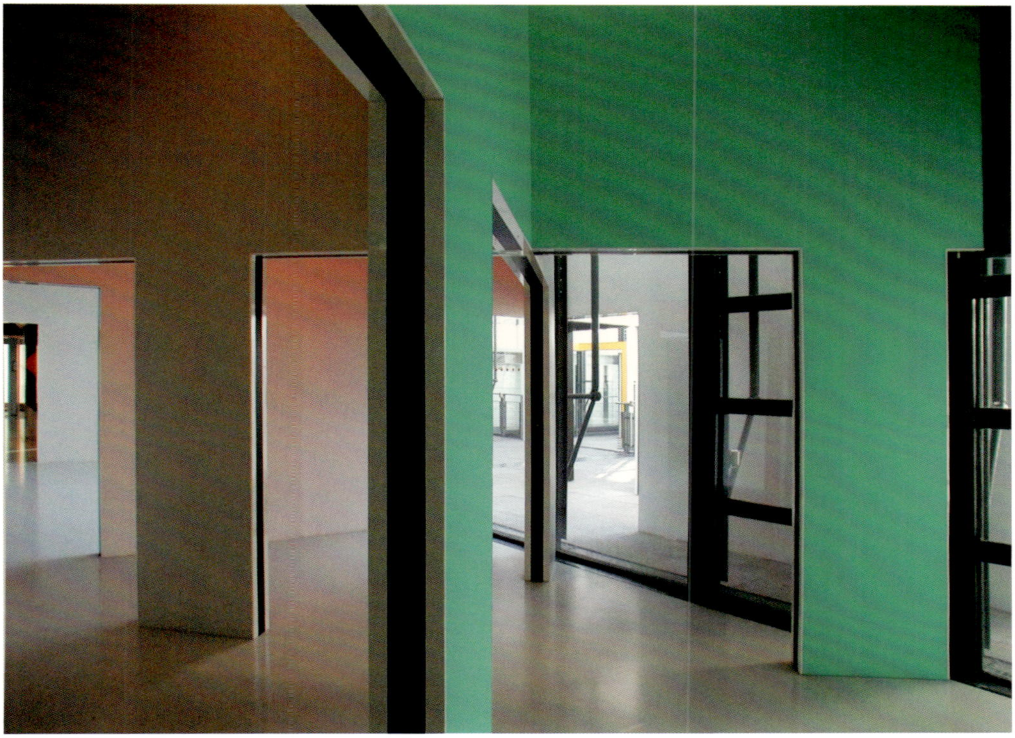

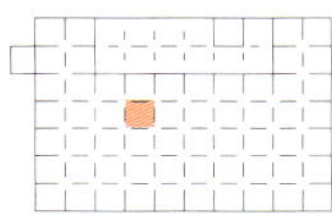

Room 37

Photo-souvenir: "45° Space", work *in situ* (inside, outside)
Sheetrock, self-adhesive vinyl, metal structure, 2 colours
Opposite, room 23, *Truncated space,* and room 19, *The framework of the rooms*

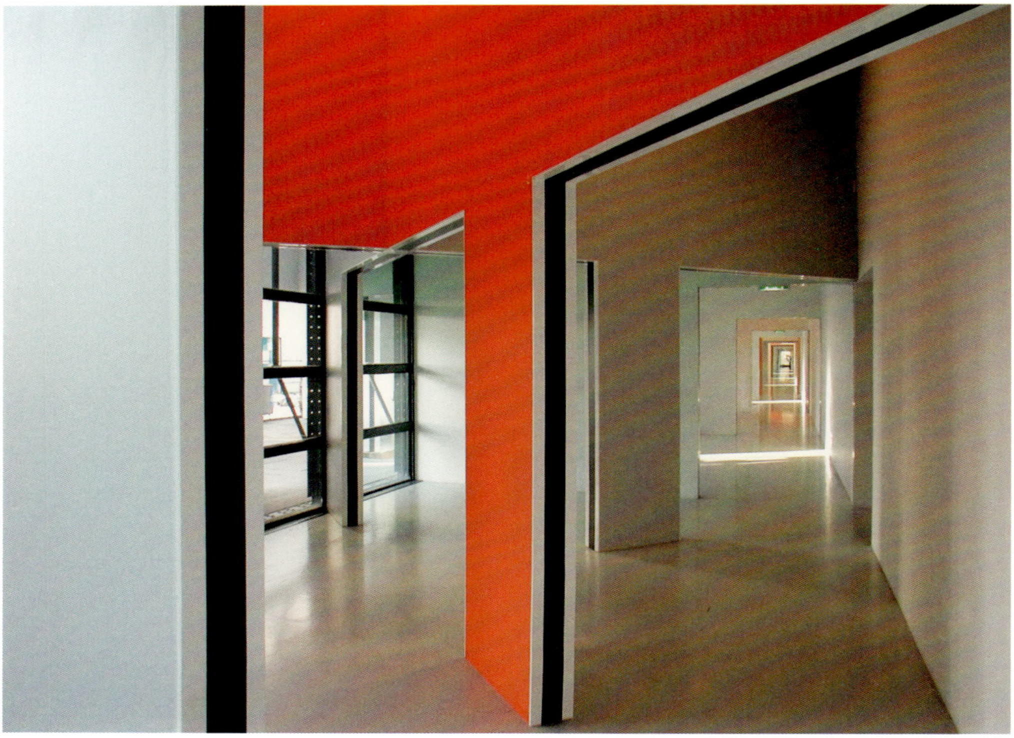

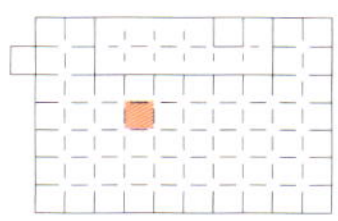

Room 37

Photo-souvenir: "45° Space", work *in situ* (inside, outside)
Sheetrock, self-adhesive vinyl, metal structure, 2 colours
Adjoining, rooms 36 to 31
In the distance, a mirror in which all the doors are reflected
Left, view towards room 25 and the outside of the museum

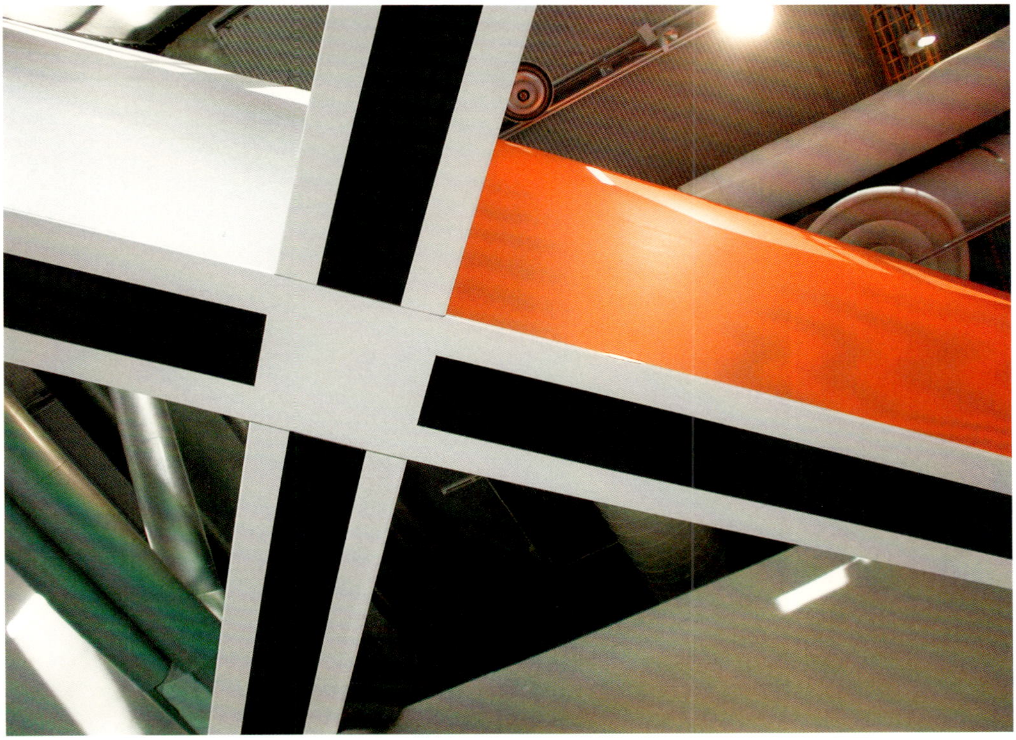

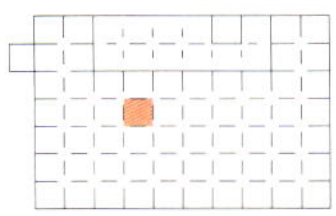

Room 37

Photo-souvenir: "45° Space, work in situ (inside, outside)
Sheetrock, self-adhesive vinyl, metal structure, 2 colours

At a time when screens are everywhere, a set of four projections made up of some forty films brought together in one and the same electronic medium on flat screens, with neither emphasis nor specific scenography, reminds us that the function and use of the "image-movement", in the sense that Gilles Deleuze intends it, lie at the heart of Buren's work.
From his earliest films made in Mexico from 1959 on to the untimely films shown on a Scopitone, slap bang in the middle of the works of the previous show left as such, for his first solo show titled *Interruption*, held at the Galerie Yvon Lambert in Paris in 1969, from *Watch the Doors*, Please, made for the one-off arrangement at the Art Institute of Chicago between 1980 and 1982, to his decidedly critical proposition for the exhibition "Les Magiciens de la Terre" held at the Centre Pompidou in 1989, for Buren film and video alike are tools whose function, like photography, have something in common with the recording and documentation of a work but in no way with the work of art as such. They are thus present at the heart of the exhibition's arrangement. They also attest to the artist's mistrust with regard to the inflation of projected images in the field of contemporary art in the 2000s.

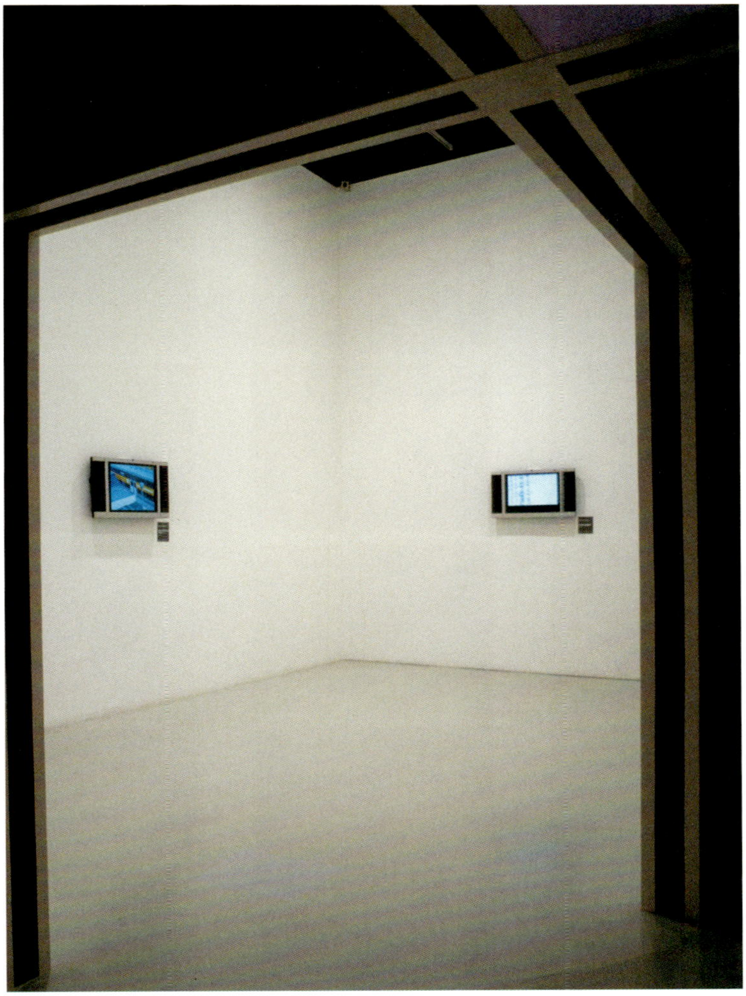

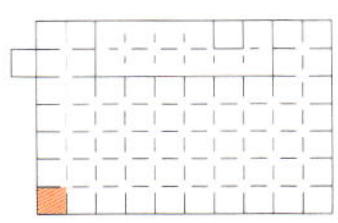

Room 61

Photo-souvenir: "Video room"
Sheetrock, paint, monitors, loudspeakers
View from room 59

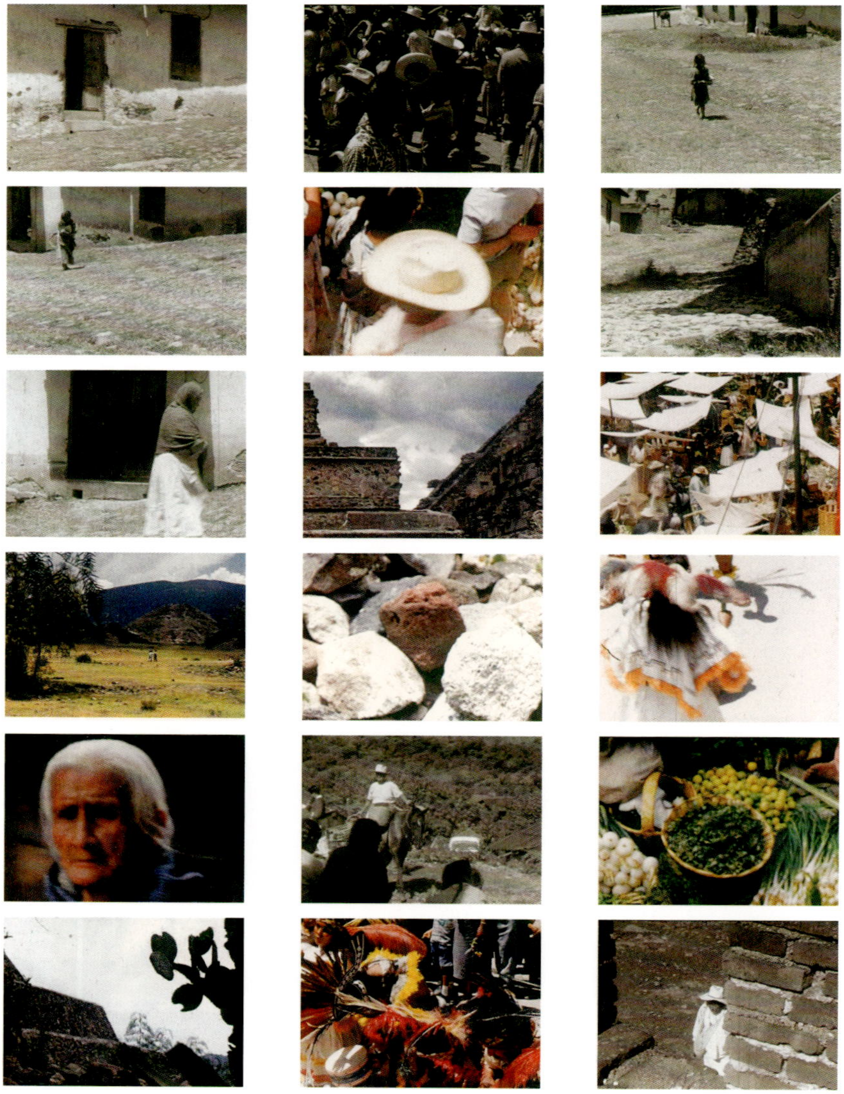

Photos-souvenirs taken from *Mexique*, 1959 (documentary film)

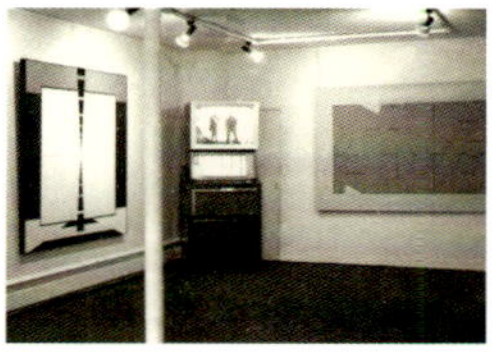

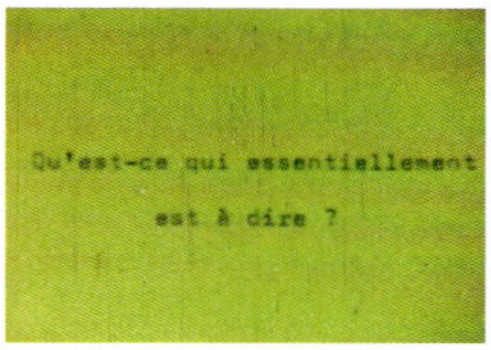

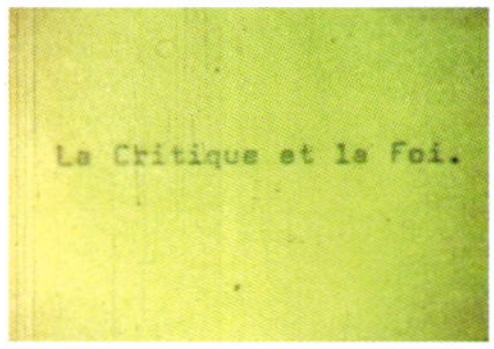

View of the Scopitone in the gallery space, seen before the exhibition proper.

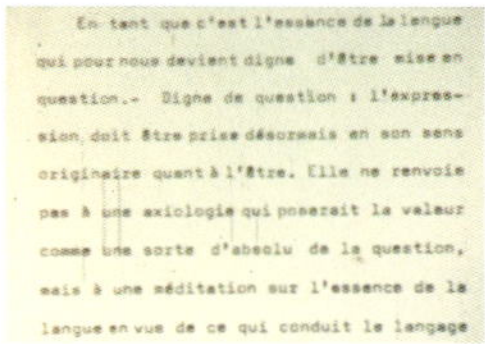

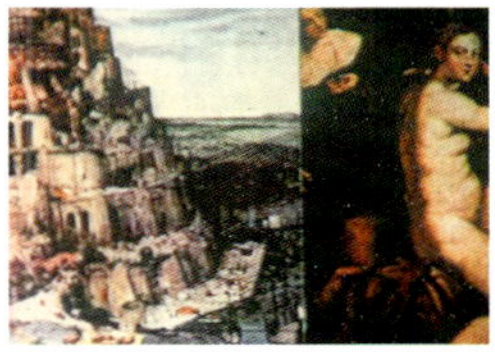

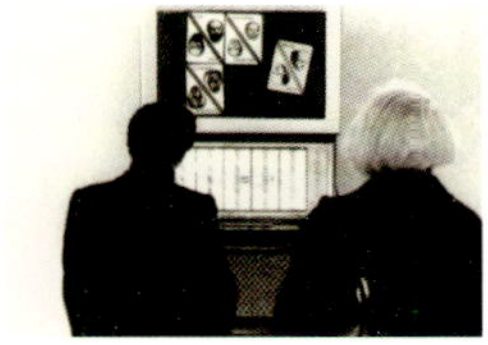

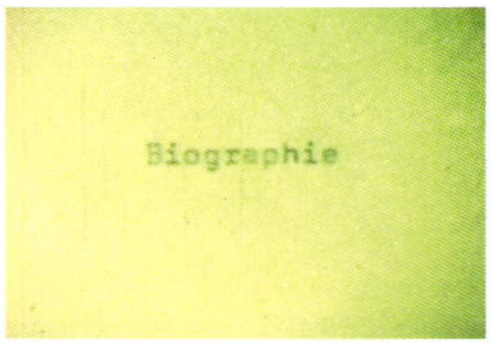

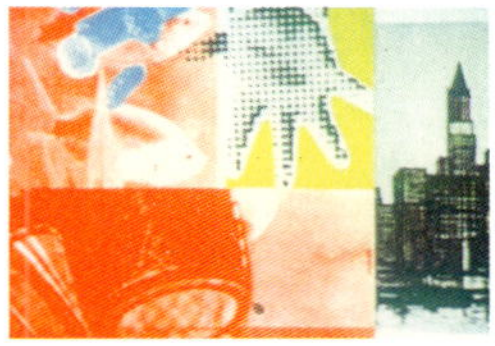

Scopitone during the projection of *The card game*, one of the eight films.

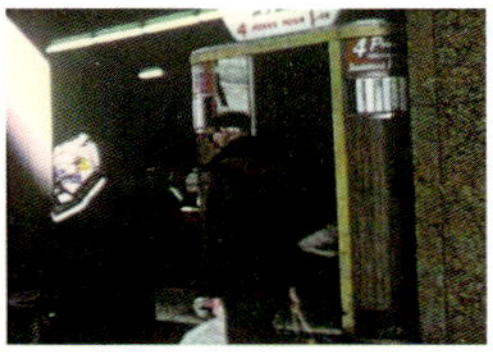

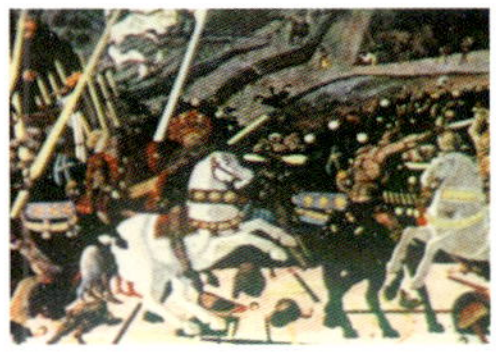

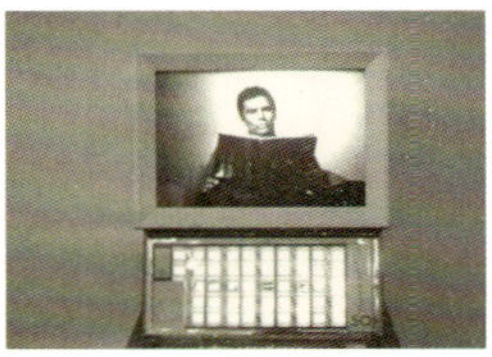

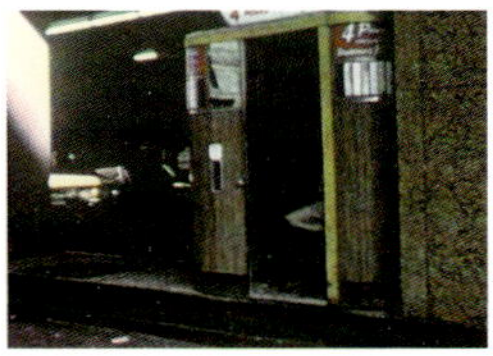

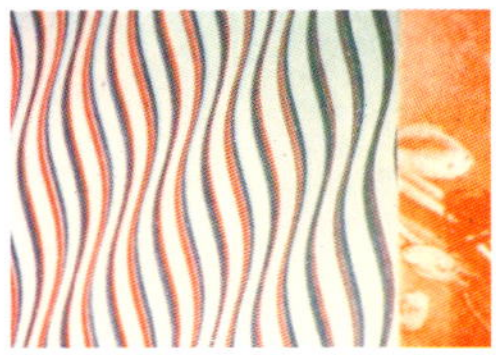

Scopitone during the projection of *Temperatures taken under cover & Probable weather development*

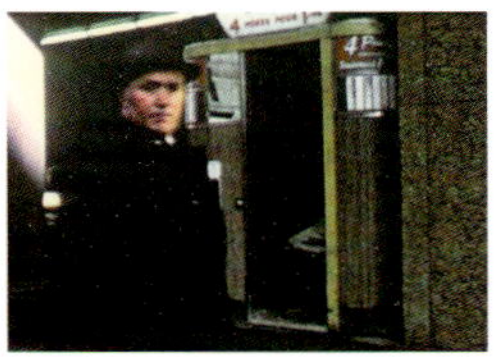

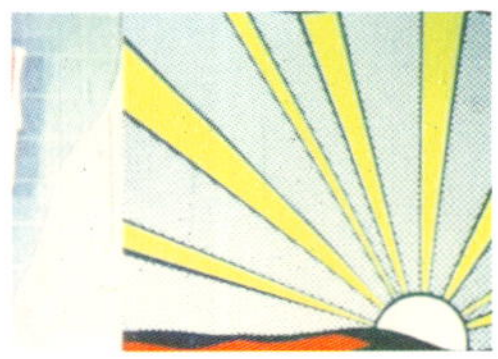

Photos-souvenirs taken from *Interruption*, 1969
(8 films shown on scopitone at the Galerie Yvon Lambert
Above: *What essentially is there to say ? Biography, Critique and Faith*)

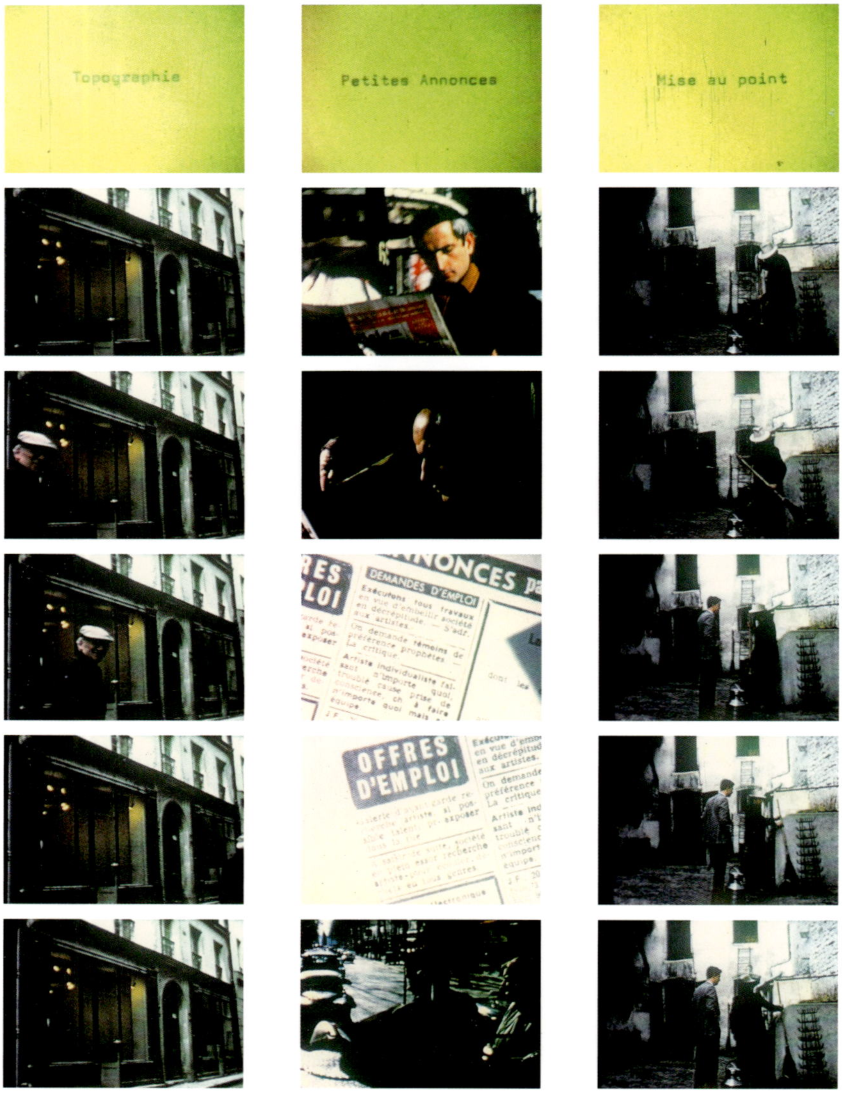

Photos-souvenirs taken from *Interruption*, 1969
(8 films shown on scopitone at the Galerie Yvon Lambert
Above: *Topography, Small ads, Focus*)

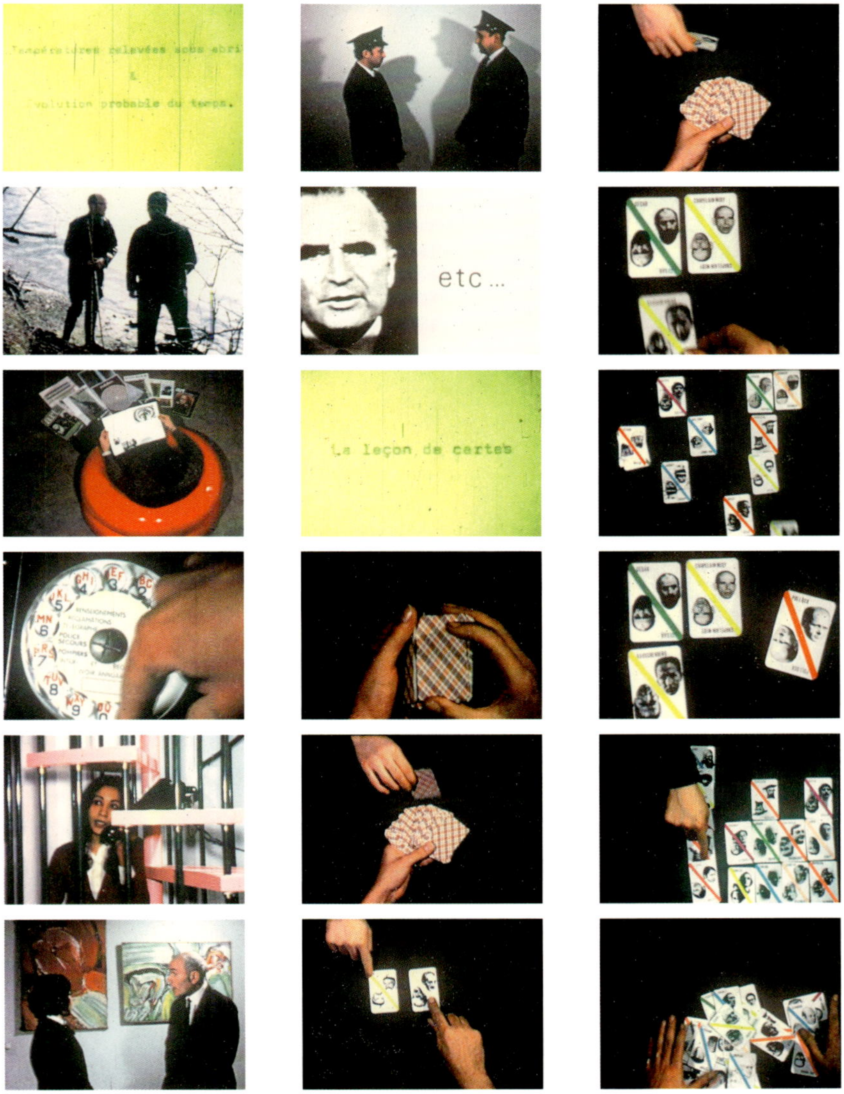

Photos-souvenirs taken from *Interruption*, 1969
(8 films shown on scopitone at the Galerie Yvon Lambert
Above: *Temperatures taken under cover & Probable weather development, The card game*)

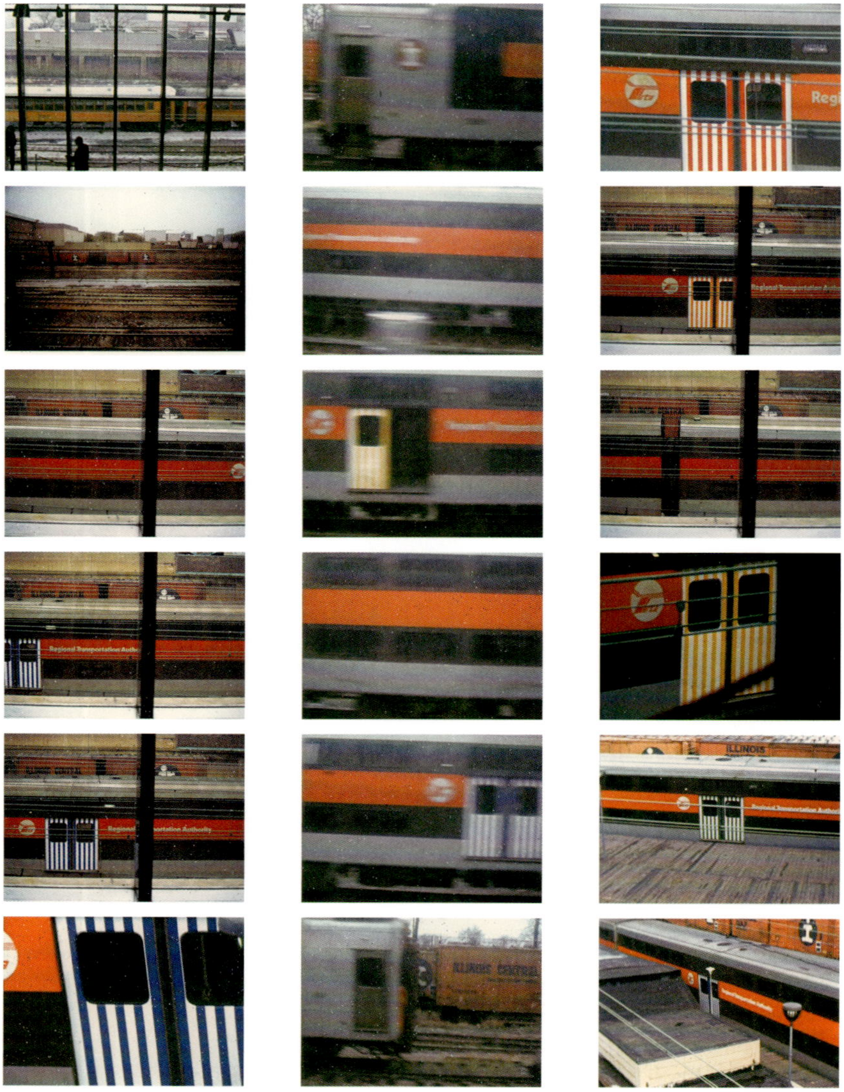

Photos-souvenirs taken from *Watch the Doors, Please!*, 1980
(film shot during the work carried out on all the trains visible from the window of the Art Institute of Chicago)

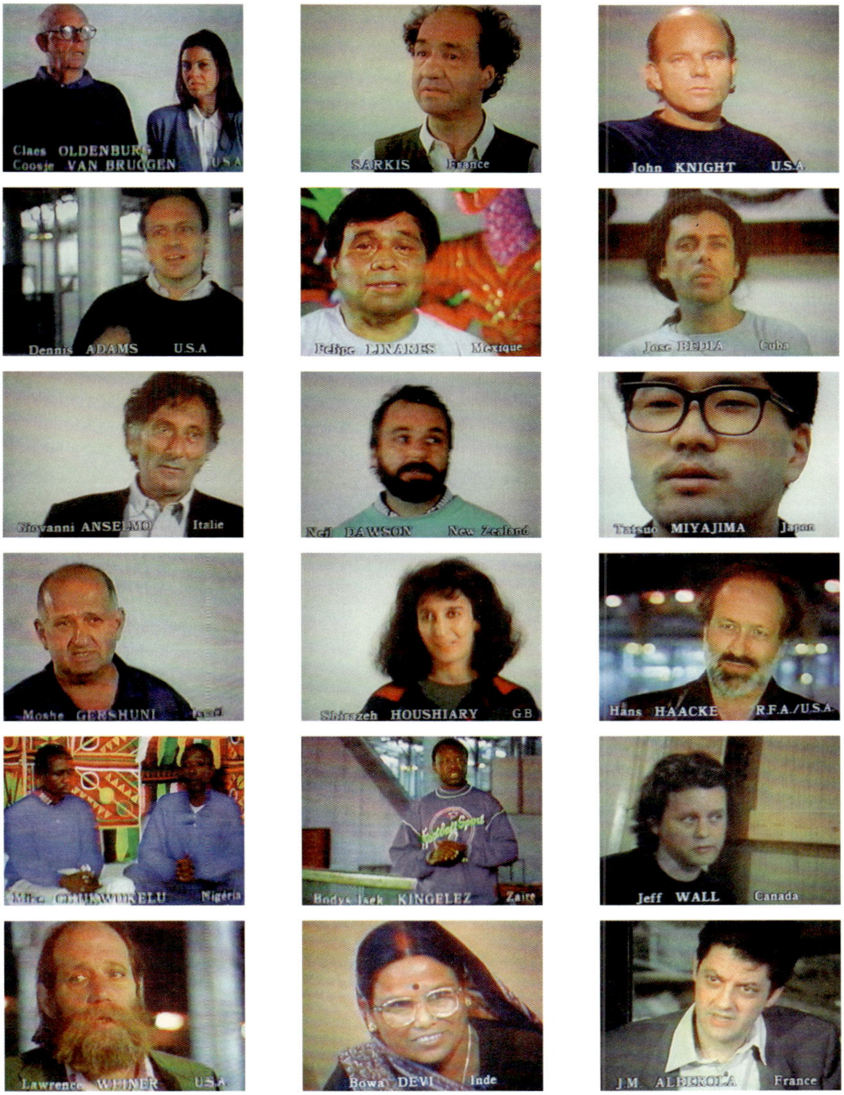

Photos-souvenirs taken from *Les Magiciens de la Terre: interviews*, 1989
(three questions put to some forty participants:
Do you feel like magician of the earth?
What do you think about the mediatisation of the visual arts by television?
What do you think about the juxtaposition of genres and cultures?)

"Le Musée qui n'existait pas" is a virtuoso demonstration in which the technical and aesthetic potential of all the materials of architecture become possible plastic media for the development of specific proposals. Here, the industrial open metal flooring, which Buren has used many a time to produce certain arrangements, environments and "cabins", like *The Galvanized Cabin*, made in 2000 for a major exhibition at the Institute of Contemporary Art in Villeurbanne, structures the space and plays on the implicit link between plastic art and architecture. The proposal's title, *The Grid*, should probably be taken in many ways. As an architectural material generally used on the ground – we should for example underscore its essential function in the structuring of the underground fountain of *Les Deux Plateaux* in the main courtyard of the Palais-Royal – it is here re-erected to divide the space into two distinct areas, and permits optical effects and interplays of cast shadows, capable of breaking the uniform chromatic unity of the partitions of the space roundabout.

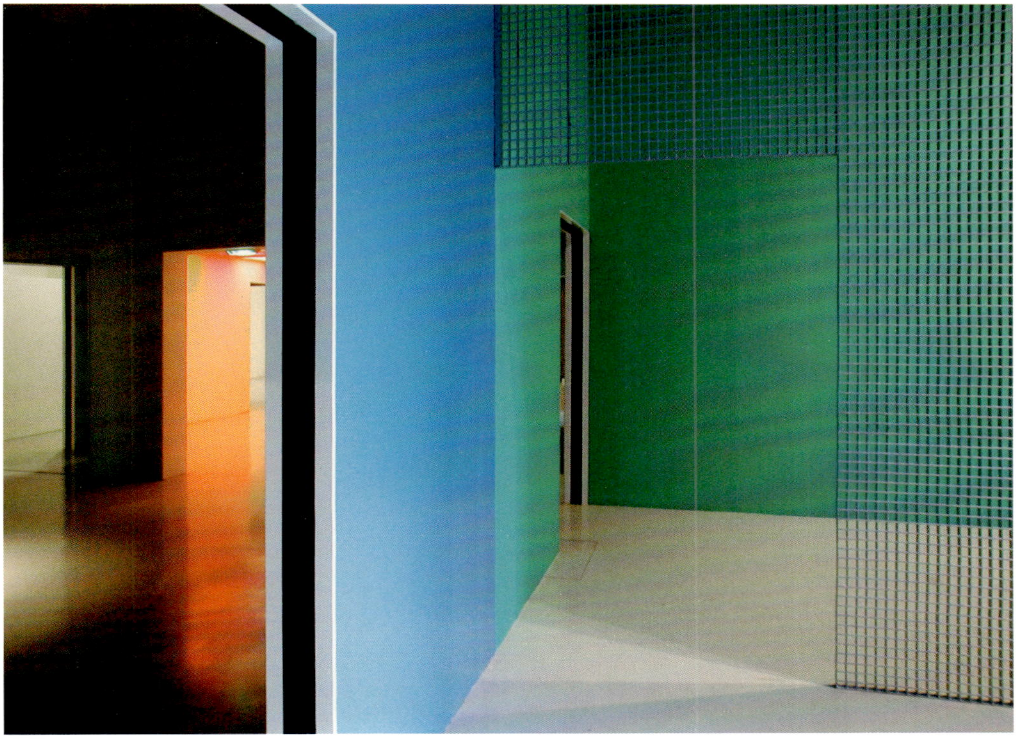

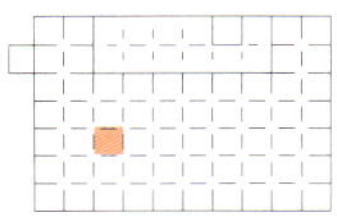

Room 43

Photo-souvenir: "The grid", work in situ
Sheetrock, steel grating, 2 colours, self-adhesive vinyl, metal structures
Left, room 58 and room 59, *The suspended ceiling*

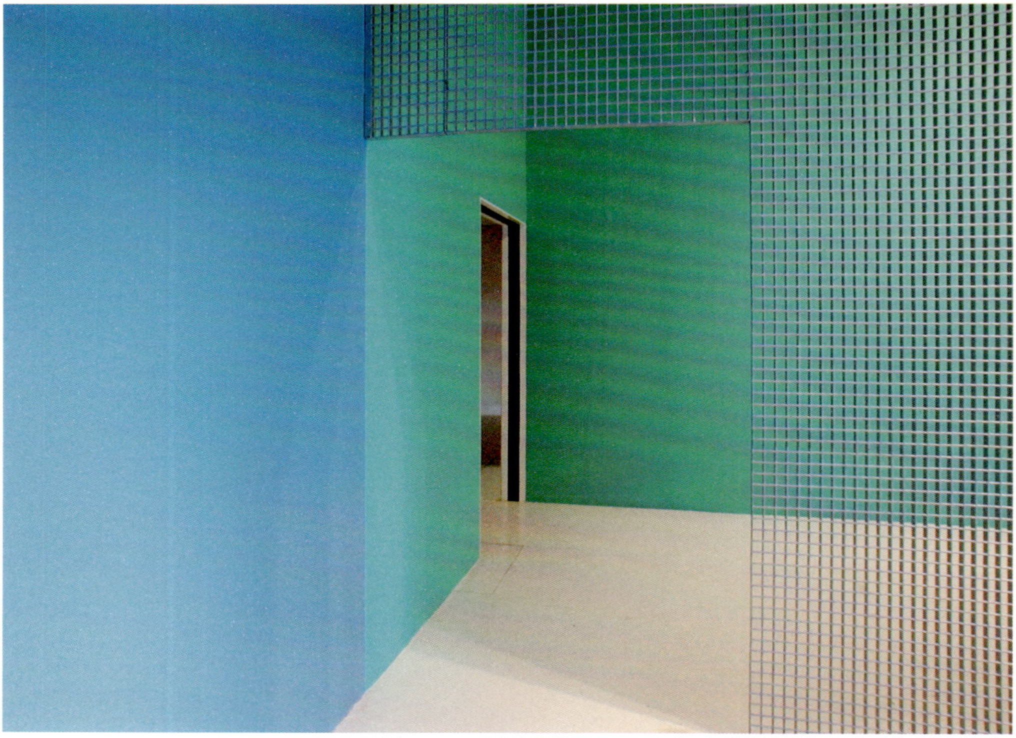

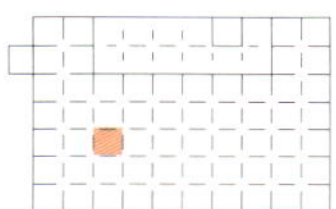

Room 43

Photo-souvenir: "The grid", work in situ
Sheetrock, steel grating, 2 colours, self-adhesive vinyl, metal structures

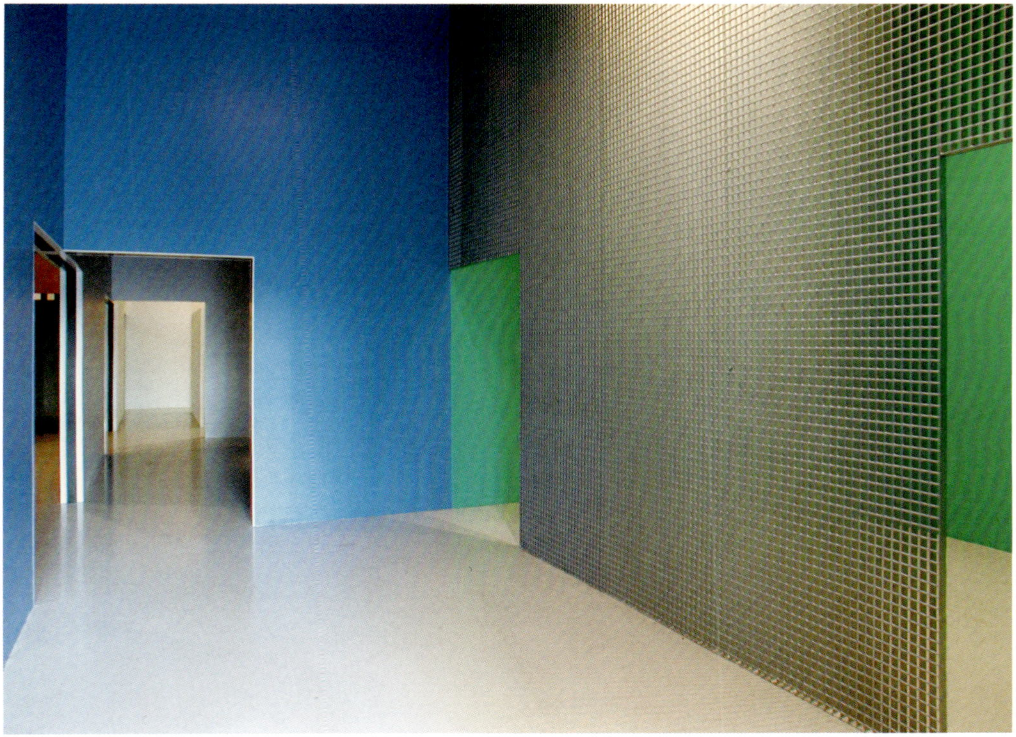

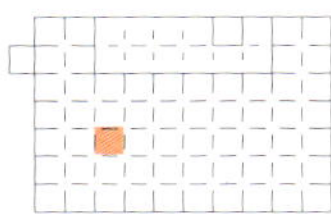

Room 43

Photo-souvenir: "The grid", work *in situ*
Sheetrock, steel grating, 2 colours, self-adhesive vinyl, metal structures
Left, adjoining, room 58 and room 63, *The colour box*

The method of "Le Musée qui n'existait pas" leads Buren to open up the space, from top to bottom, to an endless number of possibilities and perspectives informing the arrangement itself, from side to side and top to bottom alike. The geometry underlying it introduces deductive propositions which, as we see, are also included in the principle of a work which is invariably asserted between repetition and difference. Buren here constructs a succession of lanterns made of paper and wood, which he affixes in such a way that they form a set of luminous modules whose image is multiplied in the mirror covering one of the walls of the space. The nature and fragility of the materials chosen like the actual structure of each lantern refer to a logic frequently used by Buren, and underscore the formal relation his work maintains with the culture of Japan.

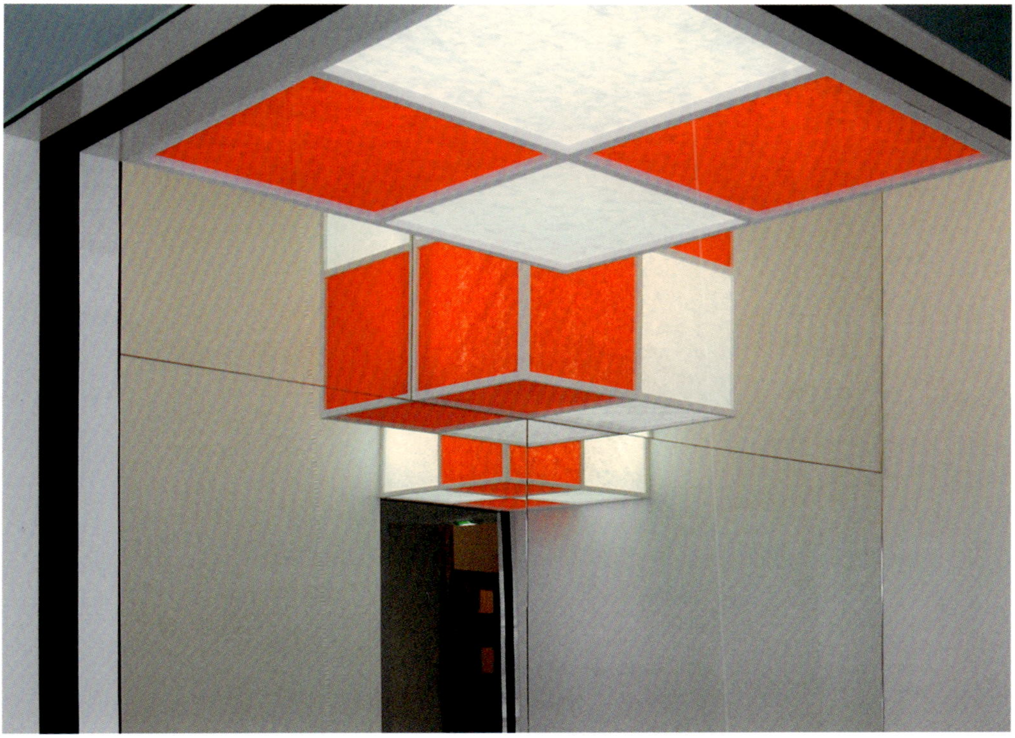

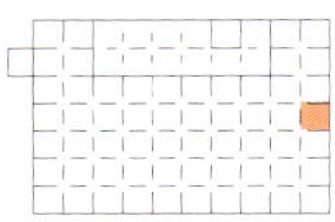

Room 31

Photo-souvenir: "The three lanterns", work in situ
Wood, paper, fluorescent tubes, mirrors, paint, self-adhesive vinyl, cables
View from room 49, *Fragmented colour*

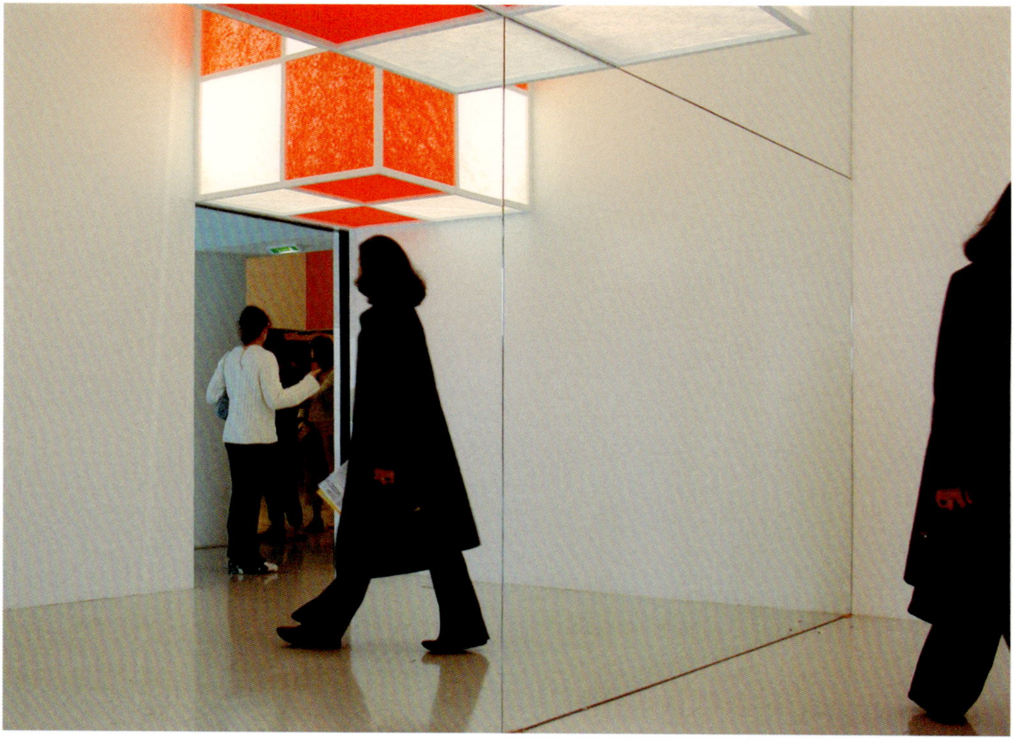

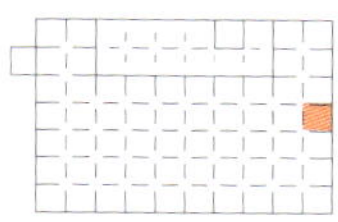

Room 31

Photo-souvenir: "The three lanterns", work in situ
Wood, paper, fluorescent tubes, mirrors, paint, self-adhesive vinyl, cables

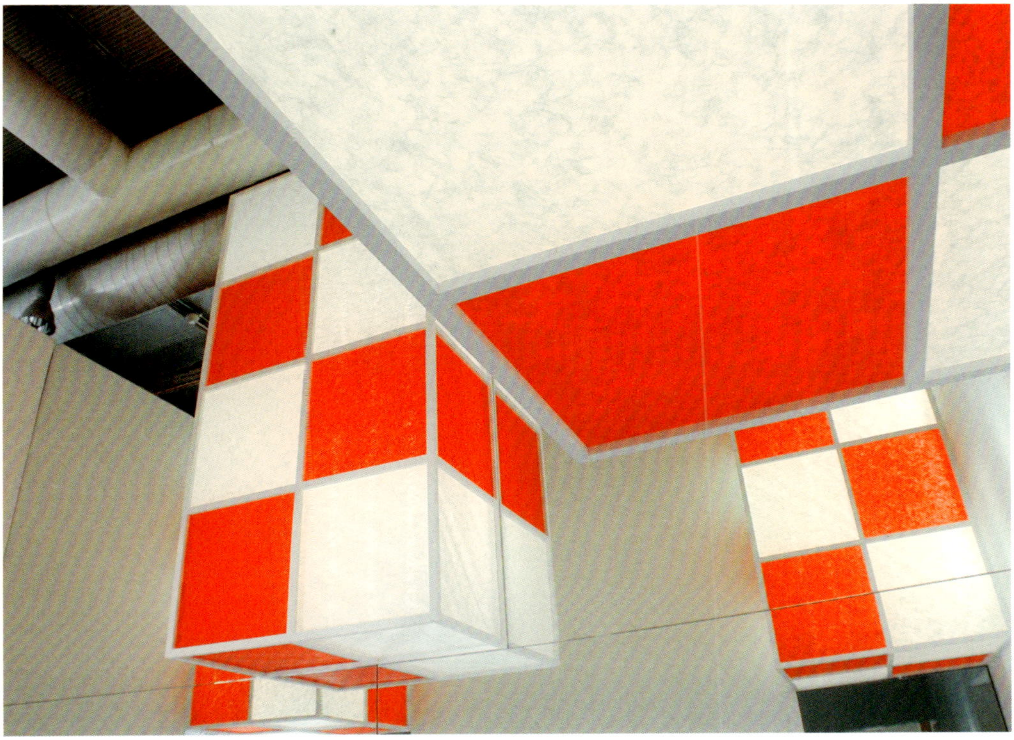

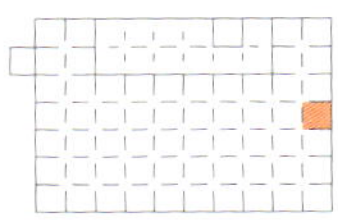

Room 31

Photo-souvenir: "The three lanterns", work in situ
Wood, paper, fluorescent tubes, mirrors, paint, self-adhesive vinyl, cables

A very large number of in situ projects produced by Buren take into account the different ceilings of the spaces in which the artist sets up his work. In 1974, Buren made a succession of interventions in several European institutions, including the Brussels Palais des Beaux-Arts, aimed at modifying the initial structure of the false ceiling by altering its configuration and the materials. This principle would then be a constant called upon many times over in his œuvre.
The Suspended Ceiling in "Le Musée qui n'existait pas" underlines the specificity of the Centre Pompidou's architecture and, by using a chequer-board of coloured, translucent sheets of Plexiglas lit from within by a series of neons, masks the building's actual technical ceiling. Buren thus lowers the proportions of the space in such a way that they break with the initial height of the picture rails and the place. The space thus seems to "process past" before the spectator's eyes and accentuates the arrangement's effect of horizontality. Lastly, it neutralizes the building's parasite-like elements, whose structure is the desired negation of the "white cube" as it is of the implicit ideology to which it refers.
It is worth noting how this motif, which Buren has also applied in many propositions, including a series of "cabins" made from the early 1980s on, has become a general factor in the work of many artists in the following generations, to such a degree did it signify the necessary adaptation of the place to the critical logic inherent in their work. Among them, the English artist Liam Gillick is undoubtedly the person for whom the "suspended ceiling" and "platform" ideas have been at the root of his thinking about place and the spectator's position in his relation to a circumscribed space within a given place.

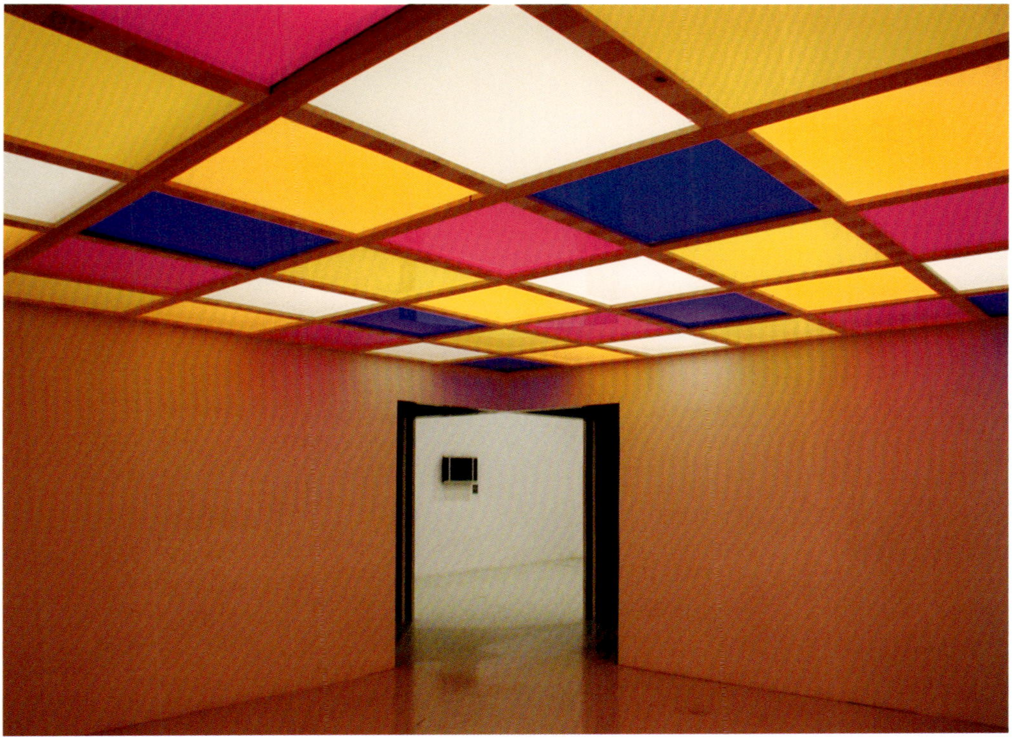

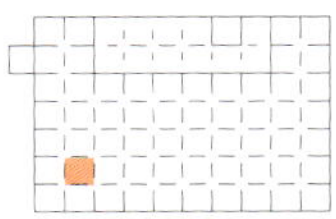

Room 59

Photo-souvenir: "The suspended ceiling", work *in situ*,
Wood, cables, fluorescent tubes, coloured and translucent Plexiglas, self-adhesive vinyl, paint, sheetrock
Opposite, room 61, *Video room*

Through the effect of the suspended mirror installed over the white cube, Buren highlights the space's invisible content. He contrasts the apparent neutrality of the outward form with the principle of an interior that is at once multi-coloured and marked on the ground by the black and white "visual tool". The arrangement thus produces nothing less than a reversal between its outer and inner structure. It comes across like a piece of optical machinery. Buren's art addresses the eye, and the way it sees things. "The arrangement, its meaning, the way it functions," says Thierry Laurent, "are to be sought actually within what it offers to the eye".

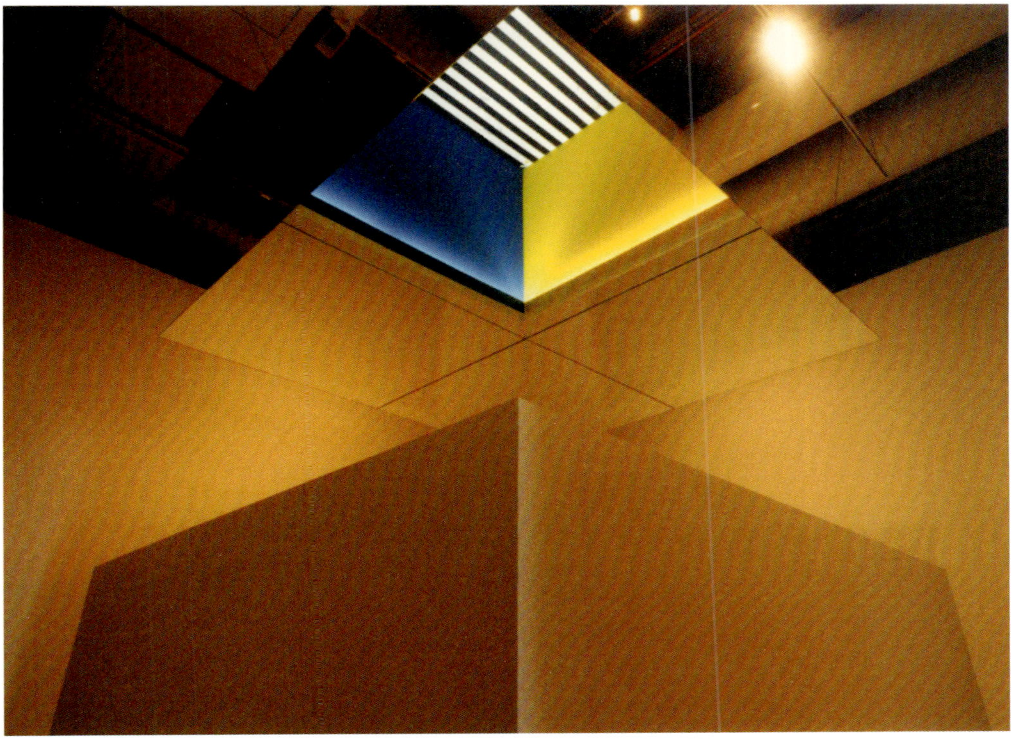

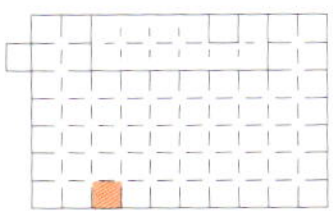

Room 63

Photo-souvenir: "The colour box", work in situ
Wood, sheetrock, paint, fluorescent tubes, metal structure, mirror, glue, cable, black self-adhesive vinyl, artificial light

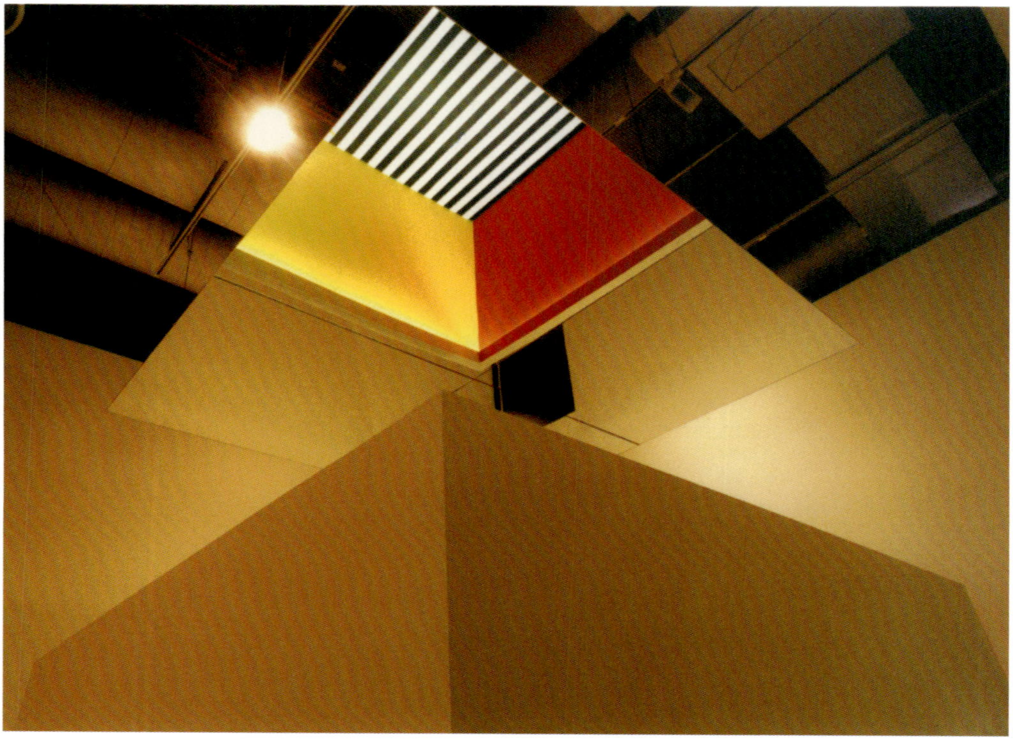

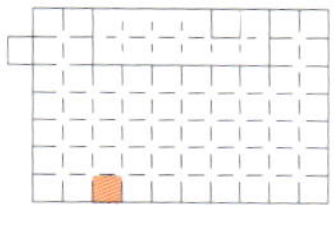

Room 63

Photo-souvenir: "The colour box", work in situ
Wood, sheetrock, paint, fluorescent tubes, metal structure, mirror, glue, cable, black self-adhesive vinyl, artificial light

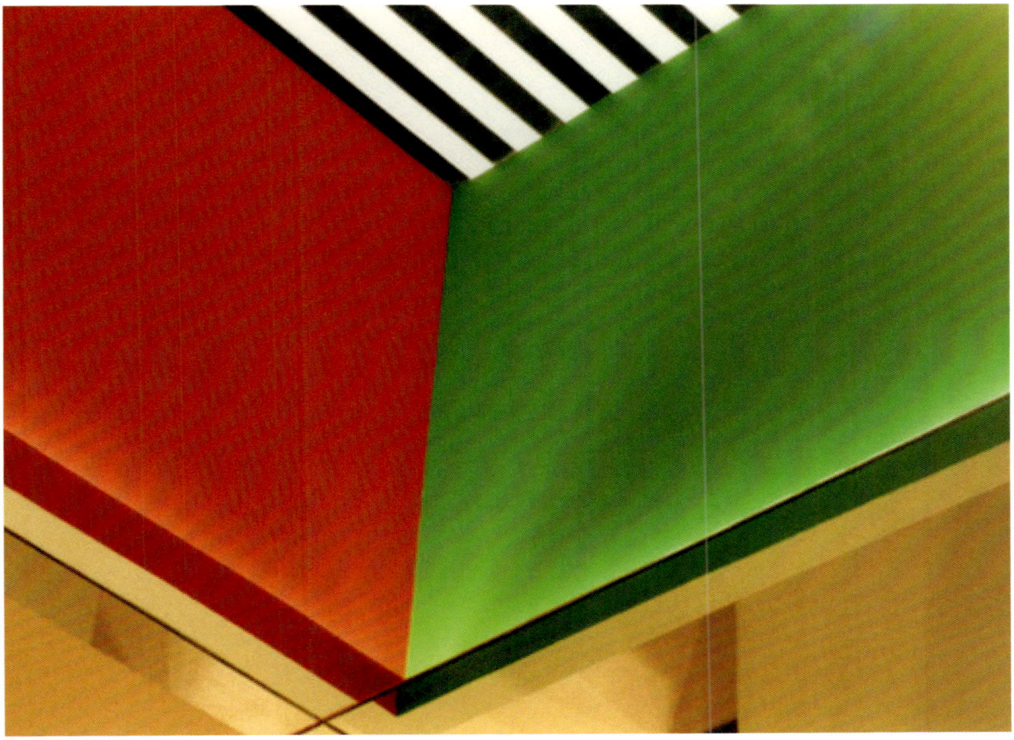

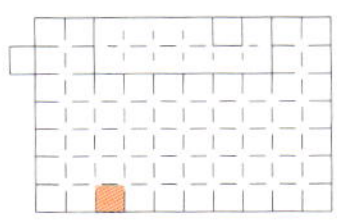

Room 63

Photo-souvenir: "The colour box", work in situ
Wood, sheetrock, paint, fluorescent tubes, metal structure, mirror, glue, cable, black self-adhesive vinyl, artificial light

The "exploded cabin" notion works like the part for the whole. It fragments the space like a chequer-board. The cell is broken and projected onto the adjacent walls. It is a fragment of the whole which is represented by the exhibition, an interplay between inside and outside and the desire that the whole literally sculpts the space. But the "exploded cabin" is first and foremost a space within the space offering the spectator a succession of visual and optical experiments, weaving a relation of reciprocity with the space which accommodates it and which it at the same time reveals. So the cabins form a work that is both *in situ* and dialectic in nature. They highlight the interdependence between two architectures: the "skin" of the cabin itself, and that of the place in which it is at once assembled and shown.
Buren uses many metaphors to describe this principle: "In addition to the interior/exterior interplay in one and the same volume, what interests me is that the movement and the appearance of this open box in the space are forever new from one space to the next, a bit like a lung which, when it inhales and exhales, fills the more or less large space of the rib cage." The "photos-souvenirs" of *The Cabin with Three Ceilings* highlight a principle which Buren has been keen to use in different places in the show, a principle consisting in working the space in both a horizontal and a vertical mode. Here, the cabin is reduced to an elementary prototype, but it is surmounted by three soffits. It asserts its dynamic by the interplay of coloured chequer-boards which explode the form above our heads. The space opens up like a game where there is an alternation of coloured and pierced planes, through which Buren underscores the building's design.

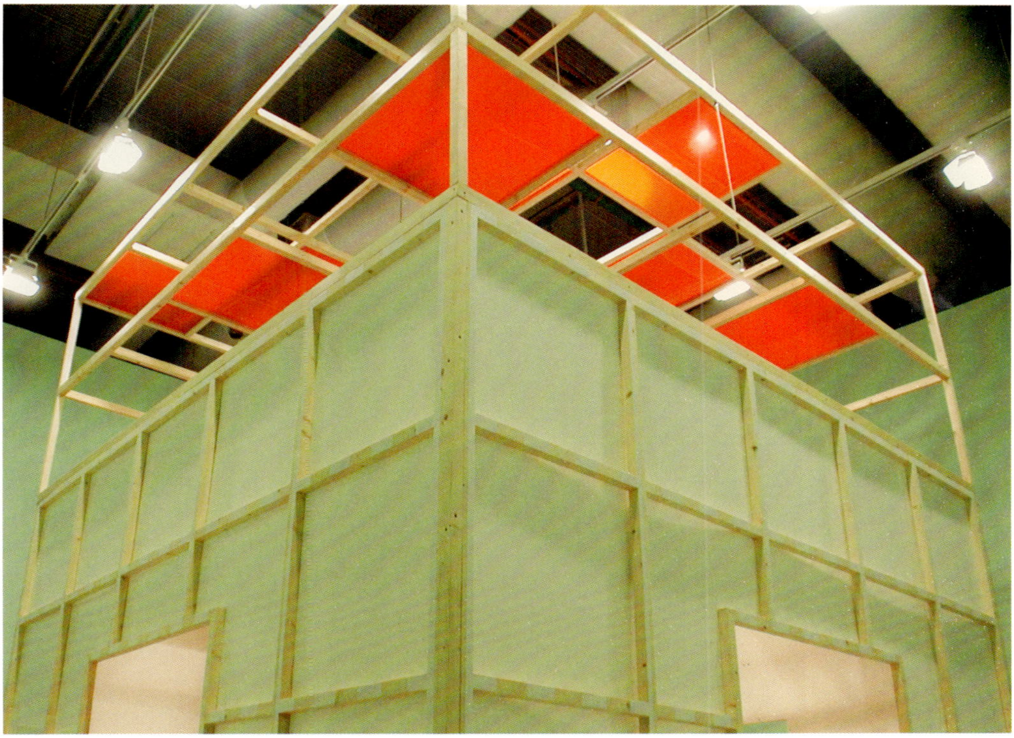

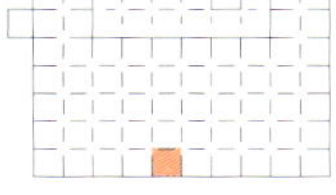

Room 65

Photo-souvenir: "The cabin with three ceilings", work in situ
Wood, fabric, rec translucent Plexiglas, sheetrock, glue, cables, artificial light

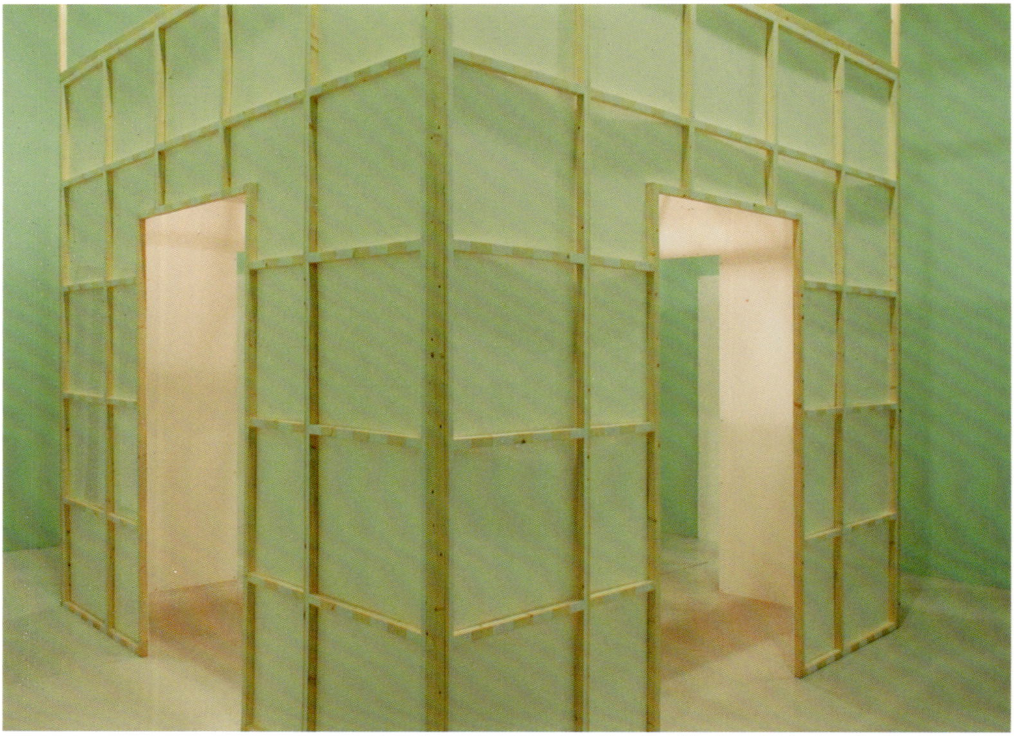

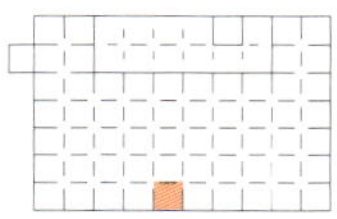

Room 65

Photo-souvenir: "The cabin with three ceilings", work *in situ*
Wood, fabric, red translucent Plexiglas, sheetrock, glue, cables, artificial light

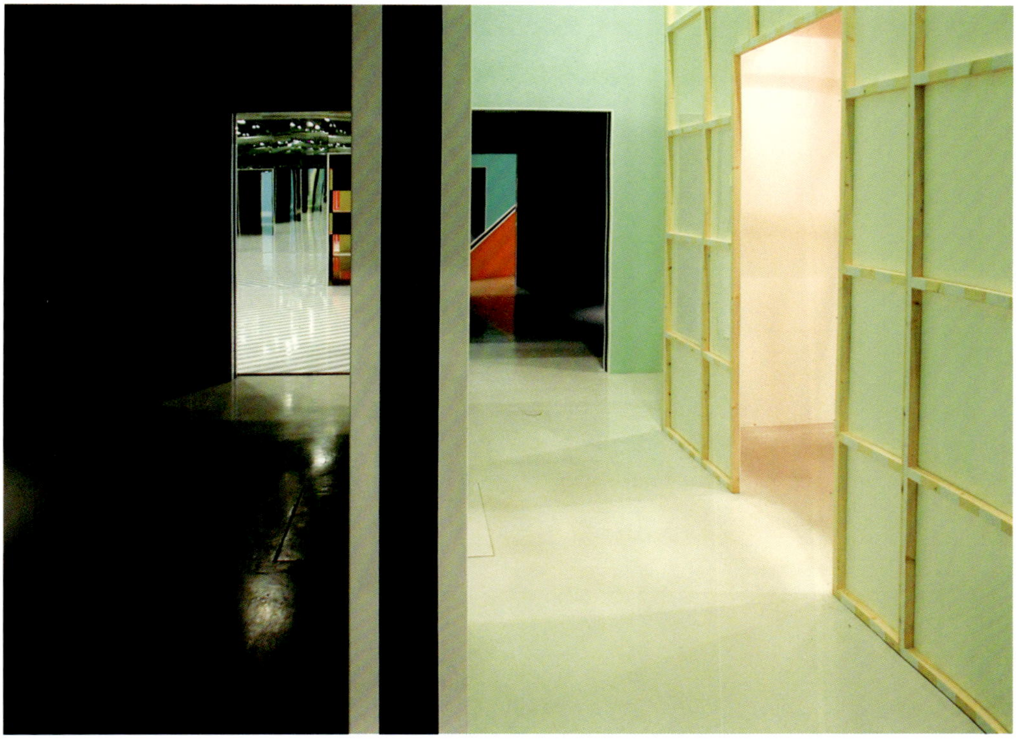

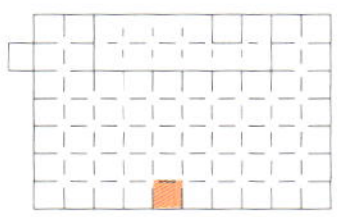

Room 65

Photo-souvenir: "The cabin with three ceilings", work *in situ*
Wood, fabric, red translucent Plexiglas, sheetrock, glue, cables, artificial light
Left, room 56 and room 55, *The endless ceiling floor*
Opposite, adjoining, room 66 and room 67, *Three colours make four: the oblique diagonal*

"Le Musée qui n'existait pas" is the place of all possible variations, and finds its unity in the principle of repetition in the different rooms gridding the whole space. It is also the space of the diversity of the materials forming it. Metal grilles and moucharabieh-like honeycombed structures permit as many discrepancies in relation to the plastic vocabulary that makes up any exhibition. The space in itself is here treated like the potential place of all inventions and discrepancies. Buren's art produces a whole host of different virtuoso effects, capable of questioning what we see.

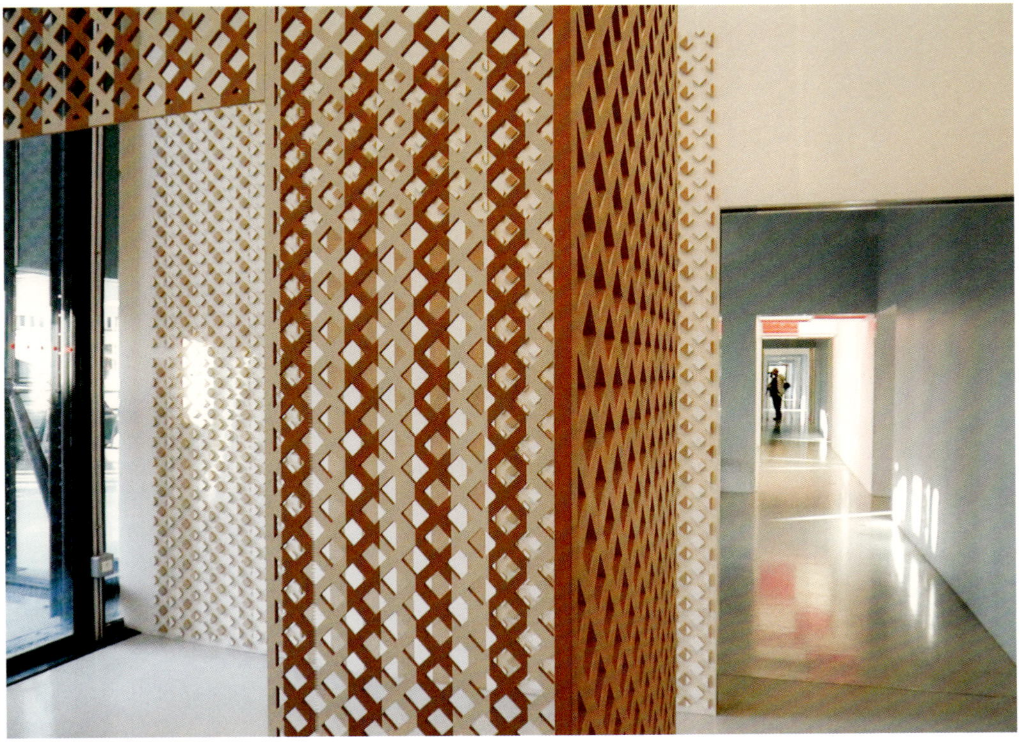

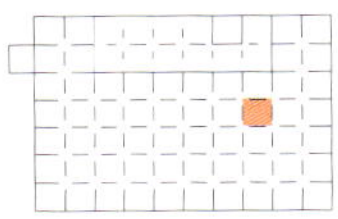

Room 33

Above and on following pages:
Photos-souvenirs: "The exploded cabin with 4,432 holes: lace", work *in situ* (inside, outside)
Wood (MDF), glue, sheetrock, paint, metal structure, daylight, artificial light
Adjoining, room 32 and room 31, *The three lanterns*
In the distance, a mirror in which all the doors are reflected

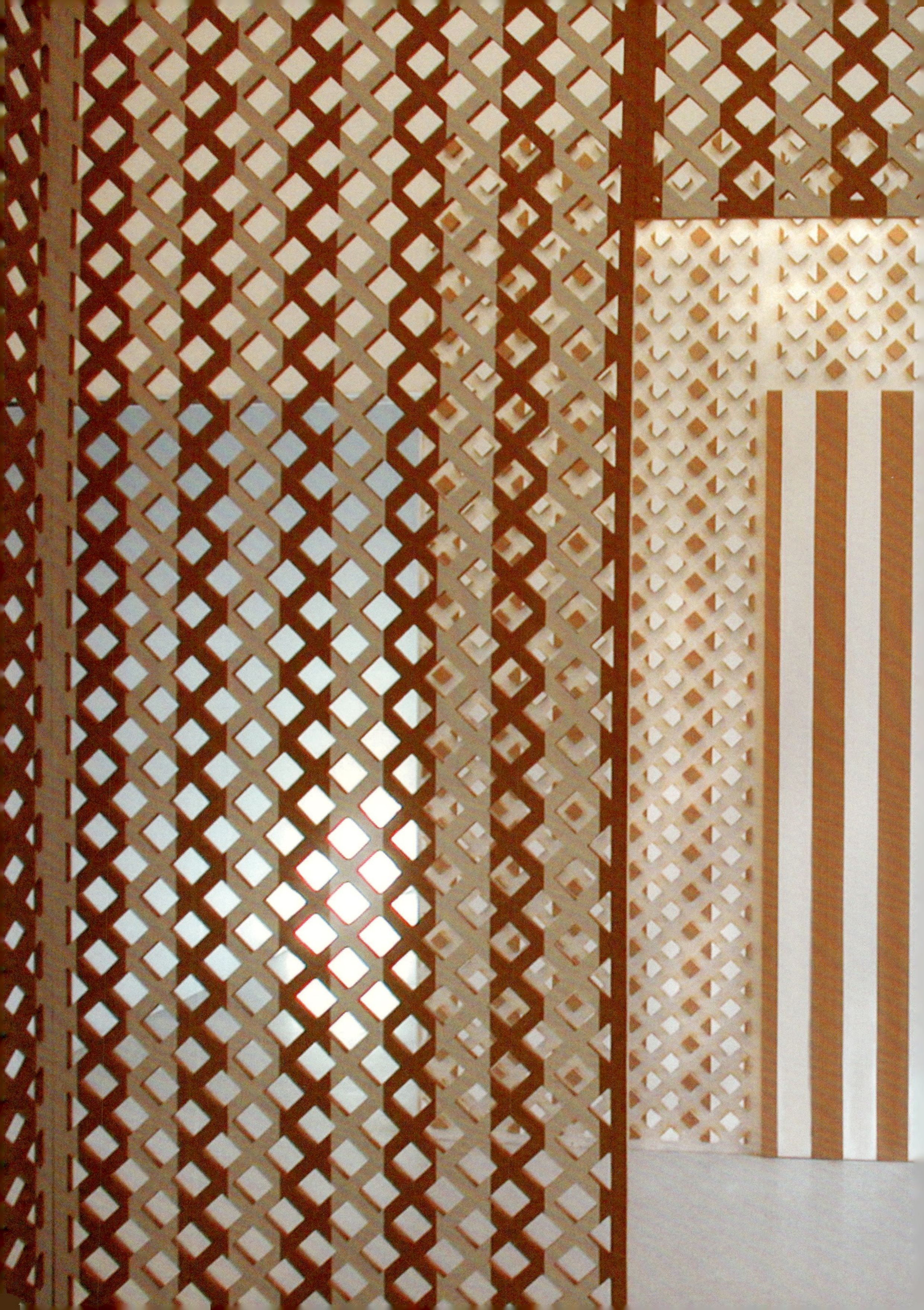

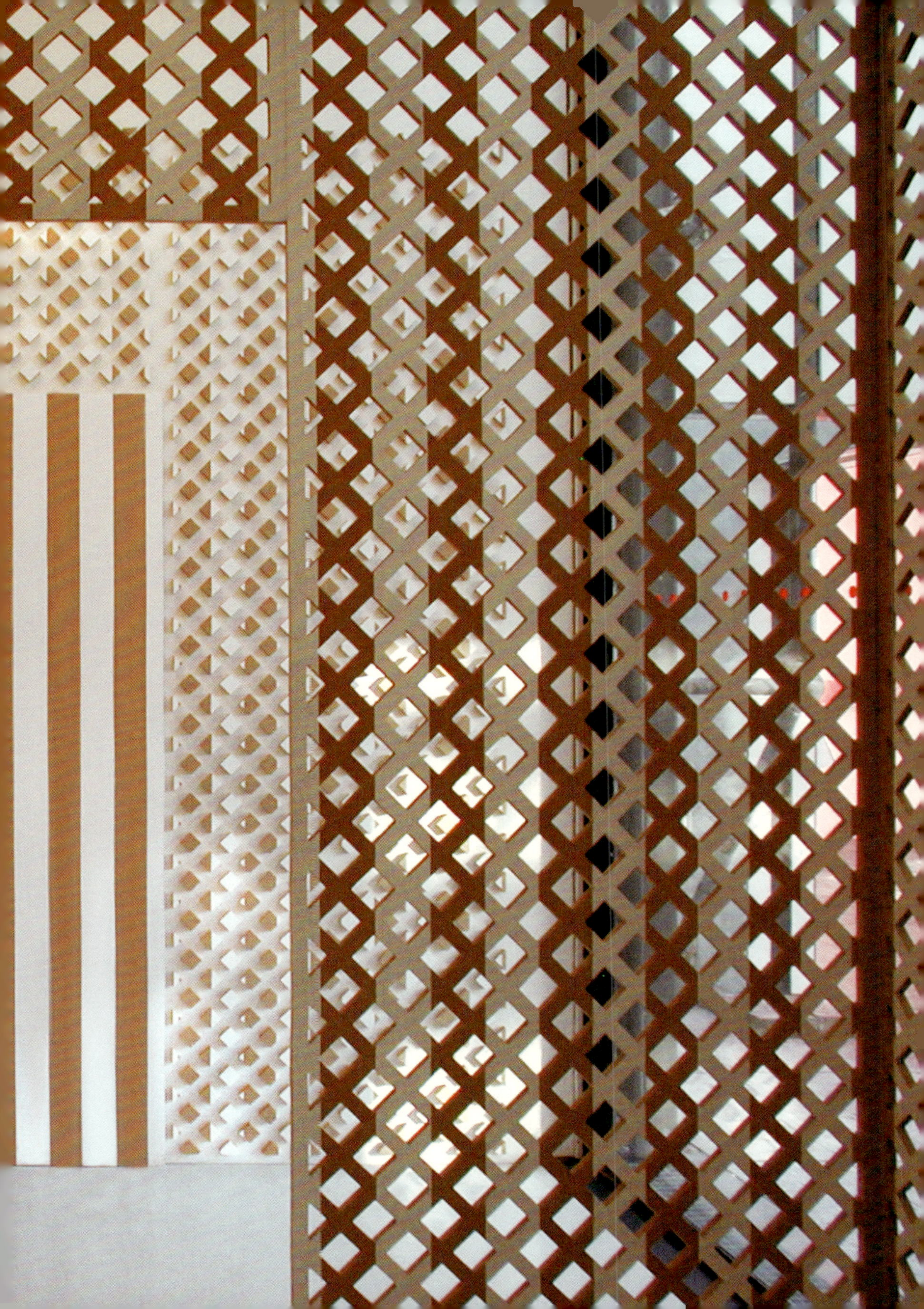

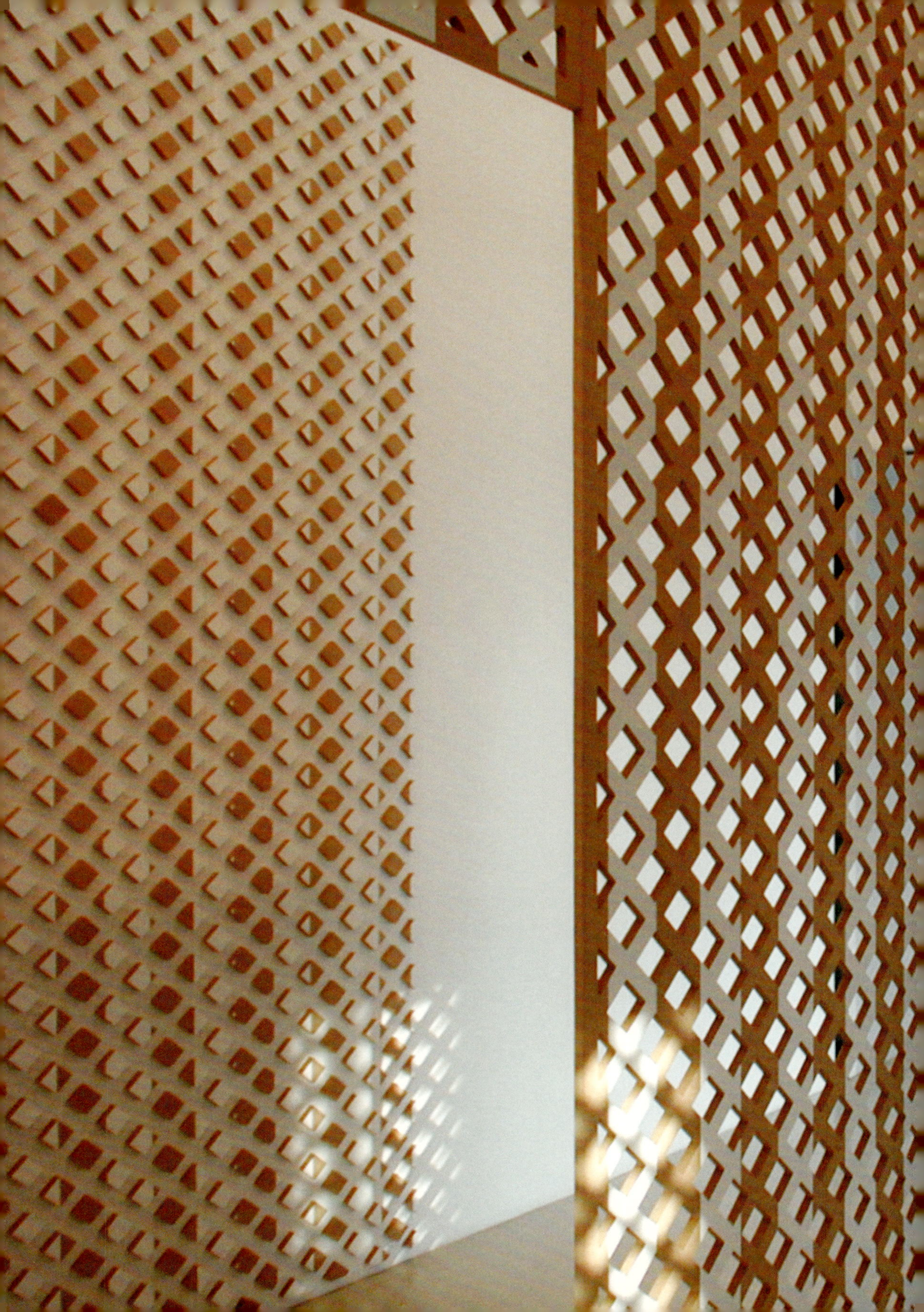

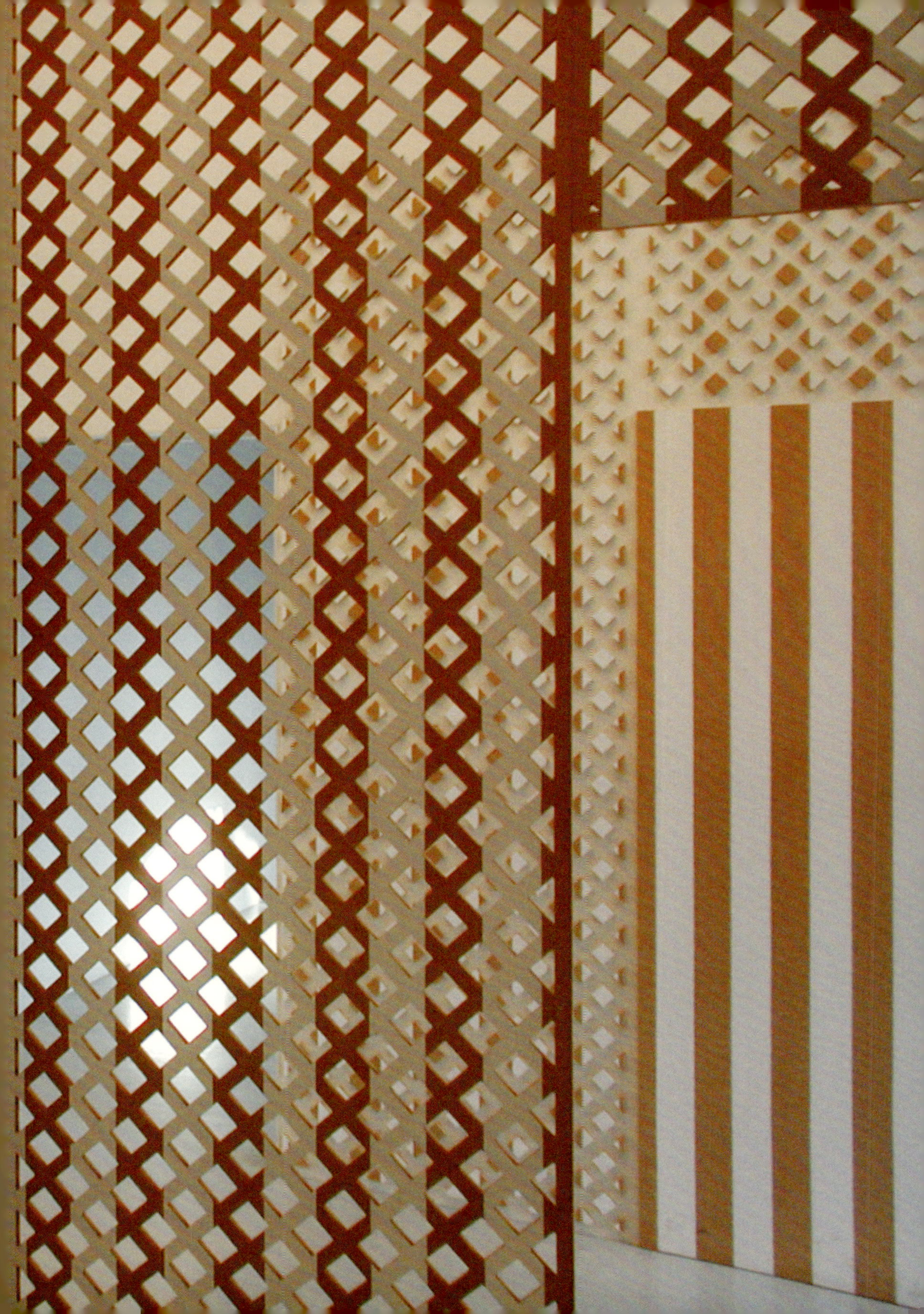

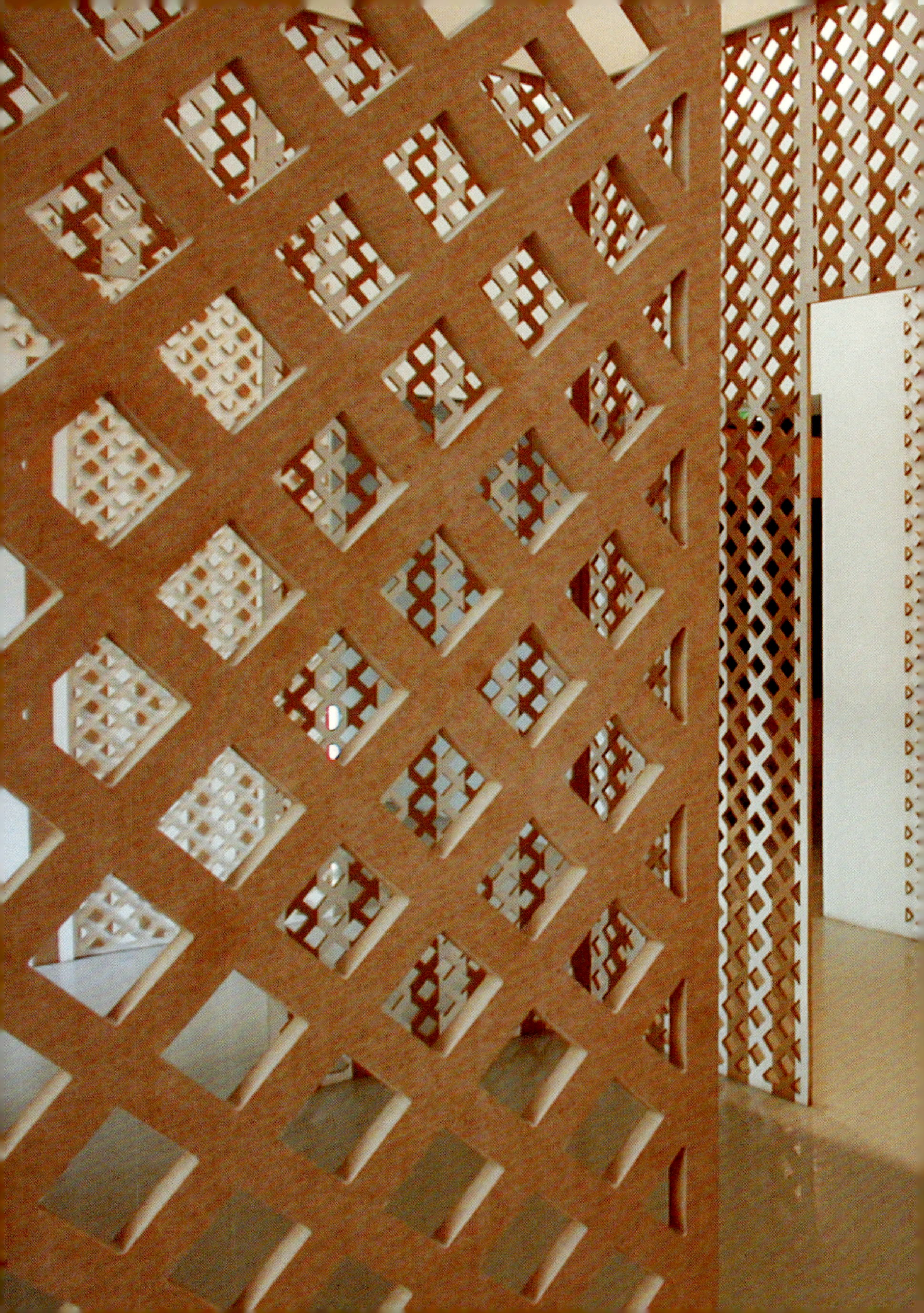

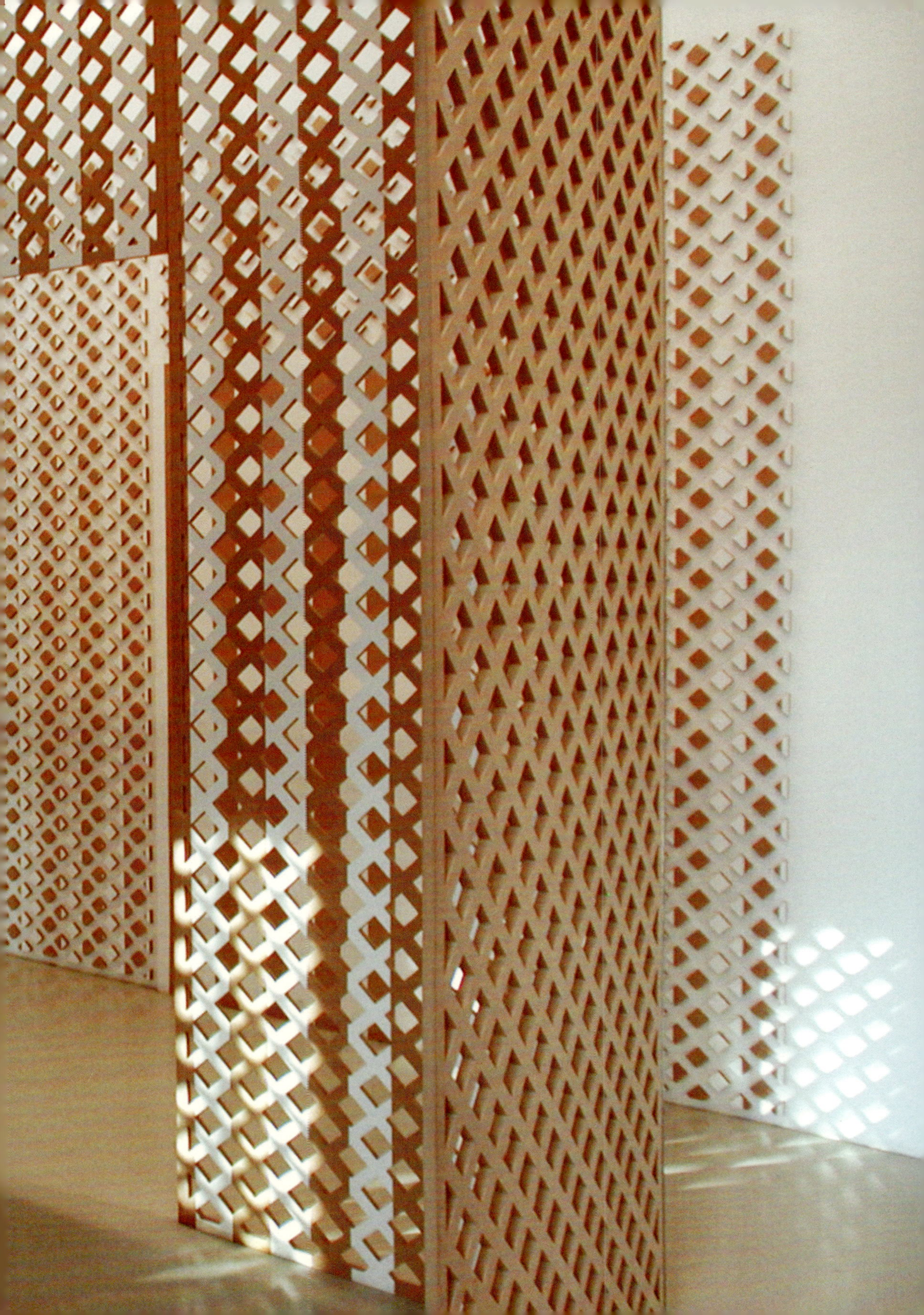

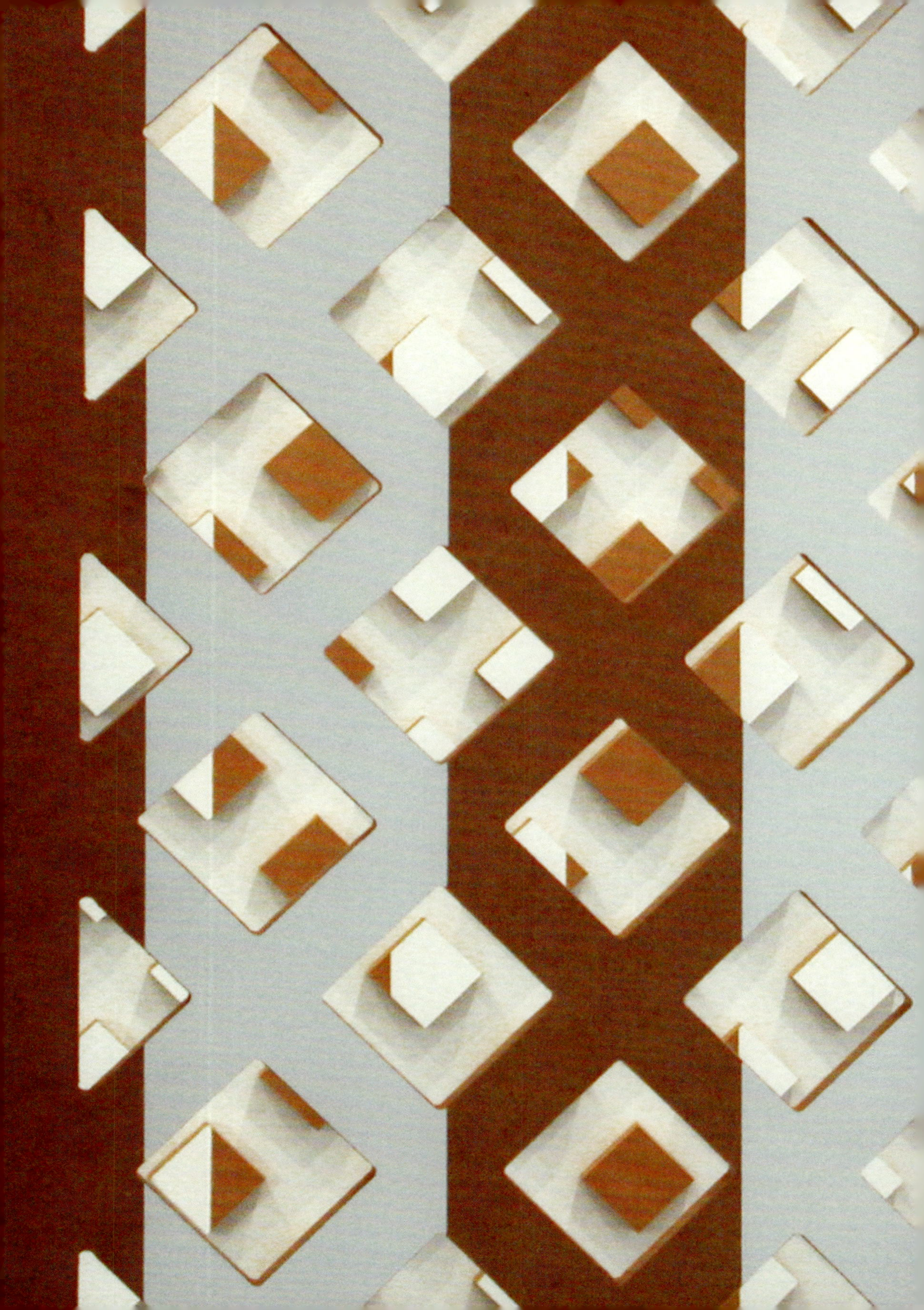

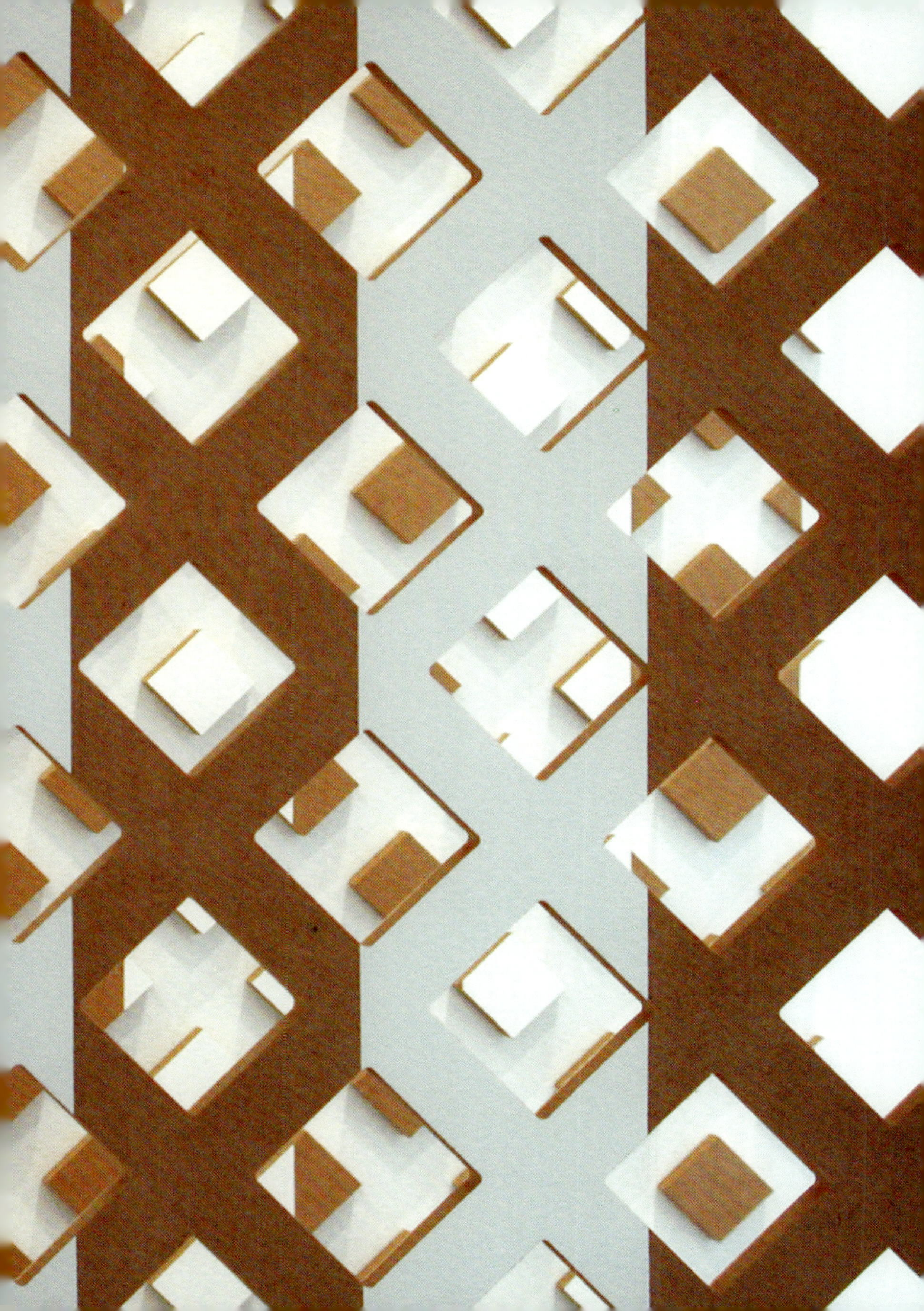

Enter-Exit

Laurent Le Bon

DAHLIA

Face-to-face

At the Centre Pompidou, as elsewhere, DB's artistic life involves a constructive face-to-face. Re-reading Sun Tzu's *The Art of War* in order to understand a bit about DB and the show.

POSTERS

Three viewpoints for a dialogue

An artist, an architect and a 1300-person strong institution, 300 of them involved in various ways in this project.
Three curators.
Three financiers.

STANDARDS

A split-second space

Finding some of the Centre Pompidou's original utopias for the duration of an exhibition. The arrangement created by DB and implemented by Patrick Bouchain combines the structure designed by Renzo Piano and his little slips with the restrictions regarding use and safety (harder at the Centre than in many other public buildings) which make any ephemeral intervention very problematic. In addition the project had to comply with the public works contracts law, which does not permit anything hasty. The building's history is one of gradual densification. DB caricatures this by showing up its contradictions, as when he decides to partly fill the empty areas on the terraces with cells on scaffolding. This had never been done since the Centre opened. With its slightly grandiloquent title, at once somewhat provocative and mixed with melancholy (use of the imperfect), DB's exhibition is an impressive attempt to create a space from scratch, magnifying a place whose architecture no longer resembles the original statements of the contractors and the commissioning authorities.

INVITATION

Gridding

After an initial suggestion made by Patrick Bouchain to create the void on the level allocated for the show, DB came up with a grid: a very dense and in the end regular grid made up of cells distributed over the entire area. Few references spring to mind, so closely does this idea resemble a UFO in the museum world accustomed to huge rooms. One thinks of the small exhibition rooms of the parallel circuits at the Alte Pinakothek in Munich and the Kunsthistorisches Museum in Vienna. This marks a return to the intimate with spaces of 30 square metres (5.6 x 6.1 m) [325 square feet (18 x 20 ft)]. Images come to mind, and mingle: archaeological remains at thermal baths and antique markets (like Trajan's), ideal city, refugee camp, Japanese dwelling, Palladian villa, prison (cells), fair stalls (DB's supreme irony, being a sworn enemy of the art market), the mosque at Cordoba, offices in Tati's *Playtime*, Billy Wilder's *The Apartment*, the Centre's old open-plan offices, glass maze at a fairground, and a bit of all that and anything else that resists references and leaves room for surprise (something that is becoming rare in museums: being surprised). The guards have almost disappeared and been replaced by a utopian closed-circuit surveillance room controlling the whole thing, including the inaccessible cells. This response to the absence of guards becomes a work in its own right, and the stuff of voyeurism.

SCAFFOLDING

From one obstacle to another

Like an application of Pascal Dusapin's work paying tribute to the *Deux Plateaux*: an alternating "yes" and "no" over two pages, DB puts pressure on the institution inviting him, so as to get helpful answers at the right time. Not without an ultimatum or two, DB is a supporter of the go/no-go in effect in private management. He only starts working when a minimum, but necessary and sufficient number of favourable conditions have been obtained.

BOOKS

Composition précis

"The visual tool is the judge of peace," DB likes to remind us. The whole arrangement is measured by the yardstick of this precision. Many battles are necessary, sometimes over a centimetre.

STRIPES

Either empty, or full

Luxury steeped in appropriateness: the artist is only using half the cells created (a distant echo of the choice made by Piano and Rogers, who had decided to build on only half the parcel offered, so they could offer visitors a piazza?). Running counter to abundance and surplus, hallmarks of museums, the visitor's eye comes to rest on empty grey cells (the colour of the Centre Pompidou's floor, chosen to paint the walls of the rooms) before entering a full cell. A new variation on the void, essential notion for many artists over the past fifty years.

UNITED

Interplay of cubes

DB had rails put up very high to transform our vision of the Centre's technical apparatus hanging from the ceiling, so as to unify it, and make it vanish. Many types of cells are created: on water, suspended, allusive, stripped bare, etc. as in a game with endless variations. Only the available space was missing and a painful choice was called for. The artist's whole repertory is there, all his materials too, but this is a plunge into the unknown he is inviting us to. The artist pulls us across his chequer-board where he directs the moves of a game whose rules he has drawn up. The visitor is free to walk through the maze. At the heart of a microcosm of simple forms, the obligatory and linear circuit is done away with in favour of intersections (*Around the return of a detour)* and dialogues between cells, between visitors, between the most hidden (*Forms: paintings*) and the most open (*The Colours: sculptures*). Squeezing the space to expand it, creating short-cuts to lengthen it, creating confinement the better to appreciate the view of the outside, these are some of the paradoxes of this temporary museum with its three-month shelf-life, but three years in the making.

REGULATIONS

Stage system

It would be a serious mistake to regard DB's proposal as architecture or, worse still, décor. This is a total work, both intellectual and material, which is incorporated like an essential milestone in his career, questioning relations between the artist and the museum, about which he is one of the greatest theoreticians. You can bet your boots that "Le Musée qui n'existait pas" will reverberate every bit as much as the censured work in the Guggenheim and the arrangement at the CAPC in Bordeaux. This is a work which touches all the limits of what is possible in an institution today, from the basement to the Parisian sky, from the ticket to the giant tarpaulin, from solid to void, and from wit to meditation.

SPACE

Diagonal for a place

One of the arrangement's surprises lies in the creation of large cross-wise diagonals: something never seen before at the Centre.

NOTES

This is how it is and more

Nothing to add.

CARS

The duplicated space

DB has conquered the territory. He is exhibiting on the main floor but not in the great gallery. So for a year he did battle to double the initially proposed area of 1,200 square metres [13,000 square feet] and obtain the same space as the great gallery.

VIDEOS

Above the basement

The contradicting choices for the re-organization of the Centre Pompidou's forum are brought to the fore by DB's proposal: disappearance of complex signs and notices, extension of the car park as the only way of using level -1, and enhancement of past work by a looped montage of photos-souvenirs on suspended televisions whose function is uncertain, but which are, in the end of the day, good conveyors of documentation on the artist.

PHOTOS-SOUVENIRS

From one narrow door to the next

Rather than doorways, DB creates a whole host of thresholds on the borderline with regard to standards for places of passage, as provided for a space open to the public. The visit is a succession of traverses and encounters.

SOUND

The large corridor

The Centre's architecture has always been hallmarked by an alignment of corridors, so many anteroom-like galleries, running the entire length of the building, used for sometimes ill-defined purposes. DB's proposition gets rid of most of these useless areas to offer other prospects.

MIRROR

Ambulatory

The exhibition offers visitors the possibility of discovering the whole building from level -1 to level 6. Pleasures of promenading, discovery and the *passeggiata*. This is another vision of the building, offered to visitors, away from the signposted circuit.

GLASS

Façade

DB, a garden enthusiast, already catches visitors off balance in the piazza where they are greeted by a huge dahlia, antithesis of the Centre Pompidou's architecture – antithesis of the exhibition to be discovered within? Passers-by might have been previously surprised by the black-and-white poster campaign (4 x 3): a nostalgic idea harking back to fly-posting, just when the artist was pitting himself against a cultural institution.

SHEETROCK

Impromptu

DB acts at a moment's notice and on the spot, which does not mean without preparation. Quite to the contrary, this is a method of revealing, at the last minute, the fruit of much mature reflection, the better to surprise people. Secrecy is the order of the day. The artist likes magic and doubt. Not without a certain anxiety?

WOOD

Restaurant Georges

As part of the reconquest of the space and the extension of the structure, DB installs a cell over the pond at the *Restaurant Georges*, public property with a concession. Pirouette: in this metal décor, the motifs of the cell's façades are imbued with something extremely classical, with, for example, a Venetian window. Restaurant-goers can leave with a drawing of one of the motifs, the better to think about this apparent contradiction.

MENU

The square of flags

DB wanted to re-install the work *The Colours: sculptures.* Since this piece was acquired by the Centre in 1977, the law has become more important, as have security concerns. One year's work for fifteen flags in the city.

TELESCOPE

Flags in the wind

The re-installation of the flags might pass for a challenge taken up by the artist for his show, because, in the past, he had had to demand that it be taken down because certain clauses in the contract were not being complied with. The artist's works in the possession of institutions call for an attention and a precision that are not necessarily guaranteed by the rules of ethics governing conservation and restoration.

BANNERS

Borrowing the landscape

The main interest of the re-installation of *The Colours: sculptures* is that it introduces a dialogue with the arrangement created on level 6, which starts and ends in the escalator track where this work is installed. From a sensation of confinement to the conquest of the city. The figure of Walter Benjamin haunts this Parisian exhibition from passage to panorama by way of Baudelaire.

METAL

Mind the colour

Once again, DB proposes colour at times outrageously, with novel hues in his work. Against almost one and all on this subject, thirty years ago, he is still sticking to his guns today.

POLES

Construction

DB's proposal comes from made-to-measure craftsmanship. By joining in the *Art Project* undertaking, he constructs the exhibition on a just-in-time basis. The content of the cells, partly prefabricated in Lyon, fits into the structure made in Paris down to the nearest centimetre.

WIND

Seen, not seen

Always in motion, DB has found that the labyrinth arrangement is the ideal terrain for sowing trouble.

PICTURES

From one shift to the next

Someone should write an essay on DB's waistcoat, symbol of his nomadism. Always on the point of going somewhere, always in action, DB goes everywhere so that he can control and inspect every aspect of a show. He cherishes independence. All the meetings hatched by the Centre Pompidou system were a pain in the neck for him.

COATING

That's it. It was done here

DB works *in situ. No comment!* From the first day to the last.

ADHESIVE

Dominating-dominated

Tensions, conflicts, compromises and no base deeds

FABRIC

Above the waves, the horizon

The exhibition opened on 25 June, on time and within its budget.

SKETCHES

Solo show about the limits of artistic freedom.

A forty-year career. Several round-the-world trips. First solo show at the Centre Pompidou. Free as a bird? Definitely, because there were only constraints.

CAMERAS

Is the work happening?

Rendez-vous *in situ.* To hell with discourse and its embellishments!

SCREENS

Heave ho!

One or two efforts were necessary to give birth to this new museum, and to understand it. An exhibition is a cultural production that calls for a great deal of time, and material, financial and human wherewithal, like any live spectacle or film. And an open door, just one! France can be permitted this luxury. Let us not forget it too fast.

SPOTS

Buren Circus

The show goes on. DB is just passing: the game carries on across the world map, punctuated by the artist's ephemeral works. A world fair of another sort.

PAINTING

Radiating

Ten thousand artists in France, and some of them different.

LIGHT

The Museum that did not exist

It disappears on 25 September, and re-appears?

Warning (in the guise of a conclusion, for once)
DB's exhibition occupies different areas, scattered throughout the Centre Pompidou. It ends with an arrangement on level 6, formed by seventy cells. Ahead of exegeses and gossip, this text is an elliptical reading in which thirty-five components (non-exhaustive list) of the arrangement alternate with thirty-five partial and ... partial notes (because of my position in the exhibition system): an allusion to the rhythm of the cell's solids and voids. Each note is preceded by a title in italics referring to one of the artist's works. The artist's concern for precision also encompasses the naming of his works. Nevertheless, after a forty-year career, a glossary peculiar to the artist has been drawn up. Like the fragments of a work, "Le Musée qui n'existait pas" may be seen through the prism of previous works, whose titles are more appropriate than any other comment. The exhibition at the Centre may be anything but a retrospective, but you will still find in this choice of title a homage to the unerring continuity of the artist's career and as many doors in this labyrinth. The order of the text is arbitrary, like the visit to Daniel Buren's proposition. Readers, and visitors, enter and exit, as they wish, and will be caught up, or otherwise, in the whirlwind of this diabolical enter-exit. An enter-exit–in French: *entre-sort* also means a fairground booth, a sort of house of horrors where monsters are on display. "Monster" derives from the Latin verb *monere:* "to remind, attract attention to, admonish, warn"; it describes something that is exceptional, astonishing, strange, marvellous, sometimes a miracle.

Laurent Le Bon, June 2002

The development of the structure beyond the exhibition spaces properly so-called leads Buren to literally enshrine the bookshop in the general area on level 6 in the building. Caught vice-like, it becomes an integral part of the arrangement. In underscoring, in passing, the relation of text to work and work to text, Buren establishes an aesthetic and functional relation between his visual idea and the exegesis on his work. The written word here finds its extension actually within the arrangement accommodating it. The arrangement of "Le Musée qui n'existait pas" also finds its extension in its use value.

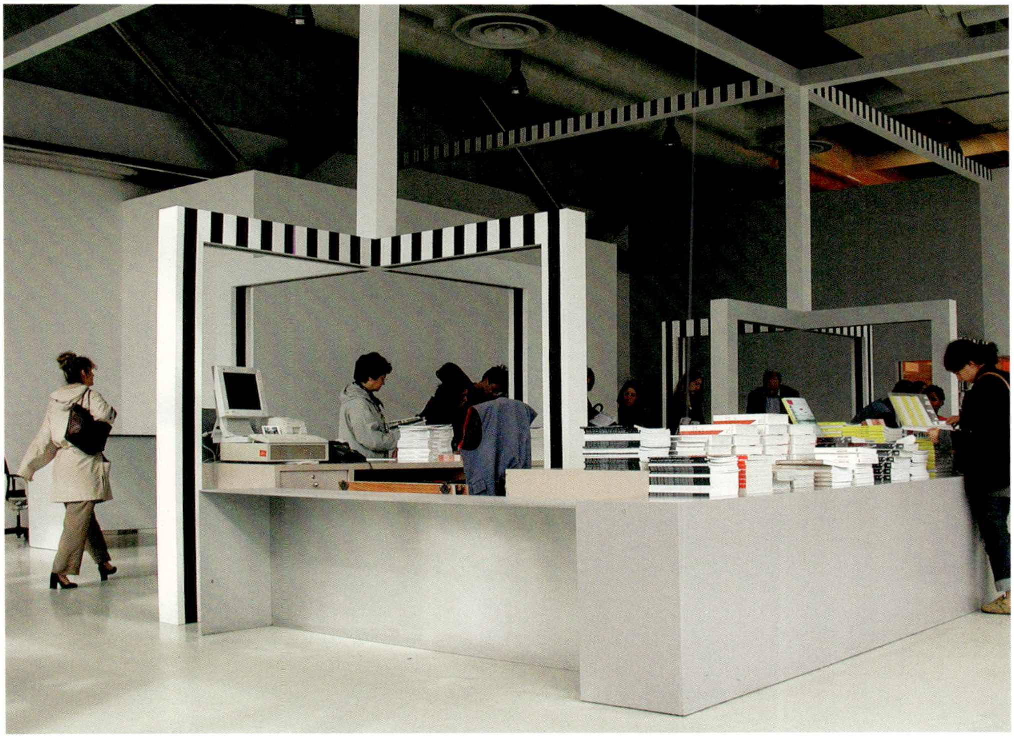

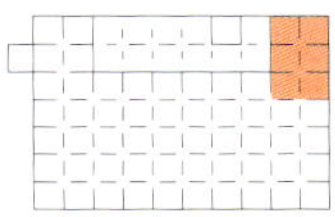

Rooms 9, 10, 11, 12, 29, 30

Photo-souvenir: "The framework of the rooms", work in situ
Metal structures, sheetrock, self-adhesive vinyl, paint, glass, steel, chairs and tables, books…

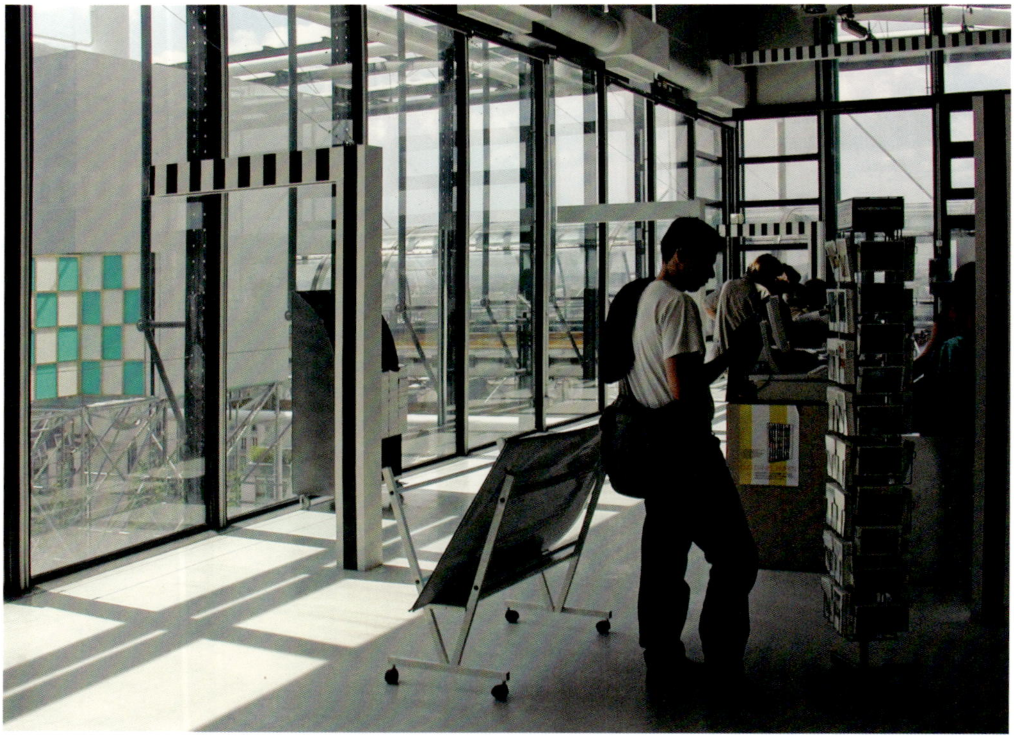

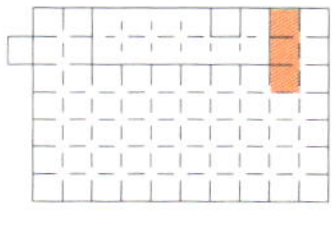

Rooms 9, 12, 29

Photo-souvenir: "The framework of the rooms", work in situ
Metal structures, sheetrock, self-adhesive vinyl, paint, glass, steel, chairs and tables, books...
Outside, room 7, *The floating island*

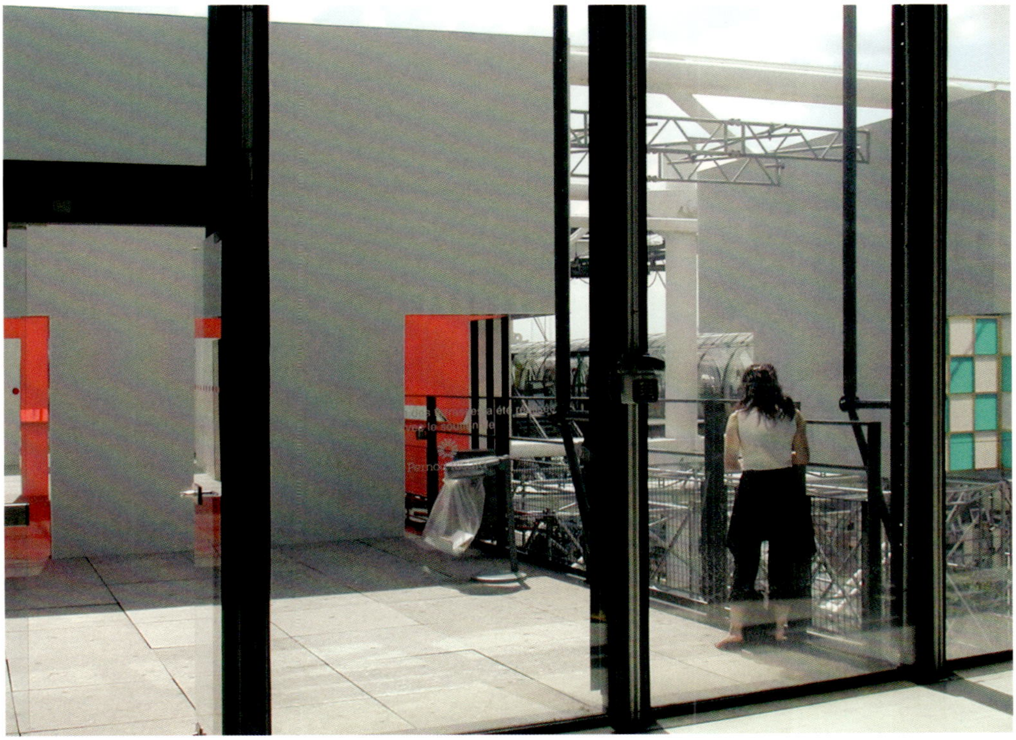

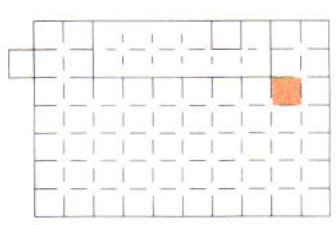

Room 29

Photo-souvenir: "The framework of the rooms", work *in situ*
Metal structures, sheetrock, self-adhesive vinyl, paint, glass, steel, chairs and tables, books...
Outside, room 27, *The transparent red roof*, and room 7, *The floating island*

A part of the arrangement rests on the scaffolding designed for the occasion, and conspicuously surveys the void above the terraces of the Musée national d'art moderne, where it is erected and is symbolically based. Buren's structure develops beyond the building's railings and spatial boundaries. It is maintained like a "moment of equilibrium" and reveals the extraordinary complexity of the Centre Pompidou's traffic and architecture. It re-asserts the construction principle inherent in the building as well as the high-tech principle of its construction. The scaffolding set up for the occasion contrasts with the interplay of the building's girders. The Centre Pompidou and "Le Musée qui n'existait pas" are "two mental and physical constructions" which the artist's system glorifies and reveals. Buren thus proposes a veritable reading, no less, of the building, its traffic and its viewpoints. On the existing architecture he overlays a provisional architecture. The Centre Pompidou is here momentarily given back its essentially modulable and larksome function. It is the place of all sorts of experiences—and experiments—which occur not so much in it as with it. Here it is the partner of the artist whom it is accommodating.

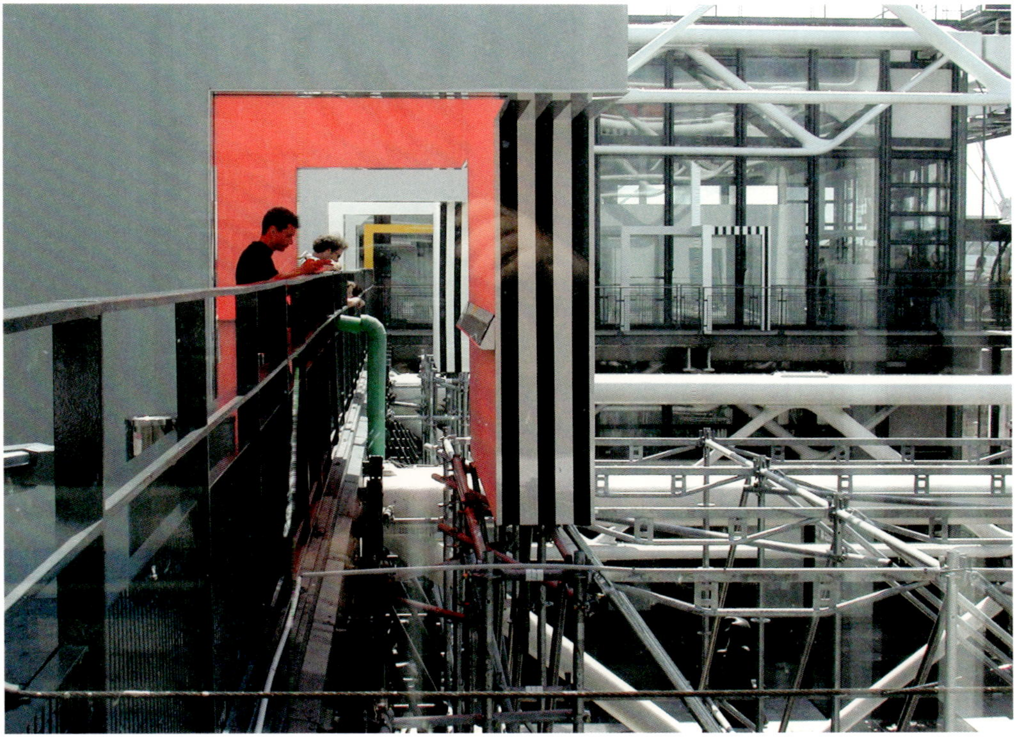

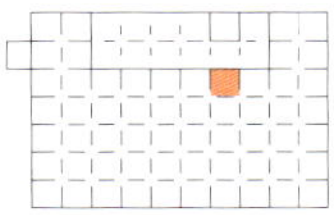

Room 27

Photo-souvenir: "The transparent red roof", work *in situ* (outside)
Coloured awning, self-adhesive vinyl, sheetrock, wood, paint, mirrors, daylight
View from room 12, *The framework of the rooms*; in the distance, rooms 2 and 19, *The framework of the rooms*

The Transparent Red Roof is one of the show's most complex ideas. It is probably also one of the ideas which most intensely transforms the space that it defines, to such a degree does its relation to colour and the effects brought on by it wreathe the space with a special light which changes as the daylight alters. The structure of the cell is surmounted by a red-coloured awning which gives transparent glimpses of the space and the architecture of the building which it diffracts and fragments. The walls are covered to a halfway point with an oblique glass frieze which reflects the architecture, absorbs and redistributes the colour. The site is nothing less than a receptacle which immerses the spectator in an atmosphere that changes with the weather. The work thus proposes a veritable phenomenological experience subject to nothing more than natural light. Buren acts here like a film director of the space and pits his proposal against both the architecture and the intensity and variations of the "chromatic ambience" he proposes.

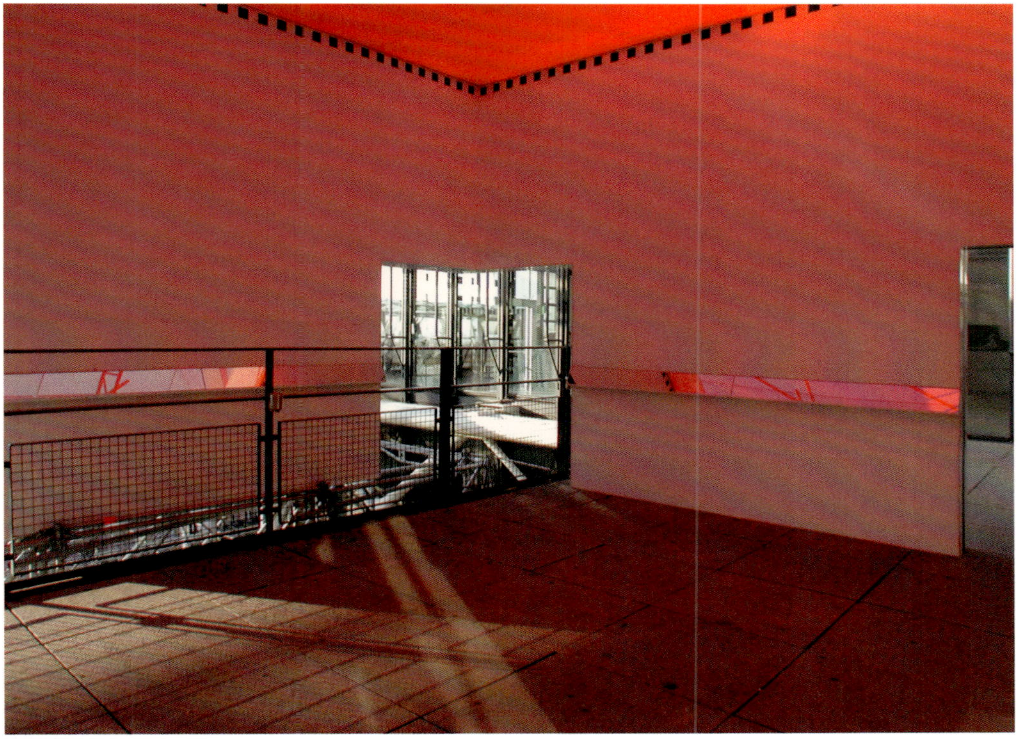

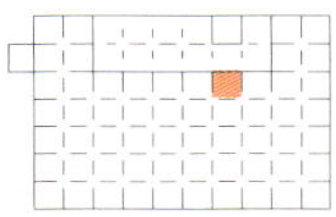

Room 27

Photo-souvenir: *"The transparent red roof"*, work *in situ* (outside)
Coloured awning, self-adhesive vinyl, sheetrock, wood, paint, mirrors, daylight
In the distance, room 9 and room 12, *The framework of the rooms*

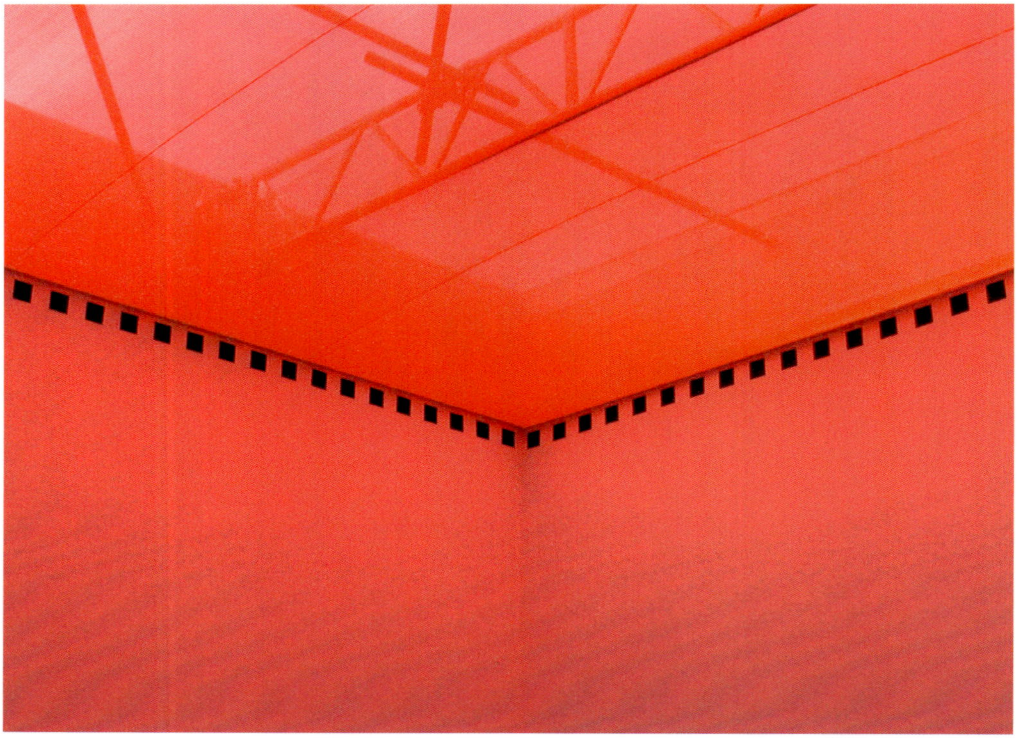

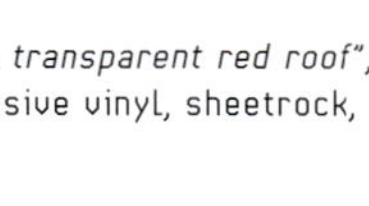

Room 27

Photo-souvenir: "The transparent red roof", work *in situ* (outside)
Coloured awning, self-adhesive vinyl, sheetrock, wood, paint, mirrors, daylight

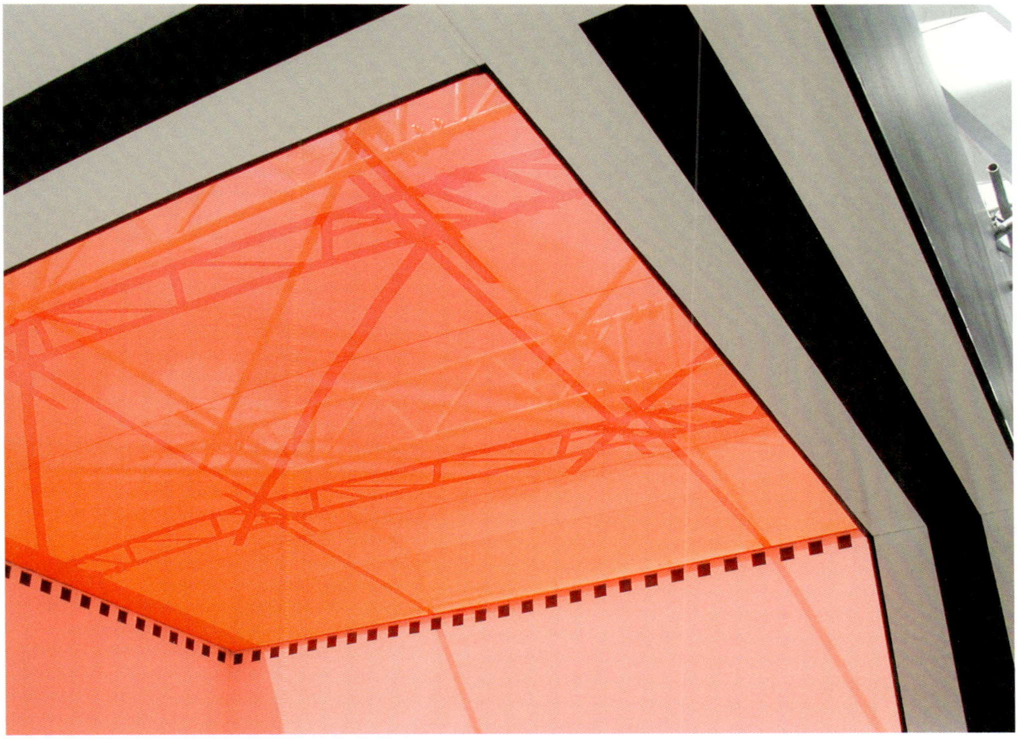

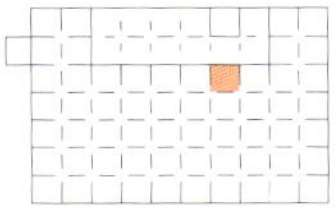

Room 27

Photo-souvenir: "The transparent red roof", work *in situ* (outside)
Coloured awning, self-adhesive vinyl, sheetrock, wood, paint, mirrors, daylight

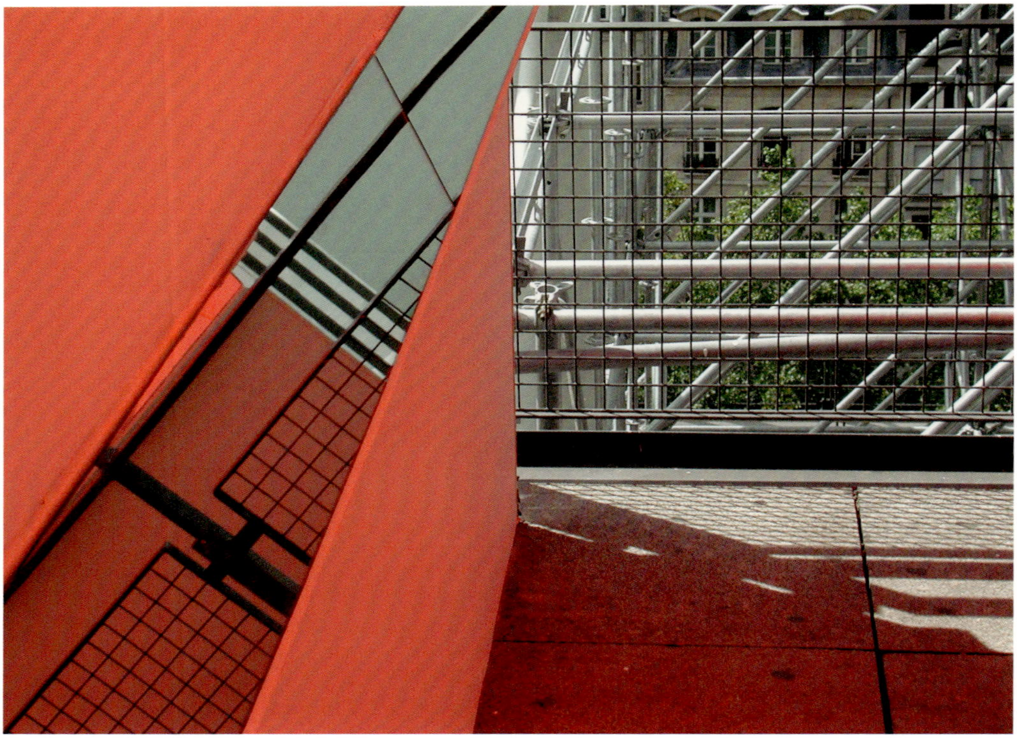

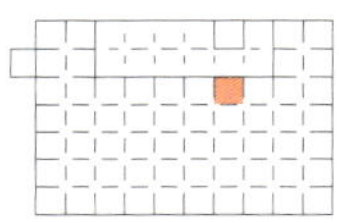

Room 27

Photo-souvenir: "The transparent red roof", work *in situ* (outside)
Coloured awning, self-adhesive vinyl, sheetrock, wood, paint, mirrors, daylight

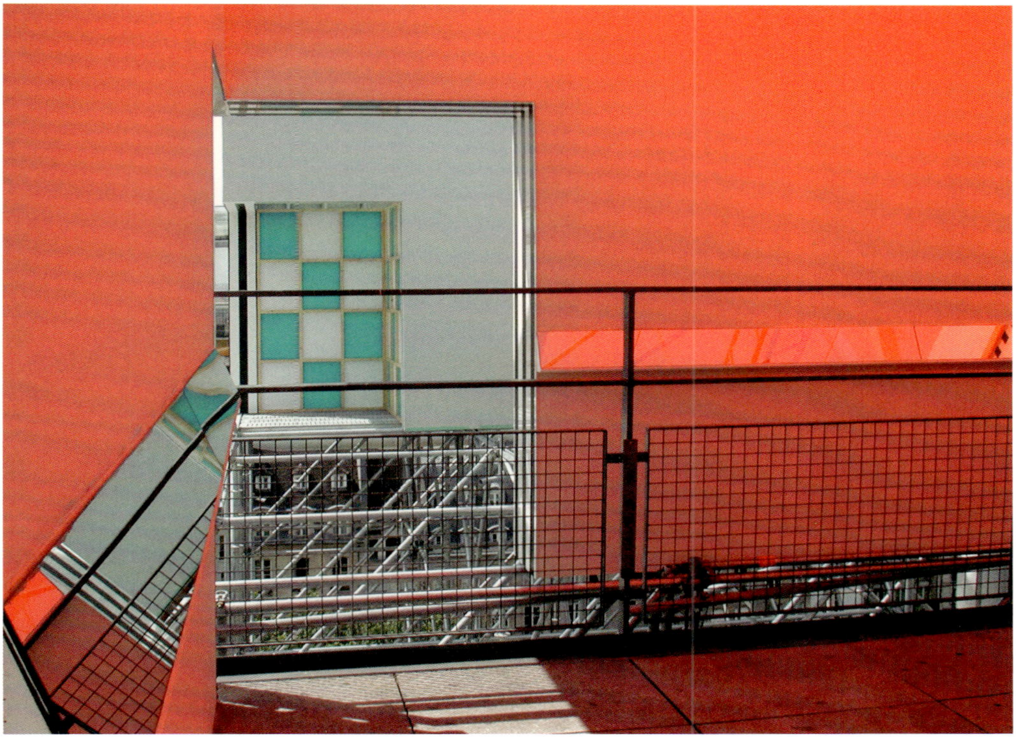

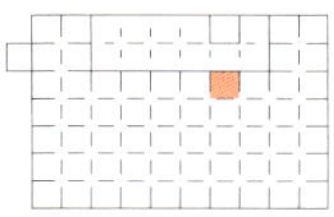

Room 27

Photo-souvenir: "The transparent red roof", work *in situ* (outside)
Coloured awring, self-adhesive vinyl, sheetrock, wood, paint, mirrors, daylight
In the distance, room 7, *The floating island*

All possible variations are developed and unfolded right onto the terraces and above the void soaring over the spaces of the Musée national d'art moderne: the praxis of art is here like a metaphorical balance between sky and earth. *The Floating Island* involves prowess, to such an extent does its construction seem like an improbable construction, resting on scaffolding rising up from the building's lower level. "Le Musée qui n'existait pas" unfurls from one end to the other and cannily finds support from the sculpture terrace of the Musée national d'art moderne, which it occupies for its own requirements. Buren plays with and ignores the space and unfurls his project like origami. He thus presents one of the modules of the exhibition from outside, all the other cells being dovetailed one with the other, while this particular one is only visible from outside and gives a precise idea of the form in question. Unlike all the other cells, *The Floating Island* is also the only one that cannot be reached and penetrated, an image, not to say a ghostlike apparition in the middle of the void it soars over. It is a clue and a sign, like a standard model distinct from all the others. In a way, it is the supreme prototype based on which one can reflect upon the entire arrangement.

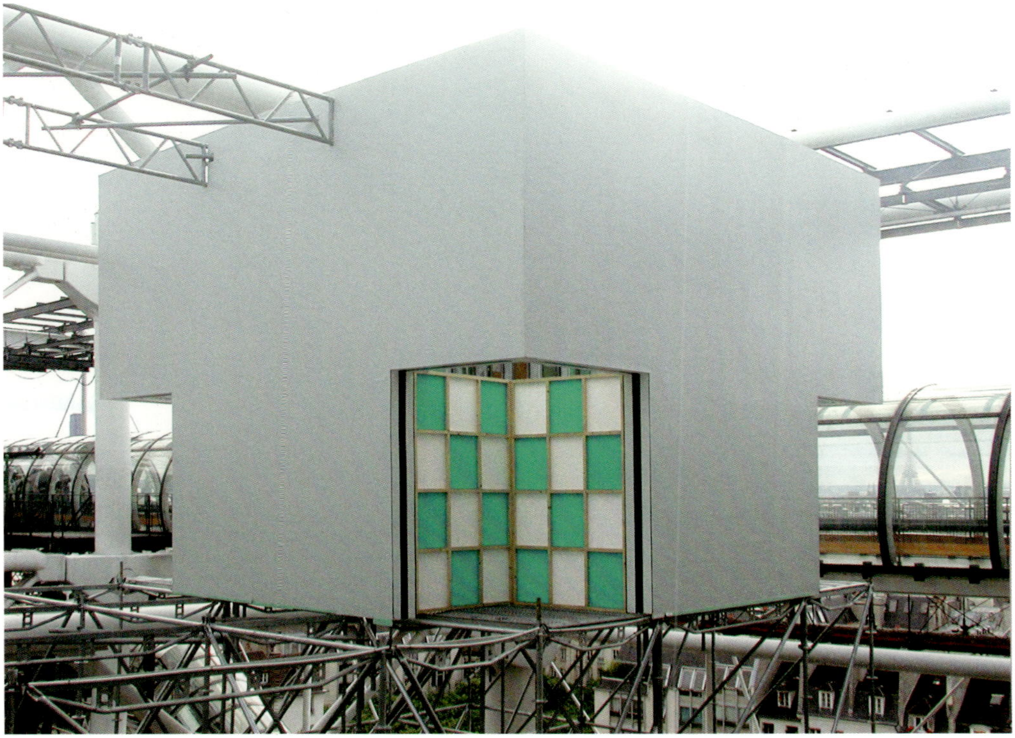

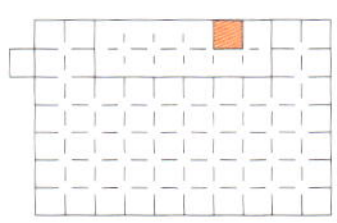

Room 7

Photo-souvenir: "The floating island", work *in situ*, inaccessible (outside)
Sheetrock, metal structure, scaffolding, coloured and white translucent Plexiglas, self-adhesive vinyl, daylight, artificial light

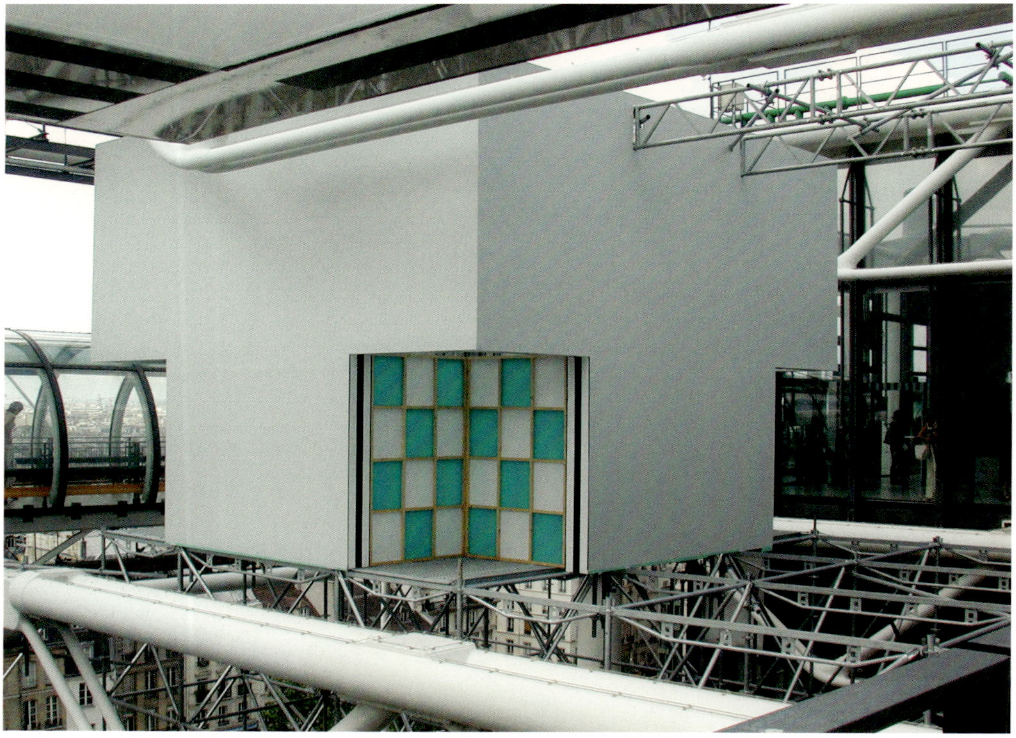

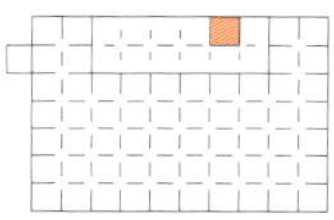

Room 7

Photo-souvenir: "The floating island", work *in situ*, inaccessible (outside)
Sheetrock, metal structure, scaffolding, coloured and white translucent Plexiglas,
self-adhesive vinyl, daylight, artificial light

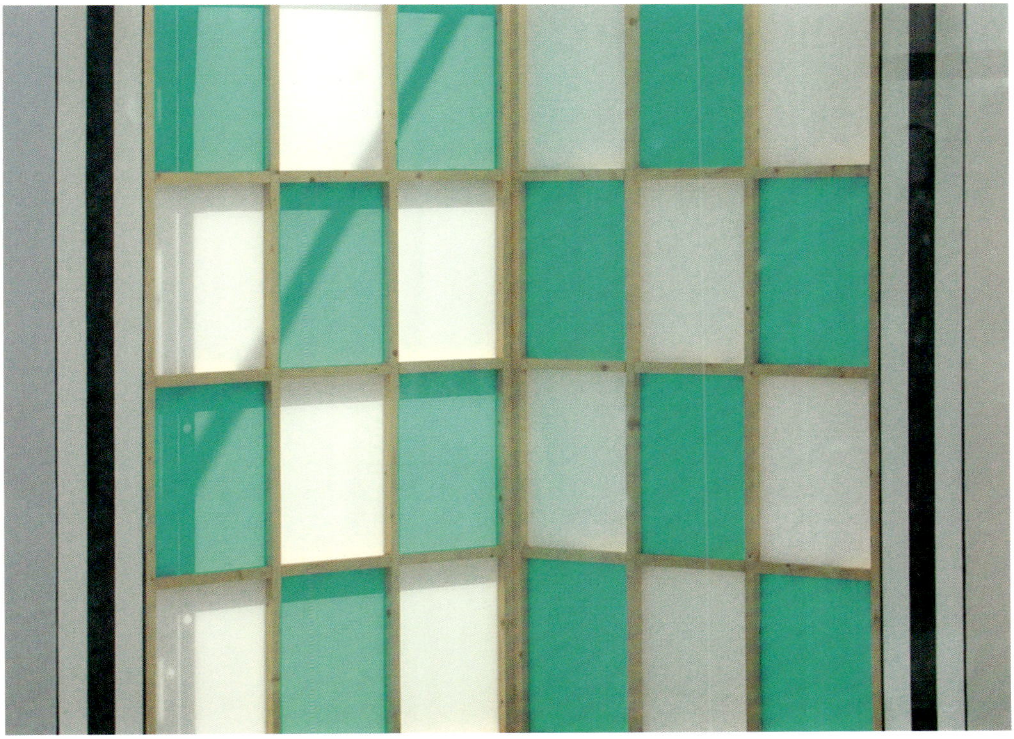

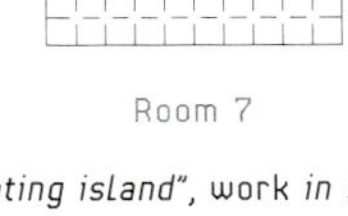

Room 7

Photo-souvenir: "The floating island", work *in situ*, inaccessible (outside)
Sheetrock, metal structure, scaffolding, coloured and white translucent Plexiglas, self-adhesive vinyl, daylight, artificial light

The principle of the portholes punctuating one of the outer walls of one of the arrangements installed on the terraces obviously calls to mind the principle of those ocean liner architectures of the 1930s and can be seen as an ironical quotation at the heart of a building that has often been likened to a vessel. Buren has nevertheless used it for many ideas and works, such as an *in situ* piece produced in Toronto in the early 1980s, among others. These round holes covered with coloured filters are here arranged in a random way, so that they let through beams of light, whose cast shadows are projected onto the different adjacent walls. They act as chromatic punctuations compared with the shadows of the forms and volumes which are traced on the space's white partitions. Buren here gives his imagination free rein and permits himself to depart from the resolutely systematic dimension on which his idea is constructed and built. This time again, the issue of the decorative crops up. Buren asserts it, lays claim to it, and presents it.

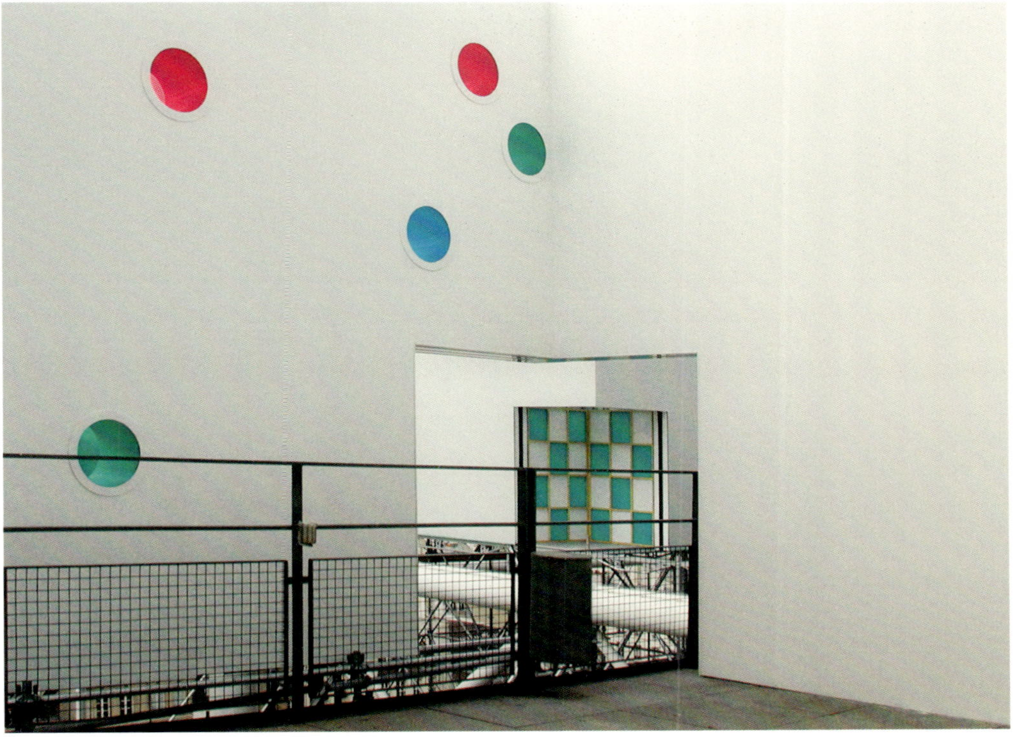

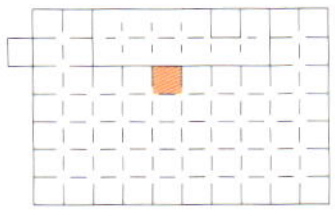

Room 25

Above and on following pages :
Photos-souvenirs: *"Colour projection"*, work *in situ* (outside),
Sheetrock, coloured transparent Plexiglas, paint, daylight
In the distance, room 7, *The floating island*

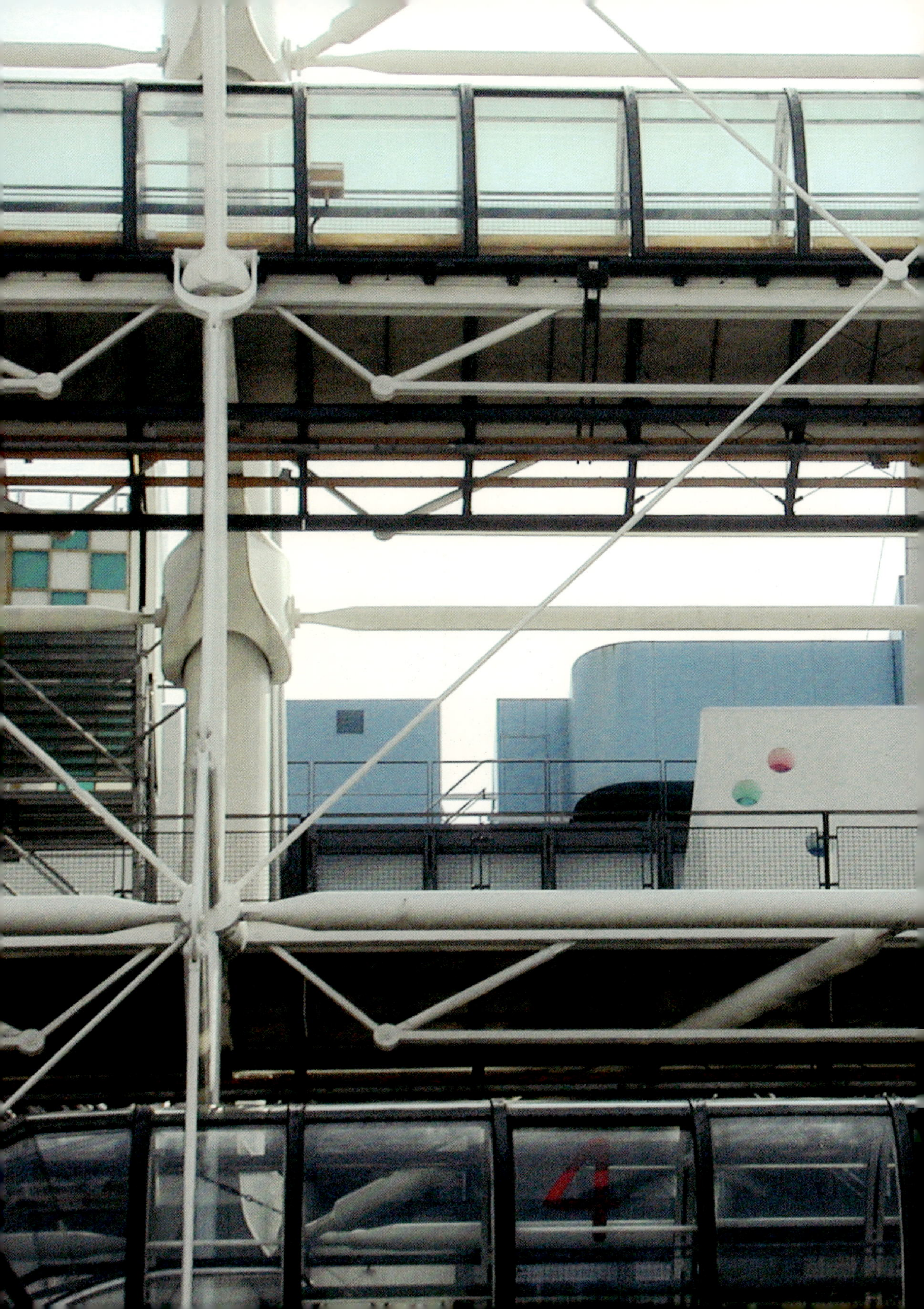
4

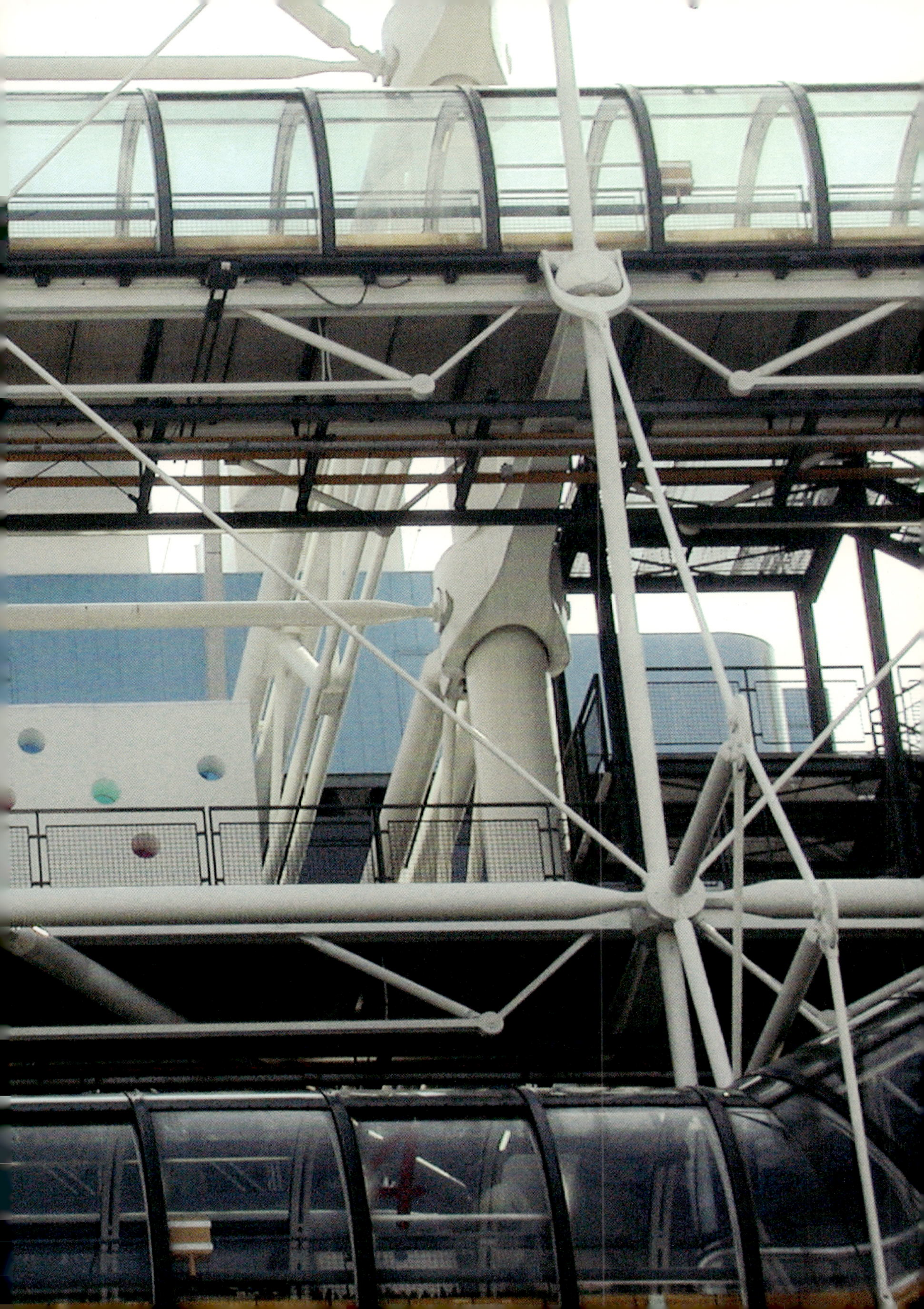

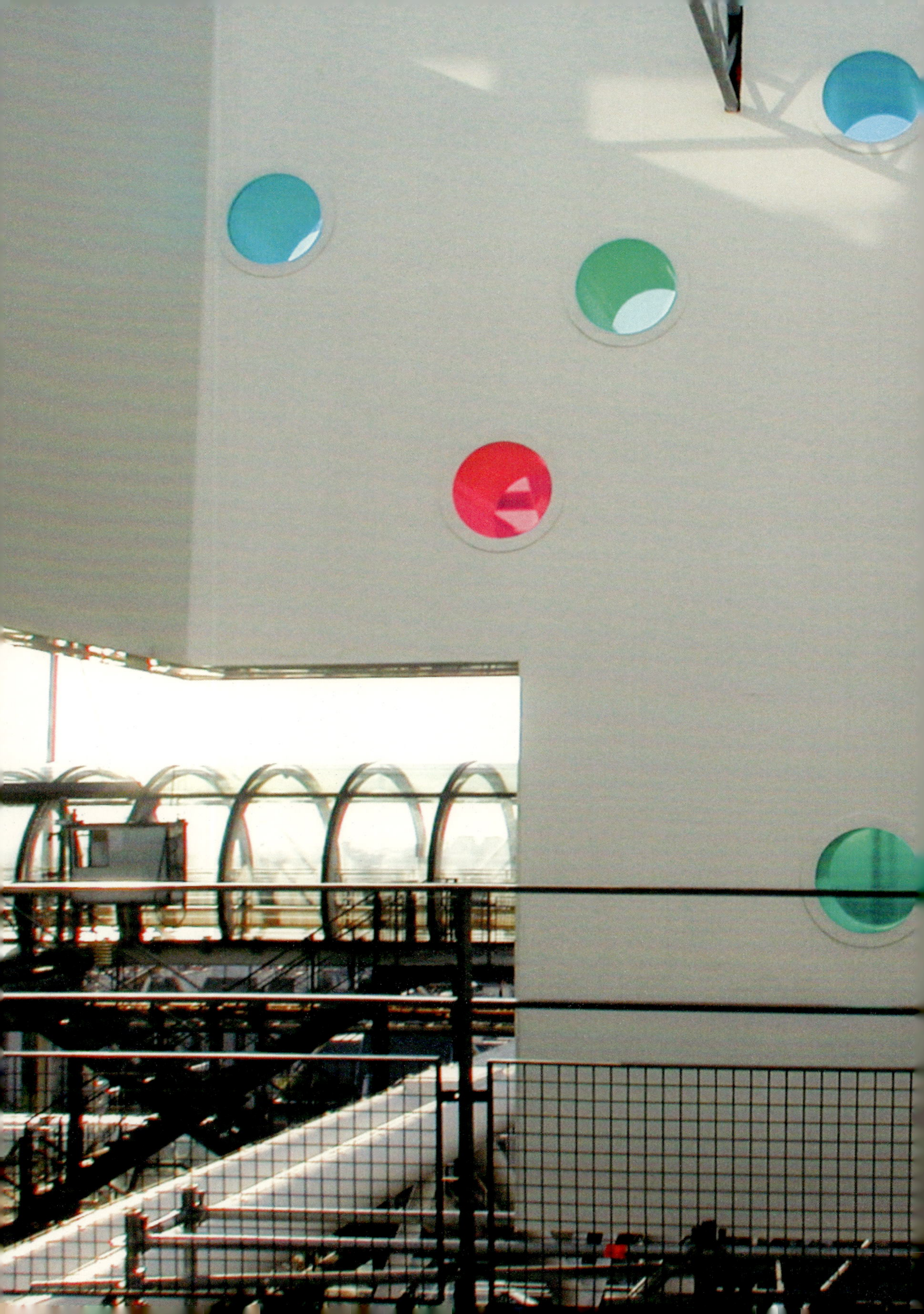

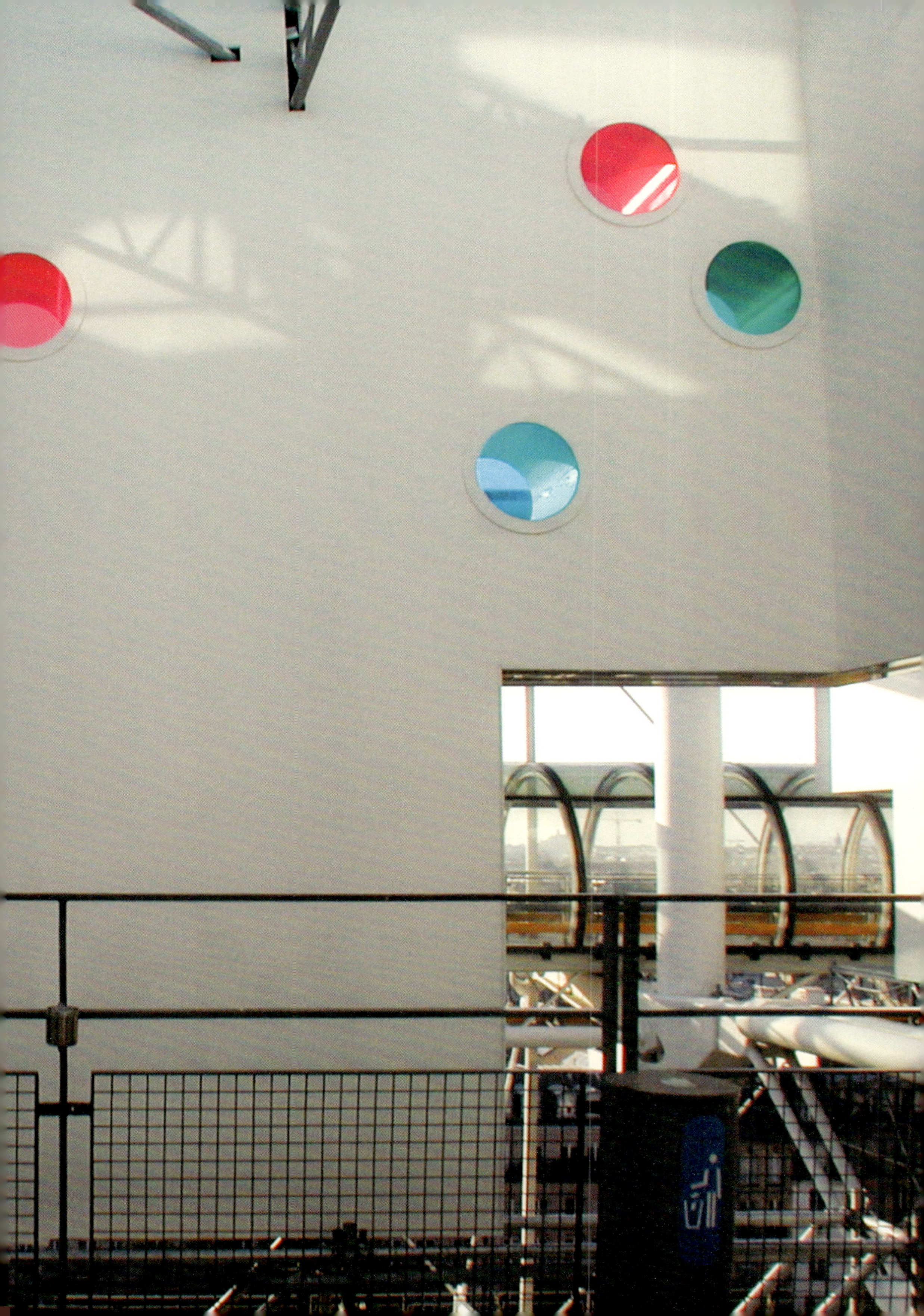

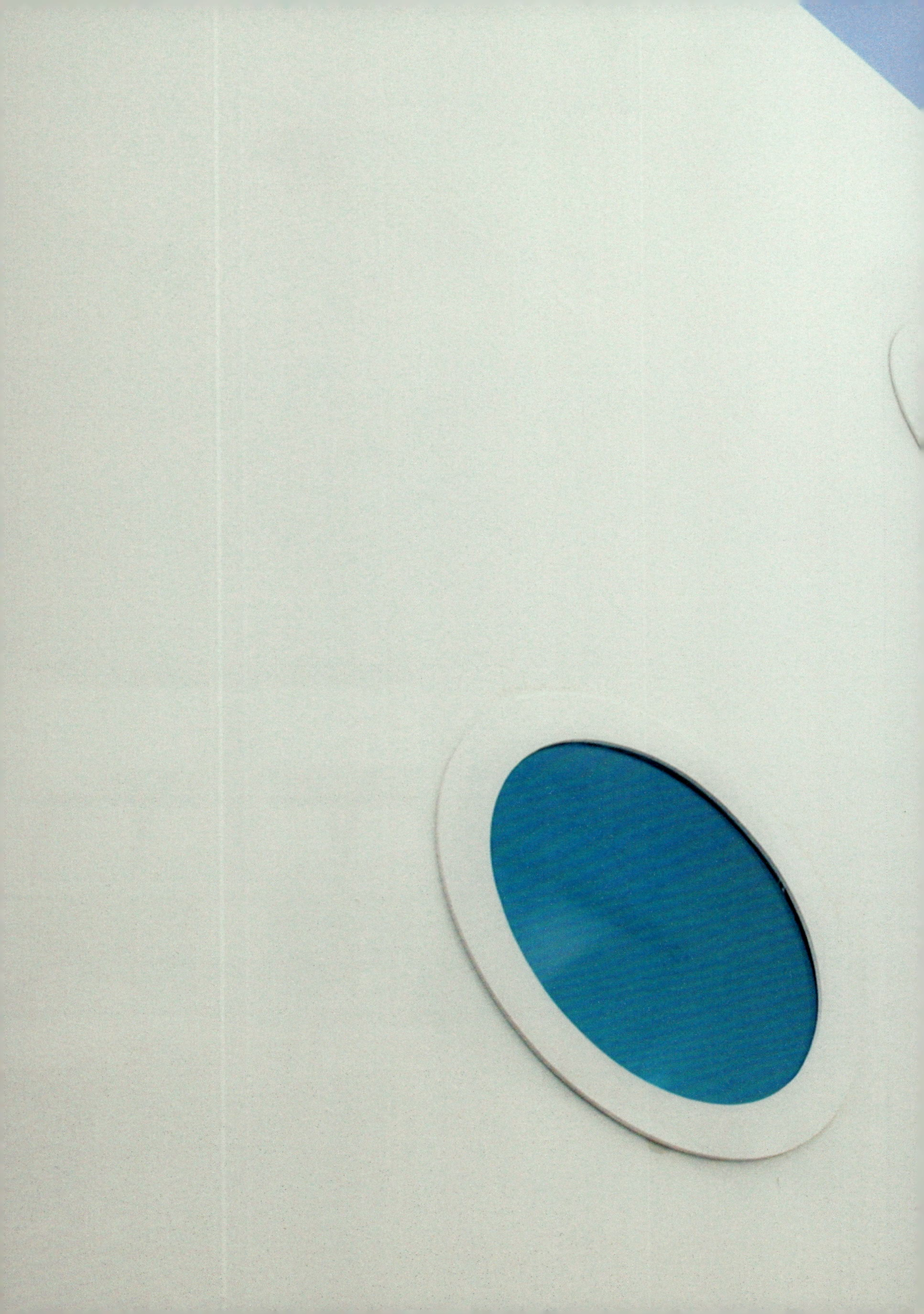

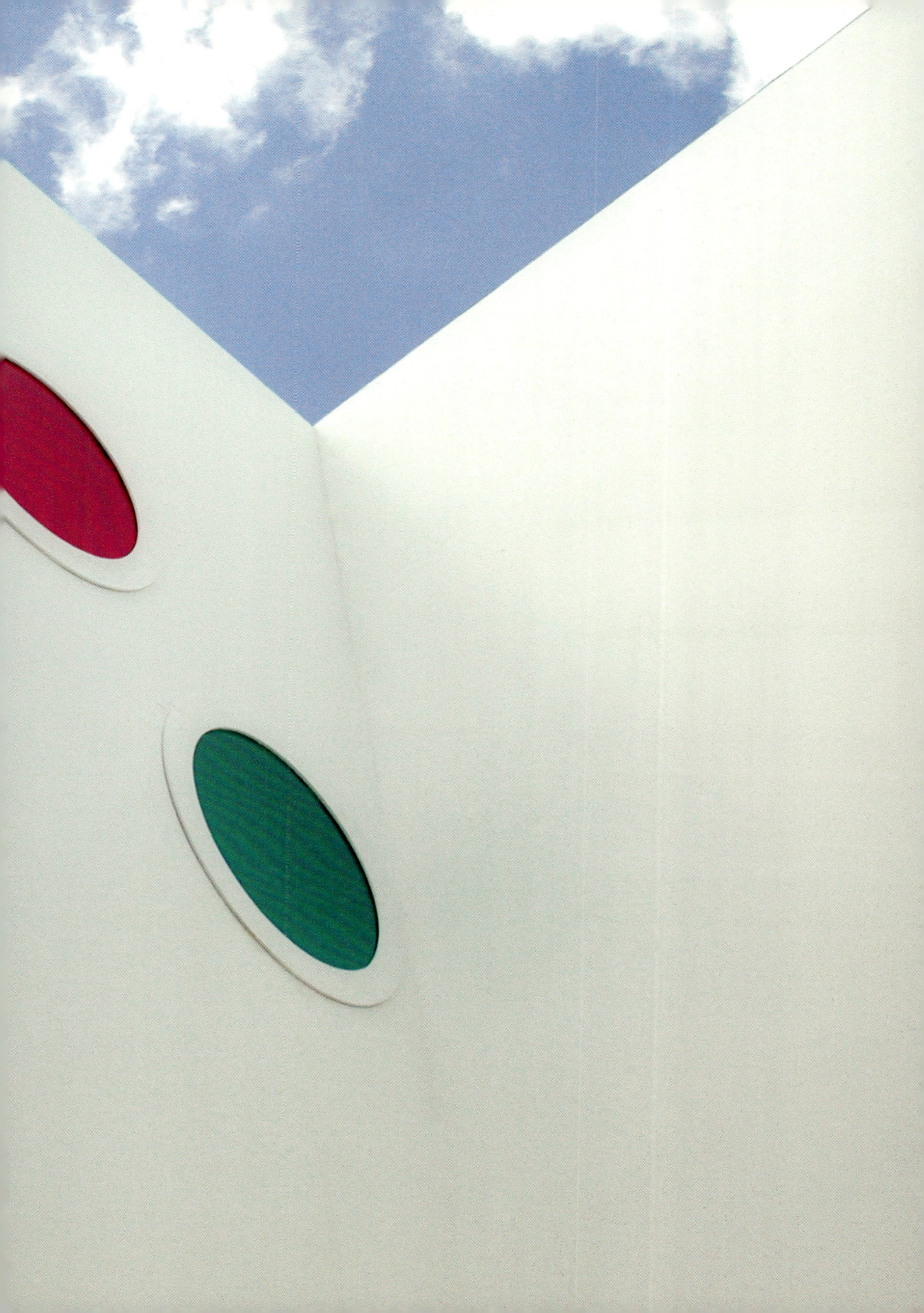

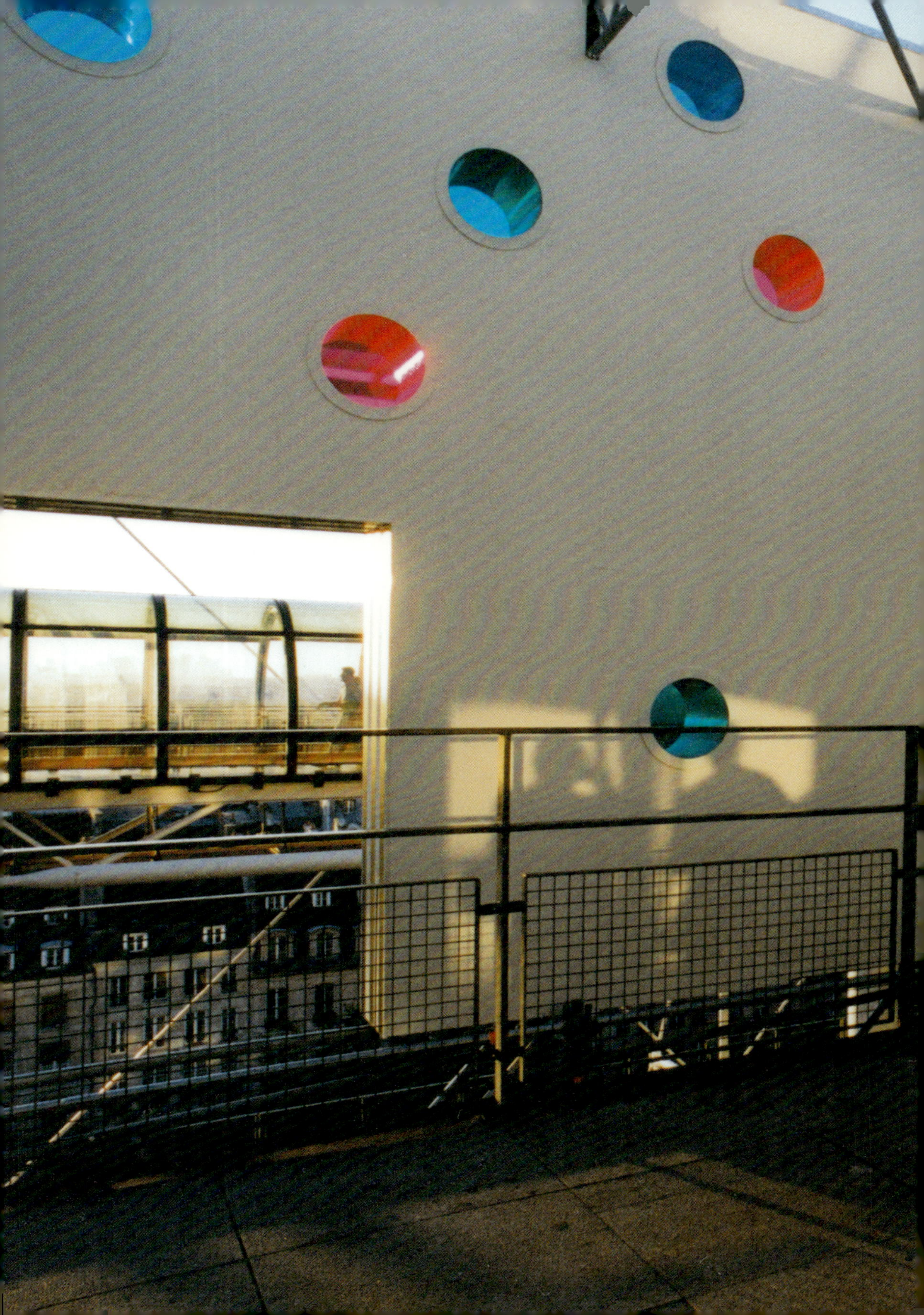

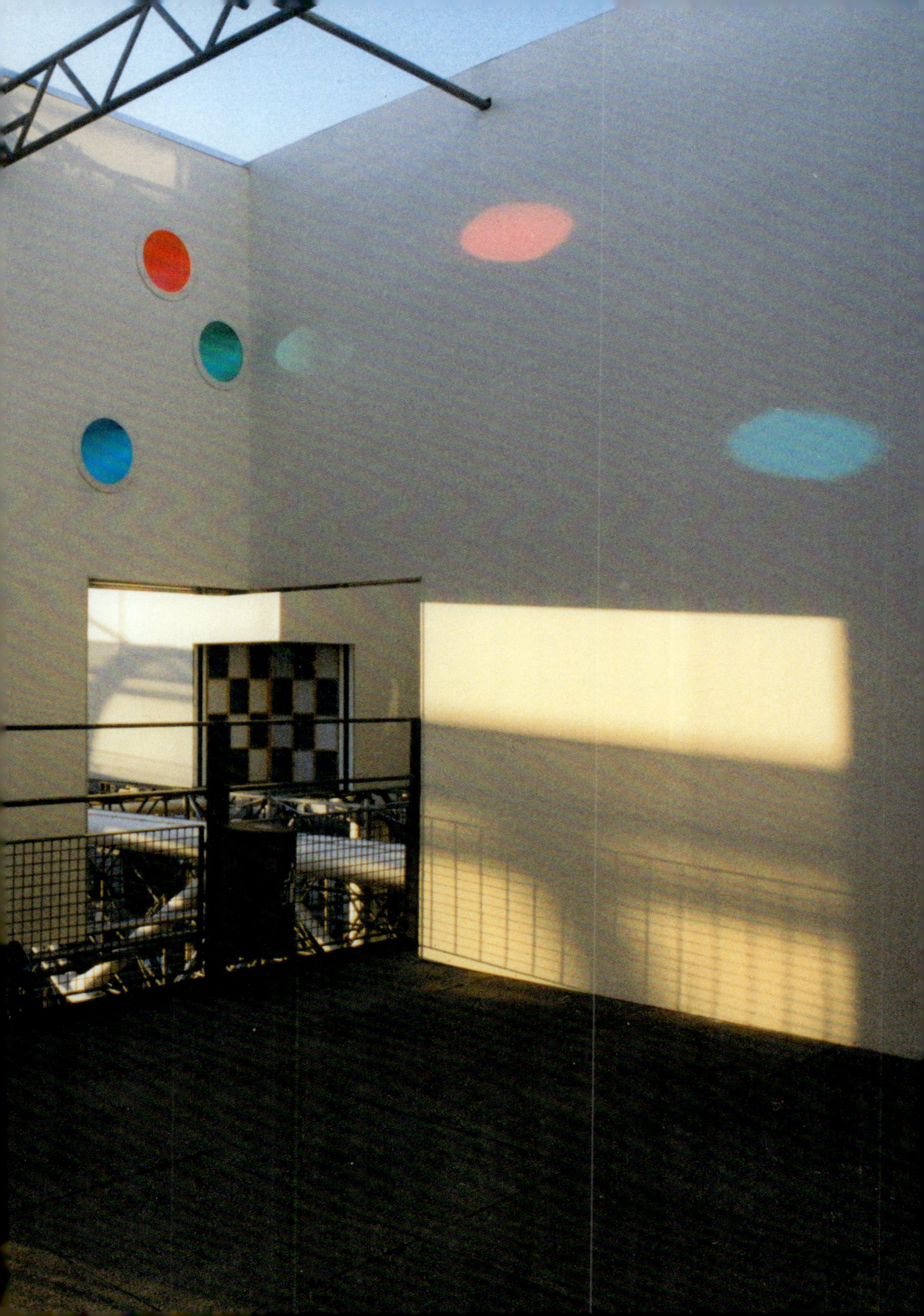

The arrangement is projected outside the exhibition limits and encompasses the public areas of the Centre Pompidou, extending out onto the building's terraces. The deductive principle peculiar to some of Buren's early two-dimensional works here finds its application in a sculptural and spatial mode. This, in a way, is what Buren elsewhere calls "the proposition's internal structure", which is developed, beyond the boundaries drawn for the show, like an implicit critique of his contemporaries' "specific objects".

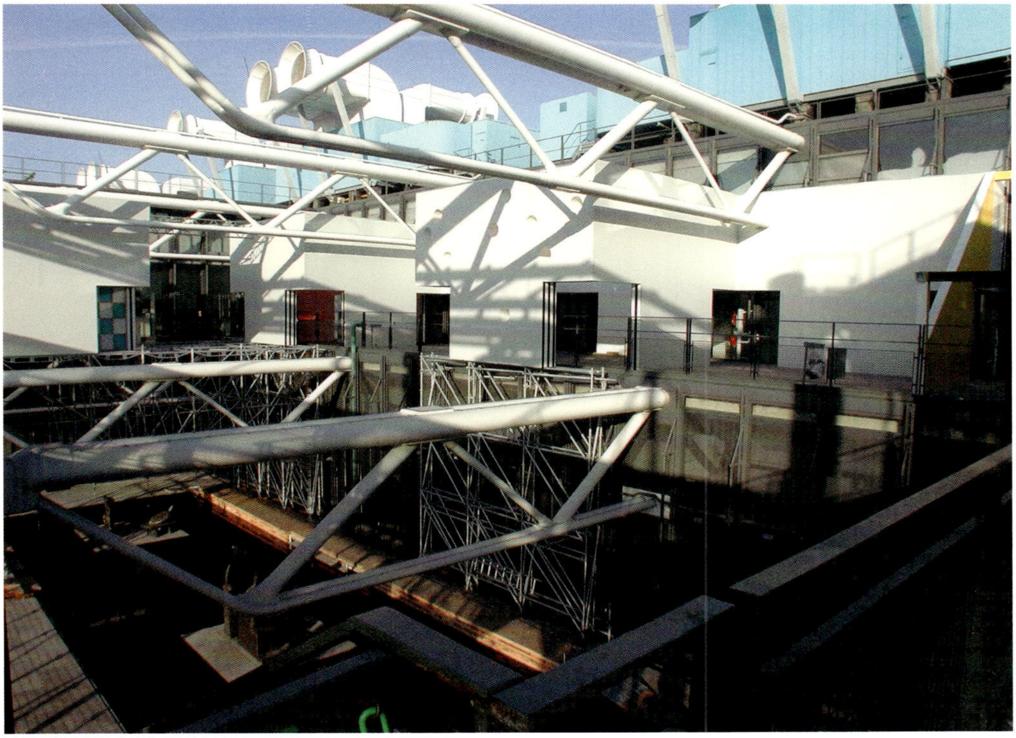

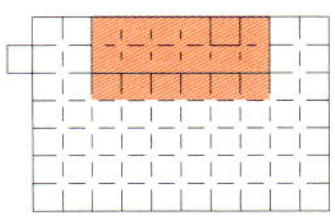

Overall view of the outside arrangement

Photo-souvenir: "The floating island", "The transparent red roof", "Colour projection", "Truncated space", works *in situ* (outside)
View of the area giving onto Level 5 from room 3

"Le Musée qui n'existait pas" is conceived as a decidedly open space, aimed at unfolding its forms beyond the usual limits allocated to shows on the Centre Pompidou's level 6. A veritable spatial and mental projection, it is constructed like a deductive system, thus spreading with a twofold movement from the inside out and vice versa. The succession of spaces it gives rise to actually breaks up on the building's terraces, playing both on the linearity and the obliqueness of the lines treated like vanishing points. The volumes "fade away" until they are no longer delimited by edges and corner posts. Buren's art is a succession of propositions and variations based on a plastic vocabulary which he pushes as far as he possibly can.
The different "photos-souvenirs" of *Truncated Space* highlight the cut of the space of the oblique line proposed by Buren. Like a polychrome sculpture, no less, the whole thing is here dealt with in a resolutely "deconstructivist" mode and draws the space, like so many lines of force echoing the nature of the place. He urges us to stroll about and multiplies the viewpoints, until he establishes a continuous resonance between closed space and open space, between the building and the city around it.

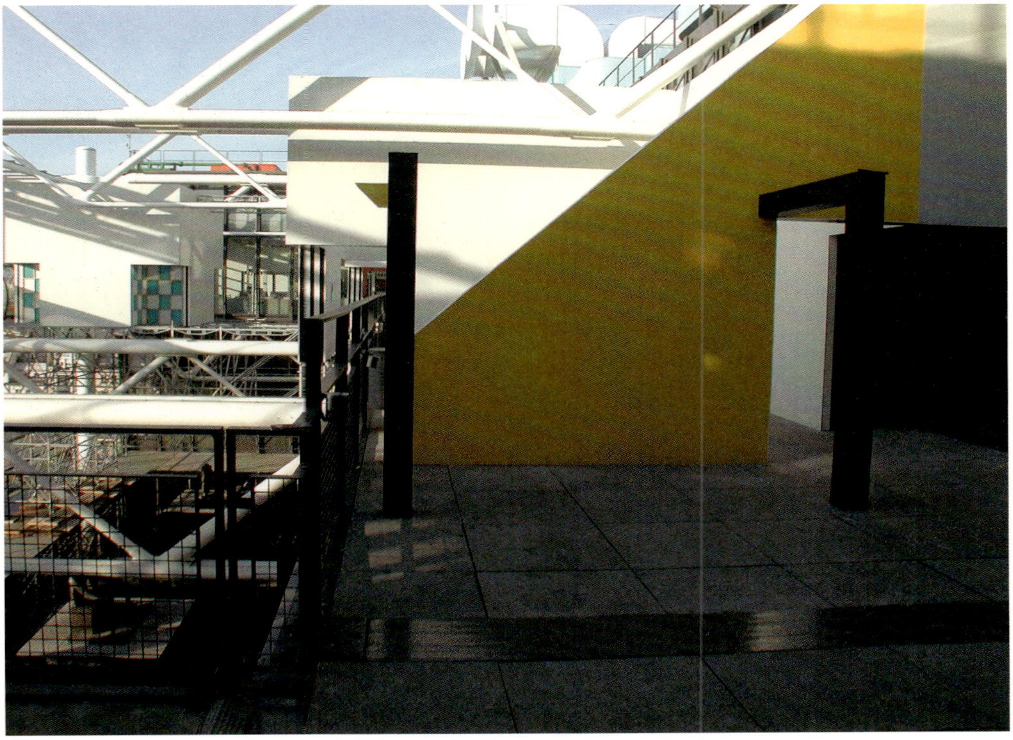

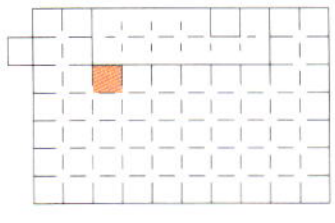

Room 23

Photo-souvenir: "Truncated space", work *in situ* (outside)
Sheetrock, one colour, metal structures, daylight
In the distance, room 7, *The floating island*

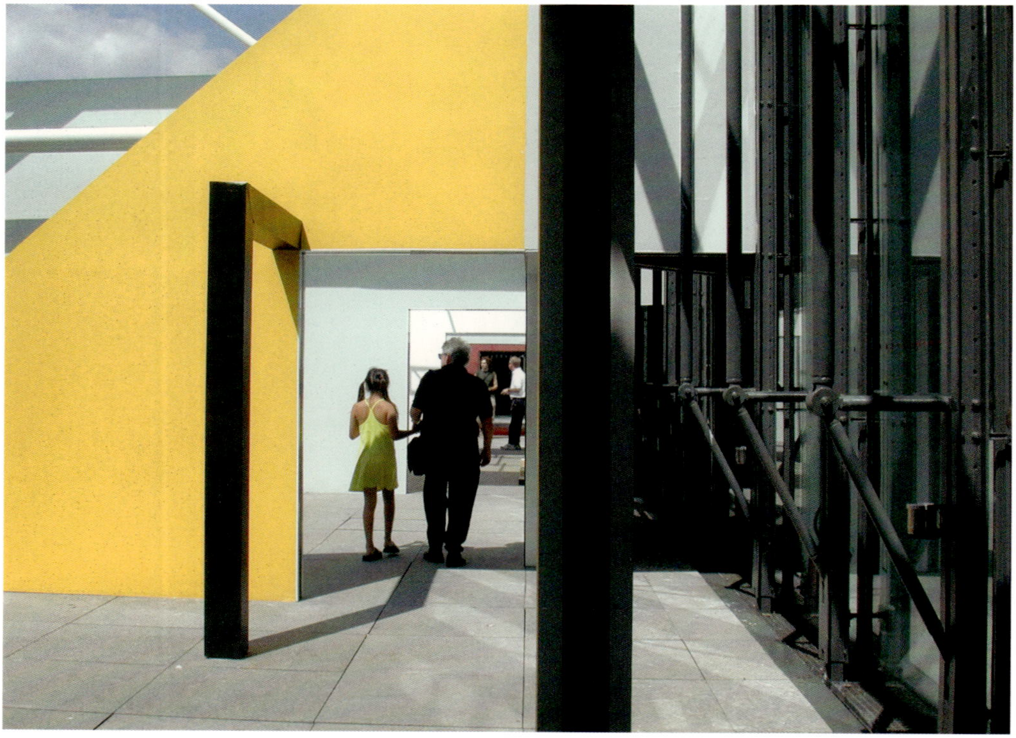

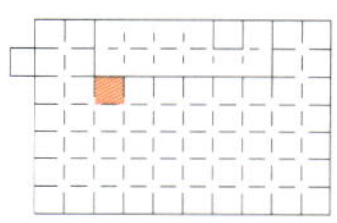

Room 23

Photo-souvenir: "Truncated space", work *in situ* (outside)
Sheetrock, one colour, metal structures, daylight
Adjoining, rooms 24 to 28

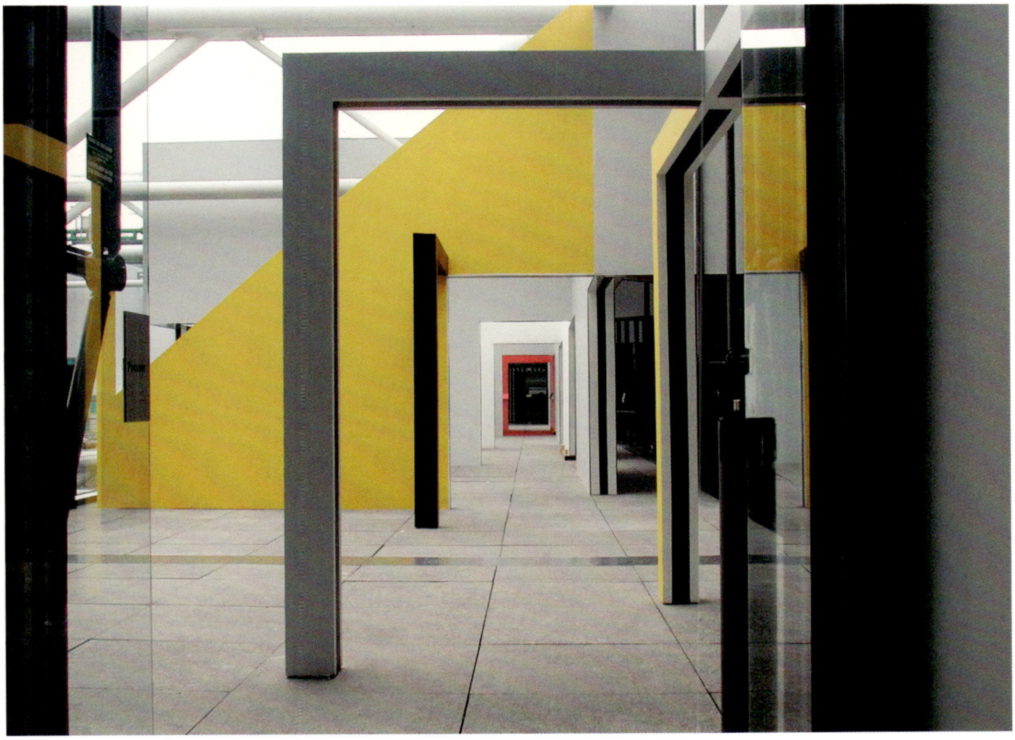

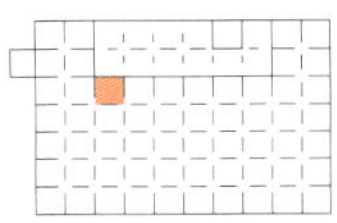

Room 23

Photo-souvenir: "Truncated space", work *in situ* (outside)
Sheetrock, one colour, metal structures, daylight
View from room 22, *The framework of the rooms*
Adjoining, rooms 24 to 28

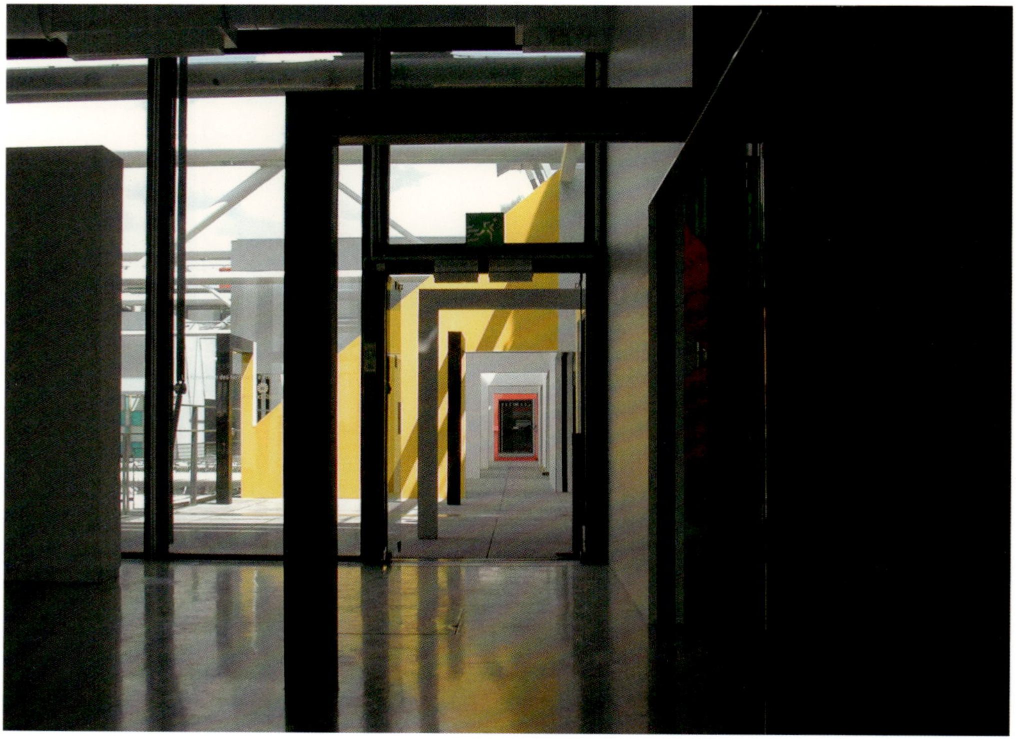

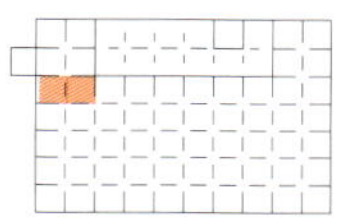

Rooms 21 and 22

Photo-souvenir: "The framework of the rooms", work in situ
Metal structures, sheetrock, self-adhesive vinyl, paint, glass, steel, chairs and tables
Adjoining, rooms 23 to 28

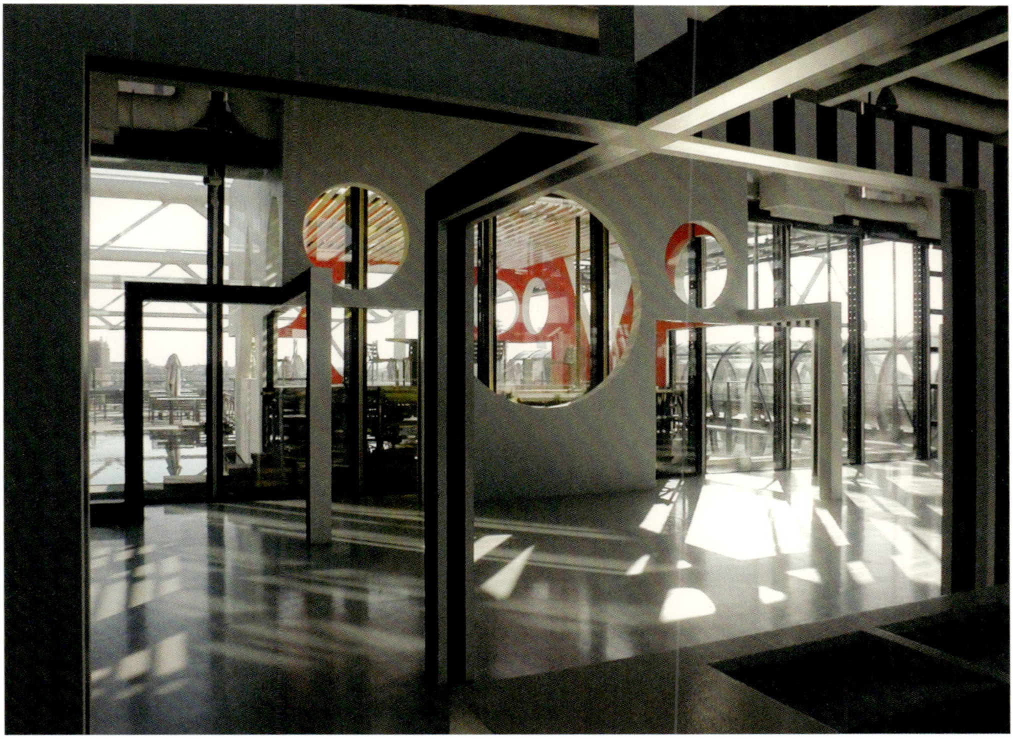

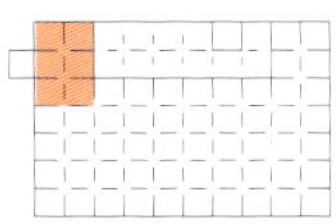

Rooms 1, 2, 19, 20, 21 and 22

Above and on following pages :
Fhotos-souvenirs: "The framework of the rooms", work *in situ*
Metal structures, sheetrock, self-adhesive vinyl, paint, glass, steel, chairs and tables
Opposite, room 71, *The dining room*

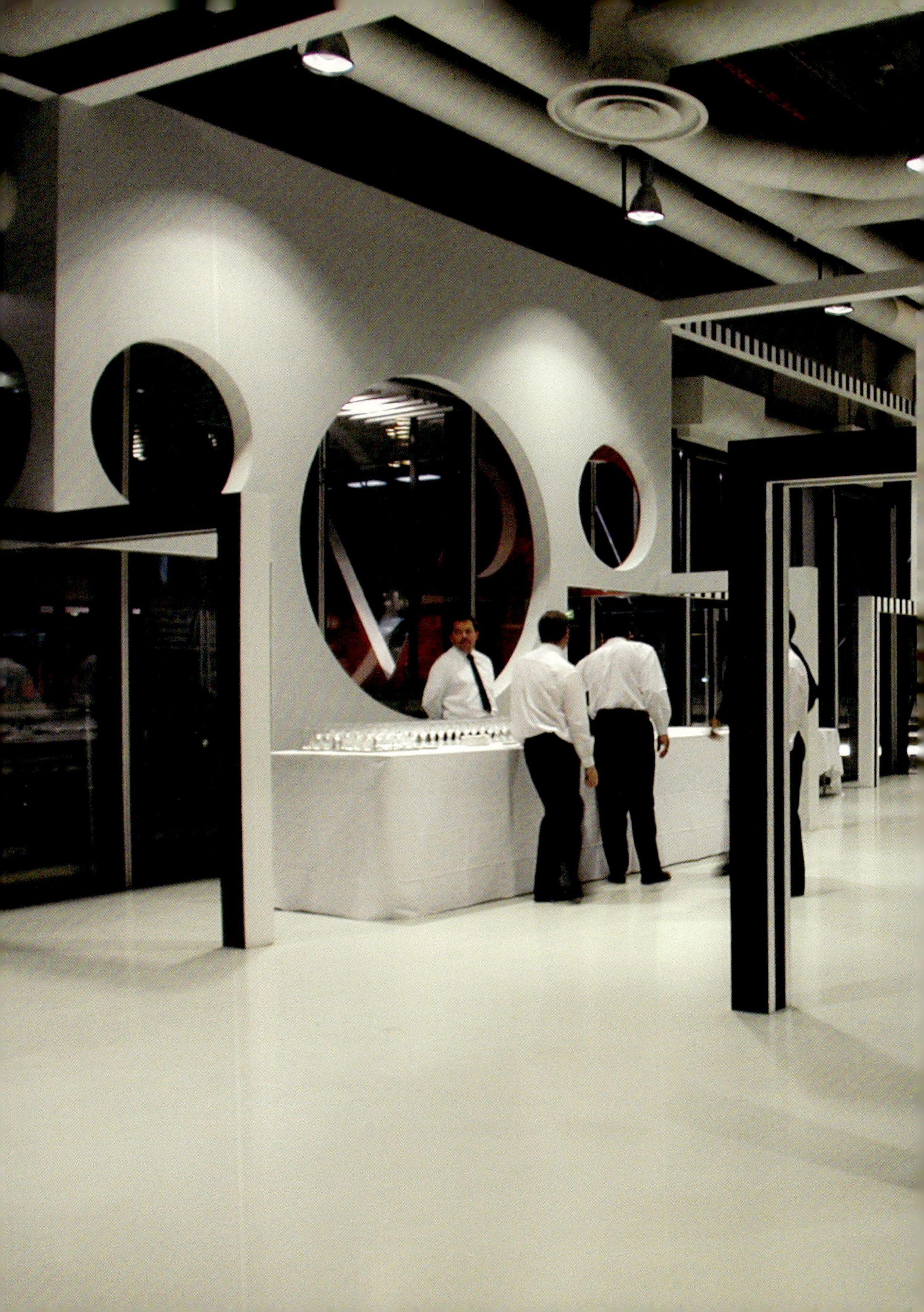

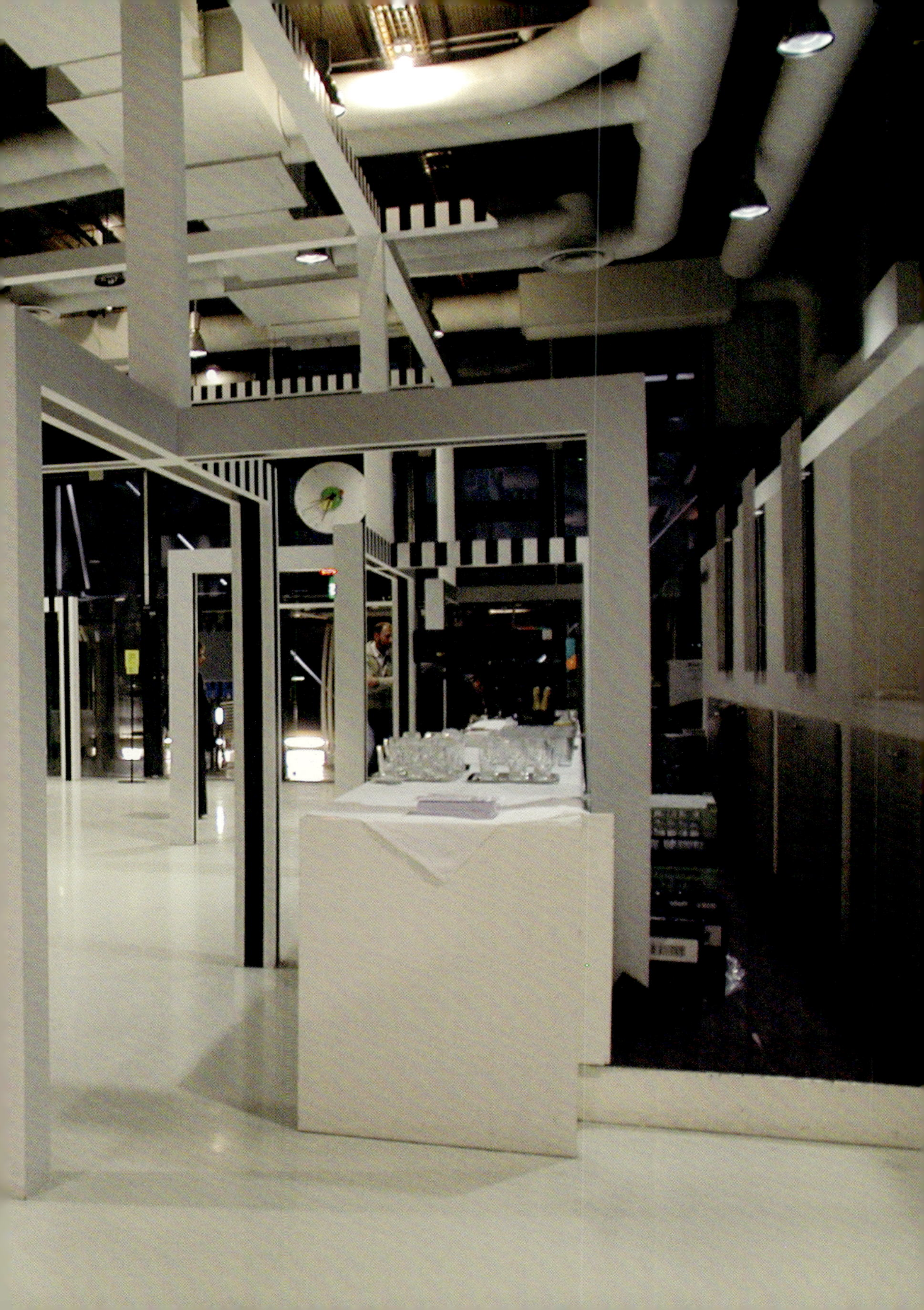

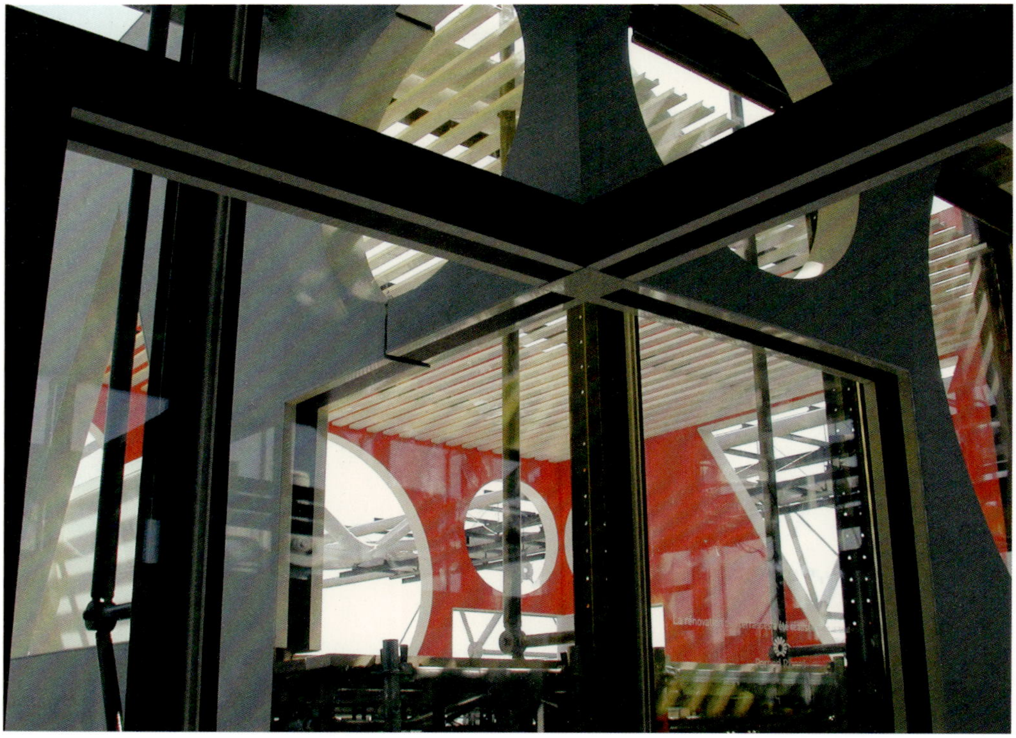

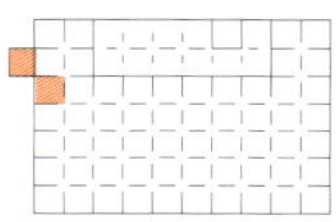

Rooms 21 and 71

Photo-souvenir: "The framework of the rooms", "The dining room", works *in situ*
Metal structures, sheetrock, self-adhesive vinyl, paint, glass, steel, chairs and tables
Metal structure, scaffolding, paint, transparent Plexiglas, water, steel, horizontal claustra, table (specially designed by Daniel Buren), chairs, stairs, daylight, candles at night

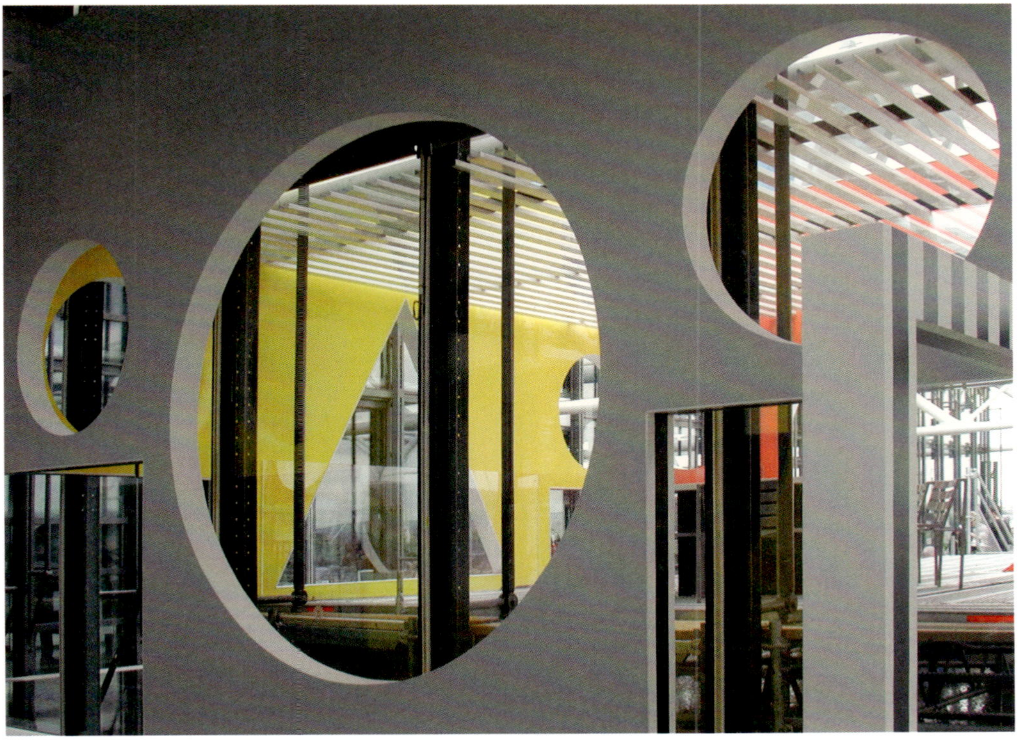

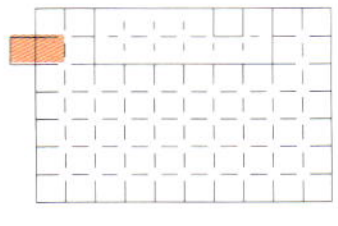

Rooms 20 and 71

Photo-souvenir: *"The framework of the rooms"*, *"The dining room"*, works *in situ*
Metal structures sheetrock, self-adhesive vinyl, paint, glass, steel, chairs and tables
Metal structure, scaffolding, paint, transparent Plexiglas, water, steel, horizontal claustra, table (specially designed by Daniel Buren), chairs, stairs, daylight, candles at night

The projection of the volumes leads Buren to invent a polychrome cell soaring over the pond at the Restaurant Georges, located on level 6 to the south of the building. The space is like a living room in the lee of the terrace opening onto the city. The oculi which form it call to mind the round and triangular cut-outs of some of Buren's works, obviously including those made to act as viewpoints for the Ushimado festival in Japan, in 1985. They "frame" the surrounding landscape. Buren emphasizes that the Japanese, whose culture and forms have greatly influenced his own work, talk for their part of "borrowing the landscape". It was worth noting, incidentally, that the striped strips are only included here thanks to the shadows cast by the "ceiling", a sort of pierced slab made of alternating bars set apart by a void and projecting onto the walls, the floor and the object (here, the table) of the actual cell.

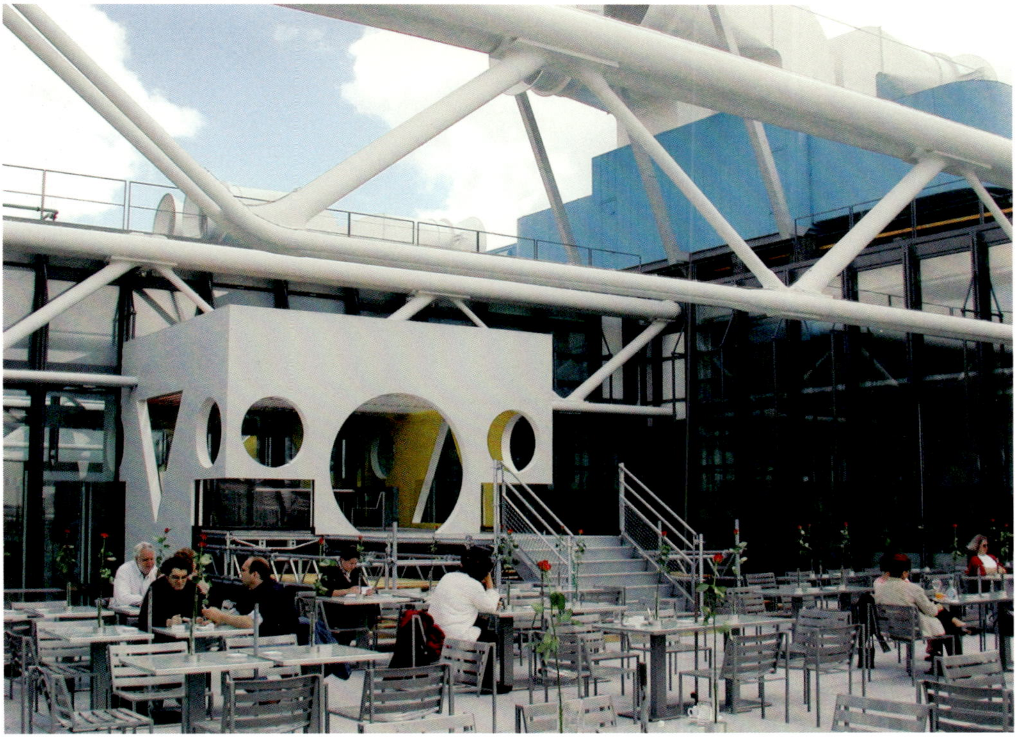

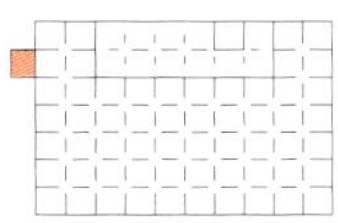

Room 71

Photo-souvenir: "The dining room", work in situ
Metal structure, scaffolding, paint, transparent Plexiglas, water, steel, horizontal claustra, table (specially designed by Daniel Buren), chairs, stairs, daylight, candles at night
View from the Restaurant Georges

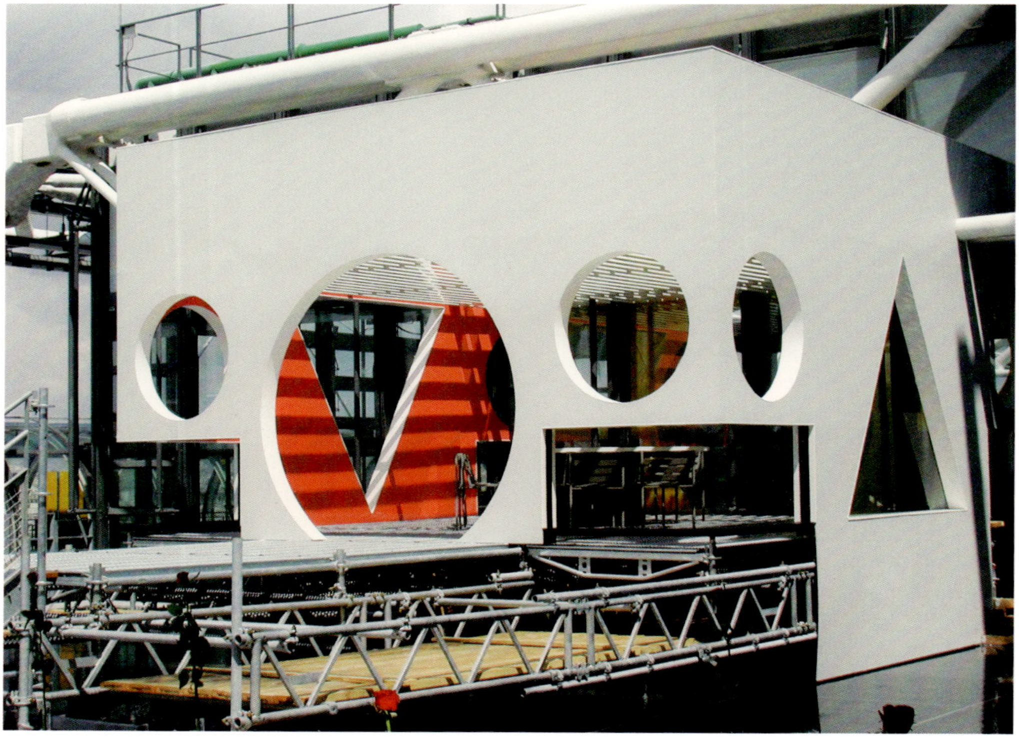

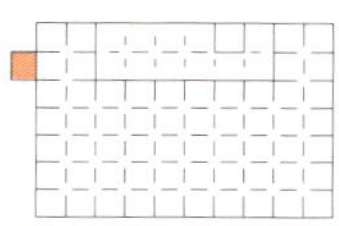

Room 71

Photo-souvenir: "The dining room", work in situ
Metal structure, scaffolding, paint, transparent Plexiglas, water, steel, horizontal claustra, table (specially designed by Daniel Buren), chairs, stairs, daylight, candles at night

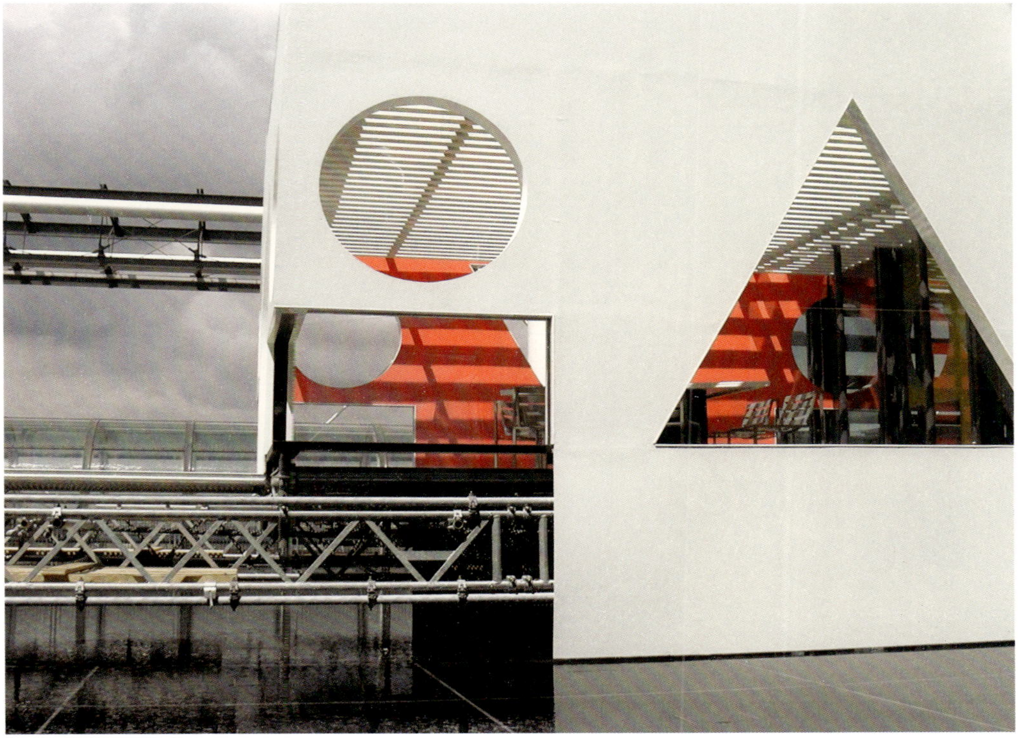

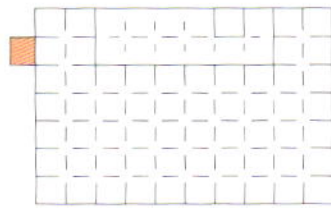

Room 71

Photo-souvenir: "The dining room", work in situ
Metal structure, scaffolding, paint, transparent Plexiglas, water, steel, horizontal claustra, table (specially designed by Daniel Buren), chairs, stairs, daylight, candles at night

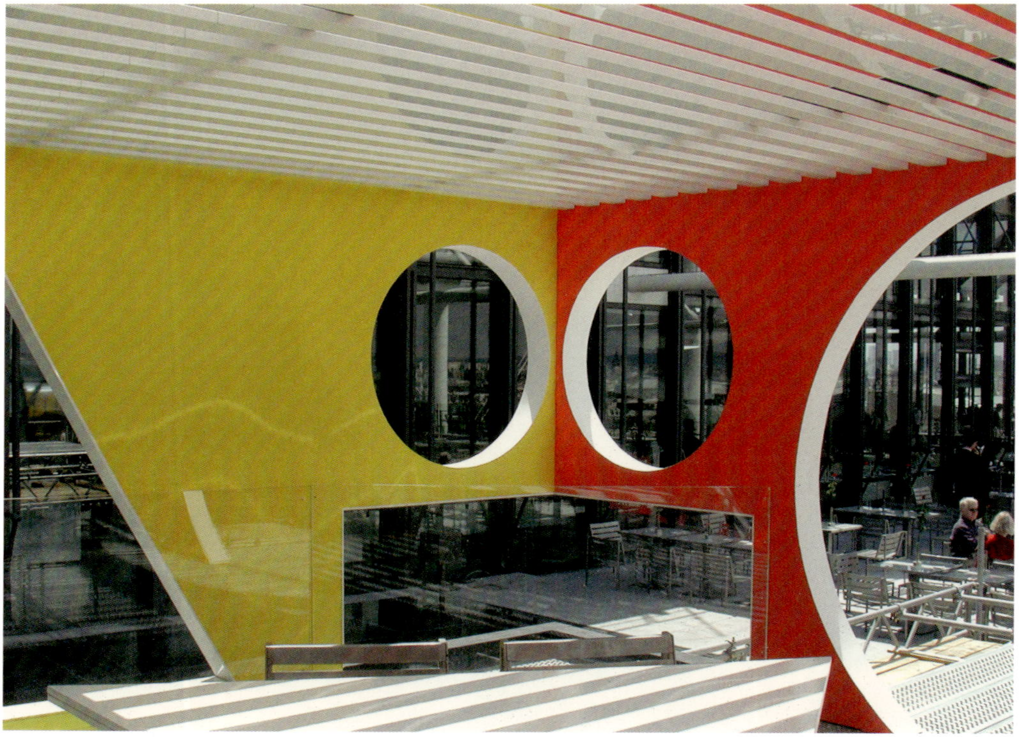

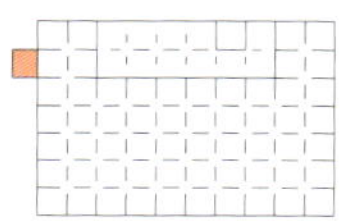

Room 71

Photo-souvenir: "The dining room", work *in situ*
Metal structure, scaffolding, paint, transparent Plexiglas, water, steel, horizontal claustra, table (specially designed by Daniel Buren), chairs, stairs, daylight, candles at night

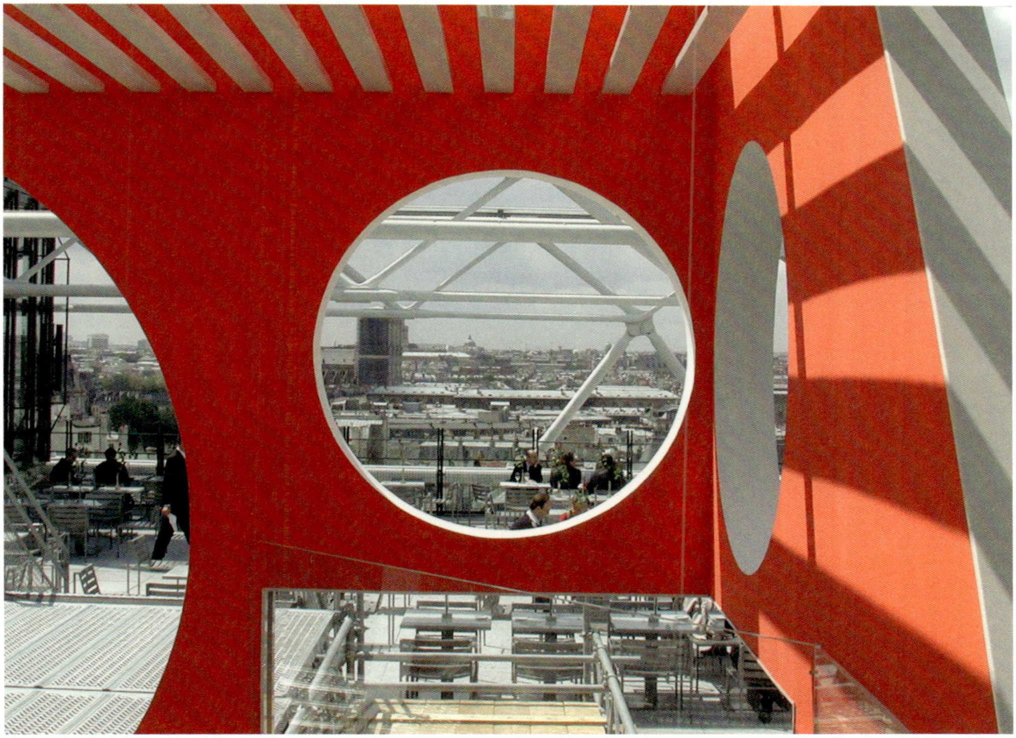

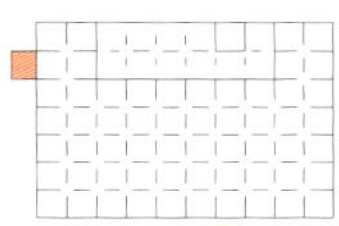

Room 71

Above and on following pages :
Photos-souvenirs: "The dining room", work *in situ*
Metal structure, scaffolding, paint, transparent Plexiglas, water, steel, horizontale claustra, table (specielly designed by Daniel Buren), chairs, stairs, daylight, candles at night

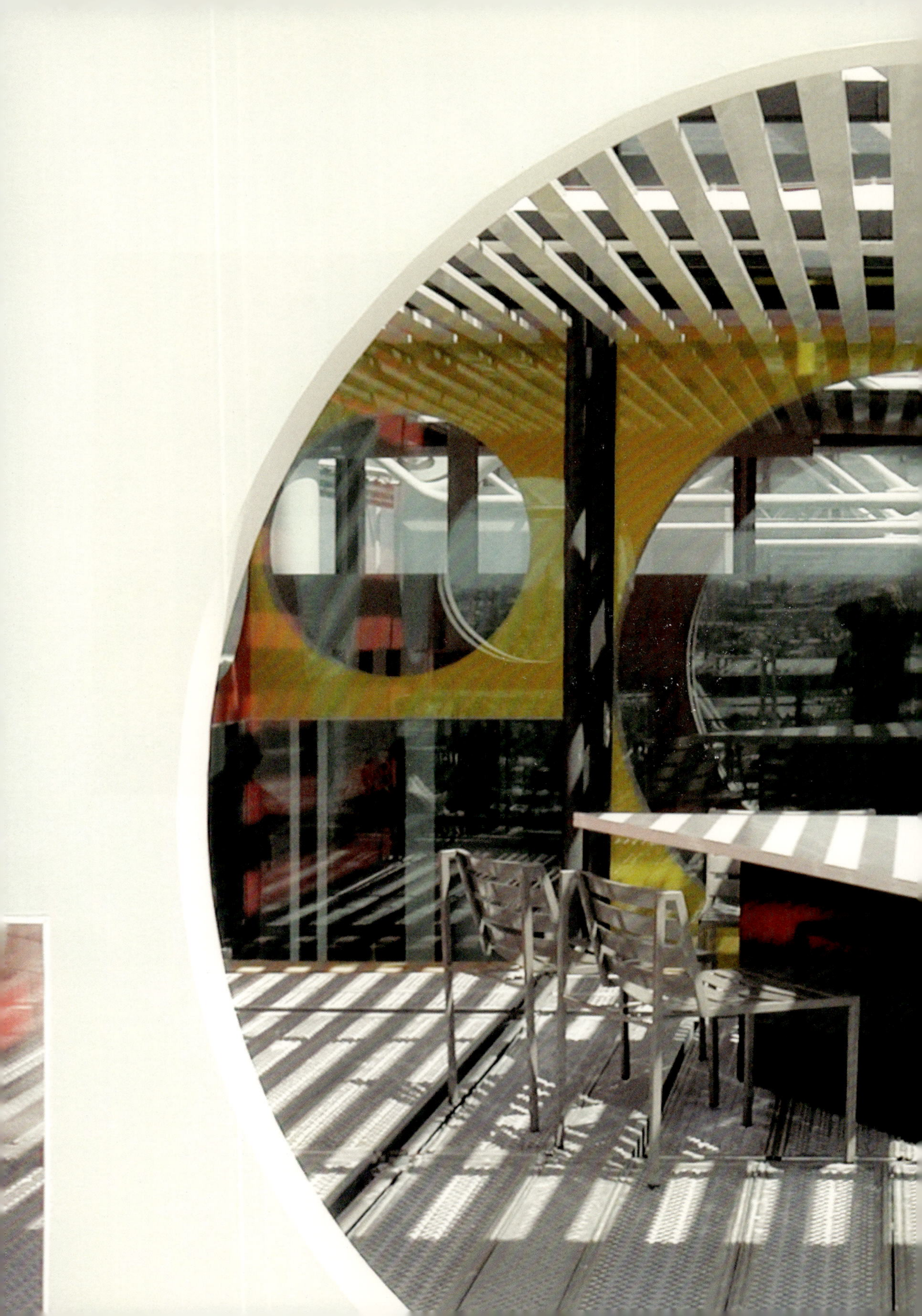

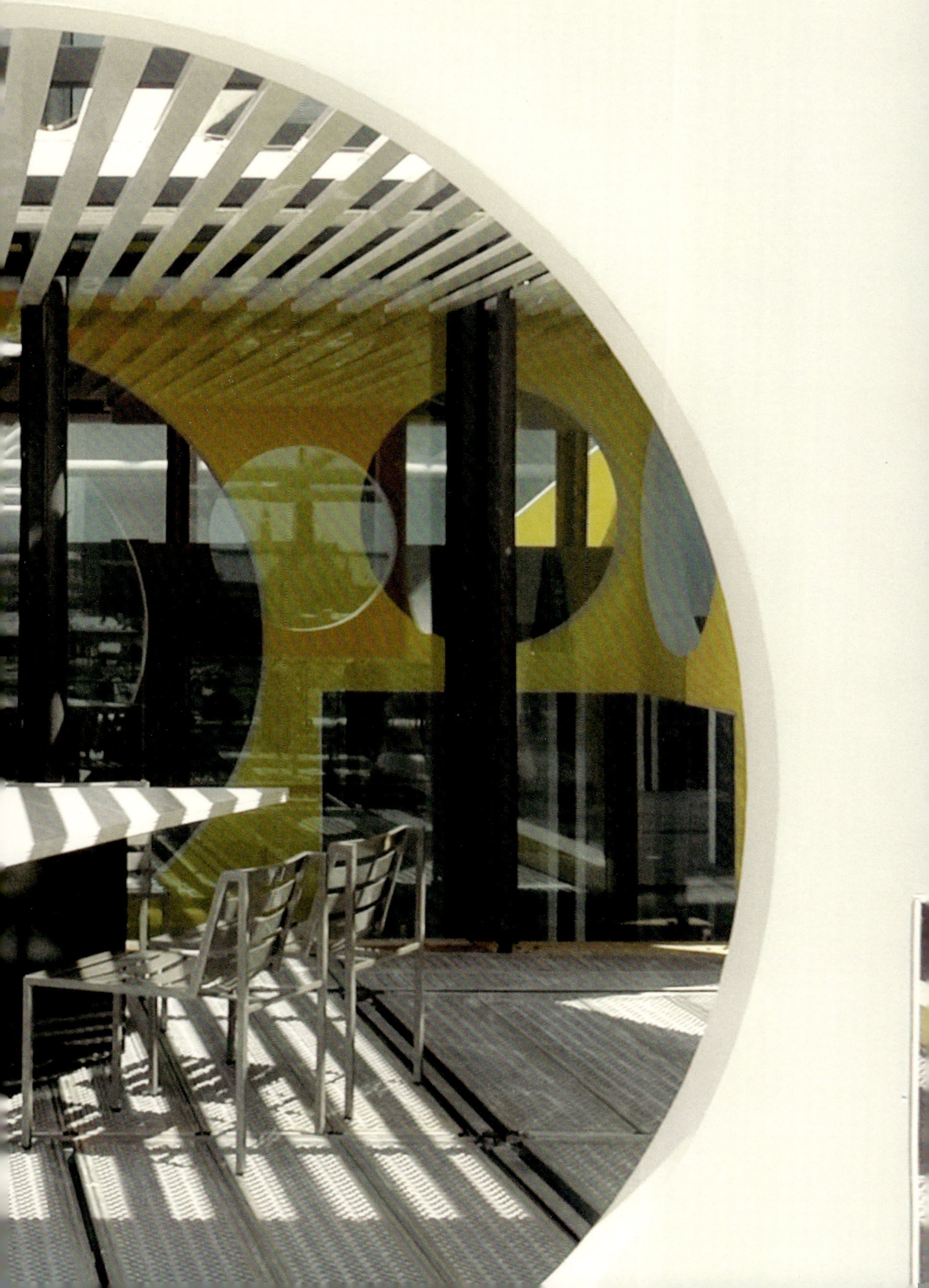

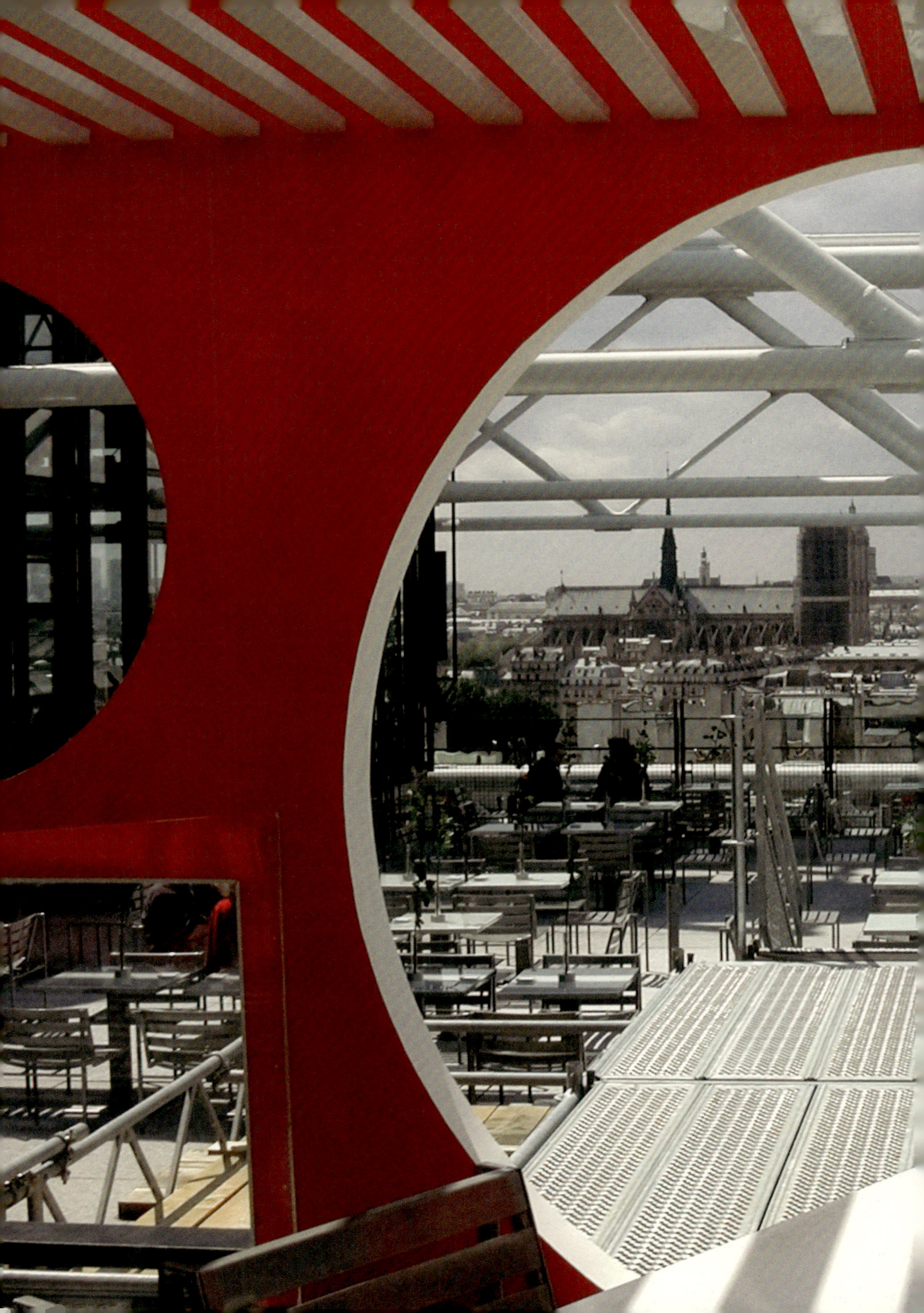

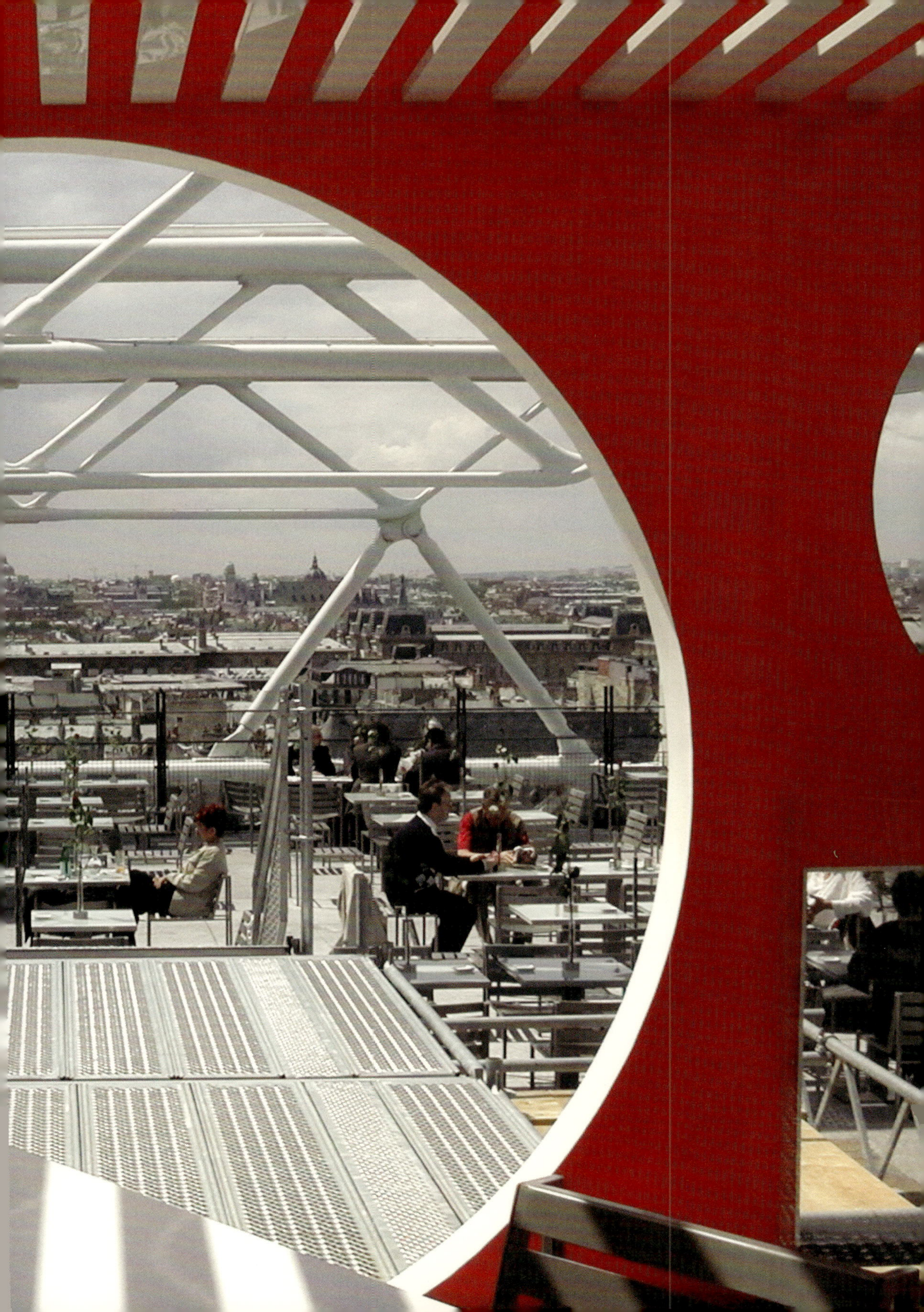

A sequence of "photos-souvenirs" records the re-installation, for the exhibition "Le Musée qui n'existait pas", of the piece acquired by the Musée national d'art moderne in 1977, a piece made up of two distinct procedures titled *The Forms: paintings* and *The Colours: sculptures*, one of which was presented inside the museum areas while the other could be seen from telescopes which had to be installed in the passageway of the Centre Pompidou's level 6. The piece forms an essential milestone in the artist's œuvre because it dialecticises the principle of the exhibition between the building's interior and exterior. It proposes a critical reversal of the ready-made principle, since the work is no longer visible in the place, but from the place. It thus exhibits the painting in the city and temporarily takes possession of emblematic and symbolic spaces: Buren's art takes place in places of power and hoists its colours over the city's roofs. It becomes heraldic. From the challenge of a work acquired in a place where it exists without being there, Buren rolls up the problem by placing the work as far as the eye can see and well removed from the person possessing it. We may recall here what was said by Jean-Hubert Martin, then curator and instigator of this acquisition: "Looking with the telescope for distant flags, barely visible to the naked eye, entails a game based on fundamental notions for painting, such as perspective and composition. The variety of colours, five in all, precludes likening them to a sign of explicit recognition, but on the contrary there is a series of questions raised about their meaning: artistic? political? advertisement-related? playful?" It is said that in 1977, at the first presentation, a president of the Republic asked, from the Palais de l'Elysée, that the whole thing be taken down as fast as possible. Oral questions to the Minister duly followed at the National Assembly.

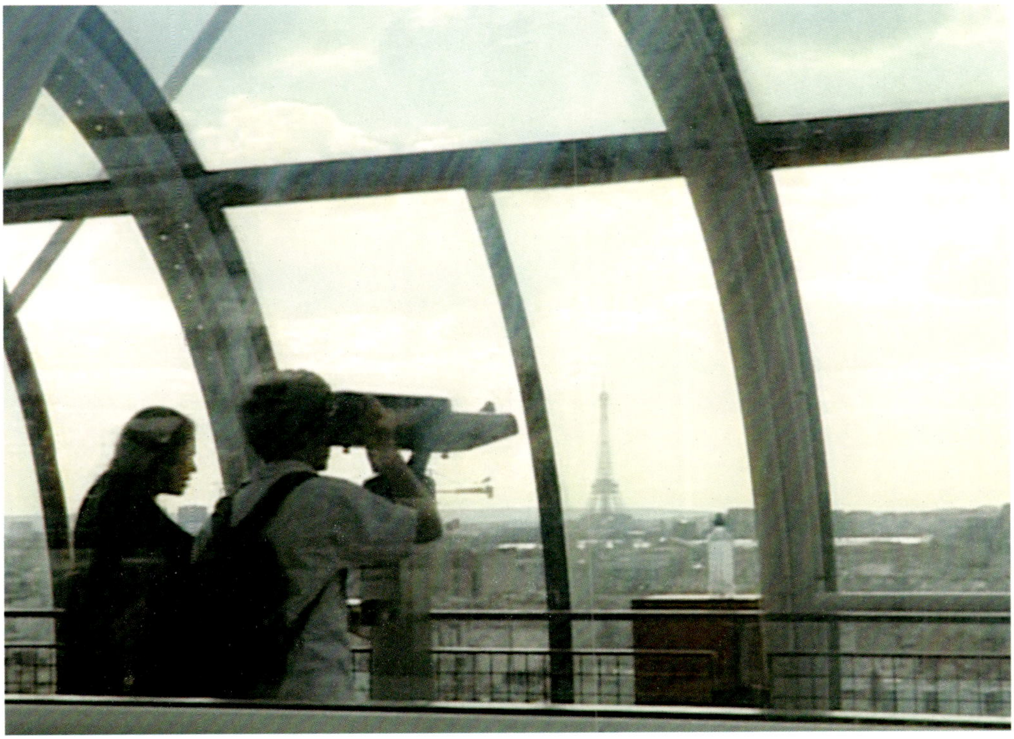

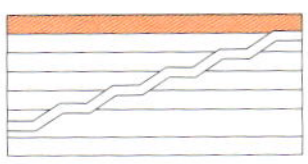

Level 6

Photo-souvenir: "The Colours: sculptures", work *in situ*, 1977-2002
3 long shots, 15 pieces of striped fabric (5 different colours)

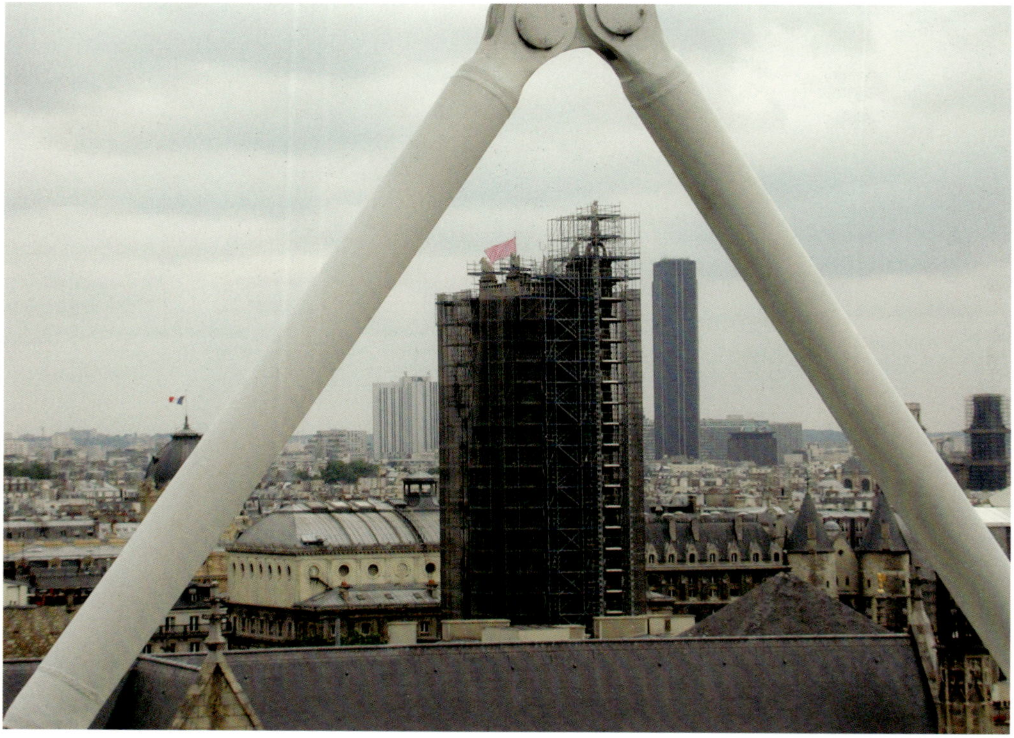

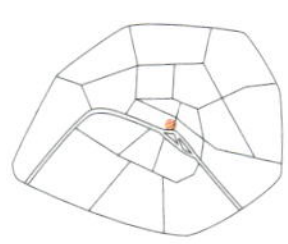

La Tour Saint-Jacques

Photo-souvenir: *"The Colours: sculptures"*, work *in situ*, 1977-2002
3 long shots, 15 pieces of striped fabric (5 different colours)

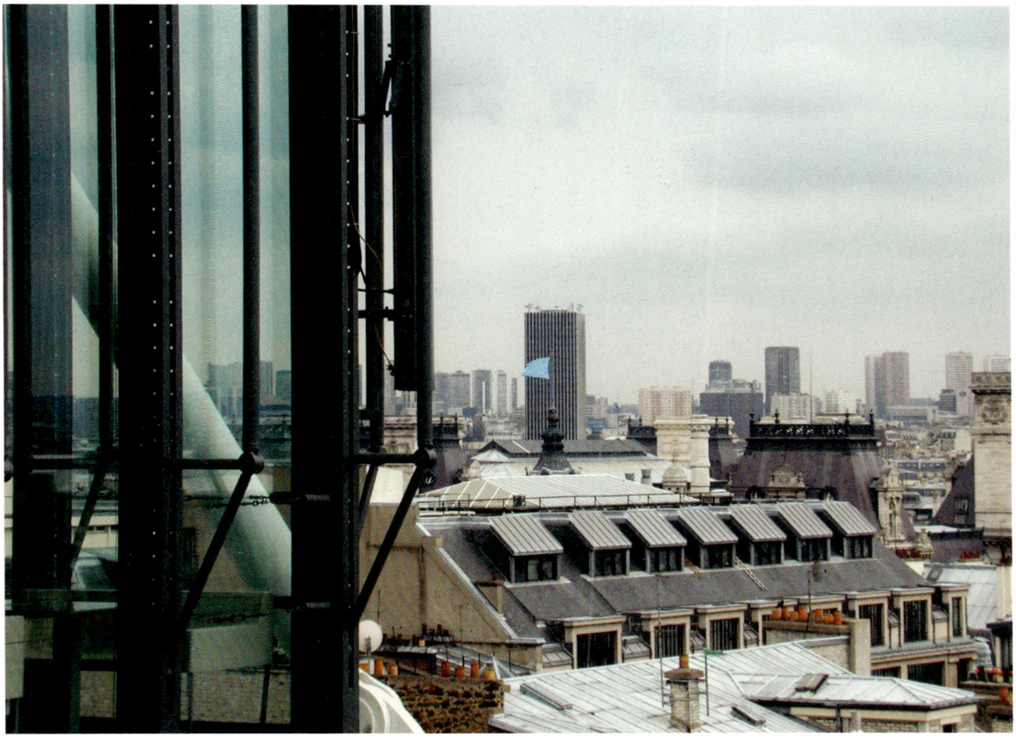

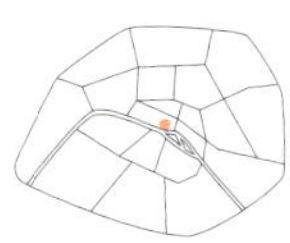

La Samaritaine

Photo-souvenir: "The Colours: sculptures", work *in situ*, 1977-2002
3 long shots, 15 pieces of striped fabric (5 different colours)

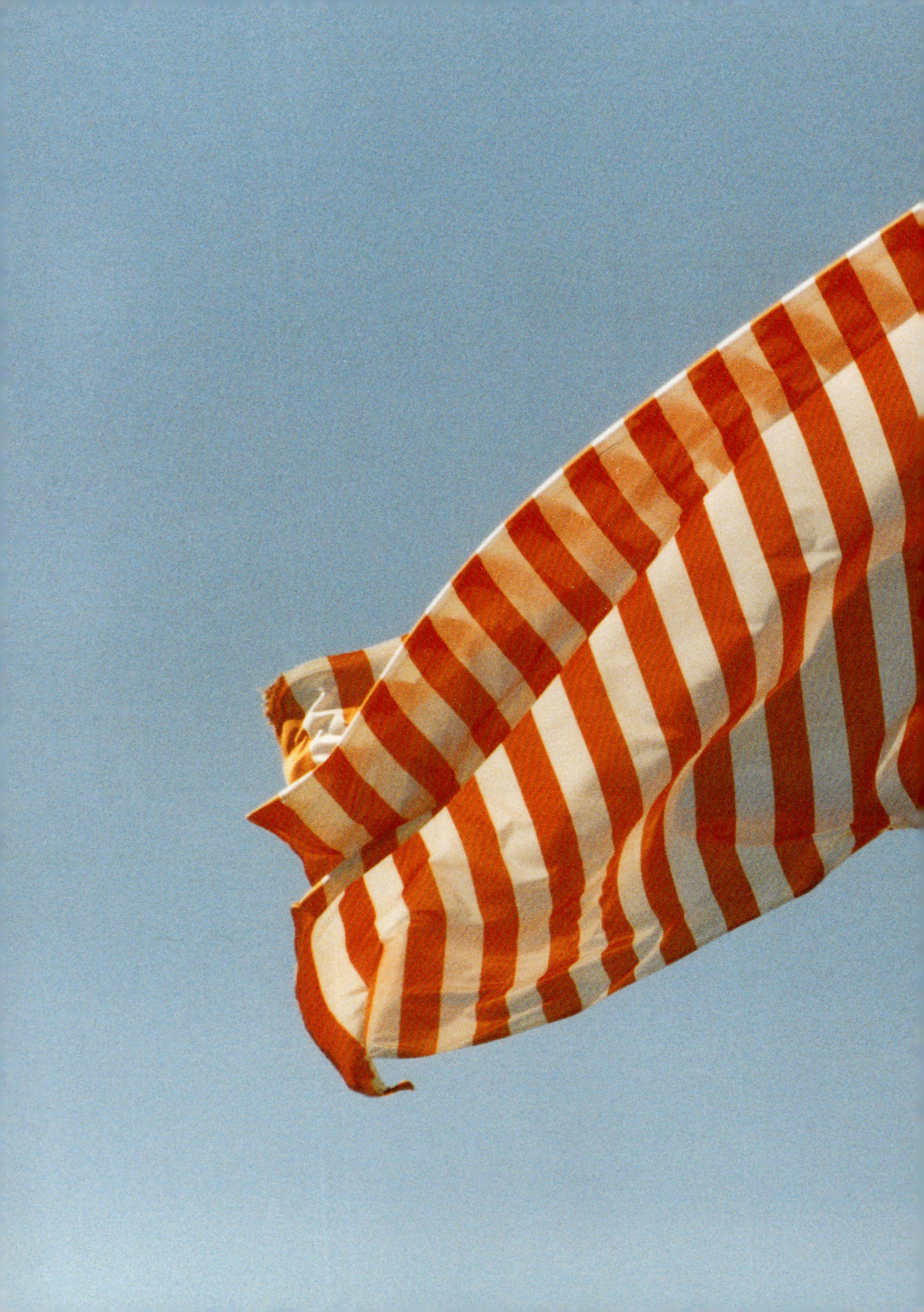

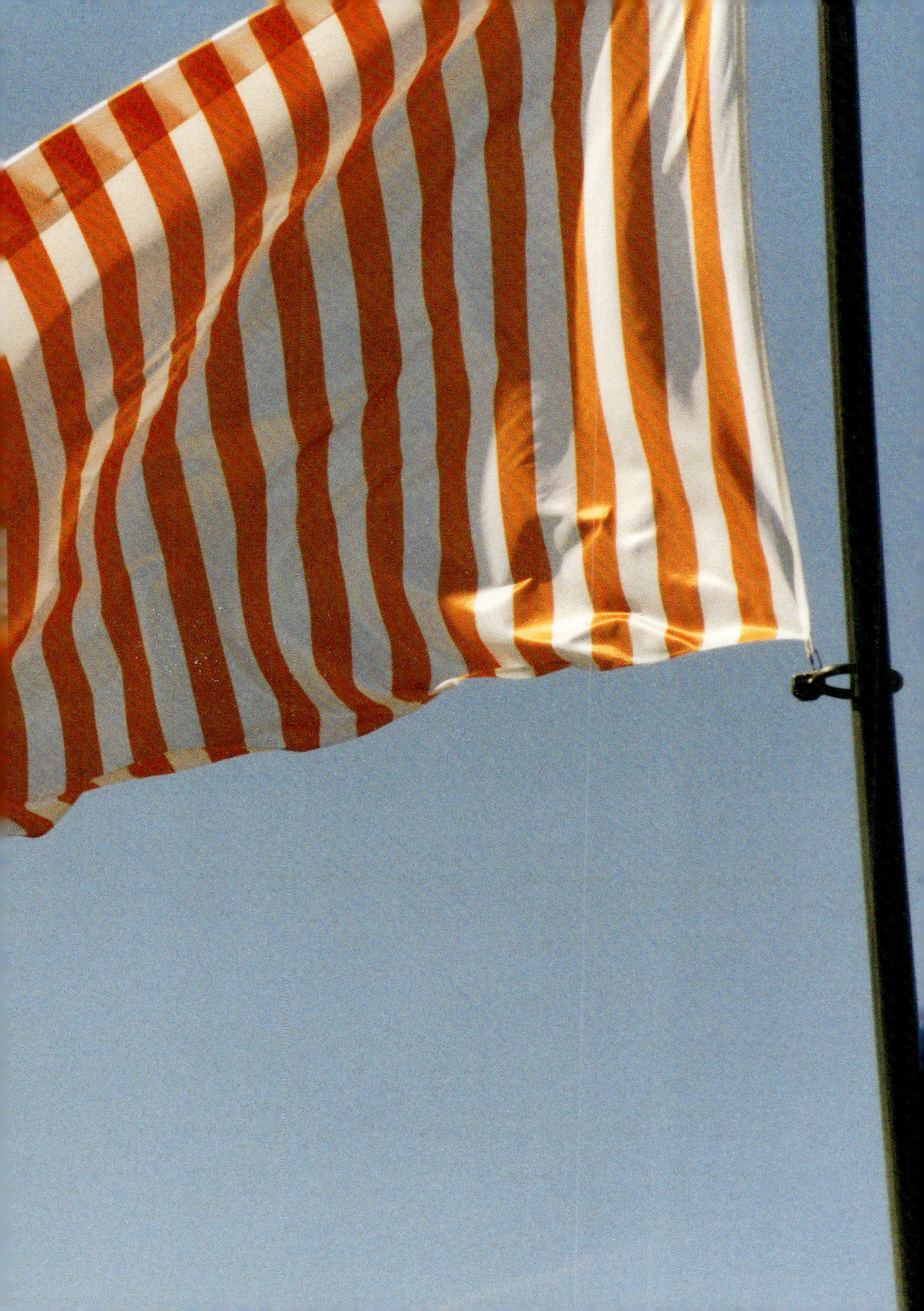

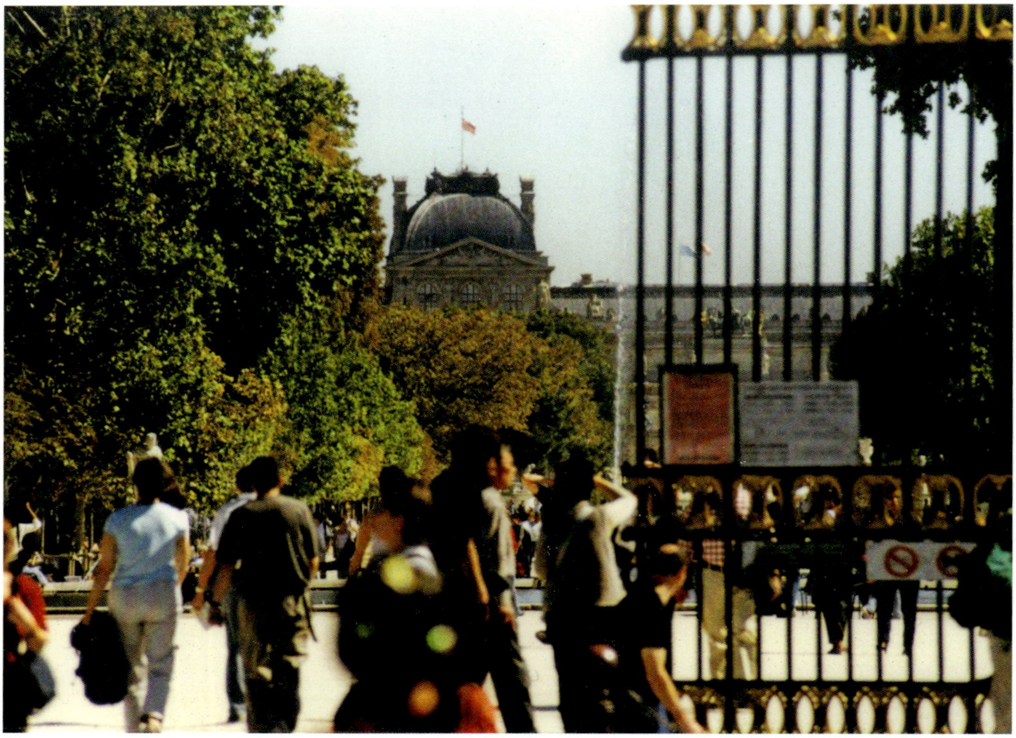

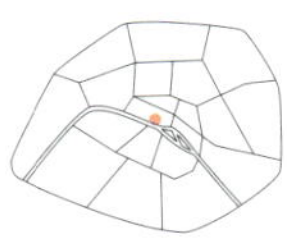

Le Louvre

Photo-souvenir: "The Colours: sculptures", work *in situ*, 1977-2002
3 long shots, 15 pieces of striped fabric (5 different colours)

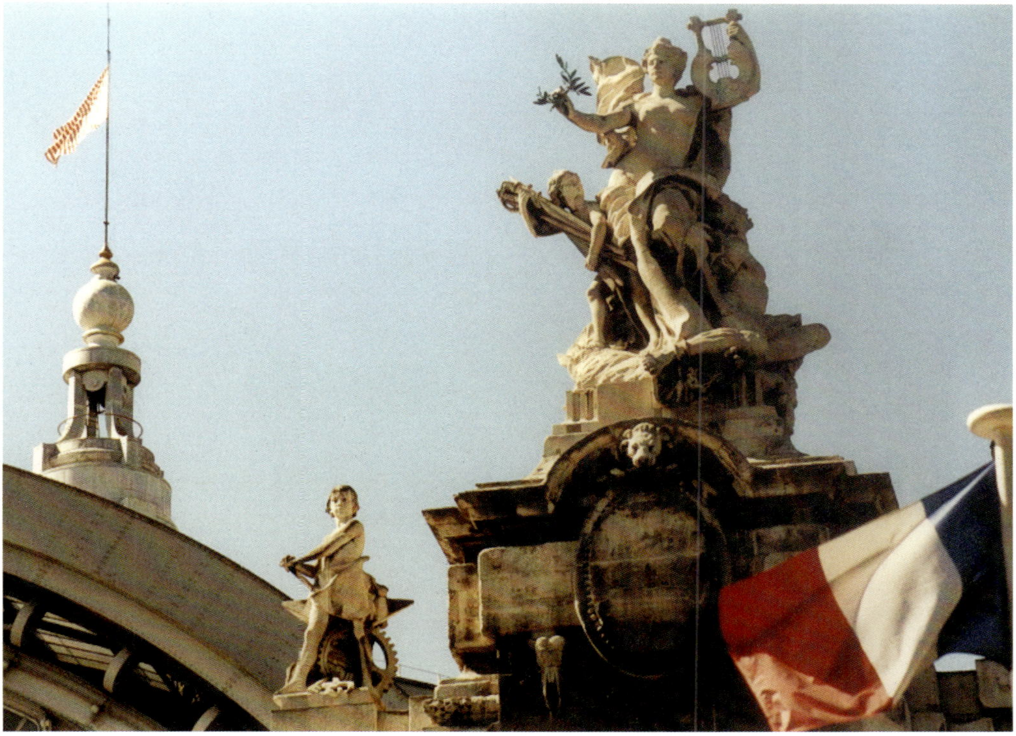

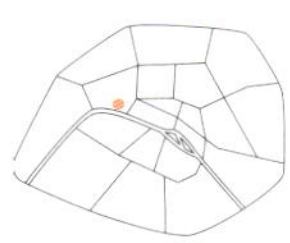

Le Grand Palais

Photo-souvenir: *"The Colours: sculptures"*, work *in situ*, 1977-2002
3 long shots, 15 pieces of striped fabric (5 different colours)

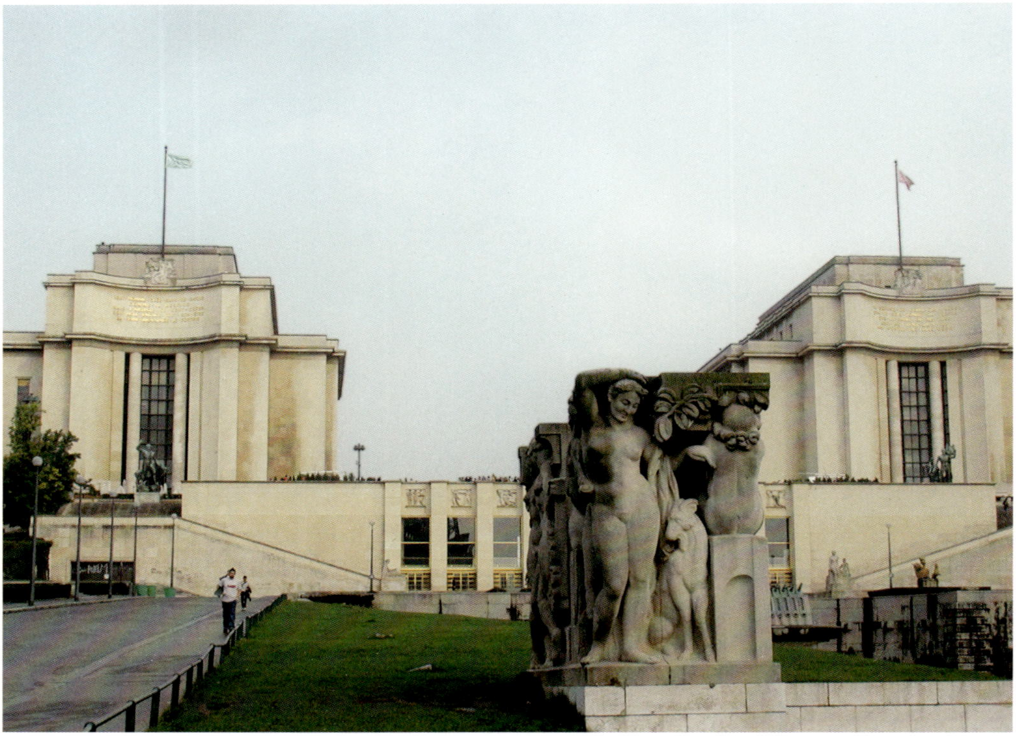

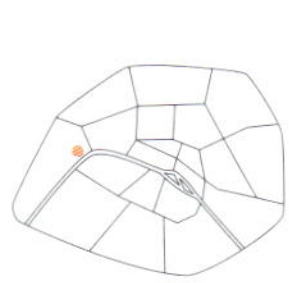

Le Trocadéro

Photo-souvenir: "*The Colours: sculptures*", work *in situ*, 1977-2002
3 long shots, 15 pieces of striped fabric (5 different colours)

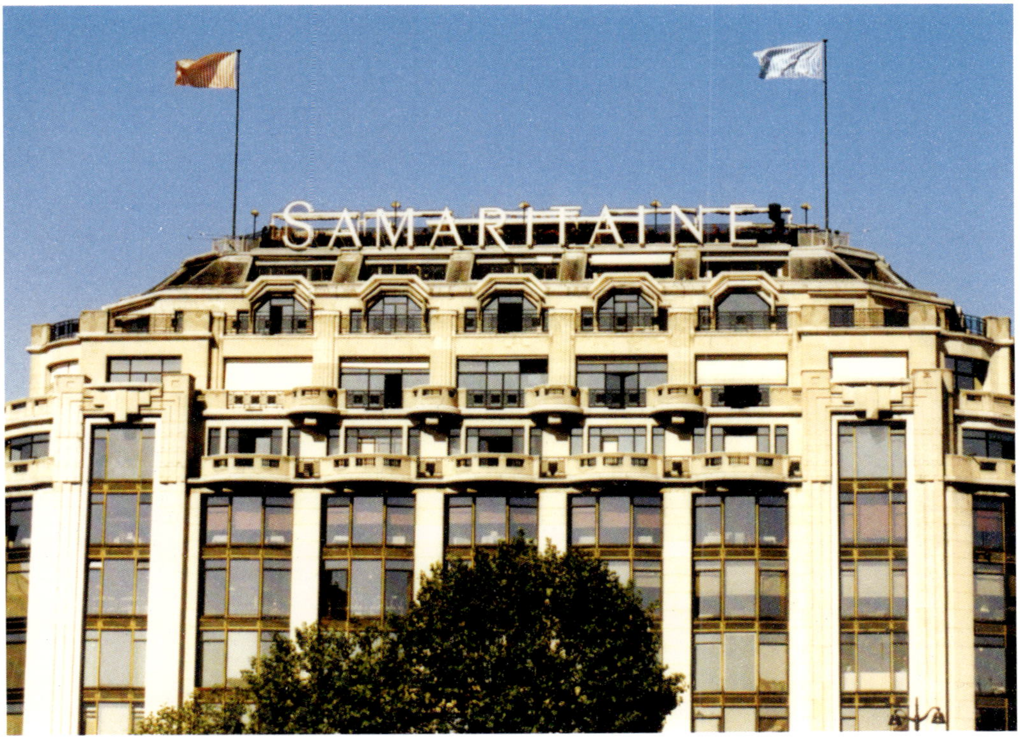

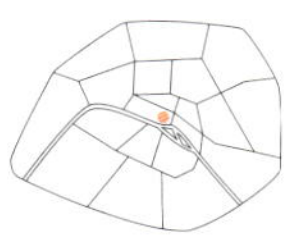

La Samaritaine

Above and on following pages
Photos-souvenirs: *"The Colours: sculptures"*, work *in situ*, 1977-2002
3 long shots, 15 pieces of striped fabric (5 different colours)

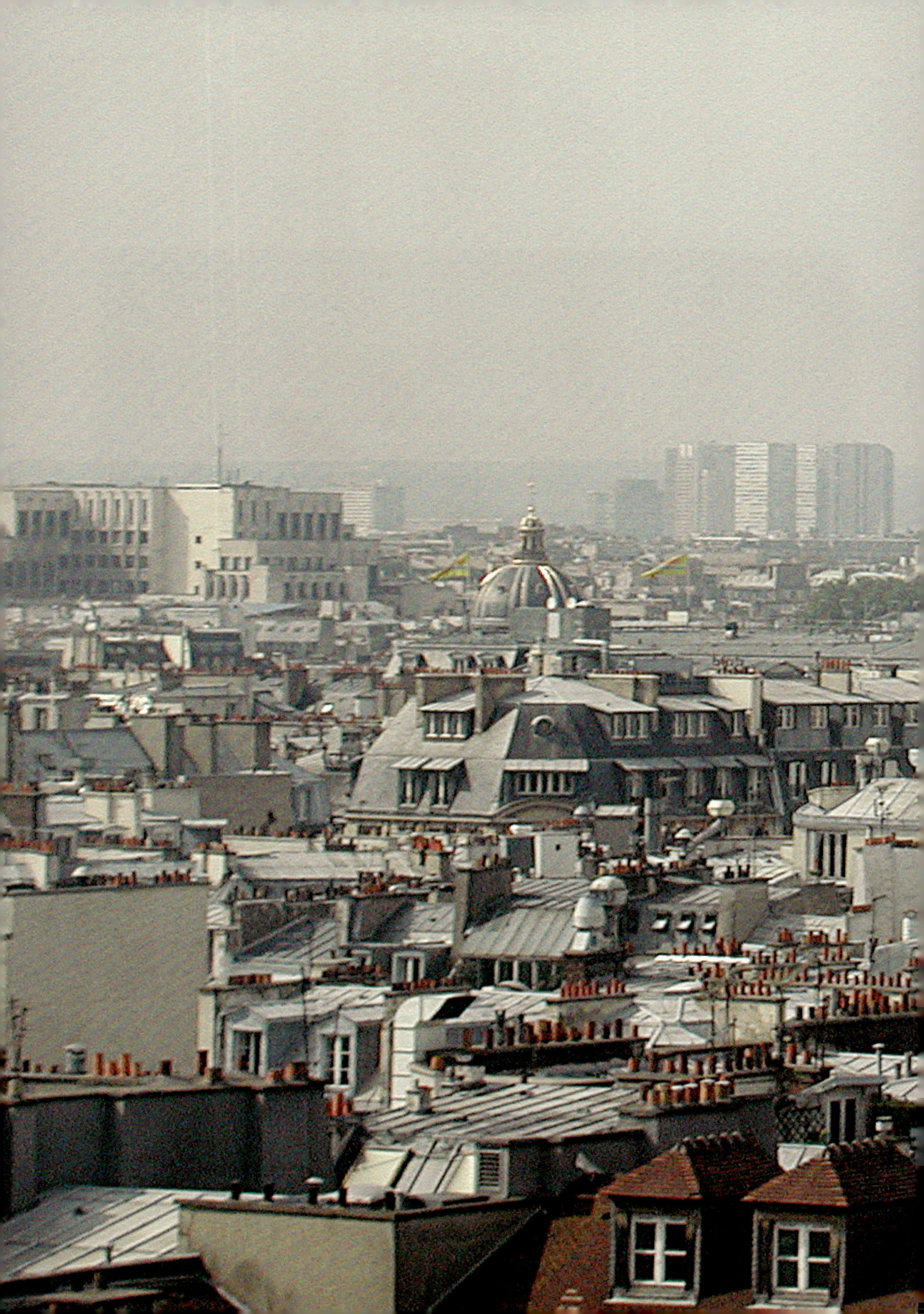

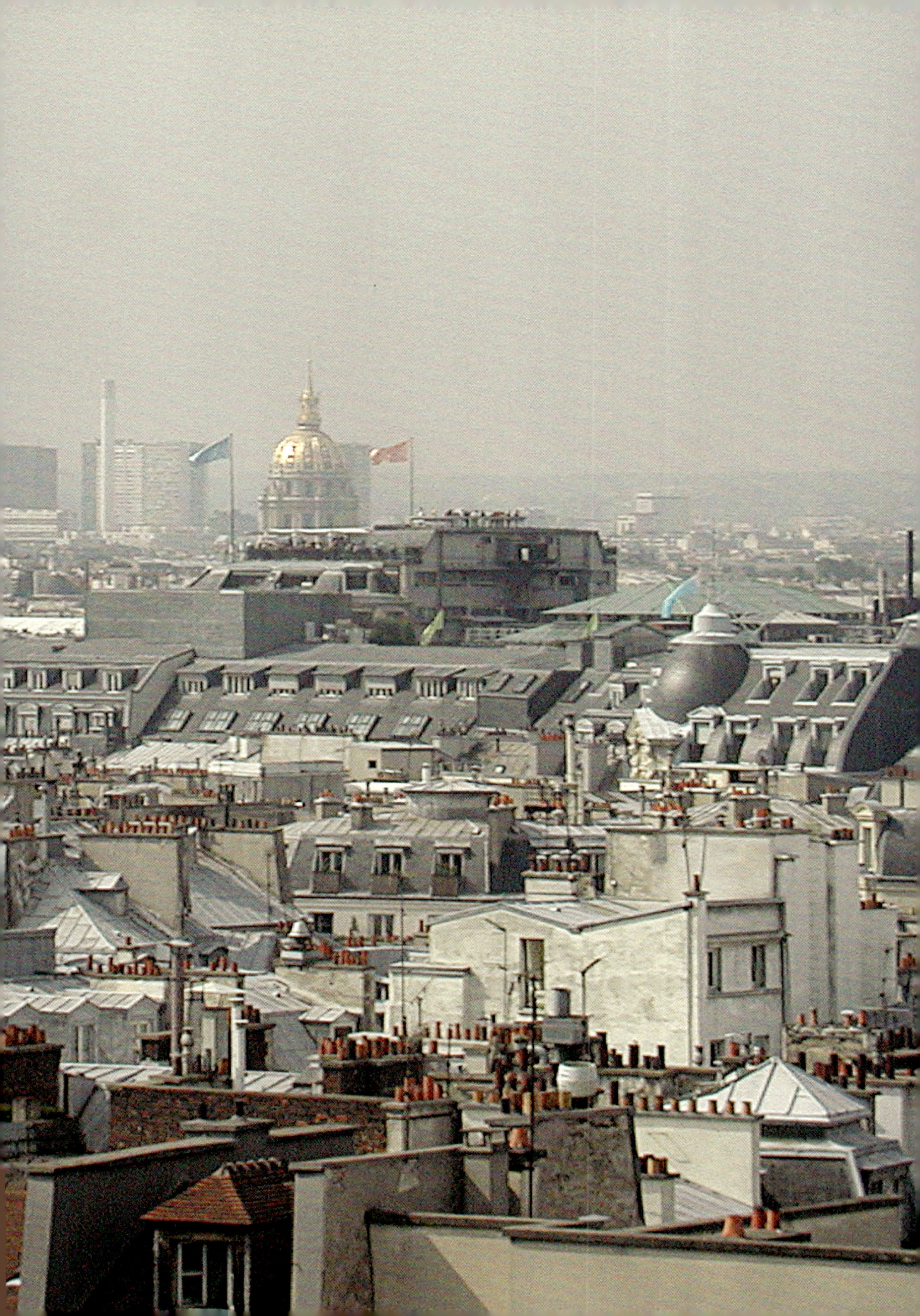

We have to go back to April 1968 to find "photos-souvenirs" recording the artist's first "Wild Billboards" in the city. Buren explained thus in 1990: "It was a gesture—a limited one—against the invasion of all those mercantile slogans in daily life, a "plastic" reaction against the consumer society. A sort of cleansing of the image at the city level."

If what was involved was a re-occupation of the public place, it was also a matter of opposing the power of the poster, the authority of a sign and a signal which, since January 1967, had become a "visual tool". Buren would thus reinstate the function of painting in its theoretical and political role. Some 35 years later, he would reverse the initial proposition by making it the official medium of the posters in his solo show at the Centre Pompidou. "The Wild Billboards" became the backdrop for the campaign to promote his own show. The images became blurred since they brought out the face of Georges Pompidou, at that time campaigning for the 1969 presidential election, and future instigator of the place that would welcome Buren into its bosom.

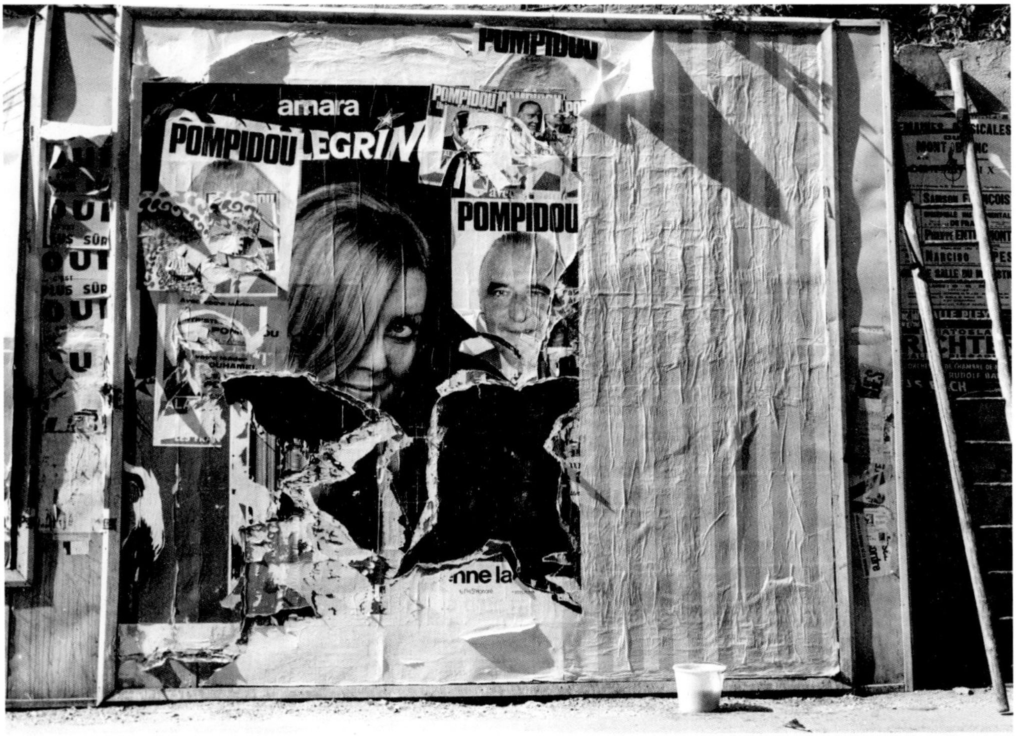

Photo-souvenir: "Wild billboard", work *in situ* and in progress
in « Summer show », July-September 1969, Paris
White and pink striped paper

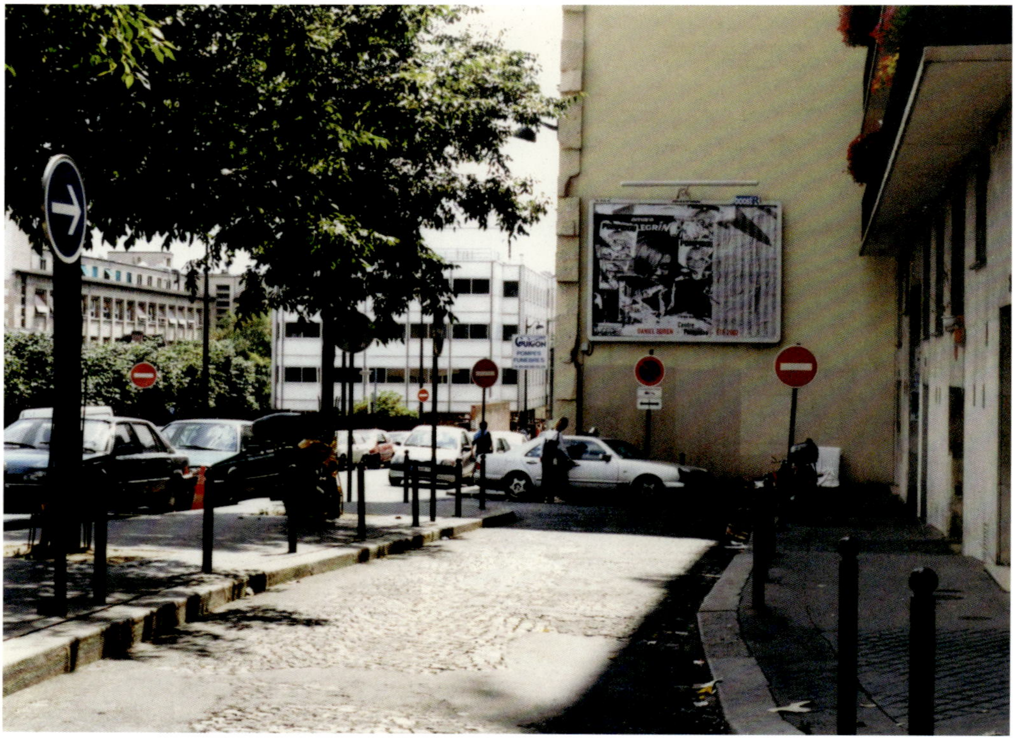

Photo-souvenir: Photo-souvenir of a "Wild billboard", 1969
Retaken on a 1 : 1 scale for the poster of the exhibition "The Museum that did not exist", 2002
Poster paper, glue, wood, signals, plaster, cement, etc.

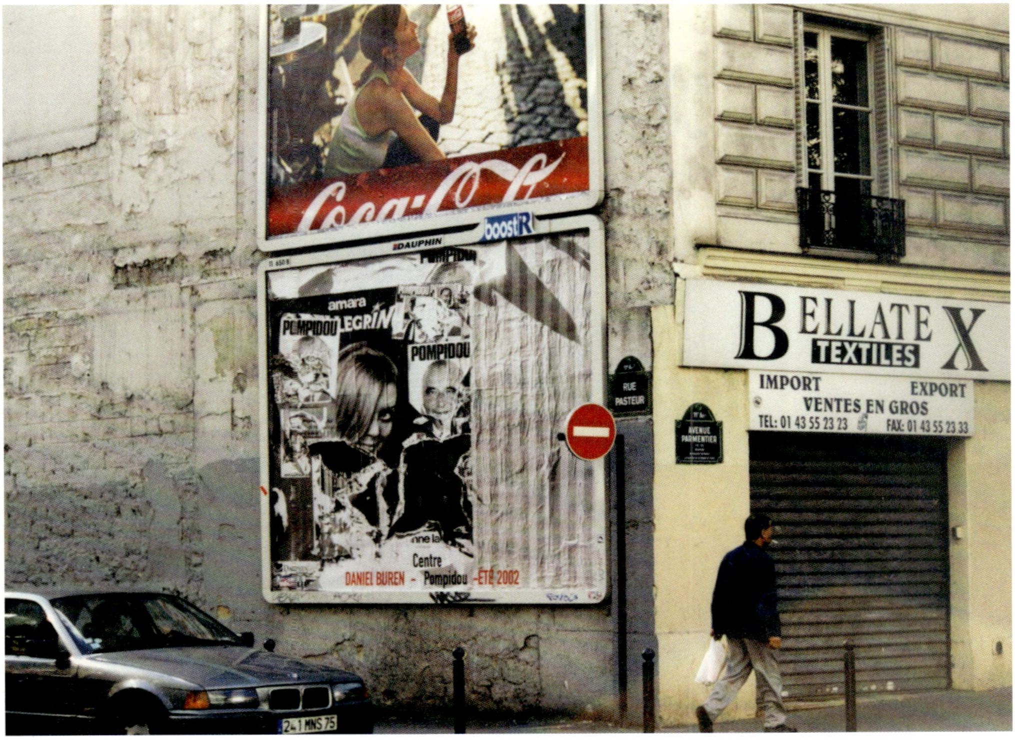

Photo-souvenir: Photo-souvenir of a "Wild billboard", 1969
Retaken on a 1 : 1 scale for the poster of the exhibition "The Museum that did not exist", 2002
Poster paper, glue, wood, signals, plaster, cement, etc.

Reconfiguring the Ritual

Dorothea von Hantelmann

It is entirely consistent with the *in situ* principle that Buren's works should elude the conventional format of a retrospective, since they are conceived to exist with and in relation to a specific place and for a specific length of time. To reproduce these works museologically in their retrospective contexts would be simply impossible. To separate individual components from their contexts and exhibit them would not only be nonsensical, but would also be contrary to the spirit of the works. For it would mean considering them as self-contained works that are autonomous and therefore also reproducible in other contexts. It is precisely this conception of the artwork, however, that Buren has opposed since he first started producing site-specific works at the end of the 1960s[1]. Acutely aware that the spatial and discursive context of an artwork is crucial to shaping its meaning, he builds this into the work's conception from the outset. It is this inseparability of work and context that characterises Buren's works. A retrospective, by contrast, would mean on the one hand disregarding the concrete context of the work and on the other hand making it necessary to subject the individual works to a history of their genesis and development. For, as a historicising show, the retrospective already implies a specific, evolutionary understanding of time, history and the development of an artistic œuvre, into which the individual artwork is integrated. One could even define it as the supreme expression of the evolutionary principle upon which the museum, in its canonical nineteenth-century form, was based. By contrast, the repetitive principle of the stripes was always the negation of a social and artistic imperative of progress. The idea was to produce a work that was based not on development and progress, but on repetition and variation. According to Buren, "from the moment when visible form is neutral it is no longer evolutive,

1 Although this approach represents a basic principle of an essential part of Buren's œuvre, there are works called *Exploded Cabins* which can be reproduced. Since the 1980s, Buren has been involved with this new type of sculptural installation. Involved are open and accessible spatio-architectural structures which can be shown in different contexts.

otherwise put, a neutral form may be followed by another neutral form, identical or different … The most important thing is our awareness of doing away with the concept of the advance of perfectibility[2]". Repetition is the principle that at once combines Buren's individual works into one work, and allows him (to a certain extent) to oppose the idea of progress and development that is inherent to the idea of an œuvre[3]. Buren's entire body of work is oriented towards creating a specific artistic spatial and temporal presence that is incompatible with the ideal of historical duration of art in museums. In this respect it seems only logical that for a long time Buren should have rejected this exhibition format for his works[4]. "It's also not about a completely arbitrary rejection of the retrospective", wrote the artist in 1975, "the statement is simply a different one and stands in the way[5]."

Yet the question remains regarding a historicising approach to this work, and with the passing of time it has become even more relevant in the light of the fact that Buren himself has now become a historical figure[6]. At some point, the retrospective view of decades of successful work comes into play, and it is not within the power of the artist to prevent or negate this. Can an artist like Buren, who painstakingly controls all the modes of presentation, documentation and sale of his work (and who has also influenced its interpretation through numerous

2 Daniel Buren: "Entrevue. Conversations avec Anne Baldessari", in: exh.cat. *Daniel Buren. Le musée des Arts décoratifs comme lieu, situation : 2*, Le musée des Arts décoratifs, Paris 1987, p. 48.

3 In many texts Buren has accentuated the constant repetition of the striped pattern in different contexts as what directs the question of its meaning away from the stripes themselves to their respective context and situation. "Repetition," he writes, "is the ineluctable means of legibility of the proposition itself." Daniel Buren, "Beware!", Studio International, Journal of Modern Art, London, 920 (1970), vol. 179, p. 103.

4 See Buren, "A partir de là" (1975) in *ibid.*, pp. 439-457.

5 *Ibid.*, p. 243 ff.

6 On this subject read in particular Buren's interview with Suzanne Pagé, in the catalogue *Daniel Buren. De la couverture*, 42nd Venice Biennale, French pavilion in the Giardini, Paris, 1986.

texts of his own)[7]. exert an influence on the historicisation of his work? How does this work, which has developed so decisively in debate with the museum – as the institution that frames, determines, enables the artwork's existence – relate to the museum as the location that preserves and recollects art and transfers it to a collective memory?

In a particular way these questions would become concrete on the occasion of Buren's 2002 exhibition at the Musée d'Art Moderne at the Centre Pompidou in Paris. For when in 2002, at the age of sixty-four, Buren was granted a large solo show in France's most important museum of modern and contemporary art for the first time, this exhibition would inevitably be perceived as a retrospective. Buren must have been particularly aware of the performative power of this convention. With this exhibition, which from the very beginning was seen by the museum as a kind of retrospective – a text by its director Alfred Pacquement confirms this[8] – Buren took on the challenge of artistically dealing with, and at the same time rerouting, this format. As Buren stated in an interview in 2000, "the retrospective is totally impossible and the problem is thus raised and settled at one and the same time by its very denial. Or else the retrospective stance is possible and what we shall see has never been seen before, in turn raising the issue of the very idea of the retrospective[9]." The Paris exhibition transformed the format of the retrospective into something new, into an original form of re-viewing a body of work through which Buren so thoroughly resets the parameters of the retrospective that the exhibition, not without justification, is entitled *Le Musée qui n'existait pas*.

7 For the past forty years Buren has been publishing texts and essays which have had repercussions on interpretations that have been made of his work.

8 Printed in: Buren, Daniel/Centre Pompidou (ed.): *Mot à Mot*, Paris 2002.

9 Daniel Buren, in: Sans Jérôme (ed.): *Daniel Buren. Au sujet de... Entretien avec Jérôme Sans*, Paris 1998, p.141.

Le Musée qui n'existait pas, 2002

The main part of Buren's exhibition took place on the sixth floor of the Centre Pompidou[10]. The artist had divided the space into 71 cubic modules in a grid system. Connected to each other via passageways, each of these spaces was constructed differently, but none of them formed an independent unit. The ensemble of spaces extended in a repetitive rhythm without beginning or end, without consolidation or focus, with no separation between artwork and frame, form and content. From space to space Buren's decorative canon repeated in endless variations and differentiations. The walls, no longer the bearers of art, were themselves part of a decorative system; the space was no longer the site of a composition taking place within it, but rather seemed to disappear entirely in its utter transformation. A new variant of the same principle was ever apparent: geometrically strong, playfully light, from the scaled-down version to opulent cascades of form and colour. Without a floor plan, which might have given some sense of the spatial dimensions, and without any thematic, chronological or otherwise recognisable ordering structure.

A dramaturgy, rather than a system, of sight lines led through the space. Openings and vistas continually appeared, through which Buren opened the space to an exterior that was brought into the interior: from the exhibition to the restaurant, from the restaurant to the exhibition, from the exhibition to the urban surroundings. Additional striped markings also extended the exhibition into the entrance lobby on the ground floor. Apart from this staged interplay between exhibition, institution and urban context, within the exhibition itself there were compositional elements that created a dynamic among the indi-

10 The basement which Burten had turned into a large car park, the escalators, and the Centre Pompidou entrance lobby had also been incorporated in the exhibition. What is more, two old Buren works from the Musee d'art moderne collection were shown once again: *Colours: sculptures* (1977) and *Forms: paintings* (1978).

vidual spaces. In the foreground and the background, in vistas and colour changes, patterns broke free and merged with one another so that the viewer's gaze was continually redirected.

This interplay of architecture and visual décor culminated in an astonishing effect: visitors to the exhibition moved continually from module to module, from space to space – but they never stood still. Indeed, there was no incentive to stand still, because the exhibition lacked a centre: a work, in the sense of something to be viewed, in which some kind of meaning or significance could be established. The endlessly varied, playfully decorative visual effects affected the eye and drew attention to themselves, but never held the gaze. One was always surrounded by something, was always *in* a situation, but never found oneself face to face with an assessable, objectifiable work of art. There were (almost) no narrative or representational elements to engage with. Buren had not only abolished the basic precondition of the museum experience – the differentiation between the space and the work – but had also deprived it of an essential feature, namely the individual object charged with significance. No meanings leading to an understanding on the part of the viewer could be found anywhere in this visual plenitude, this excess of joie-de-vivre. So one moved on, without standing still. Referring to his exhibition at the Kunsthaus Bregenz in 2001, Buren spoke of "adding a second rhythm to the building's already existing one[11]." In Paris it seemed as if Buren had given the exhibition a distinct continuous rhythm, which became manifest in the way the visitors moved through the spaces. The individual modules were small enough to shift the gaze onto the overall context, providing an inducement to keep on walking, as one wanted to know how long the show would go on. On the other hand, the individual openings were large enough to allow one to guess the approximate number of distinct

11 Daniel Buren in conversation with Eckhard Schneider, in: *Daniel Buren. Les Couleurs Traversées, Arbeiten vor Ort*, Kunsthaus Bregenz, Köln 2001, n.p.

spaces, providing a motivation for carrying on walking in order to be able to manage the dimensions. In this way the viewer's span of attention was calculated into Buren's spatial planning of the exhibition space. Although artistic operation on such a level of perception and spatial experience necessarily remains uncertain and uncontrollable, Buren had provided the stimulus to move through the exhibition in a calculated manner. One had the impression of literally being shoved through a spatial-decorative arrangement.

In his book *The Relevance of the Beautiful* Hans-Georg Gadamer emphasises the significance of the way in which we pause before a work of art. He says that every work of art (not only the so-called time-based ones like music or dance) has its own temporality, which it imposes on the viewer. "In the experience of art we must learn how to dwell upon the work in a specific way. … The essence of our temporal experience of art," according to Gadamer, "is in learning how to tarry this way[12]." This kind of "dwelling" in front of a work of art did not occur in Buren's exhibition. There was more of a choreographed striding through it, which did not pause in contemplation of a particular work[13]. A striding that, because it was not oriented towards a work, gave one the feeling of not being in an exhibition, or rather, of being *differently* in an exhibition, of somehow being in a different temporal and spatial relationship to art.

In *The Practice of Everyday Life,* Michael de Certeau writes that the act of walking is to urban space what utterance is to language[14]. Similarly to the way in which an abstract system of linguistic rules is realised through speech, urban space realises itself by being walked through.

12 Hans-Georg Gadamer: *The Relevance of the Beautiful and other Essays*, Robert Bernasconi (ed.), Cambridge, 1998, p. 45.

13 Buren himself has spoken of "choreography" in relation to the staging of his work. See Sans, *Buren. Au sujet de…,* p. 115.

14 Michel de Certeau: *The Practice of Everyday Life*, Berkeley/Los Angeles, 1988, p. 97.

In both cases, a structure, a particular systematic order is realised and actualised through its use. Can we make a similar claim for the exhibition? What exactly is it that becomes concrete in the form of walking through a museum? A possible answer derives from an examination of the history of the museum and its specific societal function.

The governmental function of aesthetic experience

The modern art museum emerged around 1800, at the same time as the concept of the public. It is the fact of accessibility to visitors that turned a collection into a museum, and here the modern art museum is particularly relevant to the question of the performative-generative effect of the museum in relation to the (political) constitution of the subject as citizen. For if it is the idea of the historical museum to subsume the individual subject into the whole (the community of the nation), i.e. to deprioritise the individual, then the task of the art museum in contrast lies in addressing subjects as individuals and constituting them as a community of individuals. The individual subject, both artist and art-viewing citizen, becomes the central category of the museum of the nineteenth century. The museum orients itself towards 'the public,' but this public is precisely not a linked group: the museum visitor is addressed as an individual; an artwork can best be observed when one is alone in quiet contemplation. In bourgeois understanding, art, or the art museum, becomes *the* place in which the subject – via an object in which the history of his or her culture is reflected – affirms his or her individuality, but also that of his or her fellow citizens.

In his book *The Birth of the Museum*, which was published in the mid-1990s, Tony Bennett discusses the way in which the museum was able, via the interplay of architecture and the display of art, to influence the formation of identity of the bourgeois subject or rather the bourgeois public sphere[15]. Following Foucault, Bennett examines the significance, or rather the performative effectiveness of the museum in relation to new forms of self-government. Foucault assumes that a fundamental transformation process takes place in the modern age, one that involves the transfer of power from its central exercise by a ruler to the individual himself, who to an increasing degree governs and regulates himself by means of norms, rules and disciplines; Tony Bennett thus investigates the role played by the museum in this context. In the museum – and this particularly applies to the art museum – two different concepts of government meet. On the one hand, the museum has a representative function: it serves to represent state power and sovereignty, or is a place in which the abstract category of the state is concretely manifest. And on the other hand, the museum is also the place where art and the cultural property of a state are made accessible to a civil public and symbolically given over. According to Bennett's thesis, the symbolic participation in the sovereignty of the state represent a challenge to the individual to fashion and cultivate his behaviour in the museum. In this sense it becomes possible to speak of the museum as a "civilising ritual" (Carol Duncan) in which new forms of a (bourgeois) code of behaviour could be created and to a certain degree taught by rote. Or, as Tony Bennett puts it, "Going to a museum, then as now, is not merely a matter of looking and learning; it is also an exercise in civics[16]." By reference to the writings of mid-nineteenth-century British social reformers, it can for example be shown how the museum visit was intended to influence the social conduct of the individual citizen, promoting decent and moral behaviour. The fact that museums were accessible to a public that was made

15 Bennett, Tony: *The Birth of the Museum*, London-New York 1995.

16 Tony Bennett: "The Political Rationality of the Museum", *Continuum: The Australian Journal of Media & Culture*, vol. 3, n° 1, 1990. http://wwwmcc.murdoch.edu.au/ReadingRoom/3.1/Bennett.html

up of different social classes also made it possible, in conjunction with a specific architectural context, for visitors to observe the behaviour of members of higher social classes from a safe distance and in a position of relative isolation and muted contemplation and thereby edge closer to them[17]. "Relations of space and vision", writes Bennett, "are organized not merely to allow a clear inspection of the objects exhibited but also to allow for the visitors to be the objects of each other's inspection – scenes in which, if not a citizenry, then certainly a public displayed itself to itself in an affirmative celebration of its own orderliness in architectural contexts which simultaneously guaranteed and produced that orderliness[18]." From this point of view the museum can be seen as a *dispositif* whose basic purpose is the fashioning and self-fashioning of the individual citizen. The exhibits themselves come to be defined merely as "props for a performance", "in which a progressive, civilizing relationship to the self might be formed and worked upon[19]." In this sense the museum is an institution in which representational (the new state is represented in its cultural achievements) and governmental functions are not merely united. One could exaggeratedly claim that the actual cultural and historical achievement of this institution lies precisely in having engineered this particular connection between representation and participation.

Specific to the art museum is the fact that these 'civilising' effects are bound up with an experience of time, history and progress. In Bennett's bourgeois conception, the museum is the place where subject knowledge is made tangible as a historical process, in other words a process that is historically determined and anchored in history. In the science and anthropological museums of the late nineteenth century,

17 *Ibid.*, p. 47.

18 *Ibid.*, p. 52.

19 *Ibid.*, p. 186.

this context attains an ideological dimension, namely the demonstration of progress. In order to illustrate this, Bennett uses the metaphor of museums as "machines of progress[20]," the ideology of progress not only being represented in a developmental history of the exhibits, but above all made tangible and comprehensible for the viewer in a staging, in a specific perceptual organisation. In general, the museum is seen as a place that is primarily organised in visual terms. However, pointing to the ritual character of the museum experience, Bennett emphasises that the concept of progress can only become effective in the literal walking through the building, i.e. in the transfer of a mental principle into a physical one. Through this ordered walking, the classification of objects in terms of an evolutionary principle is physically imitated and gradually becomes comprehensible. "New institutions of social training", argues Bennett, "were governed by what Foucault calls evolutive time. The marking out of time into a series of stages comprising a linear path of evolution; the organization of these stages into an itinerary that the visitor's route retraces; ... via the construction of a series of stages that were to be passed through by means of the successful acquisition of the appropriate skills, individuals were encouraged to relate to themselves as beings in incessant need of progressive development[21]".

Also in the art museum the model of progress is realised performatively. The chronological arrangement of the artworks is not enough to make this model effective. The spatial and discursive structure of the museum is realised in the act of walking, through which the visitor both mentally and physically recapitulates the historic development of art. Bennett quotes Phillip Fisher in this connection: "That we walk through a museum, walk past the art, recapitulates in our act the motion of art history itself, its restlessness, its forward motion, its power

20 *Ibid.*, p. 10.

21 *Ibid.*, p. 46.

to link[22]." It is the idea of ritual which Bennett introduces here into the museum. Progress is experienced through one's own physical (and mental) progression. Within the museum's performative dimension, aimed at the self-fashioning of the individual (as a politically mature citizen), lies a historical and cultural achievement that not only includes viewer participation, but is even exclusively oriented towards it. The question is whether and how the ideological goal of this combined impact of architecture, artwork, and viewer can be artistically formed and altered.

Structuring and restructuring the ritual – Buren's *peinture-sculpture* (1971)

In 1888, at the British Association of the Advancement of Science, the military general and anthropologist Henry Pitt Rivers came forward with a suggestion as to how to give spatial form to the relationship between progress and differentiation[23]. He spoke of an "anthropological rotunda," through which the course of evolution from simple to complex life forms could be understood as a kind of cycle. In the following discussion, this suggestion was widened. The spatial model of a continual spiral would be better than a rotunda, as it would represent the gradual development of human evolution without breaks.

Almost 70 years later, the American architect Frank Lloyd Wright built one of the most famous art museums in the world: the Solomon R. Guggenheim Museum in New York, completed in 1959, the architecture of which is dominated by the motif of an upwardly winding spiral, an even better model than the rotunda for presenting the gradual development of human evolution. From the very beginning, the

22 Quoted in: *Ibid.*, p. 45.

23 Quoted in: *Ibid.*, p. 182.

form of the spiral, with its curved walls and ramp, attracted criticism, most vehemently from artists, who saw the building as unsuitable for the presentation of paintings[24]. For his part, Wright spoke of an "uninterrupted, beautiful symphony" that would come about between the works of art and the architecture[25]. Here, as his biographer Vincent Scully puts it, the visitor would experience a "journey through time and space," in which the upward ramp suggests the conquest of time itself[26].

In this museum, more precisely in what is indeed called the rotunda, Daniel Buren realised one of his first large international *in situ* works in 1971, sparking off a controversy that still resonates today[27]. Buren's work was dismantled before the opening as the result of pressure from several of the artists whose work would also be on view in the same exhibition. Buren had produced a monumental, 20 x 10-metre striped canvas that hung from the ceiling and filled the entire central space. With this work Buren radically intervened in the impact of the museum. His work referred to the architectural context, but did not subordinate itself to it. It was not the artwork that was integrated into the architecture (whose pronounced meaning Buren had recognised), but the architecture into the artwork: the otherwise dominant architecture became the set for a staging that was now dominated by Buren's work, the effect of which was intended to deplete Wright's concept of its inherent evolutionary principle. One went spiralling from floor to floor with a continually changing perspective of the same thing – Buren's striped intervention.

24 In 1957 Wright received a letter signed by several artists (including Robert Motherwell and Willem de Kooning) which said that the building's curved exterior walls and upward ramp would make the presentation of paintings impossible. See Bruce Brooks Pfeiffer (ed.), *The Guggenheim Correspondence*, Fresno and Carbondale 1986, p. 223.

25 Wright, quoted from Bruce Brooks Pfeiffer (ed.), Frank Lloyd Wright in the Realm of Ideas, Carbondale and Edwardsville 1988, p. 13.

26 Vincent Jr. Scully, *Frank Lloyd Wright*, New York 1960, p. 30.

27 For details and background to this conflict see Alexander Alberro: "The Turn of the Screw: Daniel Buren, Dan Flavin, and the Sixth Guggenheim International Exhibition", in: *October*, 1997, 80, pp. 57-84.

Buren's work was attacked in particular by Dan Flavin and Donald Judd. Apart from the fact that it probably made every other piece in the exhibition look like a toy, Judd might have seen Buren's contribution as an affront to his own principle of the "specific object[28]." The work, whose outermost stripes were painted white, was entitled *Peinture-Sculpture*. Depending on one's point of view (and because of the rotunda, this constantly changed), it looked like either a painting or a sculpture. From the front or behind, the canvas could be perceived as a surface, but from either side it was more like a cut through space. It appears that Buren wanted to conceive of a viewer-oriented counter-project to Judd's "specific objects," which were intended neither as painting nor sculpture. Judd insisted on the non-relational, non-compositional type of Minimalism, on the integrity, compactness, and object-ness of form, and on the reality of the space and time in which this object would be experienced. The term "specific" was intended to describe these qualities. For Judd, art was an essentially pictorial endeavour. In his text *Specific Objects* he describes the transition from painting to three-dimensional form in space, but he thinks about this space, similar to an image, as a primarily visual composition.

For Buren, however, the art space has a functional context and impact that is ideologically loaded. The essential conflict with Judd consists in the understanding of what it means to stage a work of art in relation to its location. For Buren this does not only mean – as he accuses Judd of doing – putting something in a space "with the precision of a watchmaker," and orienting it towards the body of the viewer[29]. For him it means referring to the conventions of the museum, recognizing its performative and implicative power, and integrating this into the work. Buren is concerned with gaining agency for art, which is why he

28 For a thoroughgoing analysis of this conflict, see: Guy Lelong, *Daniel Buren*, Paris 2001, pp. 40-45.

29 "Donald Judd's shows are a good example: a discourse completely based on rigour and precision, which, as a result, is just a surface discourse pushed to its consequences, reliant on a mercantile hoax…" (Buren in: Sans, *Daniel Buren*, *op. cit.*, p. 115)

proceeds from the aspect that most strongly governs and restricts this – in the case of the Guggenheim work, the spatial structure of the building in which a notion of progress manifests itself that will always be reproduced by the artwork in as much as it remains untouched by it. It is because Buren understands his work as a part of this correlation of architecture, specific conventions, and the ideologies inherent to them that he proceeds from the architectural motif and its forming effect on the viewer. In New York he realised a work that was able, precisely through the way it related to the principle of the spiral, to deprive the architectural motif of its inherent ideology. Instead of propagating an ideology of progress, it now, through Buren's work, proclaimed the constant variation of the same. One may take issue with Buren's critique of progress, but it is interesting how he realises it performatively. Through operating with the conventions materialised in the architecture, Buren intervenes in their effect and function. He acts like a director trying to transform the dramaturgy of the building, even to reverse it. A strategy that was apparently so effective that it fell victim to censorship[30].

Naturally a single artistic work cannot derail a museum's spirit of progress. This would mean attributing to it an individual and intentional power, which Buren would have already denied it. It's rather a question of recognising (and using) an agency with this in view, to the extent that the individual artwork, the individual artistic statement always reproduces such an ideology along with it. Artistic action for Buren means mining the depths of precisely this relationship between artistic self-determination and contextual heteronomy.

30 "[In the case of Buren's installation] the limits of what was acceptable were exceeded. At that point ... the tacitly existing rules had to be re-invoked" writes Thomas M. Messer, one of the curators of the April 1971 exhibition. Quoted from: Alberro, *October*, loc. cit., p. 57. In this connection it is interesting to note Buren's exhibition *Eye of the Storm*, which took place at the Guggenheim Museum in spring 2005, and in which he – this time in a major solo show – pursued a similar strategy to that used back in 1971. He erected a mirror construction in the Guggenheim's rotunda, so that the individual levels of the ramp fractured in the mirror and the continuity of the ramp was disrupted.

A different retrospective

Buren pursues a comparable principle in his Parisian exhibition *Le Musée qui n'existait pas* – to which I would now like to return – with regard to the format of the retrospective. Here too Buren is concerned with the interlocking of repetition and difference, (artistic) intention and its framing by means of conventions. I do not think that Buren's project represents the "refusal of a retrospective," as Alison Gingeras has claimed[31]. Buren does not simply deny the principle of the retrospective because he is more than aware of the power of these conventions, and knows that this exhibition – independently of whether it is described as one or not – will be viewed as one. Buren's strategy is, in my opinion, a different one: he undermined the performative effectiveness of this exhibition as a retrospective, in the sense of a linear, historical development. I have already mentioned the recognition factor that the exhibition offered visitors who were familiar with Buren's work over the previous decades. Apart from the fact that two older works by Buren were integrated into the exhibition (*Les couleurs: sculpture* and *Les formes: peinture*, both from the collection of the Musée d'Art Moderne), apart from the references to Buren's project for the Palais Royal, and apart from several videos that documented *in situ* works from 1959 to 2002, one often had the impression of recognising certain conceptual elements of Buren's œuvre. Parts of the exhibition alluded to the decorative canon of earlier works, despite the fact that these associations never crystallised into "works" or an "œuvre." One space led into the next, one element of the décor referred to another. In this way it was impossible to isolate individual works. The show was instead staged as a *gesamtkunstwerk* in which everything was compositionally related to the same idea. What was on view was not divided into discrete units, but was instead a continual, circular, repetitive, varying

31 *cf.* Gingeras, Alison M.: "The decorative as strategy", in: *Parkett*, 2002, 66, p.84.

flow. The category of the individual artwork – in the sense of a distinct unit, and the matter of its placement within an œuvre – had been abandoned.

The essential artistic strategy through which Buren denied the show's effect as a retrospective was the experience of aimless walking. The decisive factor was of course not in the walking itself, but the fact that there was no incentive to stand still. Buren gave the exhibition a different rhythm, which was not defined by a purposeful movement from beginning to end, from early work to the present, but by a flow, an excursive circulation within a fragmented space. In a conventional retrospective, one walks through a life (an œuvre) from beginning to end; one passes through stages, emphases, and highpoints; in short, a conventional retrospective mirrors the historical developmental dynamic that Buren recorded. No matter how far one walked, there was neither a beginning nor an end to this exhibition; no progress and no development, only the constant differentiation of the same. This is the "different retrospective" that Buren integrated into the museum as archive, as storage. This walking, in which the narrative of history and of progress becomes both mentally and physically concrete, converted into a different idea of history and progress: a "retrospective" in the form of repetitive, differentiating snapshots of the movement of a work, not as fixed points brought to standstill. Buren developed an exhibition format that was composed like a piece of music and defined by a rhythm of continuous progress, repetition and difference; a retrospective with no beginning or end, no chronology or system.

In the manner of the Situationists, with whom Buren always felt a strong connection, one could speak here of a "constructed situation," but one that is no longer a counter-project in opposition to the work; it *is* the work, which dissolves the boundaries of a practice of which it still nonetheless remains part – which is however recognised and organised to a new extent as a field and sphere of activity. This situation is not only determined spatially, temporally or discursively. It is constituted to a significant degree in the physical as well as mental participation of the viewer (whether male or female), whose perception and experience is shaped by the *dispositif*, just as, conversely, the *dispositif* itself is shaped by the viewer. Buren seizes on the potential of this form of participation and attempts to alter and reconfigure its effects.

The meaning of the decorative

The reception of Buren's work is marked by a more or less explicit break that took place in the 1980s. With his large and spectacular projects, e.g. for the French pavilion at the Venice Biennale in 1986, Buren became a favourite of the public, but fell from favour with the critics. This break can be explained by reference to the early and misconceived classification of Buren under the banner of conceptual art or indeed institutional critique, which has made it difficult to see his more recent (and older) works beyond the critical parameters that privileged these artistic phenomena[32]. Those who, in the 1970s, had declared him to be at the front line of institutional critique had particular difficulty with the colourful and formal opulence, the playfulness and the monumentality of his later work. The initial visual tool, used in a radical gesture of revealing a context, now only served a decorative playing around with colour and form, so the argument went. For many critics, Buren's obvious interest in beauty and visual pleasure

32 See Alison M. Gingeras, "Who is Daniel Buren?" in Solomon R. Guggenheim Museum (ed.), *The Buren Times*, New York, 2005, Section 3A. As has been demonstrated by the art historian Blake Stimson, this reception of Buren's œuvre tallies with general trends in the way of dealing with the neo-avant-garde of the late 1960s and 1970s. "The problem with conceptual art is that it was regularly thought to be different from the other art movements of modernity in its approach, and more determined and comprehensive in its refusal. Its stake, concept-wise, meant, in principle, not only the rejection of specific aesthetic pleasure but also the rejection of aesthetic experiences as such." (quoted in *ibid.*)

could only mean an aberration in the direction of effect and spectacle[33]. Since then the accusation has been made that Buren's works have become "merely decorative." But what does this accusation mean? Apparently that his work no longer has any content. But did it ever? Was the striped pattern not intended to replace such a conventional level of symbolic meaning with a referring function? In my opinion, Buren's recent works have not become "uncritical," but the way in which their critical stance is realised has changed significantly.

A comparison between Buren's exhibition *Le Musée qui n'existait pas* and a well-known, earlier work by the artist illustrates this change. *A partir de là...* was created in 1975 for the Städtisches Museum in Mönchengladbach, where Buren covered the walls of the museum with striped wallpaper into which he cut gaps corresponding to the works which had once hung there, so that these works emerged in their absence as breaks in the striped pattern. This work evokes a complex relationship between the museum, the present or absent work, and the presence of Buren's intervention. It marks an intervention that brings the institution's form of presentation to the fore, and that marks, modifies and generates the relations between artworks, their location and the practices of showing them. An intervention occurs – but one that is relatively easy to put into words and to interpret in terms of its function as institutional critique. Although the striped pattern does not have a semantic level of meaning, this work includes a referential dimension that enables it to be read as critique. Beyond its reference to a location and surroundings, it contains a recognisable discursive level. It points to something, makes something visible that was not previously perceived as such, and in doing so it puts the conditions of artistic production and reception that precede the indi-

33 In 1997, Benjamin Buchloh said that Buren's critical stance amounted to nothing more than "comply[ing] with (culture) industry standards and yet maintain[ing] the avant-garde gesture of refusal to deliver meaning to the apparatus of domination", Benjamin H.D. Buchloh, "Sculpture Projects in Münster", *Artforum*, 9 (1997), p. 116.

vidual work into a critical perspective. By marking the space between paintings, it highlights these very conventions, literally "pointing them out." Through marking the frame or parameters within which they are manifest, the conventions themselves become present as a reference within the work. *A partir de là ...* exhibits the idea of a painting, the conventions of its presentation, and its inherent narrative, but in this demonstration it also repeats these references – albeit as a shadow of themselves, as a blank, an index. It is exactly this repetition that makes the conventions present within the work – and that makes the work readable, in and as a relation to these conventions.

This is different in Buren's more recent work, such as the Paris exhibition *Le Musée qui n'existait pas*, for example. There is no longer the level of critical reference to the circumstances. *Le Musée qui n'existait pas* did not refer to the conventions of the museum in which it took place (on the contrary, the institution almost vanished from the consciousness of the viewer), but transformed the space in such a way as to bring forth a different museum, the one *qui n'existait pas*. Buren's work is fundamentally characterised by an awareness of being part of a functional context, to which it refers. But the significance of this reference changes from the earlier to the later works. The early works such as *A partir de là ...* are constituted in their reference to a location and its conditions. The work, it could be said, *is* the reference. In *Le Musée qui n'existait pas* there is also a thematic reference, namely to the organising principles of the retrospective, i.e., the linear sequence of individual works. But as a work (and in my opinion, the exhibition as a whole can be described as a work) it is not constituted as a reference, a "critical view" of specific conventions, but as a construction, a different principle, with which Buren counters the conventional format of the retrospective. In the former case the work tends towards aesthetic reference and quotation, in the latter towards aesthetic position. This shift from critical reference to the configuration of a performative power to posit does not mean that a work has no meaning. But to discern it requires a methodologically different view of the artwork: as long as its performative effectiveness is not recognised as significant and as a producer of meaning, the work seems to mean nothing – it stays "merely" decorative. The meaning of this work cannot be "read"; it is not something hidden within that must be discovered. Rather it is manifested in an experience that proceeds from exploring and perceiving the exhibition. In *Le Musée qui n'existait pas* it is not the thematic reference to the principle of the retrospective that becomes explicit, but the concrete experience of aimless walking. Or to put it more precisely: the subject matter of the work is the way in which a retrospective usually, i.e. habitually (to follow the sociologist Bourdieu, the dedicatee of Buren's book for the exhibition), becomes concrete in experiences and physical activity. This type of shaping of experience — Buren himself talks of his works as "exemplary experiences[34]" — is of course much more difficult to grasp, because its subject matter cannot be objectified independently of one's own perception and experience.

What however makes possible this shaping and unshaping of art experience, which we have described with reference to *Le Musée qui n'existait pas*, is that very decorative quality of Buren's works. In replying to a 1954 questionnaire devised by René Magritte, the *Internationale Lettriste* wrote: "The deliberate use of décor will bring about continually regenerating forms of conduct[35]". Therein lies, in my opinion, a starting point for understanding Buren's relationship to the decorative. Seen positively, the accusation of "decorative" is not only correct, but even applies to a central aspect of Buren's concept of art, namely the re-conception of the art object as décor – décor that is intended to have an effect and to effectuate. Pierre Huyghe has described Buren's works as "hollowed out objects" that can be experienced visually but not be

34 *cf.* Buren in: Sans, *Daniel Buren*, *op. cit.*, p. 126.

35 Quoted from German: Roberto Ohrt: *Phantom Avantgarde. Eine Geschichte der Situationistischen Internationale und der modernen Kunst*, Hamburg 1990, p. 79 (Herv. orig.).

appropriated as meaning[36]. They are objects, says Huyghe, that, contrary to the general functional principle of a work of art, do not "produce an attraction but open a space for distraction, hence for thinking elsewhere[37]." They initiate something more like a perpetual interplay, in which the eye of the viewer is attracted only to be redirected. Buren forms and composes this interplay with the aid of the object as décor. In this sense all of his works can be characterised as decorative, for they take up a particular mode of functioning that is inherent to décor. Gadamer, who links the concept of the decorative to the question of the nature of the image, describes this mode as follows:

"The nature of decoration consists in performing that two-sided mediation: namely to draw the viewer's attention to itself, to satisfy his taste, and then to redirect it away from itself to the greater whole of the life context which is accompanies[38]." Gadamer's accentuation of the double orientation towards a viewer and a place exactly corresponds to the functional principle of Buren's striped pattern. It halts, interrupts and blocks the gaze, but also, because it cannot be read as a sign, opens the gaze up to something else, causes something to occur[39]. This "two-sided mediation" makes décor basic to the specific functioning of Buren's art. In this sense the following words by Gadamer can be applied almost directly to these works:

"Certainly it should not invite us to linger and notice it as a decorative motif, but should have a merely accompanying effect. Thus

36 Daniel Buren in conversation with Pierre Huyghe, *Parkett* 66, 2002, p. 108.

37 *Ibid.*

38 Hans-Georg Gadamer: *Truth and Method*, trans. by W. Glen-Doepel, London 2006, p. 151.

39 "These stripes have two contrasting qualities. One that obstructs, firstly: without any effort on the part of the onlooker, you dwell on these stripes, without seeing anything else; they block the gaze. Then, the quality of creating precisely the opposite effect: once you produce the effort required consisting in reading this work by considering these alternate stripes as signs permitting a reading, there is the visual discovery of something that we are not acquainted with seeing." (Daniel Buren, in, Sans, *Daniel Buren*, *op.cit.* (note 9), p.112).

in general it will not have any representational content, or will so iron it out through stylization or repetition that one's eye glides across it[40]."

The phrases "not ... to linger," "the eye glides across it," also precisely describe the perceptual experience of *Le Musée qui n'existait pas*. Buren's décor halts the gaze, but does not hold it; the eye is directed on, led through the space in continual attraction and relinquishment so that one never stands still and never becomes immersed in the unified context of meaning that a single object accumulates. In this sense all of Buren's works can fundamentally be described as decorative. Décor for Buren is a device by means of which he arrives at a different notion of the object. With the object as décor Buren takes one step back behind the idea of the 'autonomous' and independent object, for as décor it *cannot* claim any independence, existing by definition only in relation to a place and as bearer of a function. Based on a creative concept that no longer derives from the idea of a self-contained work, but much rather from the reality in which it exists and is perceived, Buren uses décor to bring about a fundamental reconceptualisation of the artwork. In this respect Buren's works are of an ontological nature. They lend art a new way of being and functioning. These are situational works, which cannot be firmly pinned down either spatially or temporally, which do not allow themselves to be appropriated either subjectively or objectively as "content" or "meaning". A work such as *Le Musée qui n'existait pas* is indeed decorative; it has no significant depth. But just and only by virtue of this meaninglessness can décor play a role in the as it were formative effect of the aimless striding that has been described in relation to the exhibition *Le Musée qui n'existait pas*. Precisely because Buren uses décor to renounce this level of a 'deep' meaning intrinsic to the artwork itself, his works challenge us to interpret them in a profoundly different way. This is how we are to understand Buren's statement that he intends

40 Gadamer, *Truth and Method*, *op.cit.* (note 12), p. 151.

neither to insert his works into the existing art system nor to stand in opposition to it. It would be much rather a question of changing the rules of the game in such a fundamental way that another, new game might be possible, *Le Musée qui n'existait pas.*

Dorothea von Hantelmann

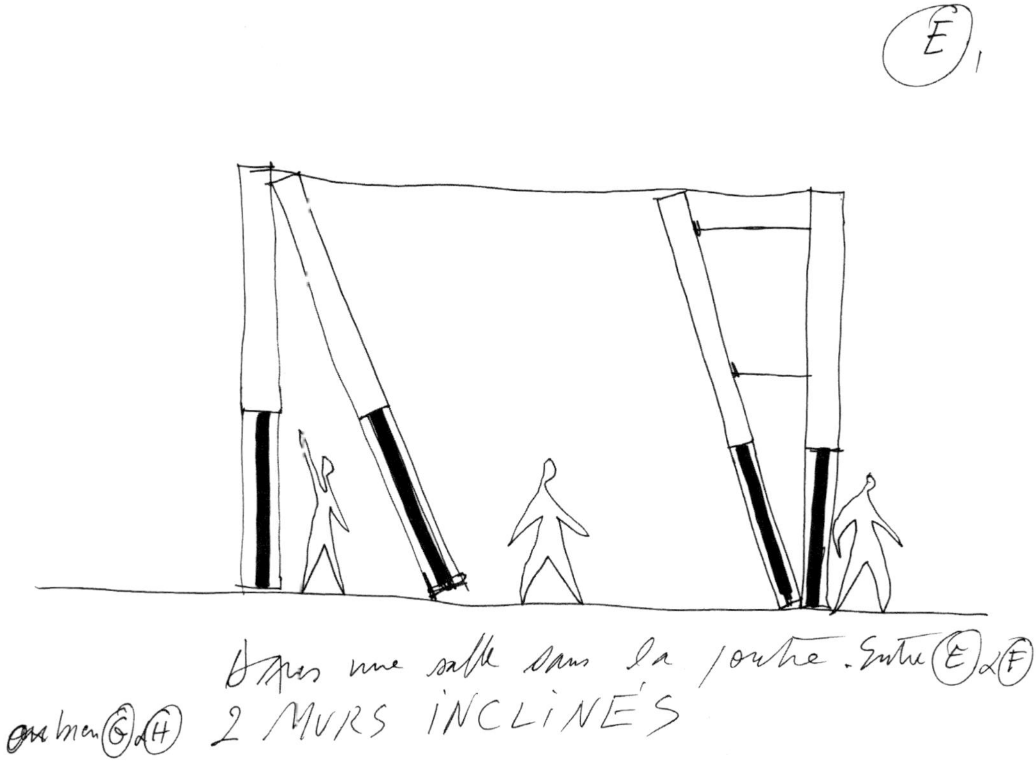

Photo-souvenir: graphic sketch for room 47

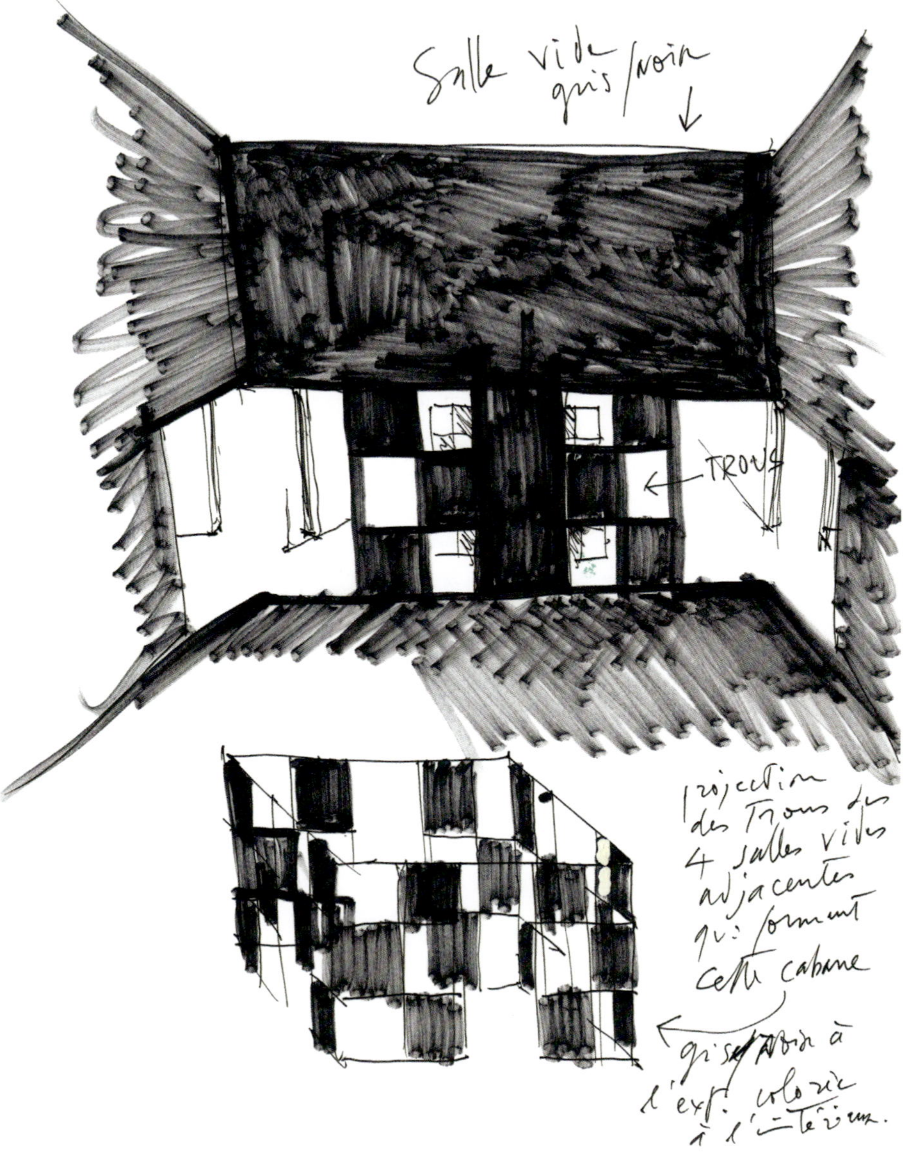

Photo-souvenir: graphic sketch for room 53

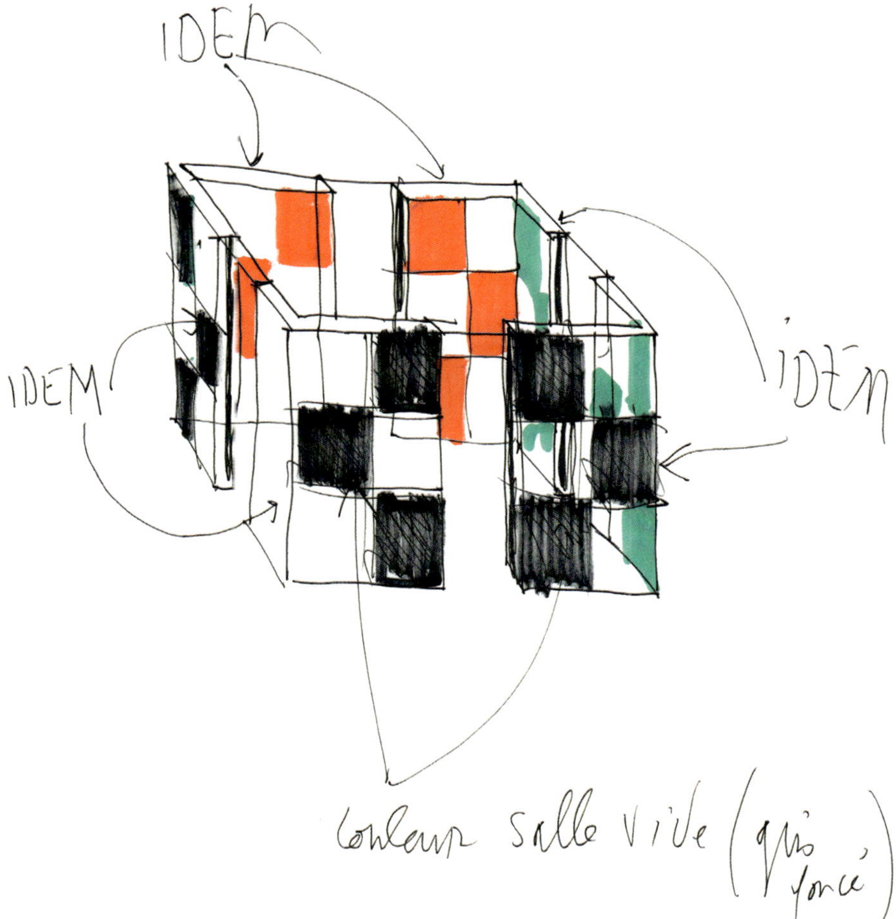

Photo-souvenir: graphic sketch for room 53

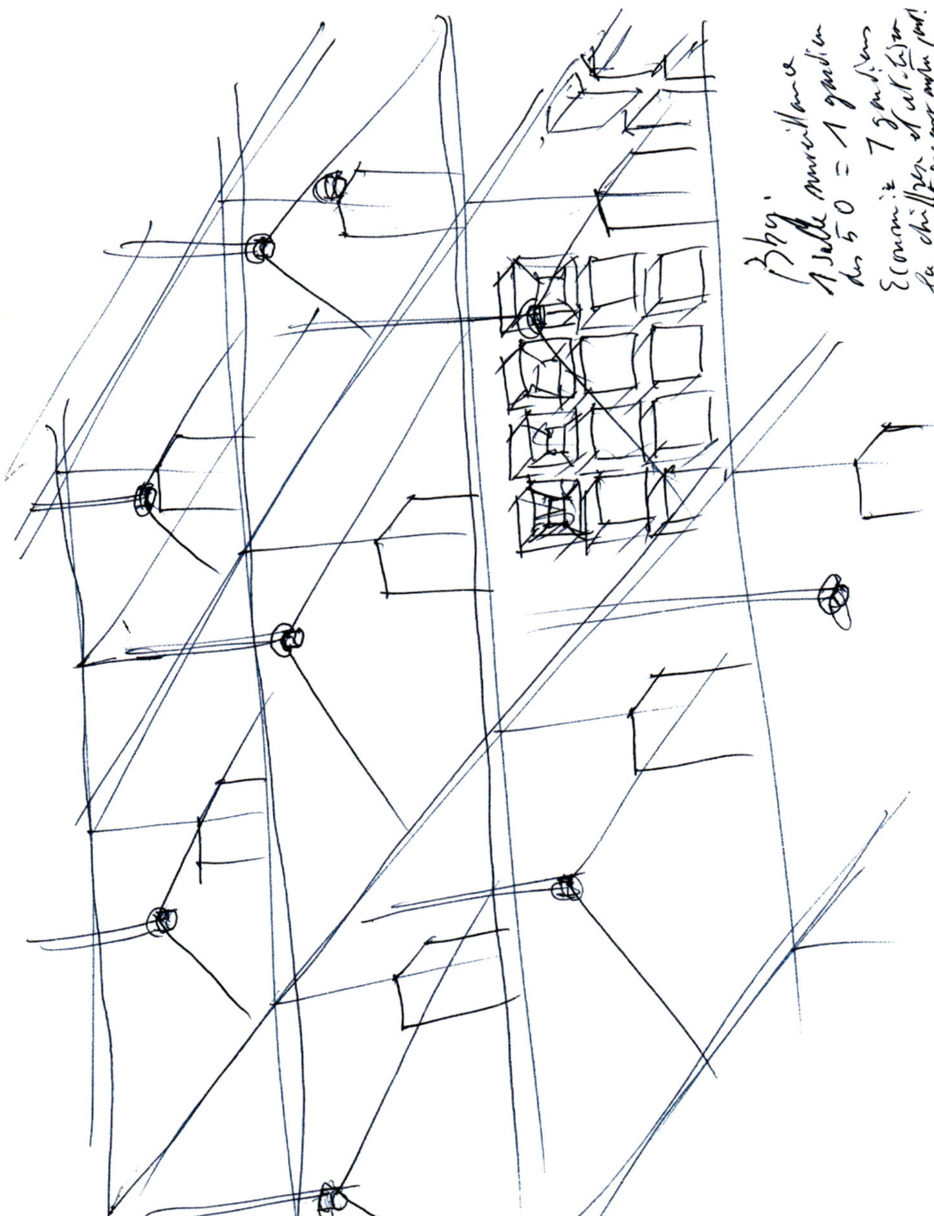

Photo-souvenir: graphic sketch for room 45

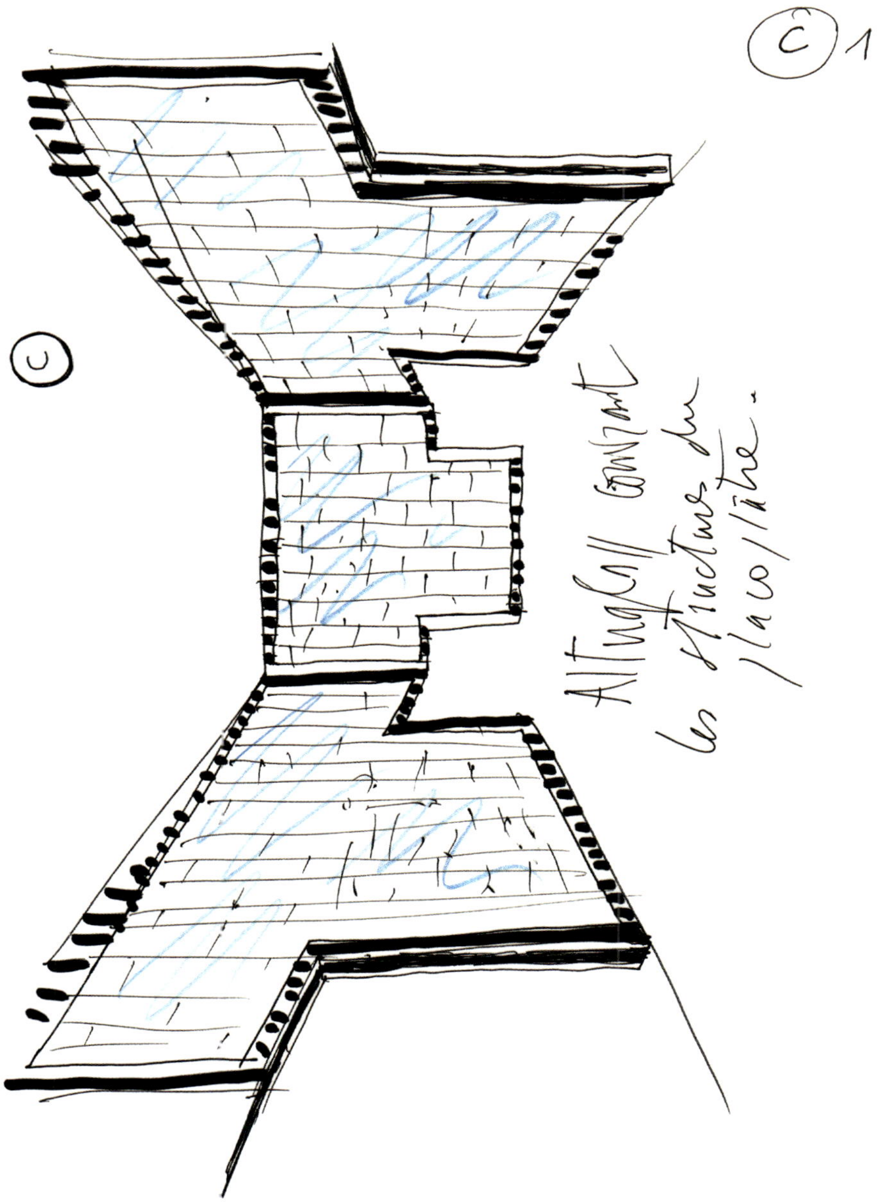

Photo-souvenir: graphic sketch for room 57

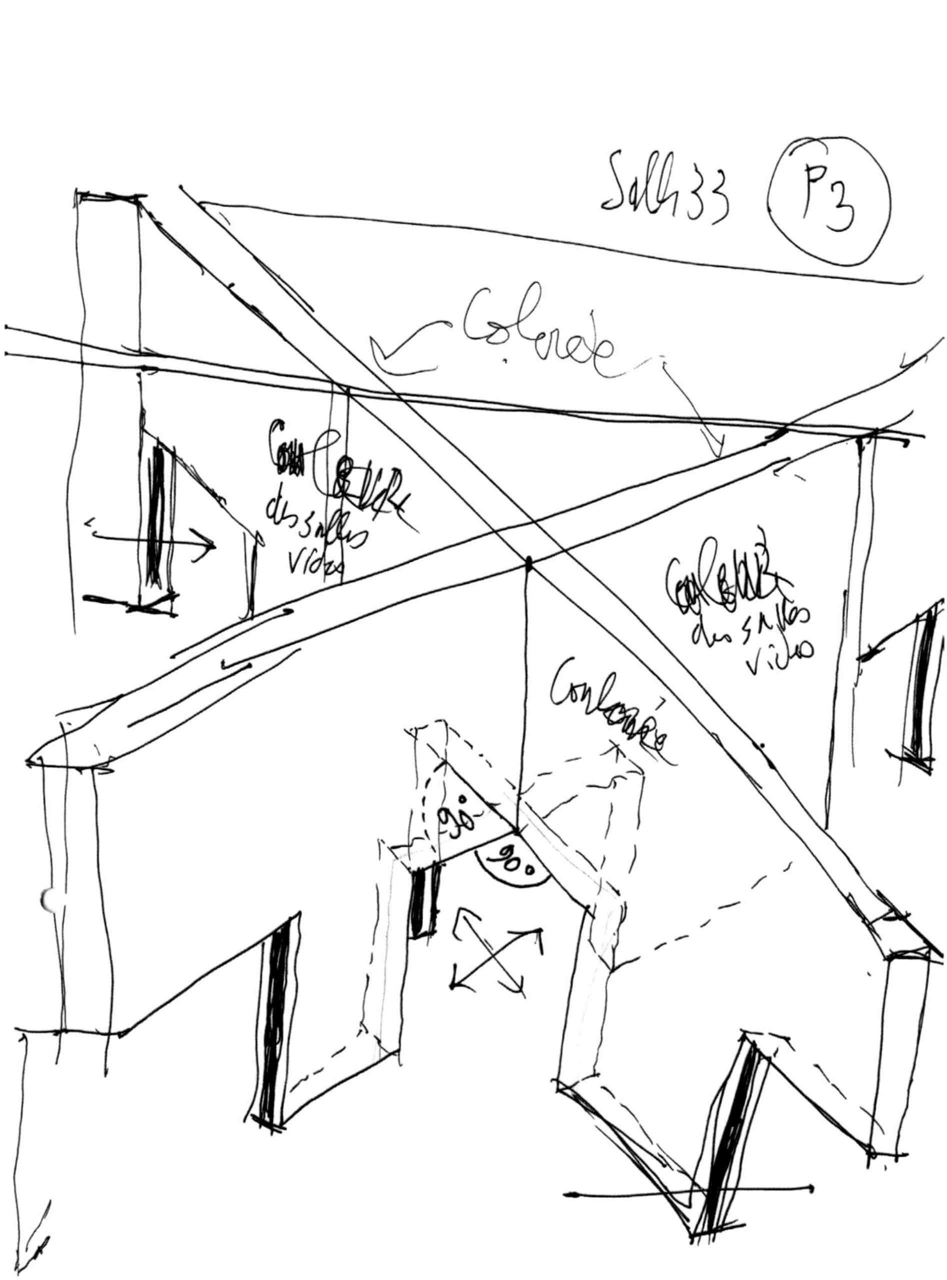

Photo-souvenir: graphic sketch for room 37

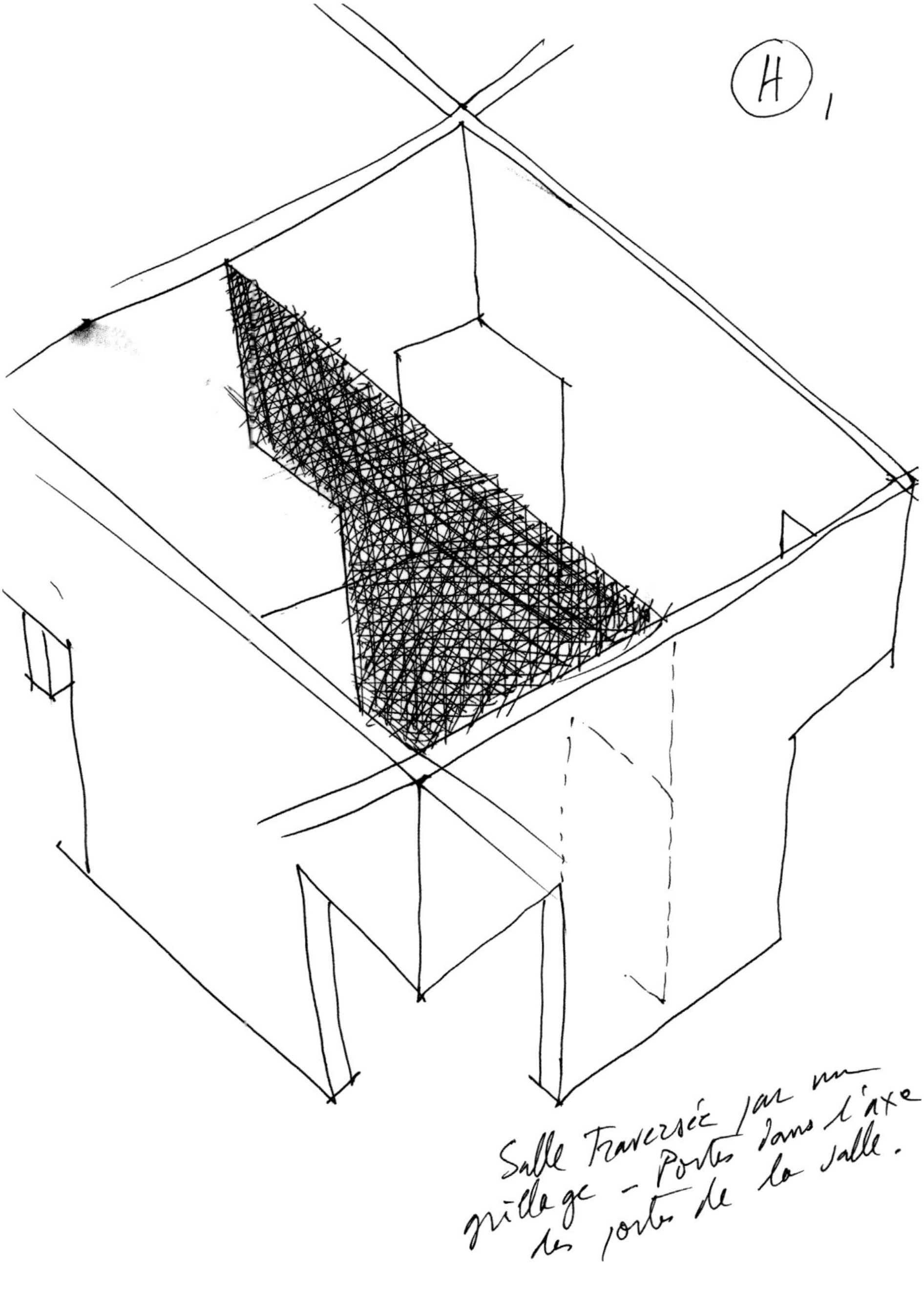

Photo-souvenir: graphic sketch for room 43

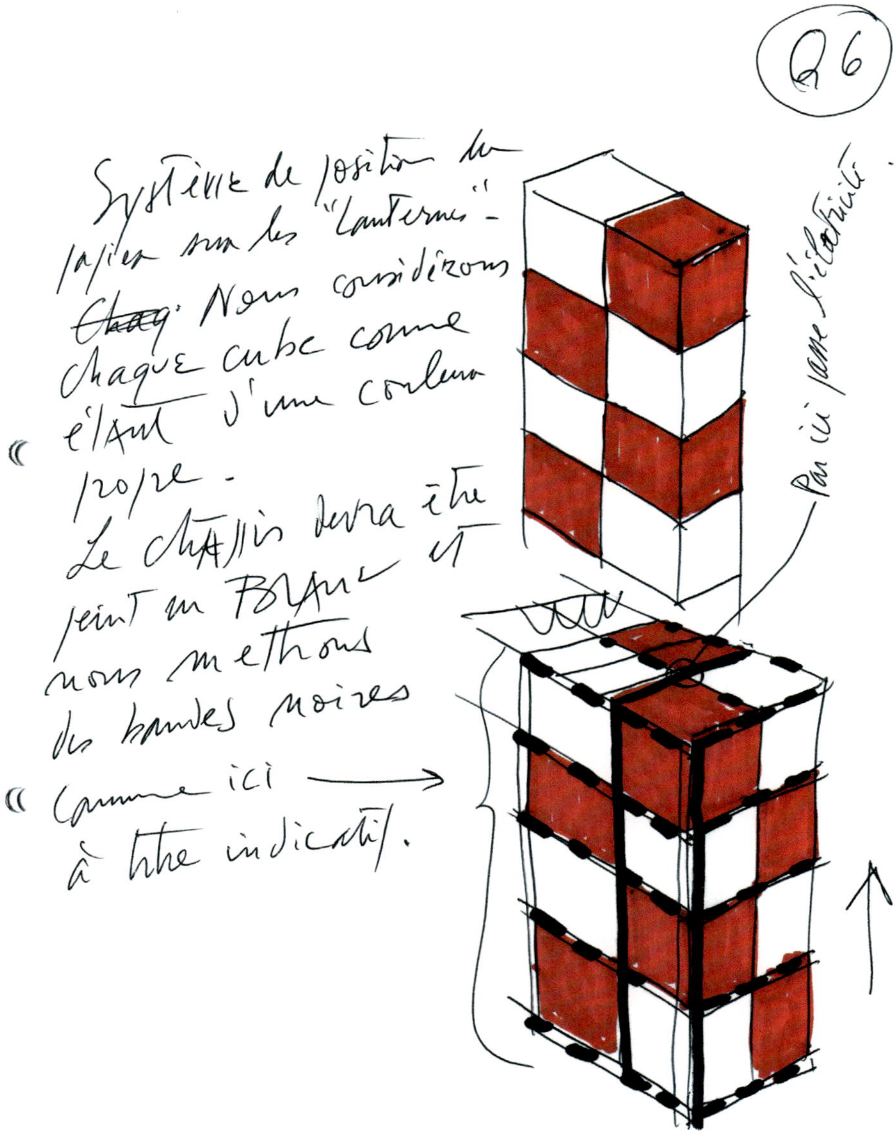

Photo-souvenir: graphic sketch for room 31

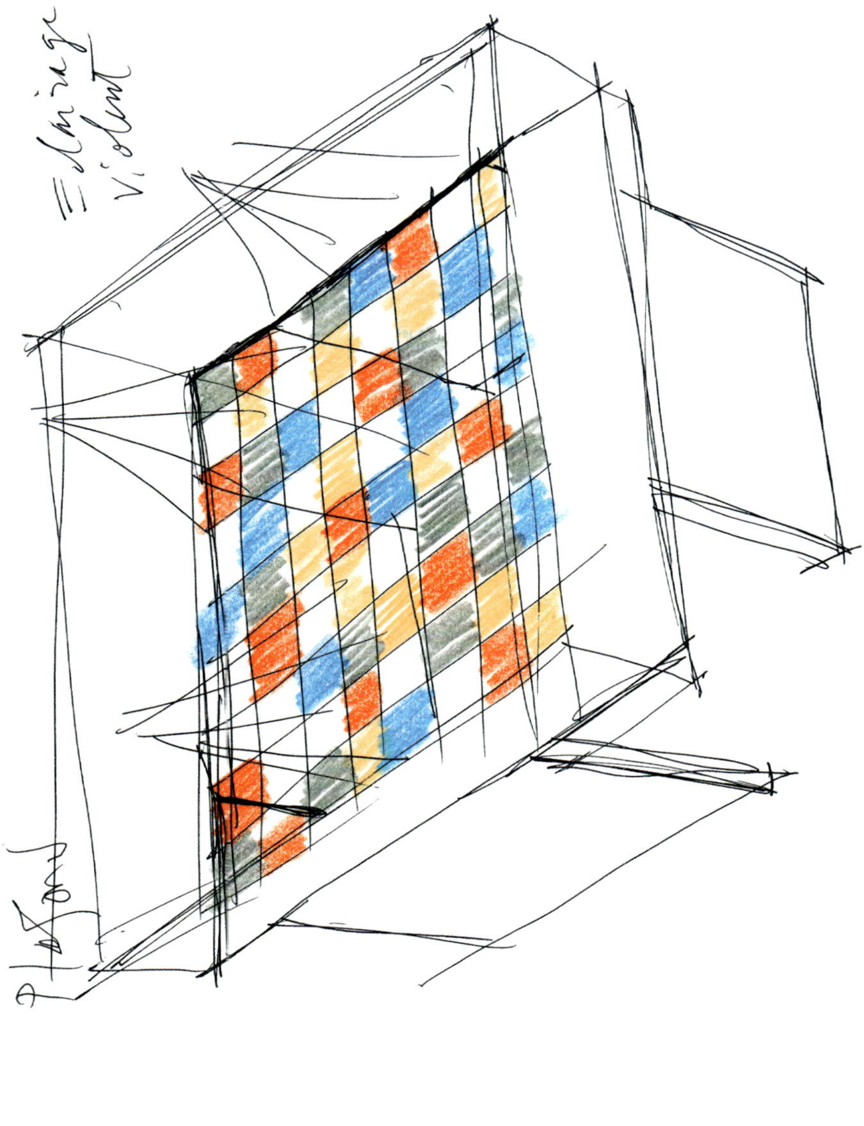

Photo-souvenir: graphic sketch for room 59

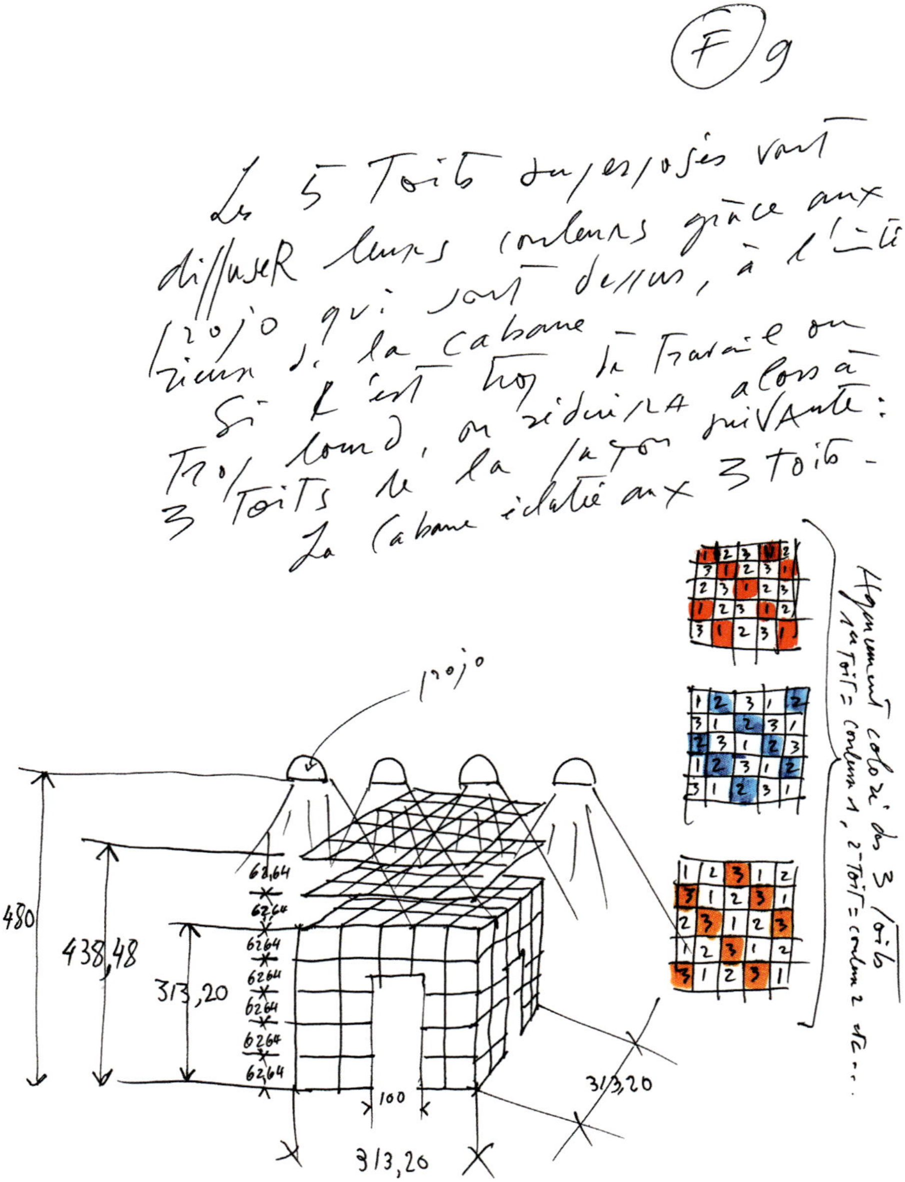

Photo-souvenir: graphic sketch for room 65

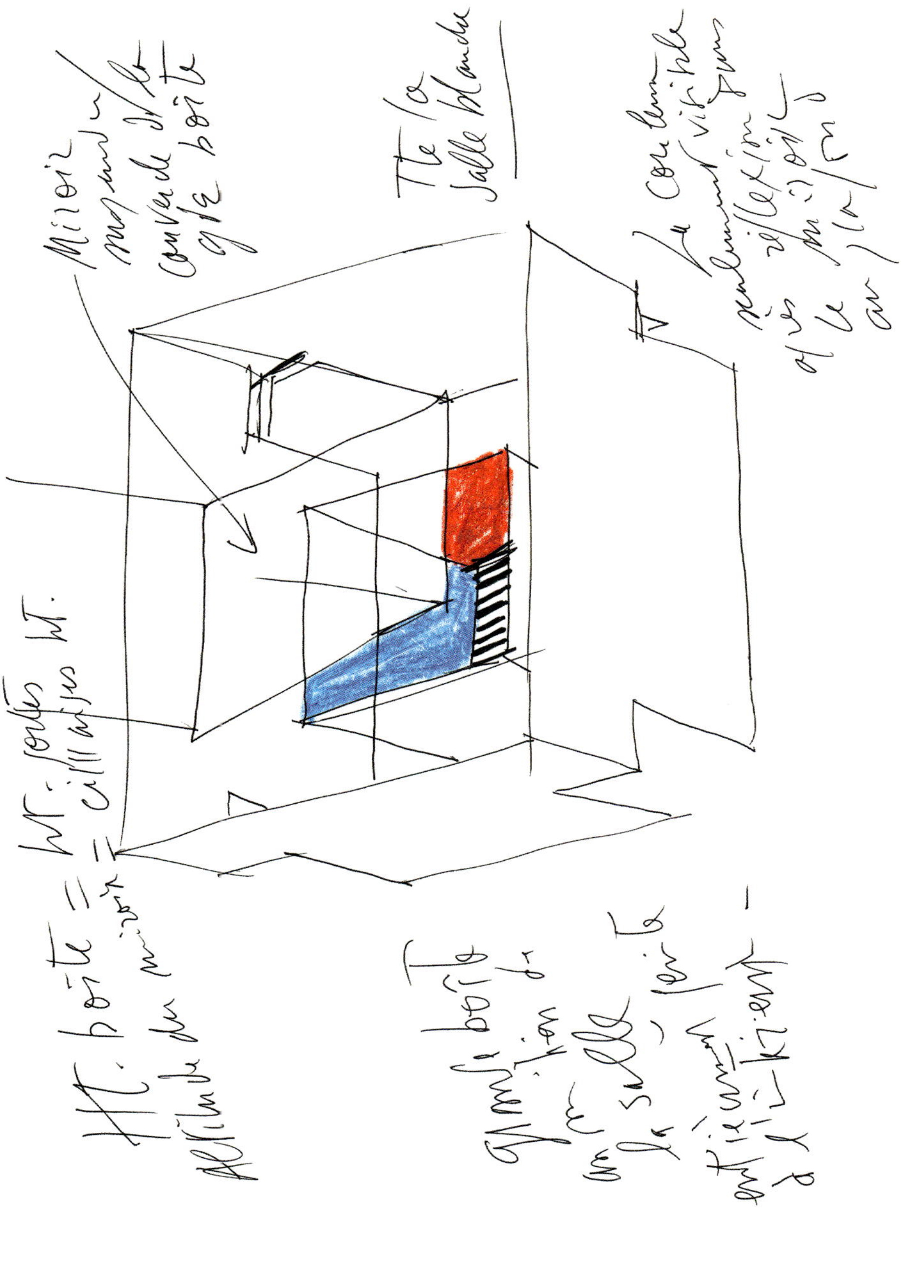

Photo-souvenir: graphic sketch for room 63

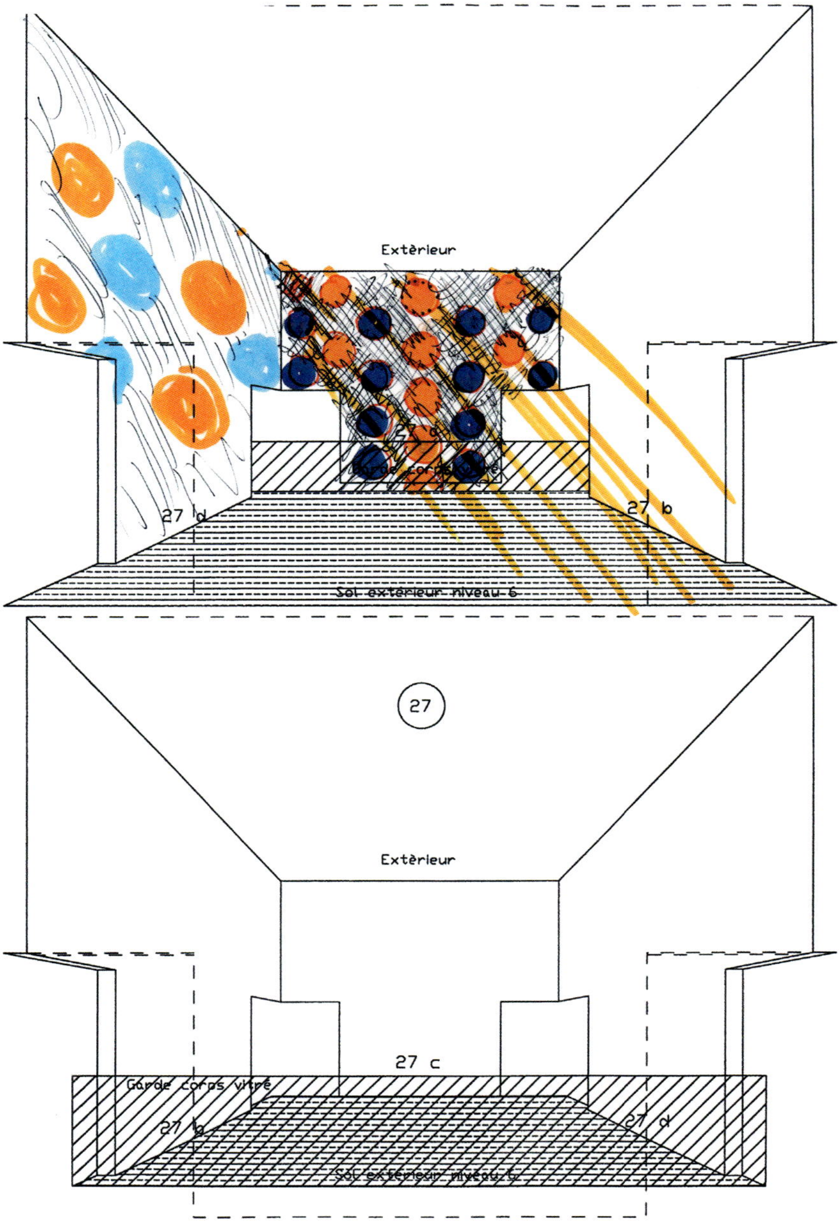

Photo-souvenir: graphic sketch for room 25

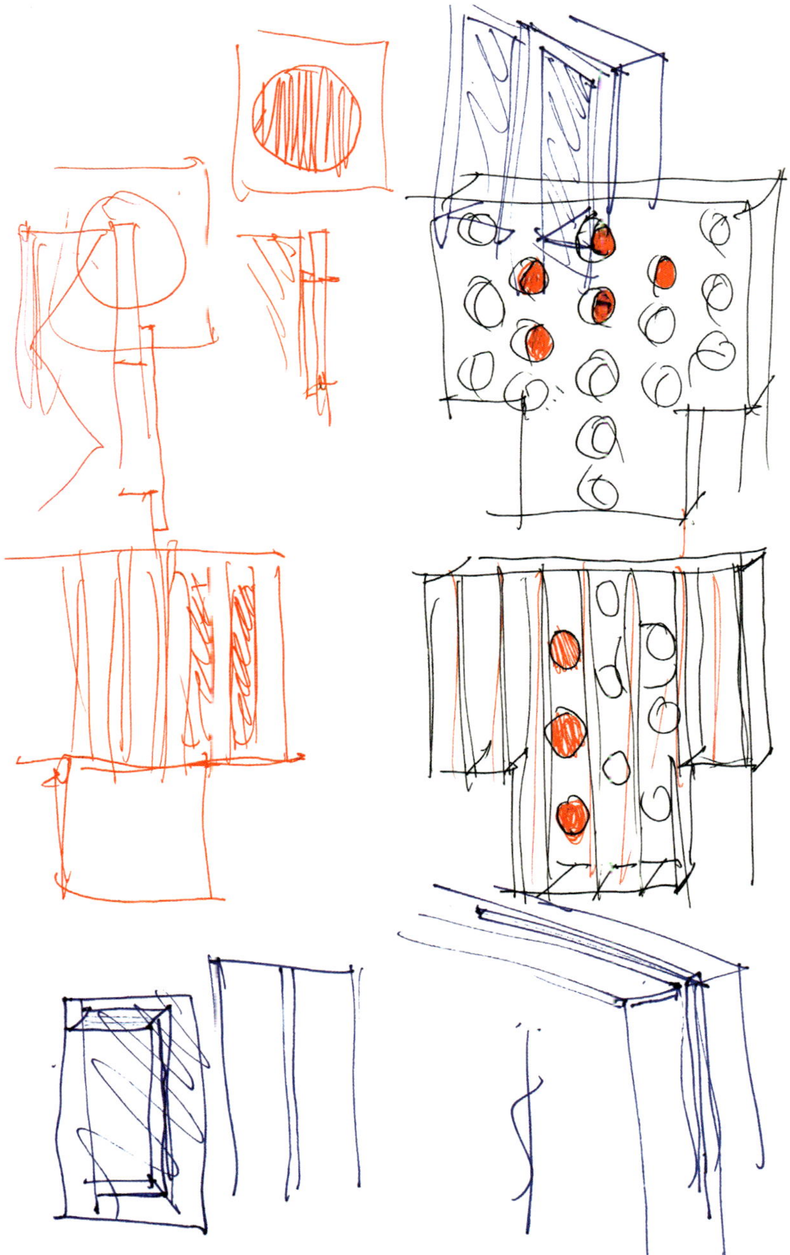

Photo-souvenir: graphic sketch for room 25

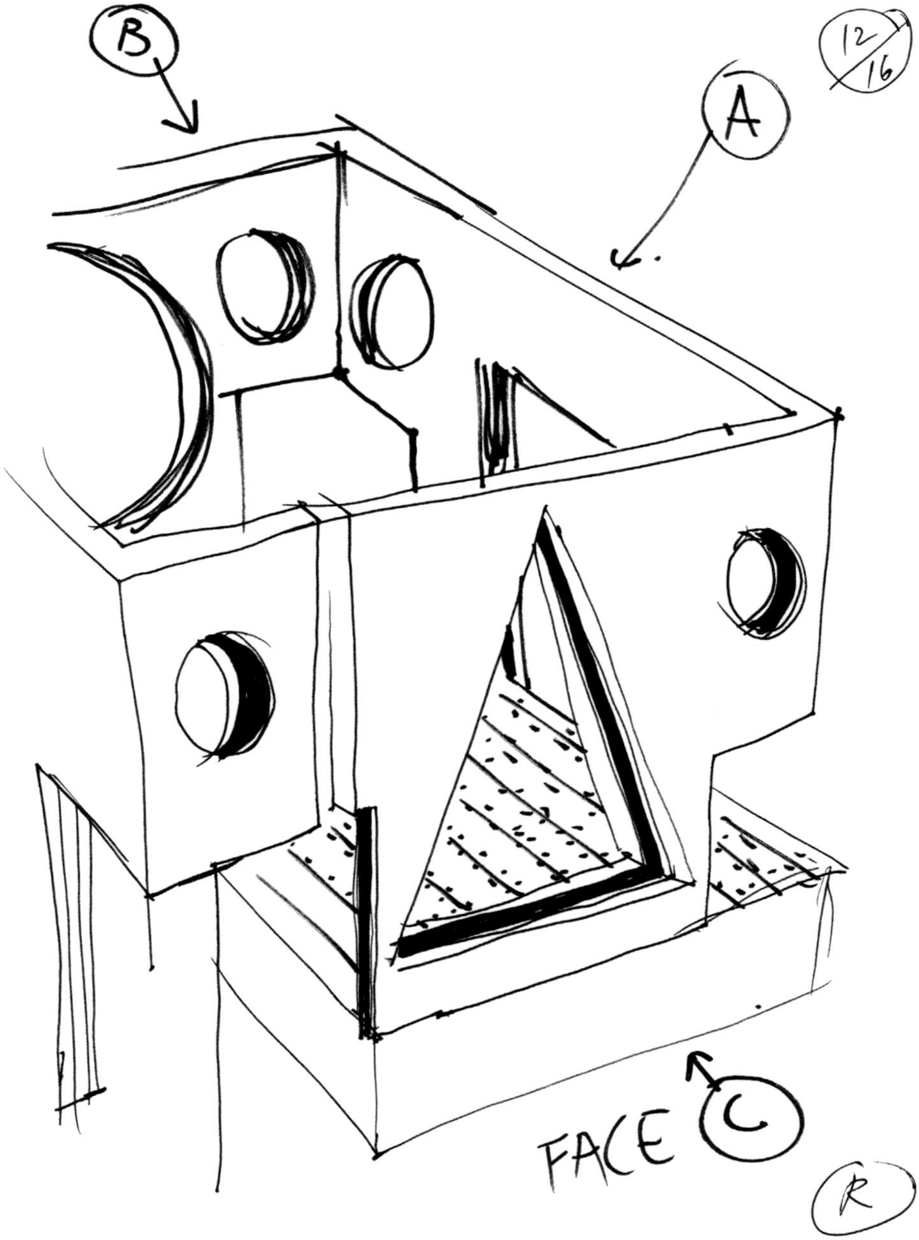

Photo-souvenir: graphic sketch for room 71

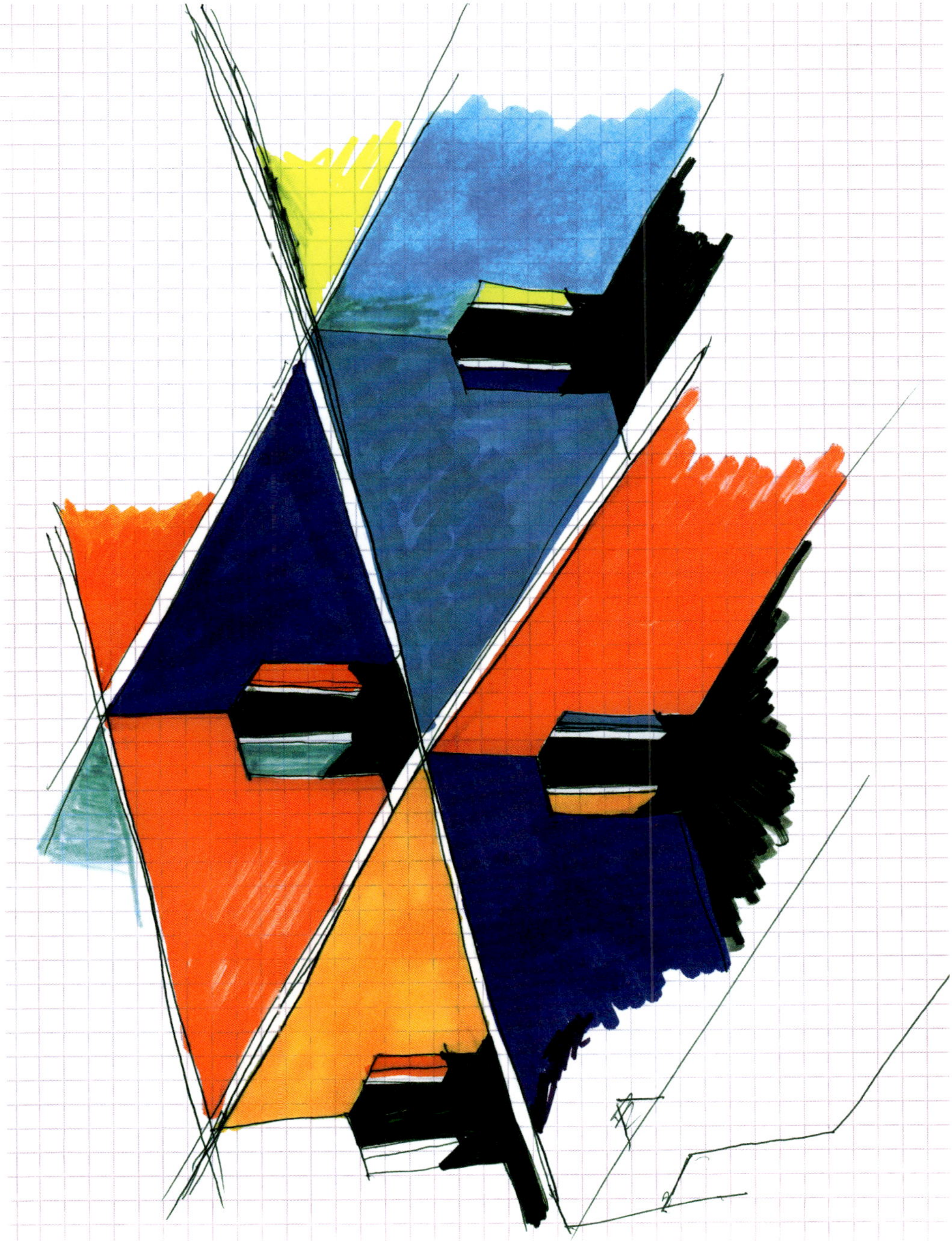

Photo-souvenir: graphic sketch for "Le Musée qui n'existait pas" (not executed)

BB suggests that DB exhibit at the Centre Pompidou (12/97)		DB thinks of PB who will bring in NC. SS will monitor the project throughout.		Official letter from Jean-Jacques Aillagon confirming the invitation (13/05/98)
	Trip to New York, meeting with Thomas Krens at the Guggenheim, possible link-up between Paris and New York provided the two shows have nothing in common (06/00)		AG asks JP to join the project. Confirmation of Pierre Bourdieu's participation (06/01)	
The building's restrictions as creative vectors. The standard: 1 person per 3 sq.m. (32 sq. ft.) At the Centre: 1 person per 5 sq.m. (54 sq. ft.), whence a capacity of 430 visitors for the exhibition.		The remote surveillance room introduced as a work into the exhibition area after the Centre's announcement about the impossibility of keeping an eye on all the cells: one attendant replaces 35.		First meeting about the catalogue: plunge into the world of DB's archives (09/01)
	DB's house transformed into a hive of activity. Arrival of JLD and CF for the catalogue documentation. Studious Sundays at Varennes with Chantal Buren as from 30/09/01.		XB, together with WvR, takes on the catalogue's artistic direction. Piere Péronnet draws the "Plastic" character for the catalogue. Michel Barréteau scans more than a thousand documents.	
Re-installation of *The Colours* as from 01/10: search for sites in Paris to install the 15 flags, loss of the telescopes, legal formalism after the storm, associations between department stores and cultural venues.		Decision about a single admission fee for the exhibition, linked with DB's intervention throughout the Centre from level -1, turned into a car park, to level 6(01/02)		Work all afternoon between Pierre Bourdieu and DB at the Saint-Antoine hospital (23/1/01). Death of Pierre Bourdieu. His essay will be published in its entirety in the catalogue with the authorisation of his family (23/01/02)
	Thursday meetings as from December 2001. Nearly 200 people at the centre are introduced to DB, including five directors. Interruptions and craziness.		Pierre Guyotat's 1989 project on *Around the return of a detour* (the Palais-Royal fences) sees the light of day in the exhibition.	
Providential patronage: the CDC. This funding permits the final constructions of the 6th floor arrangement. (03/02).		Patrick Ferragne and Art Project produce the entire contents of the rooms for the arrangement as from March 2002 in their workshops near Lyon, and install them in Paris.		The entries "Hors vue", "Kaleidoscope", "Hors champ", "Trame", "Hors jeu" are removed in favour of "Off" which traces the exhibition process.

XB XAVIER BARRAL, **BB** BERNARD BLISTÈNE, **PB** PATRICK BOUCHAIN, **DB** DANIEL BUREN, **NC** NICOLE CONCORDET, **HD** HERVÉ DEROUAULT, **CF** CÉCILE FERREIRA, **YF** YVON FIGUERAS,

	Letter from DB to BE saying that he is giving up on the exhibition because of the Centre's indecisiveness (15/02/99). BB persuades DB to be patient. First draft of the contract (12/05/99).		AG curator (10/99) Final version of the contract (08/11/00)	
xhibition area of 1,100 q.m. (11,836 sq. ft.) offered, eemed too small, doubled y DB's artistic proposal, ack to the area initially romised. Meeting at JJA, onfirmation of an area arger than planned.		Idea of gridding which increases the space by taking the building's original grids into account. The first progressive grid proposed by PB becomes regular, creating a rhythm. Creation of perspectives and diagonals (06/01)		Seventy cells are created following a square grid encompassing the entire space, as well the void of the museum's terrace. It is planned to occupy just half the doubled area.
	Promising meeting between DB and XB at BB's prompting. XB suggests La Martinière as partner (11/01)		The principle of a catalogue proposed by AG and BB in four parts (painting, visual tool, architecture, decorative) is questioned by DB who prefers a large number of entries. The graphic decision veers towards the facsimile.	
he Centre's architect esigns, followed by the rrival of KS on a half-time asis at first, then full-time 12/01)		Joint curatorship validated by official decree (15/02/02). BB/AG/LLB threesome.		Budgetary reduction by the Centre, intervention of the DAP which saves the project; the commission of the commission. The exhibition like a score performed by the Centre.
	Conquest, reconquest, pragmatism. The artist, the architect and the politician-cum-administrator. Jules and Sid.		The HD and YF production team at work under the direction of François Belfort.	
War council at Atalante because of the explosion of the catalogue: more than 1,000 pages and 1,500 photos instead of the original 488 pages planned 05/03/02)		Opening of the folds: the partition item is part of the outline budget (10/04/02)		The Dahlia as communication medium (invitations, posters, tickets). Renault vehicles in the car park thanks to François Trèves and Marie-Stéphanie de Sercey (04/02)
	The project is completed (24/06/02). Official opening, *Mot à mot* is in bookshops, along with a new volume of the catalogue raisonné, prepared by Annick Boisnard (25/06/02). DB's crazy day (26/06/02)		The "Le Musée qui n'existait pas" disappears, to reappear? (25/09/02)	

AG ALISON M. GINGERAS, **LLB** LAURENT LE BON, **JLD** JULIEN LE DOARE, **JP** JULIE PELLEGRIN, **WR** WIJNTJE VAN ROOIJEN, **KS** KATIA SAMARI, **SS** SOPHIE STREEFKERK

The Centre national d'art et de culture Georges Pompidou

is a national public establishment under the supervision of the Ministry of Culture (Law n° 75-1 of 3 January 1975)

Publication

CENTRE POMPIDOU
Director of publications
Nicolas Roche

Assistant director
Jean-Christophe Claude

Editorial division
Françoise Marquet

Commercial division
Benoît Collier

Management of rights and contracts
Claudine Guillon,
Matthias Battestini

Administrative and financial management
Nicole Parmentier

Sales administration division
Josiane Peperty

ÉDITIONS XAVIER BARRAL
Publications
Xavier Barral, Céline Moulard

Design and graphic production
Atalante/Paris, Coline Aguettaz

Photogravure
Printmodel, Paris

STUDIO DANIEL BUREN

Vesna Antic
Annick Boisnard
Sophie Streefkerk

Exhibition

"Le Musée qui n'existait pas / The Museum that did not exist"
Exhibition held at the Centre Pompidou from 26 June to 23 September 2002

Daniel Buren

CENTRE NATIONAL D'ART ET CULTURE GEORGES POMPIDOU
Jean-Jacques Aillagon
President

Bruno Maquart
Director general

Alfred Pacquement
Director of the Musée national d'art moderne - Centre de création industrielle

Jean-Pierre Marcie-Rivière
President of the Association pour le développement du Centre Pompidou

François Trèves
President of the Société des Amis du Musée national d'art moderne

Jean-Paul Ollivier
Administrator of the Musée national d'art moderne - Centre de création industrielle

CURATORSHIP
Bernard Blistène
Inspector general of artistic creation, Visual Arts Commission

Alison M. Gingeras
Curator at the Musée national d'art moderne - Centre de création industrielle, Centre Pompidou

Laurent Le Bon
Curator at the Musée national d'art moderne - Centre de création industrielle, Centre Pompidou

Hervé Derouault,
Assisted by Yvon Figueras
Production managers

Julie Pellegrin,
Assisted by Julien Le Doaré
Sophie Streefkerk,
Assisted by Cécile Ferreira
Research and editorial coordination

Annick Boisnard
Responsible for the catalogue raisonné

ARCHITECTURE
B et H
Patrick Bouchain
Architect

Nicole Concordet, assisted by Arnaud Bailly, Ludovic Bost, Jean-Christophe Denise
Katia Samari
Architect for the Centre Pompidou

EXECUTION
Art Project
Patrick Ferragne
Thierry Sagnes
Manuel Dacunha

PRODUCTION
François Belfort
Director

Cléa Richon
Deputy

Martine Silie, assisted by Valérie Millot
Head of the events department

Annie Boucher
Head of the artworks management department

Florence Turner
Manager

Catherine Duruel
Head of the collections department

Merja Laukia
Collections assistant

Yannick Château
Collections assistant

Katia Lafitte
Head of the architectural department

Colette Oger
Production manager

Of the architectural department
Anne Baylac-Martres

Head of the audiovisual department
Gérard Chiron

Technical and artistic manager of the audiovisual department

Vahid Hamidi
Manager of the operating unit

Myriam Bezdjian
Production manager

Patrick Arnold
Multimedia director

Noël Viard
Che

Head of the workshop and technical department
Alain Chaume

Exhibition area manager
Michel Boukreis, Philippe Chagnon, Philippe Delapierre, Pascal Dossat, Philippe Fourrier, Patrig Le Jeanne, Emmanuel Gentilhomme, Toni Réga
Administrative management

PHOTOGRAPHERS
Jean-Claude Planchet
Georges Meguerditchian

Daniel Buren is especially grateful to Patrick Bouchain for
his valuable support, Patrick Ferragne and his whole team for their
magnificent work and, needless to add, all those without whom
this exhibition would not have seen the light of day.

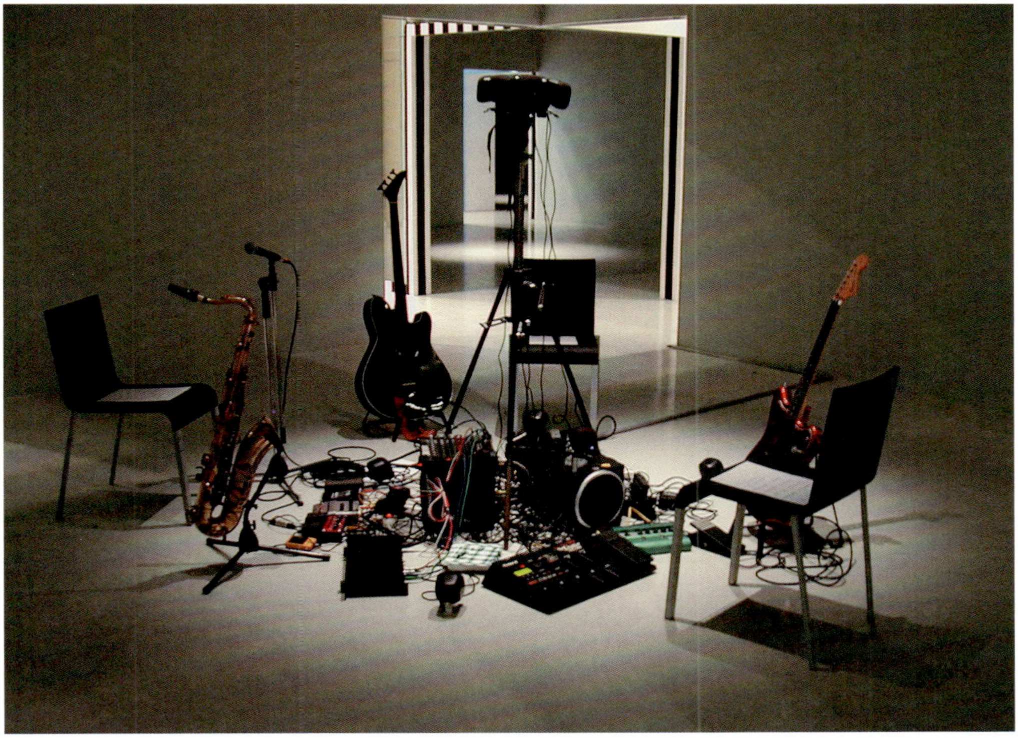

In one of the central grey rooms, 10-minute concert every half-hour
Music written and played by "Les Trois 8" (Fred Costa, Alexandre Meyer, Frédéric Minière)

The Museum That Did Not Exist

This catalogue has been published on the occasion of the exhibition: "Daniel Buren, Le Musée qui n'existait pas", presented by Centre Pompidou from 26 June – 23 September 2002

RANDOM HOUSE GmbH – PRESTEL VERLAG
Königinstrasse 9
80539 Munich
Tel. +49 (0)89 24 29 08-300
Fax +49 (0)89 24 29 08-381

Prestel Publishing Ltd.
4 Bloomsbury Place
London WC1A 2QA
Tel. +44 (0)20 7323 5004
Fax + 44 (0)20 7636-8004

Prestel Publishing
900 Broadway, Suite 603
New York, NY 10003
Tel. (212) 995 27 20
Fax (212) 995 27 33

www.prestel.com

Prestel books are available worldwide. Please contact your nearest bookseller or one of the above addresses for information concerning your local distributor.

Library of Congress Control Number: 2010929467
British Library Cataloguing-in-Publication data: a catalogue record for this book is available from the British Library.
The Deutsche Bibliothek holds a record of this publication in the Deutsche Nationalbibliografie, detailed bibliographical data can be found under: http://dnb.ddb.de

Translated from the French by Simon Pleasance & Fronza Woods
Project Managers: Stefanie Penck and Déborah Engel
Copyedited by: Jane Michael
Design and layout: Éditions Xavier Barral

Printing: on the Cantz presses, Germany
Printed in July 2010

ISBN : 978-3-7913-4499-7

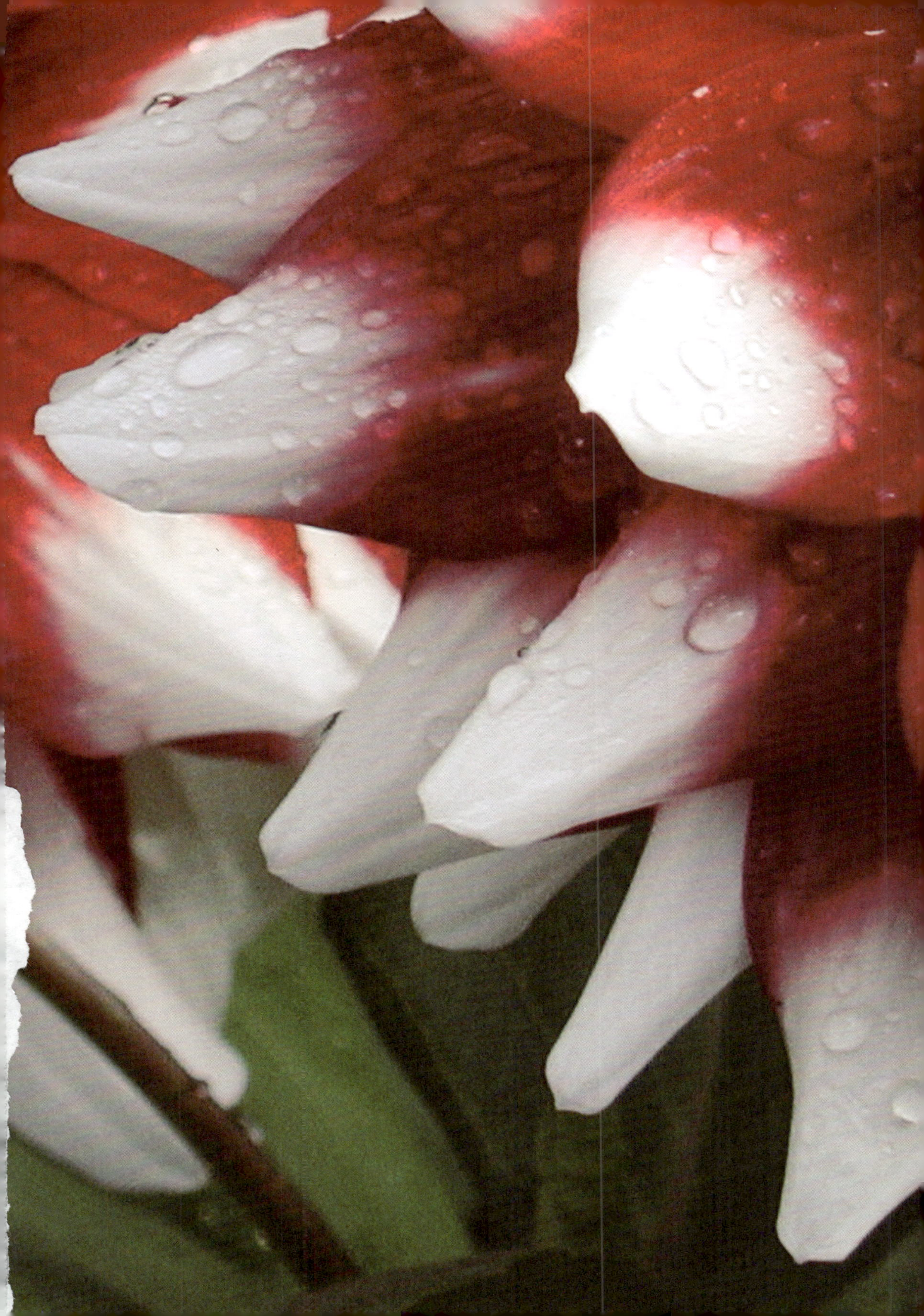

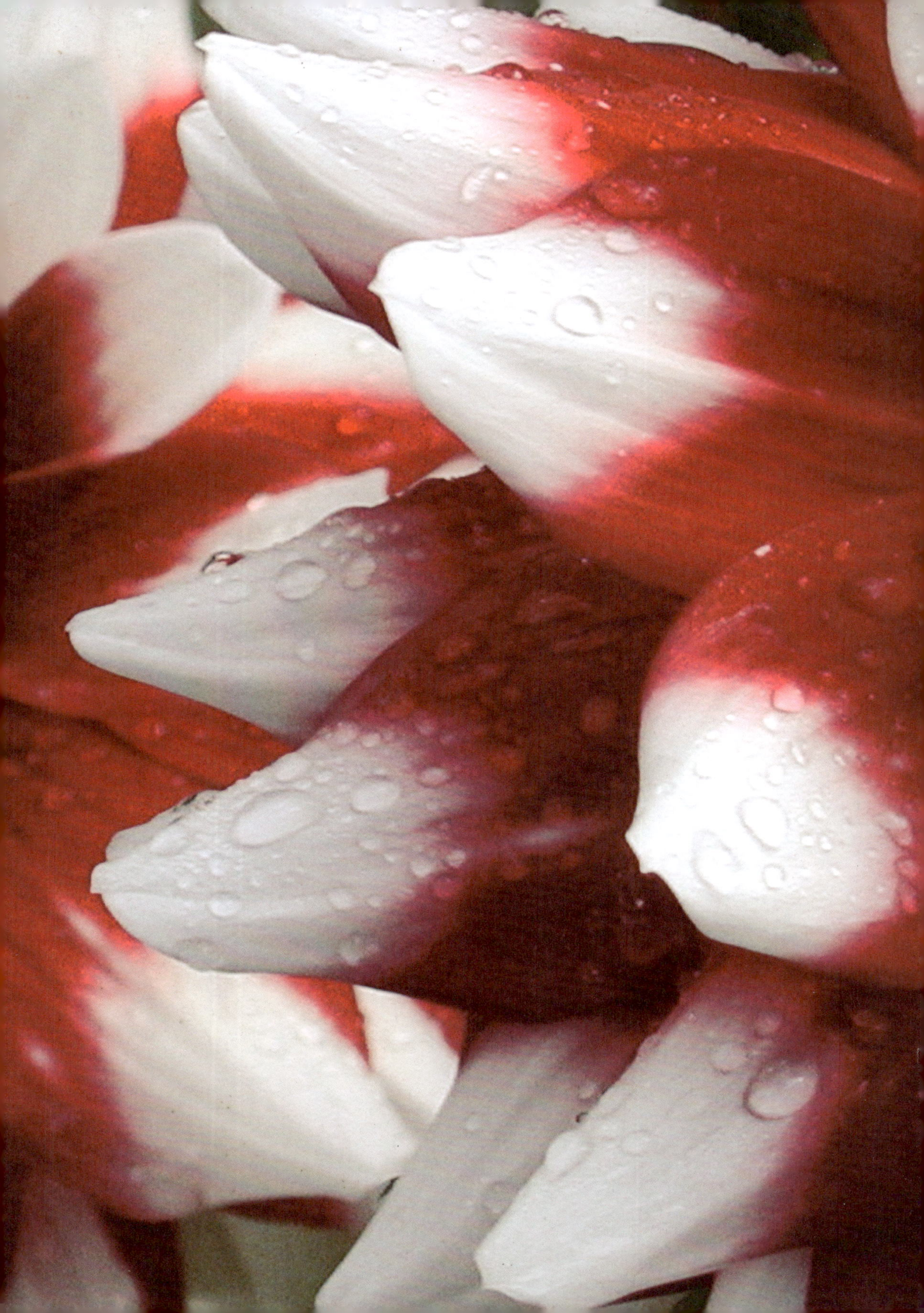